JOHN DEMOS

THE UNREDEEMED CAPTIVE

ॐ

JOHN DEMOS was born and raised in Cambridge, Massachusetts, graduated from Harvard College and received his professional training at Oxford, the University of California at Berkeley and Harvard. He has taught at Brandeis University and at Yale, where he is currently Samuel Knight Professor of American History. His previous books include *A Little Commonwealth: Family Life in Plymouth Colony, Entertaining Satan: Witchcraft and the Culture of Early New England* (for which he received the 1983 Bancroft Prize) and *Past, Present, and Personal: The Family and the Life Course in American History*.

ALSO BY JOHN DEMOS

A Little Commonwealth:
Family Life in Plymouth Colony

Entertaining Satan:
Witchcraft and the Culture of Early New England

Past, Present, and Personal:
The Family and the Life Course in American History

THE UNREDEEMED CAPTIVE

THE
UNREDEEMED
CAPTIVE

A Family Story From Early America

JOHN DEMOS

PAPERMAC

First published 1994 as a Borzoi Book by Alfred A. Knopf, Inc., New York

First published in Great Britain 1996 by Papermac
an imprint of Macmillan General Books
25 Eccleston Place London SW1W 9NF and Basingstoke

Associated companies throughout the world

ISBN 0 333 65010 7

1 3 5 7 9 8 6 4 2

A CIP catalogue record for this book is available from the British Library

Printed and bound in Great Britain by
Mackays of Chatham Plc, Chatham, Kent

No human being, who has not experienced a similar misfortune, is capable of conceiving the horror which thrilled through my frame upon finding myself a captive to these ruthless barbarians. . . . Bred up with an instinctive horror of Indians and Indian cruelties, it was a situation which, of all others, I had most deprecated.

—*Charles Johnston, returned captive (1790–91)*

ᚼ

The moment that [the captive] enters the lodge to which he is given . . . his bonds are untied. . . . He is washed with warm water to efface the colors with which his face was painted and he is dressed properly. Then he receives visits of relatives and friends of the family into which he is entering. A short time afterwards a feast is made for all the village to give him the name of the person whom he is resurrecting . . . and from that moment, he enters upon all his rights.

—*J. F. Lafitau, Jesuit missionary*
to the Kahnawake Mohawks (1712–17)

ᚼ

[Captivity is] an awfull School for Children When We See how Quick they will Fall in with the Indians ways. Nothing Seems to be more takeing. In Six months time they Forsake Father & mother, Forgit thir own Land, Refuess to Speak there own toungue & Seeminly be Holley Swollowed up with the Indians.

—*Titus King, returned captive (1755–58)*

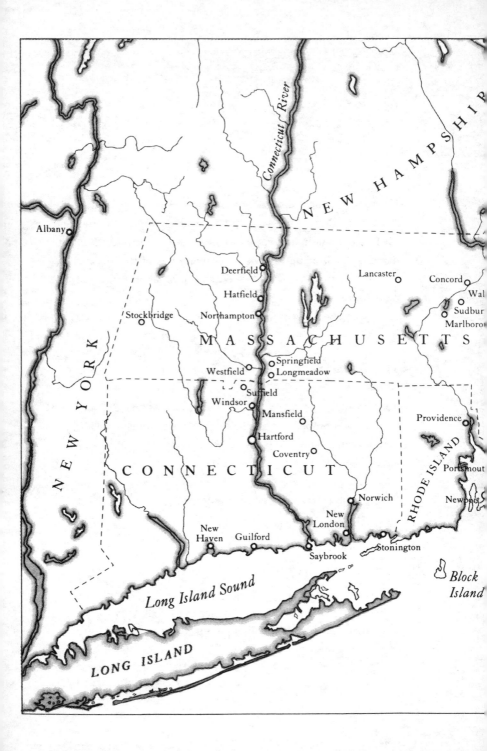

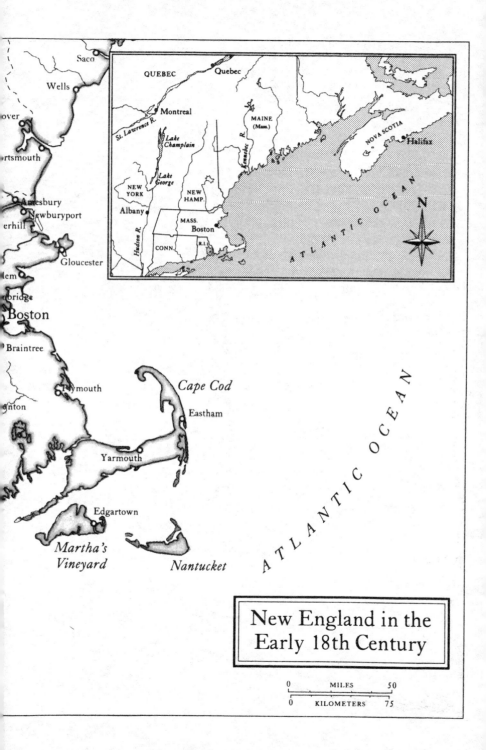

New England in the
Early 18th Century

PREFACE

じ

MOST OF ALL, I wanted to write a *story*.

じ

As a CHILD in school, I had been drawn to history by the stories.
Yet my subsequent training (and practice) followed a different track.
"Narrative history" was in deep eclipse during the time of my professional coming-of-age. So I, like many others, professed a "new social
history," in which analysis and interpretation became the main—if
not the only—thing. Then in mid-life old loyalties, old pleasures,
reasserted themselves. Almost as if by accident, a narrative voice crept
into another book (previous to this one). And, realizing at last the
strength of my wish, I resolved to yield to it fully.

I made a second resolution as well. Having studied for years the
early "colonists"—those English men and women who "settled"
America, and their immediate descendants—I would try this time to
confront the people who were "already here." It seemed, in retrospect,
astonishing how completely I had missed (ignored? discounted?
avoided?) the various host-groups. ("Native Americans" we have recently come to call them. Yet the term feels strained, unfamiliar. In
most of what follows I reluctantly retain the old misnomer "Indians.")

Together these two aims gave me a certain direction. But they did
not by themselves identify a topic. And, for months, I simply searched.
Bit by bit, I explored the new academic subfield of "ethnohistory,"
where Indians finally appear as central players. There were conferences to attend, and sites to visit, and much fine scholarship to read.
Eventually I moved on to "primary sources": for example, the extraordinary compilation published several decades ago as *The Jesuit Relations*. The early Jesuit missionaries, I came to think, had seen—truly

seen—Indians more fully than other "white" colonists. I sampled, too, the fictional portrayals, and took special inspiration from Brian Moore's *Black Robe*. Moore, I thought, had done better than scholars—better than anyone—with an obviously fundamental task: showing the strangeness of Indians (from a European standpoint) while still reflecting their basic humanity.

Through all this my focus narrowed and sharpened. Increasingly I fixed on the matter of "Indian captivity." In some respects the process seemed a retreat; the "captives" in question were colonists, not Indians. But, to be candid, I felt incapable of understanding Indians well enough to place them right at center-stage. (The colonists, too, have been hard to understand; but after many years of trying, I do think I know them. Indians present a deeper, more daunting challenge.)

Anyway, I compromised. My chosen story would be a captive's story, in its time the most famous of many such. Indians would be included, though not exactly featured. The subject—the frame and meaning of the story—would be the larger business of "contact," of "encounter," between these immensely different human groups. Captivity, after all, meant "contact" of a particularly vivid sort.

Moreover, I heard echoes reaching far through time. Contact across the lines of race and culture remains a lively, often painful, theme in our modern "global village." What another scholar calls "the contest of cultures in colonial North America" has obvious twentieth-century equivalents. Captivity itself retains a quite specific resonance: witness Tehran, witness Lebanon, witness "hijackings" of many sorts, witness (in our own country) sensational events like the capture and "redemption" of Patty Hearst.

᠊ᠣ

BUT ENOUGH; from here on the story must carry itself. It remains to acknowledge the range and depth of the *help* I've been given in every stage of this project.

June Namias was perhaps the first of my helpers; it was her dissertation (now a book) that introduced me to Eunice Williams and mapped the entire field of "captivity" studies. Soon thereafter I received important guidance from leading practitioners of ethnohistory: James Axtell, Denys DeLâge, William N. Fenton, Daniel Richter, and Dean Snow.

My several visits to the Kahnawake reserve were powerfully aided and abetted by Brian Deer, Léon Lajoie, and the late Henri Béchard.

Father Béchard's kindness and inexhaustible knowledge of the early Canadian missions have left an especially warm memory.

Deerfield, Massachusetts, was a second major site for my research. There the way was smoothed by Donald Friary, president of Historic Deerfield, Inc., David Proper, staff librarian, and historians Kevin Sweeney, Richard Melvoin, and Alexander Medlicott. Professor Sweeney, in particular, became my final authority on the many intricacies of Williams family history.

The project took me also to the Massachusetts town of Longmeadow, where Mabel Swanson and Virginia Flint, custodians of the local historical society, offered valuable assistance. I will long remember the afternoon when Mrs. Swanson casually produced the Rev. John Williams's personal firearm—itself a part of the story—from inside an old file drawer.

In each of these places, and a good many others, I availed myself of institutional help as well. The institutions included the American Antiquarian Society (Worcester, Mass.); the Archives de la Compagnie de Jésus (St. Jérôme, Canada, and Chantilly, France); the Archives de la Séminaire de Saint Sulpice (Montreal); the Bibliothèque Centrale (Montreal); the Bibliothèque Nationale (Paris); the Boston (Mass.) Public Library; the Dartmouth College Library (Hanover, N.H.); the Genealogical Library of the Church of Jesus Christ of Latter-Day Saints (Salt Lake City, Utah); the Historic Deerfield Library (Deerfield, Mass.); the Historical Society of Pennsylvania (Philadelphia, Pa.); the Houghton Library, Harvard University (Cambridge, Mass.); the Kanien'kahaka Raotitionkwa Cultural Center (Kahnawake, Canada); the Library of Congress (Washington, D.C.); the Longmeadow (Mass.) Historical Society; the Massachusetts Historical Society (Boston, Mass.); the Missouri Historical Society (St. Louis, Mo.); the New England Historic Genealogical Society (Boston, Mass.); the New York Public Library (New York, N.Y.); the New York State Archives (Albany, N.Y.); the New-York Historical Society (New York, N.Y.); the Newberry Library (Chicago, Ill.); the Public Archives of Canada (Ottawa, Canada); the Springfield (Mass.) City Library; the State Historical Society of Wisconsin, Area Research Center (Green Bay, Wisc.); the Sterling and Beinecke Libraries, Yale University (New Haven, Conn.); the Stockbridge (Mass.) Library Association; and the Richard S. Storrs Memorial Library (Longmeadow, Mass.). I am grateful to all these places for able ministrations by staff—and for permission to quote from original documents in their possession.

PREFACE

I pumped friends, colleagues, and complete strangers with questions on many specific points of research: Ross Beales, Nancy Bonvillain, Jon Butler, W. J. Eccles, Cornelius Jaenen, Edna Lemay, James P. Lynch, Frederick J. McGinness, John Merriman, Kenneth Minkima, Marianne Mithun, Nancy Roelker, Robert Schwartz, Jonathan Spence, William Starna, Lee Wandel, and Eleazer Williams.

Individual chapters were read and helpfully criticized by Richard D. Brown, David Brion Davis, Alison Demos, David Hackett Fischer, Alexander Keyssar, Sarah LeVine, Gerard McCauley, Richard Ross, Neal Salisbury, Harry Stout, and Laurel Ulrich.

In addition, six people have been through most, or all, of the final manuscript. Marybeth McCaulley endured the typing process with unfailing patience and good humor. Ashbel Green saw the project through, on the publisher's side, from start to finish. Jane Kamensky managed the delicate task of being simultaneously my student and my most effective line editor. Elinor Langer gave me full benefit of her uniquely acute "writer's eye." William Cronon offered suggestions both large and small; more than anyone else in recent years, he has helped me to grasp why history matters. And, as on so many occasions before, Virginia Demos infused all my efforts with her extraordinary powers of human—and humane—understanding.

To each and every one of these people my debt is large, and my thanks compounded accordingly. I am grateful also to the National Endowment for the Humanities and the American Council of Learned Societies for major fellowship awards, and to Yale University for a timely travel grant.

Learning, I have been reminded yet again, is a wonderfully cooperative enterprise . . .

J.D.
Watertown, Massachusetts
31 December 1992

Textual Note: In all of what follows, quoted passages are rendered with the original spelling and punctuation—except for a few cases where "modernization" seemed necessary to avoid ambiguity or outright misunderstanding.

THE UNREDEEMED CAPTIVE

Seal of the Massachusetts Bay Company 1629

BEGINNINGS

ॐ

WHERE DOES the story begin?

PERHAPS IT IS in the old university town of Cambridge, England. In the summer of 1629.

A group of English "Puritans," religious reformers increasingly at odds with the established church of their land, are meeting to plan a new settlement overseas. They have recently gained the necessary charter from the king and are about to move themselves and a few hundred "like-minded" followers to a place called Massachusetts Bay.[1]

Their view of this place, before they leave, is neatly expressed in the image they choose for their official seal. At its center, facing front, stands an Indian—naked apart from a small skirt of leaves covering his loins. His hands are spread; in one he holds a bow, in the other an arrow. He is flanked on both sides by trees, in obvious reference to his woodland "wilderness" environment. From his mouth rises a carefully lined bubble, enclosing the words "Come over and help us."[2]

In short, the Massachusetts Bay Colony is to be a charitable project (among other things): the native peoples will be "helped." From the "darkness of heathenism" they will be drawn toward the bright light of Protestant Christianity. From their lowly state of "savagery" they will be raised to the heights of English "civility." Religion, technology, clothing, personal deportment: all are included here in a sweeping vision of cultural change. This in turn will be linked to a process of ecological change: English settlers "taming the wilderness" and remaking America in the image of their motherland.[3]

The process will begin from the moment of their arrival. Each new village founded, each field planted, every tree cut down and sawed to boards (for houses, barns, fences, or furnishings) will be a step toward their ultimate goal. The project with the Indians will also move apace: quite soon, for example, there will be special "praying towns" for native converts.[4]

However, neither process nor project will go as smoothly as the colonists hope. There will be occasional searing setbacks—like "Indian wars." There will be periods of difficulty and "deadness," when Nature itself seems to fight back: droughts, storms, crop blights, winter cold beyond anything they have known before. And at some deeper (mostly unacknowledged) level, there will be growing worry that the process might reverse itself—so as to make the currents of change run the opposite way. Instead of their civilizing the wilderness (and its savage inhabitants), the wilderness might change, might *un*civilize, *them*. This they will feel as an appalling prospect, a nightmare to resist and suppress by every means possible.[5]

In fact, experience will sometimes enlarge the worry and make it acutely specific. Towns will find themselves unable to support schools or ministers; learning and piety will suffer as a result. Unattached and undisciplined individuals will gravitate to frontier sites where the fist of authority cannot reach; there "riotous living" will flourish without check. Moreover, in the continuing struggles with Indians, certain colonists will be captured and physically removed from the "abodes of civilized life." Reduced thereby to the status of prisoners, they will have to adjust to the "brutish ways" of their "masters." (Indians as *masters*: another, deeply shocking inversion.)[6]

But even this is not the worst of it. The worst is that some captives will come to *prefer* Indian ways—and will refuse subsequent chances for repatriation. Here will be seen a direct fulfillment of the nightmare prospect: civilized people willingly turned savage, their vaunted "Old World" culture overwhelmed by the wilderness.[7]

None of this, of course, is in the minds of the Puritan leaders planning their journey to Massachusetts in 1629. "Come over and help us," says the Indian on their seal—and that is all he says. It seems so simple, so straightforward, in the anticipation. And will prove so enormously complicated in the result.

৵

PERHAPS IT BEGINS in the villages of the Iroquois heartland (what is today upstate New York). In the decade of the 1660s.

Oneida villages, Cayuga villages, Onondaga villages. And, most especially, Mohawk villages. In many of these places the 1660s are a time of particular crisis. War has become a regular feature of life: war against other Indian groups (Susquehannocks to the south, Mahicans and Sokokis to the east, Algonquins to the north), and war, too, against the French colonists in Canada. In 1665, the French conclude a truce with most of the Iroquois tribes. But the Mohawks decline to join—and soon pay for it. The following year brings two separate military expeditions from Canada, deep into Mohawk territory. The first yields only a standoff, but the second is crushingly successful. The inhabitants of the native "castles" (fortified settlements) flee before the advancing army—which then proceeds to burn their houses and despoil their food stores. Soon thereafter the Mohawks, too, sue for peace.[8]

Epidemic disease—carried to America in the boats and bodies of the European colonizers—is an equally crippling factor. Smallpox, typhus, measles, and various forms of respiratory illness: each takes a relentless toll. To make up their demographic losses, Iroquois communities frequently absorb and "adopt" the prisoners taken in their various wars. But this creates internal complications—of ethnic, linguistic, and (sometimes) religious difference.[9]

For some years, too, in the intervals between wars, French Jesuit missionaries have been laboring to turn the Iroquois toward Christianity. Their experience has been uneven. Some are welcomed into the castles; others are expelled; a few are tortured, executed, and thus "martyred" (from the Catholic point of view). But they do make converts, as their work goes on. By now, many Iroquois villages are divided into bitterly antagonized factions: newly professed Christians on the one hand, versus staunch "traditionalists" on the other.[10]

Economic pressure—and economic opportunity—also bring disruption. For decades the Iroquois have been moving into the orbit of European commerce. Their involvement in the fur trade, for example, has been massively consequential. As huntsmen, as traders, as arbiters and enforcers in the trade of other tribes, their role is central; their so-called beaver wars are a direct result. But even where they are most successful, they pay a price in growing dependence on foreign markets and external supply. Indeed, the very integrity of their culture hangs in the balance: the authority of their chiefs, the ritual knowledge of their shamans, the traditional responsibilities of their clans, their finely calibrated relationships to Nature.[11]

Amid so much turmoil and change, individual people increasingly decide to leave. Some are Christian converts, driven out by traditionalist opponents or lured away by Jesuit mentors. Some are captive adoptees, seeking a safer, less dominating host community. Some are entrepreneurs: men, and women too, eager to exploit the new possibilities of intercultural trade. And some aim simply to escape. Moreover, in such a fluid situation personal factors may more easily lead to removal: feuds, embarrassment, all manner of localized "discontent."

Their leaving, of course, may take them in many directions. But the biggest number go north, following lines of movement already laid down by missionaries and traders. These lines will carry them, eventually, to Canada. There they will reorganize themselves into new communities. And will collectively become known—to the colonists farther south—as "the French Indians." In time, the term itself will acquire an aura of deep menace and terror.

ꝛ

PERHAPS IT BEGINS in the Massachusetts town of Dedham. On May 22, 1670.

The townsmen have gathered in the parlor of one of their leaders, Lieutenant Joseph Fisher, to take a series of steps toward creating a new community. They have been, for the past several years, beneficiaries of an unusual "gift" from the Massachusetts General Court: 8,000 acres of land "in any convenient place . . . where it shall be found free from former grants." They have chosen a particularly fertile tract at a place called Pocumtuck, on a tributary of the "Great River" (today the Connecticut), eighty miles to the west. This grant comes as compensation for lands lost, within their own borders, to a recently established "praying town" of Indians.[12]

In fact, what Dedham has lost to one group of Indians it is taking from another. Pocumtuck was, for generations, the home of a small tribe by the same name. But in 1664, its people were attacked and devastated by Mohawk enemies from eastern New York; their surviving remnant lies helpless to resist further incursions. By the end of the decade, their ownership rights have been bought or bartered away, and their land itself has been carefully reconnoitered by "explorers" from Dedham.

The object, that morning at Lieutenant Fisher's, is to divide the lands of Pocumtuck "severally" among all Dedham property owners.

The process is not simple—and will require additional meetings to complete—but within weeks there are settlers on site. Over the next few years the population will grow steadily, to a total of about 200. Fields will be planted, town government established, a minister hired: customary stages, all, in the evolution of New England towns.[13]

But Pocumtuck's evolution will soon depart from the customary. In the spring of 1675, New Englanders, native and colonist, will plunge into a horrific race war—King Philip's War, as it will subsequently be known, after its Indian leader.[14] The fledgling community of Pocumtuck is immediately vulnerable; within weeks it will be attacked, overwhelmed, and abandoned. When, in the following year, the English side emerges victorious, efforts at resettlement will begin—but slowly and with much caution. Not until a decade has passed will the town regain its prewar size and condition. By then it will have a substantially different population—and also a different name: *Deerfield*. (Perhaps its prior, Indian name carries too many painful associations.)

For a brief period in the 1680s its prospects will seem moderately bright—with a new minister, a new meetinghouse, a new mill, a cadre of newly arrived craftsmen, and a new structure of local governance. But soon the picture will darken again, as a new war brings the threat— then the reality—of violence back to Deerfield. This time it is a European war (the so-called War of the League of Augsburg) with an offshoot in colonial America: New France (Canada) versus New York and New England.

The Massachusetts frontier will be a primary target, and Deerfield will become a fortified village. Six times in the 1690s the town will sustain direct attacks; all will be repelled, though at a considerable cost in bloodshed. Finally, in 1697, the various European powers will make peace—for themselves, and for their colonial "dominions" as well. But the peace will prove short-lived.[15]

⁂

PERHAPS IT BEGINS in the "borning room" of a particular house at Deerfield. In September 1696.

The house belongs to the local minister, the Reverend John Williams. This man is thirty-two years old; he has been in Deerfield for more than a decade. He was raised in Roxbury (near Boston), as the fourth child (second son) of Samuel and Theoda (Parke) Williams. His father was a farmer, shoemaker, and "ruling elder" in the Roxbury church. (The minister of that church was the Reverend John Eliot, founder of the "praying town" carved from lands at Dedham, and widely celebrated as New England's foremost "Apostle to the Indians.")[16] His paternal grandfather, Robert Williams, had also been a shoemaker (or "cordwainer," in the parlance of the time). Robert was actually the first of the Williamses to live in Massachusetts, having arrived from England in 1637 as part of the Puritans' "Great Migration." Further back, the family tree reached to the region known as East Anglia—and possibly to Wales.[17]

If John Williams's pedigree seems certifiably Puritan, his wife's is even more so. She was born Eunice Mather, daughter of the Reverend Eleazer Mather, pastor of Northampton, Massachusetts; as such, she is linked to the colony's premier line of religious leaders. The famous Boston ministers Increase and Cotton Mather are, respectively, her uncle and first cousin. There are ministers, too, on her mother's side— for example, her grandfather, the Reverend John Warham, one of the founders of colonial Connecticut. Her father died when she was still a child. Her mother then married the Reverend Solomon Stoddard, her father's successor in the Northampton pastorate and an eminent "divine" in his own right.

These connections, plus John's education, plus his position as minister, establish the Williamses as Deerfield's foremost family. And the family is growing—with the births, at regular intervals, of children. Six have arrived prior to the summer of 1696 (though only four are still living); another is on the way. There is, no doubt, some apprehension as Mrs. Williams approaches the end of her pregnancy; an infant son has died just weeks before. But on September 17 she bears an evidently healthy daughter. Who is herself named Eunice, after the mother.

In the years to follow, this child will start the "pilgrimage" of life in ways that reflect her Puritan heritage, her family's elevated status, and her sex. She will learn—probably from her parents, and possibly, too, at the local "dame school"—to read, to pray, to recite Scripture. She will perform small chores in the household, alongside her mother and older sister. She may also take some part in the care of younger siblings. For her family will continue to grow—with the arrival in 1698 of her brother John, in 1699 of another brother, Warham, in 1701 of her twin sisters Jemima and Jerusha (these, however, will die in infancy), and in January 1704 of a sister also named Jerusha.

At this point she will rank as the fifth of her parents' eight living

children. She will begin to look forward to her later childhood, and
even to her adult life as a Puritan "gentlewoman." In the middle of
her eighth year the way ahead will seem straight, predictable, and
unusually promising. But in this place, at this time, no child's future
is secure.

᠊ᢌ᠊

PERHAPS IT BEGINS in the royal palace, in Madrid, center of the
sprawling Spanish Empire. In the autumn of the year 1700.

The king, Charles II, is dying. ("The Sufferer," he is sometimes
called.) He has no heir, and with his passing, his family line—the
Spanish Hapsburgs—will be extinct. Around him rise old tides of
controversy: Who will follow him to the throne? As his condition
worsens, he writes a will—*his* will on the matter of the succession.
His choice is a young French duke, Philippe of Anjou, grandson and
protégé of the Bourbon "Sun King," Louis XIV.

Death takes him on November 1st. Louis moves to assert the claims
of the duke—who is, in due course, installed as Philip V, King of
Spain. But elsewhere in Europe this joining of two crowns, two empires, in the Bourbon line arouses deep anxiety. Within the year a
"Grand Alliance," led by King William III of England and the Holy
Roman Emperor Leopold I, will form in opposition. The result will
be a bloody ten-year conflict, known to history as the War of the
Spanish Succession. England and France are, as on several previous
occasions, principal antagonists. William III dies in 1702, but the war
will be vigorously pursued by his successor, the Princess (now Queen)
Anne.[18]

Fighting begins in various parts of Europe, and once again leaps the
Atlantic to the colonies on the other side. In autumn 1703, a Canadian
force—combining French soldiers and officers with hundreds of
"French Indian" warriors—attacks English settlements in an outlying
region of (what will later become) the province of Maine. Lives are
lost, prisoners taken, houses burned, fields destroyed. And apprehen-
sions rise all along the New England frontier.

᠊ᢌ᠊

TO RECAPITULATE: Cambridge (England), Iroquoia, Dedham,
Deerfield, Madrid. In short, *multiple* beginnings: none of them truly

"first," each of them contributing, in one way or another, to the story that follows.

To this list of five could certainly be added others—indeed, an almost infinite number. As with all the stories that together form "history."

ONE

ॐ

DEERFIELD, MASSACHUSETTS. October 1703. Harvest over.
First frost. The valley ablaze with autumn color: reds and yellows at
the sides (along the forested ridges of East Mountain and the lower
hills to the west), green of the meadows in between. The river low
and languorous, a glassy rope snaked through the center. The most
beautiful month, sunset of the year.

Do the townspeople notice? No, they are fixed on the night ahead.
Danger grows in darkening corners. *Night of winter, night of want,
night of war.*

They have, already, shocking news "from the eastward": the "mis-
chief" done by French and Indian enemies along the Maine frontier.
Will it be their turn next? They make what preparations they can. For
some years past, Deerfield, like other exposed villages, has maintained
a protective "fort" (or "stockade"). Within this central area of roughly
ten acres, enclosed by a tall picket fence, the entire populace can be
gathered in case of attack. The fence, however, has rotted in some
places. And the housing within the fort falls far short of current need:
perhaps a dozen regular dwellings, plus a few "cellars" and "small
houses." (This, for a community of roughly 300.) So, they must
rebuild the fence and create additional shelter inside.[1]

But even before they can begin this work, the war reaches them.
On the evening of October 8th, two young men "went into ye meadow"
to tend their cows, and "were ambushed by indians . . . beyond Frary's
bridge." The attackers "fird at them, but missed"; however, while
trying to flee, they were captured and "carried to Canada." Nor was
this the first such encounter: "My father escaped narrowly ye night
before at Broughton's hill." The writer of these lines (years later) was
only a child at the time.[2] But the darkness to come—no respecter of

age—would take him heedlessly, along with the rest. His father, too: lucky once, but not again.

The father is John Williams—the "Reverend Mr." John Williams—minister of Deerfield, and, in effect, town leader. On October 21st, he writes a long letter to "his Excellency Joseph Dudley his Majestie's Governor for the Province of Massachusetts Bay," with much affecting description of Deerfield's current plight and fears for the future. The townspeople have abandoned their homes for the safety of the fort, where their crowded situation prevents "indoor affairs being carried on to any advantage." They have "in the alarms, several times been wholly taken off from any business, the whole town kept in"; their children they dare not send into the fields at all. They feel so vulnerable to attack that some among them "would freely leave all they have & go away." Indeed, "strangers [say] . . . they would not live where we do for twenty times as much as we do."

The letter has a specific purpose: to explain and to justify the town's wish for "relief" from provincial taxes. It requests, as well, a subsidy toward rebuilding the fort. Finally, there is the matter of the young men captured two weeks before, whose "sorrowful parents and distressed widow . . . request your Excellency to endeavour that there may be an exchange of prisoners to their release."[3]

This insider's view of the situation at Deerfield is confirmed in a separate letter sent from the neighboring town of Northampton a day later. The writer, Solomon Stoddard, is John Williams's pastoral colleague—and kinsman (stepfather-in-law). "Their circumstances," he declares, "doe call for commiseration." In fact, "their spirits are so taken up about their Dangers, that they have little heart to undertake what is needful for advancing their estates." Stoddard, too, believes that Deerfield should be "freed from Country Rates [taxes] during the time of the war." And he advances a further suggestion: that New England's soldiers be "put in a way to hunt the Inds. with dogs." Stoddard knows that "it might be looked upon as inhuman to persue them in such a maner . . . if the Indians were as other people are." But—the point is—they are *not* as other people are. Their methods of waging war are especially barbarous: "they don't appear openly in the field to bid us battle, [and] they use those cruelly that fall into their hands. They act like wolves, & are to be dealt withall as wolves."[4]

A severe indictment, very severe. But an accurate sign of popular feeling as winter approaches. *Night of wolves.*

To these appeals from (and on behalf of) Deerfield, the Governor and his Councillors respond with sympathy. Taxes "abated." And a special allowance to be "paid out of the publick Treasury towards the support of the ministry in . . . Deerfield." And "sixteen soldiers" to be stationed "at the garrison" there. Spirits rise along with the new fortifications. The town feels stronger now.[5]

Then, a kind of lull. November, December, January: a season of more-than-ordinary cold, and deep snow, all across New England.[6] Deerfield does not immediately relax; its people continue for a time "taken up about their dangers." There are rumors of war, but no actual fighting. In early December the "garrison soldiers" are withdrawn. And, probably about then, some of the families housed temporarily within the fort go back to their homes outside.[7]

Has the danger truly passed? Some remain apprehensive—for example, the minister, described (in one later account) as "strongly possest that the Town would in a little time be destroyed." But others "make light of [such] impressions." Occasionally "intelligence" arrives from elsewhere. Albany is a major conduit of trade—and of information—from Canada; one source there forwards a warning of "designs of the enemy" upon the frontier towns. Yet this, too, is disputed in "a letter from one of Westfield, who sojourning that winter in Albany, and loath his wife should be under fear, signifyed that altho there was such advice, yet but few took notice of it." Back and forth, to and fro. No one can be sure.[8]

In mid-February, the mood swings sharply toward vigilance. Hard news, again, from the east: Parties of Indians have attacked Berwick, Haverhill, and Exeter, and there are casualties ("some killed & some taken captive"). Colonel Samuel Partridge, military commander in the Connecticut Valley, expects "ye Enemy to come Over into our parts"; and then "our Upper towns will be in danger . . . in speciall Derefield." Meanwhile, too, there is the possibility of direct attack from the north (Canada): "we are prserved yet & hope for respitt till ye Rivers break up & the great Body of Snow yet with us & up the River [be] drawn down," but after that "we look for troubles." Time, in short, to refurbish local defenses—and on February 24th twenty "muskiteers" are reassigned to the "garrison" at Deerfield.[9]

There is also response of another sort. John Williams, gripped more than ever by a sense of impending crisis, announces a day of prayer and fasting in the Deerfield church. Two services, two programs, two sermons. "In the forenoon," as Williams will remember later, he preaches from the thirty-second chapter of the Book of Genesis: "I am not worthy of the least of all the mercies and of all the truth which thou hast showed unto thy servant. Deliver me, I pray thee, from the hand of my brother, from the hand of Esau, for I fear him, lest he will come and smite me and the Mother with the children." And, "in the afternoon," Williams takes another verse from the same Scriptural chapter: "He said, 'let me go, for the day breaketh'; and he said, 'I will not let thee go, except thou bless me.' "¹⁰

For the members of John Williams's congregation these texts are immediately resonant. Both refer to the figure of Jacob, following his estrangement from his older brother, Esau. In the Biblical story, Jacob practices a deception to obtain their father's blessing, which belongs, as a birthright, to Esau. He flees, and hopes for an end to Esau's righteous anger, and eventually prepares to return. The theme here is unworthiness and fear. And the people of Deerfield, like many New Englanders of their time, may indeed feel unworthy. Inheritors of the spiritual traditions of their forebears (the founding "fathers"), they have—so their preachers insist—gone increasingly astray; in a sense they, too, hold a false blessing.¹¹ This, in turn, might well make them afraid—for themselves and for their families ("the Mother with the children"). Perhaps they *deserve* "smiting" by an avenging hand. But perhaps, like Jacob, they will be spared that fate—thanks to a merciful God.

And so, to the second of the sermon texts. As Jacob awaits his meeting with Esau, he finds himself wrestling in the night with a powerful stranger. Though exhausted and injured, he hangs on till morning—when the stranger demands to be released. This part of the story emphasizes persistence, the refusal of despair—and is no less apposite than the other. For, surely, some of John Williams's hearers are inclined to lose heart and "let go," as the fear-filled winter drags on. And is there also a broader meaning, for all "settlers" on the New England frontier—wrestling, as they repeatedly are, against strange, largely unseen forces? And a meaning, even, for all Puritans—struggling, in their spiritual lives, for signs of "assurance" and "grace," against seemingly unknowable odds? Thus do religion, ecology, and present circumstance converge on Deerfield's day of fasting in February 1704.

There are, in addition, some unusual portents. (Or so say the later accounts.) A night when the people of Deerfield are "strangely amused, by a trampling Noise round the Fort, as if it were beset by Indians." (In the morning, however: no Indians, no tracks, nothing.) And an evening in the adjacent town of Hatfield when "a black cloud" appears, which "on a sudden [is] burned as red as blood." Another kind of convergence: *noise, burning,* and *blood.*[12]

⌇

MONTREAL, CANADA (NEW FRANCE). OCTOBER 1703. Same autumn, same look. But different people, and an entirely different mood. Here the news from the Maine frontier gives much satisfaction. An official communiqué, sent to the Ministry of the Marine (in Paris), describes "the war-party sent out towards the region of Boston." Governor Pierre de Rigaud, the Marquis de Vaudreuil, "believes it has succeeded very well"; the specific results include "more than fifteen leagues of countryside . . . laid waste" and "more than three hundred persons . . . captured or killed." Moreover, the governor's aim in organizing the expedition—to render the Abenaki Indians and the English colonists "irreconcilable enemies"—has apparently been realized.[13]

As the war intensifies, the interests of French Canada depend on a delicate balance of forces. The actual French settlers—the *habitants*— are vastly outnumbered by their English counterparts to the south. But their leaders, in Quebec and Montreal, have managed over the years to build a wall of protective relationships with the surrounding tribes of Indians. The Abenakis are an increasingly important bulwark; indeed, some among them have come to live in the St. Lawrence Valley, as virtual clients of New France. The "Five Nations" Iroquois, for their part, have given up their traditionally hostile stance; a recent and celebrated treaty leaves them neutral in the Anglo-French conflict. Moreover, like the Abenakis, the Iroquois have yielded recruits for the migrant communities in the Valley. (Migrant communities, which are also *mission*-communities; for they lie within the ambit of resident Catholic priests.) Increasingly, these "domiciled Indians" (*sauvages domiciliés*) are linked to New France by ties of trade and political advantage. And, when need be, they provide the French with scores of fighting men skilled in the ways of wilderness war.[14]

The August attack on New England is only a starter. Quickly, the English strike back, devastating half a dozen Abenaki towns. This prompts a delegation to Quebec: "they informed us [of their losses] and asked us at the same time for help." Vaudreuil fairly leaps at the chance. By year's end, he is laying plans for a new "expedition": an unusual wintertime thrust "over the ice" toward another part of "the region of the Boston government." The specific target is "a little village of about forty households (*feux*)," a place misnamed in the French records "Guerrefille."[5] (An ironic twist just there: "Deerfield" becomes "Wardaughter.")

The commander will be a young "lieutenant" named Jean-Baptiste Hertel de Rouville, scion of a family already renowned for military prowess and described by the governor as "very proper for such an expedition." The force will include some four dozen Frenchmen, soldiers and officers (four of them brothers of Hertel), plus an additional 200 of the "domiciled" Indians. The latter are Abenakis from the village of St. François (east of Montreal), Hurons from the mission at Lorette (still farther east), and Mohawk Iroquois from Kahnawake (to the southwest).[16] They make, all in all, a motley group—consider the language problem—embracing a variety of hopes and goals. The Abenakis, we know, will go for the sake of revenge. The Hurons and Kahnawake Mohawks have no such direct motive; but they think of themselves as "brothers" to the Abenakis and "children" of the French. Too, there will be chances for "plunder" and captives—a traditional incentive among these groups. As for Vaudreuil himself: his aims (*raisons*) are of several sorts. To cement further the system of native alliances. To carry the fighting far to the south. To keep the enemy off balance and preoccupied with problems of defense. And, probably, to take an important English prisoner.[17]

This last deserves our special consideration; never acknowledged in so many words, it nonetheless is implied by subsequent events. Probably—and we must retain that qualifier—Vaudreuil has his sights set straight on the Reverend John Williams. Why? Because the English are holding a key French prisoner: a curious, notorious, and quite mysterious figure known (on both sides) as "Captain Baptiste." Born Jean-Baptiste Guyon, this man is either an extraordinarily skillful "privateer" (the French view) or a heinous pirate (the English one). Whichever, there is no disputing the havoc he has wrought with English shipping: the boats sunk, the cargoes taken, the lives lost, through at least a dozen years. In 1702, his career is interrupted: captured that summer off the coast of Maine, he has since been confined to a Boston jail. But Vaudreuil wants him back—and badly. How to make this happen? With a prisoner exchange. An exchange for whom? For someone no less valued by the other side. Like John Williams.

And so—again, probably—the governor concocts a special plan. It will not do to have a noncombatant clergyman seized directly by French military forces. But what about the Indians? With them the case is different. Quietly, perhaps secretly, Vaudreuil approaches the leaders of the mission Indians. His plan is discussed, his terms accepted. Three trusted warriors are designated to take the minister, and return him to Montreal; for this Vaudreuil will pay them well (in effect, a ransom). Then: Williams for Baptiste. Another important *raison*.[18]

᪥

SOME THINGS we have to imagine. The gathering of the "expedition" members, presumably at Montreal in early February. The feasting and dancing, and speech-making, before they set out. Their progress south, largely on frozen rivers and lakes, with one hard leg across the Green Mountains. They have snowshoes for walking, and sleds to carry their supplies, and dogs to pull the sleds. The lower part of their route follows the Connecticut River Valley, till it reaches a point near (what would later become) the town of Brattleboro, Vermont. Here they will strike off into the woods to the south, leaving dogs and sleds (probably with a small guard) for their return. They are barely a day's march (twenty miles) from their objective. The rest they will cover as quickly and quietly as possible. Surprise is their most potent weapon.[19]

And Deerfield will indeed be surprised. The "day of fasting," the portents, the warnings received from east and west: these have aroused a general apprehension. But of specific dangers—specific, real, and now very imminent—they know nothing. The recently arrived soldiers are distributed here and there: several to Captain Thomas Wells's "fortified house" (fortified, apparently, with its own palisade fence), three to Sergeant Benoni Stebbins's house, two to guard the minister's family, and so on. (Wells and Stebbins are officers in the local militia.) Several families from the north part of town continue to board, or at least to sleep, with friends and relatives inside the fort. But those who live to the south feel less exposed; they remain in their own homes. There are lookouts in the "mounts" along the main fence, and a "watch" to walk the streets at night. And Colonel Partridge keeps occasional "troops" prowling the woods nearby. But all this—to repeat—is for general, not specific, protection. Presumably, then, on the evening of Monday, February 28, the town goes to sleep in the usual way.

Midnight. Across the river to the west the expedition members are making final preparations for their assault. Loading weapons. Putting on war paint. Reviewing plans. (The layout of the town is, apparently, known to them, from visits made in previous years by Indian hunters and traders.) Presently, a scout is sent "to discover the posture of the Town, who observing the Watch walking in the Streets" returns to his comrades and "puts them to a stand." Another check, a short while later, brings a different result. The village lies "all . . . still and quiet"; the watch, evidently, has fallen asleep. It is now about four o'clock (a.m.). Time for the attackers to move.[20]

Over the river, on the ice. Across a mile of meadowland, ghostly and white. Past the darkened houses at the north end of the street. Right up to the fort. The snow has piled hugely here; the drifts make walkways to the top of the fence. A vanguard of some forty men climbs quickly over, and drops down on the inside. A gate is opened to admit the rest. The watch awakens, fires a warning shot, cries "Arm!": too little, surely, and far too late. (John Williams will subsequently describe him as "unfaithful" and warn "all watchmen" to avoid his example, lest they, too, "bring charge of blood upon themselves.") The attackers separate into smaller parties, and "immediately set upon breaking open doors and windows."[21]

The townspeople come to life with a rush. Some find opportunities to escape, by jumping from windows or roof-lines. Several manage to flee the stockade altogether and make their way to neighboring villages. (For example: "[Goodman] Allison & his wife escaped out the great gate meadow-ward & ran to Hatfield; she was frozen in her feet very much . . .") In half a dozen households the men leave families behind, in order to rally outside as a counterforce. ("Deacon Sheldon, Godfre Nims & a souldier escaped to Capt Wells' forte.") In others there is a frantic attempt to hide. ("Ebenezer Brooks & family went down into thir cellar & so did Serg. Mun in his house run down into the cellar & so were not found the houses left unburned.")[22]

The minister's house is a special target, singled out "in the beginning of the onset"; later, John Williams will remember (and write about) his experience in detail. Roused "out of sleep . . . by their violent endeavors to break open doors and windows with axes and hatchets," he leaps from bed, runs to the front door, sees "the enemy making their entrance," awakens the pair of soldiers lodged upstairs, and returns to his bedside "for my arms." There is hardly time, for the "enemy immediately brake into the room, I judge to the number of twenty, with painted faces and hideous acclamations." (They are "all of them Indians [Abenakis] and Macquas [Mohawks]"; no Frenchmen in sight as yet.) The minister does manage to cock his pistol and "put it to the breast of the first Indian that came up." Fortunately—for both of them—it misfires. Whereupon Williams is "seized by 3 Indians, disarmed, and bound . . . naked, as I was in my shirt"; in this posture he will remain "for near the space of an hour."

With their chief prize secured, the invaders turn to "rifling the house, entering in great numbers into every room." There is killing work, too: "Some were so cruel and barbarous as to take and carry to the door two of my children and murder them [six-year-old John Jr.. and six-week-old Jerusha], as also a Negro woman [a family slave, named Parthena]." After "insulting over me a while, holding up hatchets over my head, [and] threatening to burn all I had," the Indians allow their captive to dress. (Very carefully, though: "keeping me bound with a cord on one arm, till I put on my clothes to the other, and then changing my cord.") They also permit Mrs. Williams "to dress herself and our children."[23]

By this time the sun is "about an hour high" (perhaps 7 a.m.). The sequence described by John Williams has been experienced, with some variations, in households throughout the fort: killings (especially of infants and others considered too frail to survive the rigors of life on the trail); "Rifleing houses of provissions, mony, cloathing, drink"; "fireing houses" (once they have been rifled); "killing Cattle, hogs, sheep, & sakeing & wasting all that came before ym."[24] When Williams and his family are finally taken outside, they see "many of the houses . . . in flames"; later, in recalling the moment, he asks rhetorically, "Who can tell what sorrows pierced our souls?"[25]

The Williamses know they are destined "for a march . . . into a strange land," as prisoners. And prisoners are being herded together—in the meetinghouse and in a home nearby—from all over town. However, one household (that of Sergeant Stebbins) in the northwest corner of the stockade has mounted a remarkable resistance. Its occupants—"7 men, besides woemen and children"—are well armed and fiercely determined; moreover, the walls of this house, "being filled up with brick," effectively repel incoming fire. The battle continues here for more than two hours. The attackers fall back, then surge forward in an unsuccessful attempt "to fire ye house." Again they retreat—this time to the shelter of the meetinghouse—while maintaining their fusillade all the while. The defenders return bullet for bullet, "accepting of no q[uarte]r, though offered," and "causing sev[era]ll of the Enemy to fall." These casualties include "one frenctch-man, a Gentile man [gentleman] to appearance," and "3 or 4 Indians."

Among the latter is a "captain" who had, shortly before, been part of the group personally responsible for seizing John Williams.[26]

In the meantime, some of the attackers, with their captives, begin to leave the fort. Heading north, they retrace their steps toward the river. Then, a stunning intervention: a band of Englishmen arrives from the villages below (where an orange glow on the horizon "gave Notice [of the attack] . . . before we had News from the Distressed people" themselves). "Being a little above forty in number," they have "hasted" on horseback to bring relief. They stop briefly in the southern—and so far undamaged—part of the town, to pick up "fifteen of Deerfield men" (probably from Captain Wells's house). And this combined force proceeds to the fort, to deliver a surprise of its own: "When we entred at one gate, the enemy fled out at the other." Now comes a flat-out chase—pell-mell across the meadow—the erstwhile attackers put to rout. (In their panic they leave "a great part of their plunder behinde them.") The Englishmen warm—literally—to the fight, stripping off clothing as they run. (Later they will seek compensation for the loss of certain "garments, which we had put off . . . in the pursuit." For instance: "one hat and a pair of gloves"; a "coat and jacket"; even "one pr new shoes and spurs.") They inflict heavy casualties: "We saw at the time many dead bodies, and . . . afterwards . . . manifest prints on the snow, where other dead bodies were drawn to a hole in the river."[27]

They make, in sum, a highly successful counterattack. But one that is "pursued to farr, imprudently," creating new dangers. For, across the river, the French commanders hear the tumult and observe the chase—and swiftly regroup their forces. The riverbank affords an excellent cover for a new stand; soon a "Numerous Company [of] . . . fresh hands" is in place there, concealed and waiting. On the Englishmen come, ignoring the orders of Captain Wells, "who led them [and] called for a retreat." On and on—the river is just ahead, and the captives are waiting on the other side—into the teeth of a withering ambush: "The Enemy . . . Rose up [and] Fired upon us." About face, and back across the meadow one more time; pursued and pursuers reversing roles. The English are hard-pressed, "our breath being Spent, theirs in full Strength." Their retreat is as orderly as they can make it, "faceing & fireing, so that those that first failed might be defended"; even so, "many were Slain and others wounded." Eventually, the survivors regain the fort and clamber inside—at which "the Enemy drew off." They will appear no more.[28]

It is now about 9 a.m. The "massacre" is ended.

A NUMBNESS settles over the village. The fires are burning down. There is blood on the snow along the street. The survivors of the "meadow fight" crouch warily behind the palisades. After some minutes the townspeople start to filter back in, through the south gate. Time to look after their wounded, and count their dead.

Viewed from close up, the carnage is appalling. Death by various means—by gunshot, by hatchet, by knife, by war club—grisly beyond words. Moreover, the torn bodies on the ground are not the whole of it; when they poke through the rubble, they find more. Casualty lists, made later, will have entries like this: "Mary, Mercy, and Mehitable Nims [ages 5, 5, and 7 respectively] supposed to be burnt in the cellar." Indeed, several of their cellar hideouts have turned into death traps; in one house fully ten people lie "stifled" that way.[29]

And then, the injured. One man shot through the arm. Another with a bullet in his thigh. Another with a shattered foot. Yet another who had been briefly captured by the Indians, and "when I was in their hands, they cut off the forefinger of my right hand" (a traditional Iroquois practice with captives). A young woman "wounded" in the Stebbins house. A second with an ankle broken while jumping from an upper-story window.[30]

There are, too, the lucky ones: quite a number who might have been killed or injured (or captured) but managed somehow to escape. The people who ran out in the first moments and fled the town unobserved. A young couple (and their infant son) whose "small house" was so small that the snow had covered it completely. A woman who lay hidden beneath an overturned tub. A boy who dived under a pile of flax. Some of this is remembered only by "tradition," not hard evidence, but is too compelling to overlook. Here is another instance, passed through generations of the descendants of Mrs. Mary Catlin:

> The captives were taken to a house . . . and a Frenchman was brought in [wounded] and laid on the floor; he was in great distress and called for water; Mrs. Catlin fed him with water. Some one said to her, "How can you do that for your enemy?" She replied, "If thine enemy hunger, feed him; if he thirst, give him water to drink." The Frenchman was taken and carried away, and the captives marched off. Some thought the kindness shown to the Frenchman was the reason of Mrs. Catlin's being left. . . . [Mary Catlin was indeed "left," the only one of her large family

not killed or captured. And this is as plausible an explanation of
her survival as any.]

Thus Deerfield, in the immediate aftermath: the living and the dead,
the wounded and the escaped. "Tradition" also tells of a mass burial
in the southeast corner of the town cemetery. Another "sorrowful"
task for the survivors.[31]

Soon additional groups of armed men begin arriving from the towns
"below." All day and through the evening they come; by midnight
there are "neer about 80." Together they debate the obvious question,
the only one that matters right now. Should they follow the retreating
enemy, to retake their captive "friends"? Some are for it—better to
try than do nothing—but eventually counter-arguments prevail. They
have no snowshoes, "ye snow being at Least 3 foot deep." The enemy
has "treble our Numbr, if not more." Following "in their path . . . we
should too much Expose our men." Moreover, the captives themselves
will be endangered, "Mr. Williams famyly Especially, whome ye Enemy would kill, if we come on."

The day after, "Coniticot men began to come in"; by nightfall their
number has swelled to fully 250. There is more debate on what to do
next. However, the "aforesd Objections" remain—plus one more.
The weather has turned unseasonably warm, "wth Raine;" and the
snowpack is going to slush. They "judge it impossible to travail [ex-
cept] . . . to uttermost disadvantage." Under the circumstances they
could hardly hope "to offend the Enemy or Rescue our Captives,
which was ye End we aimed at in all." And so they "desist" once again.
They give what further help they can to "ye Remayneing Inhabitants"—help with the burials, and with rounding up the surviving
cattle. They leave "a Garrisson of 30 men or upwards, undr Capt.
Wells." And the rest return "to our places."[32]

⸙

BEFORE THEY GO, Colonel Partridge gathers information for a
report to his superiors in Boston. Completed and sent a few days later,
this "Account of Ye Destruction at Deerfd Febr 29, 1703–4" has
remained in a public archive ever since—the only such artifact of the
massacre known to have come straight down from that day to this.[33]
Inevitably, a scholar who holds it in his hands sees more than the
words on the page: sees the rough (but remarkably strong) qualities

of the paper, the occasional blurriness of the ink, the clear and steady penmanship of the writer (clear and steady in spite of the horror). Sees also, behind the pen and paper, the figure of the Colonel moving amongst the survivors, comforting and questioning (and writing) by turns. The pastness of history briefly dissolves—or, rather, re-forms as the succession of present moments it was (and is). The scholar feels that bygone present simultaneously with his own. 1704, 1990; Deerfield then, Boston now; the snowy street of a shattered village, the genteel appointments of a modern library: juxtaposed—no, joined—by the document, at once theirs and ours.

Of course, information is also part of the joining. And Partridge's "Account" gives information that can be found nowhere else. Of special interest is an elaborate "Table of Losses," with entries for every household in each of four categories, "Captivitie," "Slaine," "Alive at Home," and "Estate Lost." Thus, to take just one example, we learn, of Samson Frary's family, that his wife was captured; that "himself & 2 children" were "slaine"; that two more children remained alive and free; and that their property losses came to £250, with "house [and] Barn burnt [and] Estate in it." Similar details are presented for another four dozen households comprising 285 individuals (including "Garrison Souldiers sent up . . . 5 [in] captivitie, 5 killed, 10 at home").

The table reveals some critical features of the massacre sequence. Twelve families came through unscathed; without exception, they lived to the south of the fort. Conversely, and ironically, those inside the fort sustained the heaviest losses; once the attackers had made their entry, the carefully reconstructed palisades became more hindrance than help. The table shows, too, a considerable number of adult men still "alive at home." Presumably, these were the ones who rushed out at the onset to try to join as a counter-force. (This put their families in extreme jeopardy; their wives and children appear disproportionately in the category of the "slaine." Similarly, their houses were generally "burnt," whereas the houses of other men who became captives remained standing.)

In fact, it is possible to compare the survival chances of several different groups. Women were more likely than men to be captured, and men (as noted) were more likely to escape altogether; their chances of death, however, were roughly the same. Infants (two years old and under) were "slaine" at a particularly high rate, and young children (ages 3–12) at a somewhat lower one, while nearly all teenagers (13–19) survived. These variations reflected different levels of vulnerability to begin with, and also the judgment of the attackers as to which prisoners would be most (and least) fitted for the return journey to Canada.[34]

There are some curious—and tantalizing—details. Among the captured were Benjamin Burt "& wife great with child." (Six weeks later, in Canada, Sarah Burt would be safely delivered of a son; but imagine her experience en route.) Among the escaped were Thomas Allison and his "mother of 84 years." Among those killed was "Andr[ew] Stephens ye Indian"; what, one wonders, was his personal story? And how to interpret this entry: "Denyon & wife & 2 Frentchmen." ("Denyon" was, apparently, one Jacques deNoyon, a Canadian trader recently married to Deerfield's own Abigail Stebbins. The additional pair of Frenchmen cannot be identified at all. But were they, just possibly, a Deerfield "fifth column," as the attackers came on?)[35]

Finally: the sum of the losses sustained, the massacre's full measure. Partridge's table is, again, the indispensable basis of computation— though his figures need modifying at certain points. (In particular, several persons he counted as "slaine" would subsequently turn up among the captives.) So here are the totals, as nearly as we can come at them. Killed "in town," 39—and in the "meadow fight," an additional nine soldiers. (Only two of the latter were from Deerfield; the rest belonged to the rescue party from the towns "below.") Thus, the "slaine" altogether make 48. Captured, and now bound for Canada, 112. "Alive at home"—that is, the survivors—140 (including the ten remaining "garrison soldiers"). Property losses, as given by Partridge (and we have no way to check his numbers for this column), £3015. The table concludes with some further particulars. "There is 17 houses with Barns to ym burnt within side and without the fort." And: "There is yet . . . standing within side ye Fort, 9 houses & without, 15 houses" (including one "well fortified, in wch is the Garrisson now kept"). The surviving "Woemen & children . . . are come off to Northampton, Hadly & Hatfield"; in addition, "the wounded men & one wounded woeman are in Hatfield undr Doctor Hastings cure." *Night of woe*.[36]

There are losses also on the other side. About these the participants, and their sponsors, give widely differing testimony. Governor Vaudreuil, in a report to Paris, admits to "only three men killed and twenty wounded"; another French official mentions "eleven French or Indians who have been killed." But both these counts seem far too low, given the fierce fighting within the fort and the initially successful counterattack in the meadow outside. Partridge's "Account" puts the enemy dead at "about 50 men, & 12 or 15 wounded . . . wch they carried off, & is thought they will not see Canada againe." And, weeks after the event, John Williams would hear in Quebec that "they lost above forty and that many were wounded." Moreover, said his source, "the French always endeavor to conceal the number of their slain."[37]

꒔

IN THE MEANTIME, the journey of captives and captors has begun: north, toward Canada, through the vast, uncharted borderland that separates New England and New France. Uncharted and unsettled by the colonizers—a "wilderness" through and through—but never *empty*; in fact, the region pulsates with activity. Home for centuries to a dozen Abenaki subgroups: Kennebecs, Norridgewocks, Penobscots, Wawenocks, Androscoggins, Sokokis, Cowasucks, Missisquois, Pigwackets, Pennacooks, and others with names impossible (later on) to recover. Refuge for remnants of the conquered tribes to the south: Mahicans, Pocumtucks, Narragansetts, Wampanoags. Hunting ground for other tribes farther out: Mohawks, Micmacs, Montagnais, and the various "domiciled Indians" of the St. Lawrence Valley. Meeting ground for all these peoples, plus "colonial" traders of several sorts: Dutch from New York, English from Massachusetts, French from Canada. Commerce, warfare, diplomacy, and the everyday business of life: the borderland has them all. The human traffic is constant. And complicated. And colorful.

The traffic follows the contours of the land. At one end there are coastal rivers: the Saco, the Kennebec, the Penobscot, the Machias, the St. Croix, the St. John. And scores of inland lakes: Winnipesaukee, Sebago, Umbagog, Flagstaff, Moosehead (among the larger ones). And mountain barriers: especially the Whites (in what would later become central New Hampshire).

Deeper in the interior—and closer to Deerfield—the Connecticut Valley forms a major wilderness corridor. And deeper still, another corridor: Lake Champlain, Lake George, and their tributaries; Indians call it "the door of the country." In between rise the Green Mountains, but they, too, may be crossed mostly on water. From their crest rivers descend on both sides: principally the Wells and the White to the east, the Winooski to the west. The latter is widely known in New England as the "French River," so much is it frequented by *habitants* from the north.[38]

The captors have traveled these corridors on their journey south. And many, French and Indian alike, know the route from before. Not

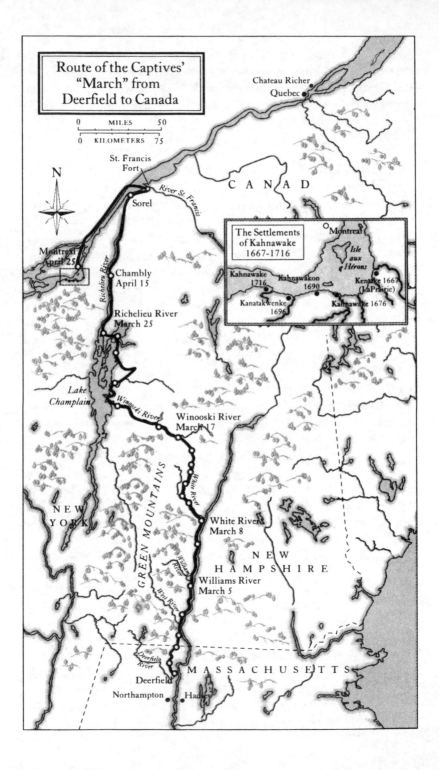

Route of the Captives'
"March" from
Deerfield to Canada

0 MILES 50
0 KILOMETERS 75

N

Chateau Richer
Quebec

St. Francis
Fort

C A N A D

Sorel

River St. Francis

The Settlements
of Kahnawake
1667-1716

Montreal

Isle
aux
Hérons

Montreal
April 25

Chambly
April 15

Kahnawake
1716

Kahnawakon
1690

Kentake 1667
(LaPrairie)

Richelieu River
March 25

Richelieu River

Kanatakwenke
1696

Kahnawake 1676

Lake
Champlain

Winooski River

Winooski River
March 17

GREEN MOUNTAINS

White River

N E W
Y O R K

White River
March 8

N E W
H A M P S H I R E

William River

Williams River
March 5

West River

Deerfield River

M A S S A C H U S E T T S

Deerfield

Northampton Hadley

so the prisoners; for them the borderland is altogether "strange."
John Williams would not forget the hour of departure "when we saw
ourselves carried away from God's sanctuary . . . the journey being at
least three hundred miles we were to travel . . . and we never inured
to such hardships and fatigues."[39]

But travel they must, and do. Perhaps they are numbed—in spirit
as well as flesh—on setting out. And perhaps, too, they find comfort
in their sharing: later Williams will describe the initial rendezvous
with "a great number of our Christian neighbors, men, women, and
children," across the river at the base of a little mountain about a
mile from town. There they remain for the duration of the "meadow
fight"—their hopes briefly rising, then shattered, with its shifting
course. There the captors "took away our shoes, and gave us, in the
room of them, Indian shoes," to prepare for the journey. It is clear
that Indians, and Indians alone, are in charge of the Deerfield contingent; the French take no part in captivity. Each prisoner has a specific
Indian "master"—except for the minister, who has two.[40]

Up the "mountain" they go; from the top they have a last glimpse
backward on "the awful desolations of our town." The captors order
another brief halt, to look after their own wounded comrades. Their
"captains" approach John Williams—they regard him as prisoner
leader—to say "that if the English pursued, they would kill us all, but
if they did not we should none of us be hurt." Yet moments later, as
if to belie themselves, they murder "a sucking child of the English."[41]

They cover perhaps five miles that afternoon. Their experiences
from moment to moment—the physical sensations large and small—
are new and unsettling. The rolling whiteness underneath, alive with
sun-gilt sparkles. The dark shapes of the forest. The blue that soars
overhead. Snow, trees, and sky: a world in three elements. Yet gradually they see more. Here and there the surface is littered with brown
refuse, twigs and cones (left by foraging squirrels). An occasional tree
stands stripped of its bark (by a vagrant moose, in search of hidden
sustenance). Often there are animal tracks (fox, rabbit, wildcat): little
dents stretched smartly toward a nearby ridge crest.

Walking on the snow is itself a problem. In open areas they find a
sharp crust; in sheltered ones lie pools of powder. Different footing,
different hazards. With the crust they break through, and fangs of ice
tear their ankles; with the powder come deep drifts and sudden "traps"
laid by buried undergrowth. They flounder, and sometimes fall, as
they proceed. They puff and pant; they sweat and shiver, by turns.
And they learn, willy-nilly, two key principles. The first is to go single-

file, so that all but the leader have another's steps to fill. (Is this why they will call their journey a "march"?) The second is to hold an even pace. Rests, in particular, must be kept brief, lest they start an inner chill. Warmth they must conserve at all costs. Cold is their enemy, no less than the "savages" alongside. Principles indeed—on which their lives depend.[42]

With nightfall the entire party stops. The Indians make wigwams and beds of spruce branches "to lie down on." John Williams, and probably others, are tied to the ground till morning. "Some of the enemy"—whether Indian or French is not known—break open the liquor they have taken from Deerfield; presently "in their drunken fit" they assault and murder the Williamses' Negro man-slave. (Is he singled out because of his race? It is hard to think of another reason.) Later that night one of the captives—a young man named Joseph Alexander—escapes and runs home. This brings a further summons to the pastor: he must inform his fellow prisoners that "if any more made their escape, they would burn the rest."[43]

Already, in these first hours, the tone of the "march" has been set. Killings, actual and threatened. Periodic physical restraint. An introduction of sorts to survival-in-the-wilderness. If they were numbed at the start, the captives are now feeling their pain. Some are elderly and infirm. Many have been separated from family members. Most are struggling with nightmare thoughts of loved ones killed and homes destroyed. And, for all, there are grave fears of the future—of "what we must yet expect from such who delightfully imbrued their hands in the blood of so many."[44]

But, in fact, the captors are themselves well short of delight. Their wounded comrades are a grievous burden. Several are apparently beyond recovery, and will soon die, including "one of chief note among the Mohawks." There is, too, the danger of English "pursuit." Encumbered as they are, and leaving an easily followed track, they have reason to fear an attack from behind. John Williams remarks the fact that they show "no great insulting mirth as I expected."[45]

It will get worse—and soon. Day two is harder; indeed, for the Williamses the hardest, the most bitter, of the entire journey. The route leads north, then east, toward the present-day boundary of Massachusetts and Vermont. The captives are stretched in a long line between special "guards" of soldiers at the front and rear.

John Williams is permitted for the first time to walk with his wife "to help her in her journey." Mrs. Williams confides that her strength is failing—she is, after all, still convalescent from recent childbearing—and that "I must expect to part with her." After a while the pastor is ordered to the front and "so made to take my last farewell of my dear wife." Together they pray briefly for "grace sufficient for what God should call us to," and separate.

The way leads across a small river, "above knee-deep . . . [and] very swift." Then there is another ridge to climb, and then a stop for rest. John Williams asks each of the captives, as they come up, for news of his wife. And presently learns the worst:

> in passing through the abovesaid river, she fell down and was plunged over head and ears in the water; after which she travelled not far, for at the foot of this mountain the cruel and bloodthirsty savage who took her slew her with his hatchet at one stroke.

Williams cannot conceal his anguish. His tears flow freely—and are "by the adversary . . . reckoned to me as a reproach."[46]

Somehow the sad "tidings" are spread among his five captive children. Together they comfort themselves with "hopes of her being taken away in mercy, to herself." At least she will not have to experience "the evils we were to see, feel, and suffer under." They hope, too, that somehow "she might meet with a Christian burial and not be left for meat to the fowls of the air and beasts of the earth." And this "God graciously vouchsafed." Her body will be recovered a few days later by searchers from Deerfield, carried home, and carefully interred in the town graveyard.[47]

When the march resumes, John Williams feels "a far heavier burden on my spirits than on my back." Like many of the captives, he is forced to carry a "pack" of supplies. There are additional killings that afternoon: another "sucking infant" and "a girl of about eleven years." According to local folklore, the infant was tomahawked and thrown into a forty-foot gorge in the present-day town of Bernardston.[48]

These killings are not, perhaps, as "cruel and bloodthirsty" as they seem to bereaved survivors; certainly, they are not capricious. Mrs. Williams herself makes a good case in point. Weak from the start, heavily fatigued, cold and wet from her fall in the river, she is simply "not able to travel any farther." Her captors must thus make a choice. They can carry her on their backs—but they are already dangerously burdened from carrying "several [of their own] wounded" plus various captive children. They can leave her by the trail—where she would soon perish from exposure and exhaustion. Or they can kill her "at one stroke"—quickly and without much pain. In the coming days they will face similar choices, and make the same decision, time after time.

Their fear of "pursuit" remains strong, so they must keep the entire group moving as fast as possible. And "their manner was"—as Stephen put it later—"if any loitered, to kill them."[49]

On the second night, John Williams will himself face the possibility of violent death, but for a different reason. An "Indian captain from the eastward" proposes "taking off my scalp." Williams prays "to God to implore His grace and mercy" and propounds to his master the blood-guilt of unprovoked murder. The master replies, a little ambiguously, that "he would not kill me." Reassured, the pastor goes to sleep.[50]

Next morning's march is delayed by a meeting of "the chief sachems of the Mohawks and Indians." The captives wait; then they, too, are summoned. Before they go, their "best clothing" is taken from them; young Stephen particularly regrets the loss of his "silver buttons and buckles." Arrived at "the place appointed," he and the others witness a dispute among their captors, "for some had five or six captives, and others none." The sachems effect "a more equal distribution," and the problem subsides.[51]

There is, however, another problem confronting the chiefs. John Williams does not know it—and apparently will never know it—but his life hangs precariously in the balance. There are ominous signs seen by all: the Indians are peeling bark from nearby trees and acting "very strangely." Frightened captives believe they are preparing "to burn some of us."[52] But the morning passes without further incident. Years later the full story of that morning would emerge in a letter from a Canadian priest to his superior. It goes like this.[53]

A chief of the Hurons, from the mission community at Lorette, has been killed in the attack on Deerfield. His kinsmen in the attack-party are greatly upset, and they respond in the traditional manner of their people. A captive—preferably someone of comparable rank to the dead man—must be sacrificed "in expiation." Typically, on these occasions:

> a relative of the dead man presents himself, and demands the prisoner; on the latter being handed over, his owner destines him to the flames, and prepares to satisfy his barbarous cruelty by torturing the wretched man. Thus the custom of the nation regulates.

But custom also requires that the matter be discussed among the entire group, before action is taken. And, in the present case:

the others murmur; the elders, although reluctantly, keep silence; the young men clamor for this right of arms, this reward of victory, this sole consolation for the chief and afflicted family.

There is one among them who strongly objects: a warrior named Thaovenhosen, much admired for his courage, his modesty, his generous spirit, and deep personal piety. Indeed, the priests regard him as "a model of Christian integrity." His skills in battle are also extraordinary: "wherever he fought, the enemy was routed, defeated, and slaughtered." And, at Deerfield, "great was his share in the victory won over the English." Thaovenhosen waits his turn; then,

> rising, although not yet honored with the dignity or the title of chief, [he] makes a speech in the assembly of the notables, and boldly pleads for the life of the Captive.

He has to be bold, for the current of feeling runs strongly against him. He is also eloquent—and determined.

> He prays, he entreats them to remember that they are Christians and citizens of the village of Lorette; that dire cruelty is unbecoming to the Christian name; that this injury cannot be branded upon the reputation of the Lorettans without the greatest disgrace.

But the dead chief's family is not easily dissuaded. Tradition—their own tradition—is on their side. They are Christians, to be sure, but are Hurons too.

> The nephew of the dead man insists; his relatives urge his claim; they allege the custom, stating that clemency shown toward a single head will bring ruin to all; that the enemies will grow more ferocious, and more audacious to harm them, through hope of impunity.

The dispute has reached its critical moment. And Thaovenhosen shifts ground. Blood and tradition will make his case as well.

> "I also," said he, raising his voice, "am related to that Chief whose fall in battle we mourn, and whose death you would avenge by an unworthy cruelty. To me also is the captive due; I claim him as my own, and I contend that such is my right."

And, finally, a direct challenge:

> "If anyone lay hands on him against my will, let him look to me for chastisement."

High drama. Taut moments of expectation. How will the others respond? There is no movement, no sound.

> Astounded at this speech, the assembly were mute, and no one
> dared to decide upon any greater severity toward the captive.

Thaovenhosen has carried the day.

The letter in which these details are found does not identify "the captive" in question. But all signs point strongly toward John Williams. There is the matter of comparable rank: the leader of the Lorette Hurons (now deceased), the leader of the Deerfield "English" (now captured). And there is the curious contretemps of the night before, as recounted by Williams himself. His execution had been proposed by an "Indian captain from the eastward"; Lorette is the easternmost of the Canadian missions. His master had said that "he [the master] would not kill me"; he did not say that another wouldn't. In fact, the pastor will not be saved until the following day, and then only by Thaovenhosen.

᠅

AS THE MARCH RESUMES, the Indians keep these matters to themselves. They are looking ahead to a new phase of the journey. Soon they reach the Connecticut River and the site of their last camp along the route south (a week before). There they recover the food they have carefully stashed away (including the carcasses of "twenty moose"), a large pack of their dogs, and a number of wooden sleds. Now they have a better way to carry supplies and wounded comrades. And, on the frozen surface of the river, they expect to move faster than before. Yet most of the party must continue on foot, and the pace is extremely demanding: "They travelled," Stephen would later say, "as if they designed to kill us all."[54]

Through four "long and tedious" days they speed northward, covering some sixty-five miles all told. The thawing temperatures, noticed concurrently at Deerfield, bring slushy conditions underfoot, with "water up to the ankles." Later the weather turns cold and "tempestuous," and Stephen's "great toe . . . [is] frozen very badly." Feet, indeed, become a special concern; Stephen's are mostly "very sore, and my ankles . . . ache much." (Meanwhile, his captors use "this argument . . . with me to travel stoutly, viz. that if I failed, they would . . . take off my scalp.") His father, too, is "lame in his ankle, which he sprained in the fall of the year." At one point the father despairs of going on, and counsels Stephen how to manage without him—"which did terrify me much." But then his condition spontaneously improves, "to the joy of [his] children and neighbors." Others are not so fortunate: in particular, eight more captive women who cannot keep up, and are accordingly "slain" at intervals along the river.[55]

There is one day of respite: the captors order a "rest" on the Sabbath. John Williams leads an impromptu worship service for his Deerfield flock. His sermon text is drawn from the Book of Lamentations: "The Lord is righteous, for I have rebelled against his commandment . . . My virgins and my young men are gone into captivity." And the group sings a psalm (44:9–14) on a similar theme: "Thou hast cast off and put us to shame . . . and has scattered us among the heathen." The Indians look on with bemused curiosity, and "upbraid us because our singing [is] not so loud as theirs." Still, the captives find comfort—even "revival"—in their wilderness devotions. The site of all this is the confluence of the Connecticut and a west-side tributary; in subsequent years the latter will be named Williams River.[56]

On March 7, a week out of Deerfield, they reach another confluence, at the mouth of the White River. This will be—in several senses—a turning point. Here the group will break into several parts, with some following the Connecticut farther north, while others swing west toward the mountains. Here the French will separate entirely from their Indian allies, heading straight for Quebec. Here the manner of "marching" will change abruptly, from its initial quasi-military mode to something much more improvised and informal. Here the various "parties" will begin to live off the land, Indian-style, as they go. Here, finally, captivity will come to feel more personal, as individuals on both sides are forced closely together.[57]

The reasons for the change are not hard to guess. The captors remain fearful of English pursuit, and their scattering will afford them cover. Travel in small groups should be increasingly advantageous as they approach the narrow "carrying places" on the mountain rivers. And food is growing extremely short; henceforth they must supply themselves by hunting, fishing, and simple foraging.

John Williams, for his part, is taken away from the valley with a small band of Indians and "two children of my neighbors." One of the latter, a girl of four, is soon killed by her Mohawk master, "the snow being so deep . . . that he could not carry the child and his pack too."

Williams feels "overwhelmed" and "almost ready to sink in my spirit," as he reflects on his own children who now "had no father to take care of them." Prayer alone sustains him.[58]

The route runs west, then north again, rising steadily with the White River and its upper branches. There are days out for hunting—on one particular Sabbath "my master . . . killed five moose"—and days also for roasting and drying the fresh meat. There are periodic encounters with other Indians, including, finally, "my master's family." The two men, "master" and captive, share an increasingly complex—and close—relationship. At one point soon after the splitting of the main group, the master approaches Williams "with my pistol in his hand." He says: "Now I will kill you, for . . . at your house you would have killed me with it if you could." But he does not pull the trigger. Later, he shows "surprising" kindness and consideration: makes for his prisoner a pair of snowshoes, provides the "best food" possible, supplies "a piece of a Bible," and allows frequent opportunities for prayer and Scripture reading. Bit by bit, the gulf between them narrows.[59]

Eventually they cross the "divide" between water systems, and reach the French River; from here it is a long descent, on the ice, to Lake Champlain. There is more ice to cover on the lake itself, and then a three-week layover for hunting in the forests just beyond. The group subsists on moosemeat, ground nuts, cranberries, and fish; in addition, "we . . . feasted two or three days on geese we killed there." John Williams is occupied mostly with cutting wood. He suffers from "lousiness" (lice) in the old clothes provided for him, but otherwise manages well. He feels almost at one with his wilderness surroundings.[60]

The journey resumes. It is April now, and the rivers are thawing; the Indians make canoes of elm-bark, and proceed by water. They reach the French fort at Chambly (some fifteen miles east of Montreal) and continue on to the St. Lawrence. En route they stop in various shoreline houses, where Williams enjoys a taste of French hospitality: "a good feather bed" and dinner at a table set with "cloth . . . and napkins." Their immediate destination is a second French fort, at the mouth of the St. François River. This is also a missionary outpost, with a group of resident Indians (Abenakis) and two Jesuit priests. Here Williams begins what will become years of intermittent struggle with the Jesuits. Arguments. Cajolings. Pressures of all sorts to "turn" (to Catholicism). His relationship with his Indian master sours badly, following his refusal even to enter the mission church. (At one point, the master "took hold of my hand to force me to cross myself, but I struggled with him. . . . He set his teeth in my thumbnails, and gave a grip . . . and then said 'No good minister, no love God, as bad as the Devil,' and so left off.")[61]

Meanwhile, the French governor, having learned of Williams's arrival nearby, sends couriers "to order my being sent up to him." One last canoe trip brings the Deerfield pastor to Montreal, where "Vaudreuil redeemed me out of the hands of the Indians." There is no reluctance on their part to surrender him, no haggling over terms—presumably because all this has been decided long before. It is eight weeks since the day of the massacre. For John Williams the "march" is over.[62]

It is over, too, for at least three of his children. Samuel (age fifteen) and Esther (thirteen) have "suffered very much through scarcity of food and tedious journeys." Nonetheless, they have been treated well by their captors: "drawn on sleighs when unable to travel," and so "carried through to Montreal." There they are "redeemed," the boy by a French merchant who "took a great deal of pains to persuade the savages to part with him," his sister by Governor Vaudreuil. (They are not, however, free to return home; that final step will require further negotiations.) Esther is sent to a hospital and "carefully tended . . . until she [recovers from] . . . her lameness." Samuel attends a French school, and comes under the spiritual tutelage of a local priest; this will be a deepening worry for his father in the months ahead. Warham, at four the youngest of the surviving Williamses, has been "wonderfully preserved" on the march from Deerfield. Marked for death several times, when those who carried him "tired with their journeys," he was always "spared and others would take care of him." Arrived in Montreal, he is seen by "a French gentlewoman," who, "pitying the child," contrives to ransom him "out of the hands of the heathen."[63]

The other two, Stephen (age nine) and Eunice (seven), remain at large. Stephen, indeed, is still far off in the wilderness, on the move with his Abenaki master. His experience of the march has been somewhat different; more than most captives he is pulled to the center of Indian life. His master's "band" has begun an extended period of hunting, on the east slope of the Green Mountains; Stephen is set to various tasks of support, such as cutting wood, and packing skins and other supplies. As summer approaches, they leave for the tribe's "planting lands" in the upper Connecticut Valley—but are deterred by the presence of enemy "scouts." They meet other Indians with other captives, including two men from Deerfield who are dying from starvation. ("Jacob Hix . . . looked like a ghost, was nothing but skin and bone, [and] could scarcely go.") Food is chronically short for all; in one period Stephen and his companions subsist on broth made from "a moose's paunch and bones," in another on "roots . . . and bark of trees." By this time the boy is fully "symbolizing" with his captors (as his father would put it); he wears native "habit," and has his hair cut "like an Indian, one side long and the other short."[64]

Eventually the group will head to Canada and Fort St. François. There Stephen will be transferred to his master's kinsman, a Pennacook "sagamore" (chief) named George. His adventures with the Indians will stretch through a full fourteen months: with more long travels for hunting, weeks of "making sugar with the sap of maple trees," winter at the fort, springtime labor in planting, brief stops at French houses here and there. Meanwhile, the French governor will be "often sending to the Indians to buy me." And, finally, in May 1705 these efforts will succeed—at the price of "forty crowns." Stephen will spend the rest of his captivity living with his father in a French village to the east of Quebec.[65]

And then: Eunice. She, like her siblings, has been treated well so far. Her father will write later, with evident gratitude, that she "was carried all the journey and looked after with a great deal of tenderness." But she belongs now to the Indians—to the Mohawk residents of the mission "fort" near Montreal called, by the French, St. François Xavier du Sault St. Louis, and, by the residents themselves, Kahnawake.[66]

Her father begs the governor for assistance in recovering her, and Vaudreuil responds sympathetically. A priest is summoned "to go along with me to see [her] . . . and endeavor her ransom." But when they arrive at the mission, "the Jesuit" in charge informs them

> that I should not be permitted to speak with or see my child . . . and that the Mohawks would as soon part with their hearts as my child.

Williams is disconsolate as he returns to Montreal and reports to Vaudreuil. The governor becomes "very angry" with the Jesuits; they will try again, he says, together. And so:

> after some days he went with me in his own person to the fort. When we came there, he discoursed with the Jesuits, after which my child was brought into the chamber where I was.

Fateful reunion. Father and child. A chance to talk, to give comfort, to reassure.

> I discoursed with her near an hour; she could read very well and had not forgotten her catechism.

At least she is safe, she is well. And her roots hold strong. But, understandably, she

> was very desirous to be redeemed out of the hands of the Mohawks and bemoaned her state among them.

The Mohawks, however, are unyielding. As the priest had previously warned, they will not part with her on any terms.

As the conversation continues, Eunice shows her bewilderment—and her pain. It is all so strange for her: the fort, the people, their words and customs. She tells him, in particular,

> how they profaned God's Sabbaths and [how] . . . a few days before they had been mocking the devil and . . . one of the Jesuits stood and looked on them.

He feels helpless, powerless. God alone has the power here. But how will He use it?

> I told her she must pray . . . for His grace every day. She said she did as she was able and God helped her. But, says she, "they force me to say some prayers in Latin. . . . I hope it won't do me any harm."

A fist in his belly, a dagger in his heart. Here is the beginning of . . . what? Of change, of "harm," as yet unmeasured. "Latin prayers," the "French tongue," "popish religion," "Indian savagery": a chain unwinding far into the future. He knows its meaning, but can only repeat what he has said before.

> I told her she must be careful she did not forget her catechism and the Scriptures she had learned by heart.

But is this enough? What does *she* think?

> She told the captives after I was gone . . . almost everything I spoke to her and said she was much afraid she should forget her catechism, having no one to instruct her.

Seven years old . . . much afraid . . . having no one: the core of her predicament.

There will be a second chance with her, a few days later. But he has nothing more to offer.

> I saw her . . . in the city [of Montreal], but had not many minutes of time with her, but what time I had I improved to give her the best advice I could.

But this, *but* that: he is floundering now. And failing from *her* point of view.[67]

A third chance? Yes, it will come. But not for a very long time.

꒰

HIS CHILDREN are not his only concern. His "neighbors," his Deerfield "flock," his fellow prisoners: they, too, must be seen, and counseled, and comforted—and, where possible, "redeemed." Who are they? And what are their stories of life in captivity? John Williams's subsequent writing will provide a glimpse here and there. Of visits to a friend taken sick and confined in a French hospital. Of secret meetings with others, and of letters exchanged "treating about religion." Of "a maid of our town . . . put into a religious house [nunnery] . . . for more than two years." Of Jesuit exasperation with "prisoners . . . [who] while . . . at Mass . . . can't be prevailed with to fall down on their knees to pray." Of Mary Brooks—she alone is named—a "pious young woman," who, while still on the march from Deerfield, suffers "an abortion" (miscarriage) and is killed by her captors after a moving prayer with her minister.[68]

They can, moreover, be counted. There are 112 of them, on setting out from Deerfield. Twenty die along the way, ninety-two reach Canada; thus the rate of survival for the group as a whole is a little better than four in five. But these numbers must be further divided to make them yield their full meaning. In fact, every individual's survival chances are tightly linked to age and gender. Infants (two years old or less) fare worst; three out of four are killed en route. These youngest of the captives are, presumably, also the most vulnerable (for example, in their dependence on mothers for nourishment). Children (ages three to twelve) do much better: thirty-one out of thirty-five will eventually reach Canada alive. They are hardier, to begin with—and yet, when unable to hold the sometimes "killing" pace, are small enough to be carried. Teenagers (thirteen to nineteen) do better still: all twenty-one of them survive. Their youthful strength and endurance bring them through; they prove, indeed, the most successful of "marchers." Adult women, by contrast, have a notably difficult time: Ten die, and sixteen survive. They are frequently unable to "keep up"; several are affected by recent or current pregnancy, others are "weakened" in more general ways. Among adult men, four will perish, while twenty-two survive. The deaths in this group are anomalous: two are from starvation, another may well be a racial killing (the Williamses' "negro man"), the fourth is (probably) caused by wounds received in the fighting at Deerfield.[69]

The moral of all this seems clear. If you are living at Deerfield in 1704, and if capture is your fate, it's better by far to be a grown man than a woman, and best of all to be a teenager.

And now, if you have indeed survived, there are other chances to think about. Above all else: your chances of returning home.

Two

⁊

THE FIRST "NOTICE" of the attack on Deerfield was conveyed
by the light of burning buildings, to Hatfield and other Valley towns
immediately below.[1] From there news traveled more slowly—by letter
and by word of mouth—on foot, horseback, and shipboard.

Word must have reached Hartford within a few hours, for by afternoon of the following day "Coniticot men" had begun arriving in
Deerfield to join in the anticipated rescue. Three days later these same
men had returned home, carrying with them a "sorrowfull" account
of the massacre. By that time the first reports were just reaching
Boston. "I but now hear of som assault upon Dearfield," wrote Wait
Winthrop in a letter begun on March 4, "and that the Govr. has a
letter from Coll. Patrick [Partridge], but know not the contents."
When the letter was finished the following Monday, Winthrop could
write more specifically of numbers killed and "caried away"; "this is
sayd," he noted, "but I suppose the Govr. will be in town today and
we shall have the certainty." On the same afternoon, a Boston merchant and Council member, Isaac Addington, was sending full details
to a correspondent in Connecticut. In fact, during the weekend—
according to Samuel Sewall—"the Slaughter made at Deerfield" became "generally known" to Bostonians. Sewall himself had been told
by the Colony Secretary and had, in turn, informed Rev. Samuel
Willard, minister of Boston's First Church. Willard evidently made a
public announcement during the Sabbath service—"by which," Sewall's diary continues, "our Congregation was made a Bochim (Judges
2: 1–5)." This Scriptural reference implies much about likely reactions
among the populace at large. Bochim was a place where the Lord had
admonished the ancient Israelites for breaking their religious covenants; in response "the people lifted up their voice and wept . . . and

they sacrificed there unto the Lord." One imagines weeping and raised voices in Boston, too, as word of the "slaughter" spread.[2]

In fact, the story of Bochim was doubly resonant to the news from Deerfield. For Bochim had been part of Canaan, the "promised land" to which the Lord had directed his followers after their long exile in Egypt. As a condition of their deliverance they were commanded to "make no league with the inhabitants [of Canaan] . . . [and to] throw down their altars." Yet, declared the Lord, "ye have not obeyed my voice . . . [Thus] I will not drive them out from before you; but they shall be as thorns in your side, and their gods shall be a snare unto you."[3] Puritans like Sewall would easily identify themselves with the Israelites, and New England with Canaan, and the American Indians with the native "inhabitants" of Scripture. The Indians had indeed become "as thorns in their side." And the analogy begged further questions, more discomfiting still. Had the Puritans made "league" with Indian peoples and left their "altars" intact? At the start of the eighteenth century it might well have seemed so. Anglo-Indian collaboration in both trade and diplomacy was an old story by then; and Puritan missions among the native peoples had borne distressingly meager fruit. Perhaps the Lord had expected—had commanded—a less compromising approach.

It is not clear, in Sewall's diary, whether Rev. Willard actually preached from the Bochim text on the question of broken covenants. But it can hardly be doubted that Deerfield figured strongly in the discourse of local churches during the succeeding weeks and months. On March 5 (the date of Sewall's first diary entry) the pastor in Windsor, Connecticut, preached on "ye awful and dreadful dispensation of God's hand at Deerfield." And four days later the General Court of Massachusetts ordered "a day of fasting and prayer" so that "ministers might implore the divine protection in the arduous affairs under present consideration." These and other declarations propounded a single theme: "The sins of a professing people" had served to "provoke God to do such things amongst them as are very dreadful." Heads were lowered in prayer—and in shame—all across New England.[4]

But the massacre evoked a broader spectrum of response than shame and religious soul-searching. There was grief: "Poor Deerfield beset by French & Indians . . . and almost depopulated," commented a diarist in the Massachusetts countryside. There was anxiety for the future, especially of the captives: their plight, wrote Sewall, "would make a hard heart bleed." There was fury: thus the venerable "Indian fighter" Benjamin Church excoriated "the French and Indian enemy" for "many cruelties . . . particularly the horrid action at Deerfield this last winter, in killing . . . and scalping, without giving any notice at all, or opportunity to ask quarter."[5] There was thirst for vengeance: Church himself would soon be commissioned to lead a retaliatory expedition against the Indians of Maine and the French in Nova Scotia—and the Massachusetts General Court raised the bounty for Indian scalps from £10 to £40 and then to £100 within a scant few months.[6]

There was, finally, an effort to assess causes and consequences, and to weigh official responsibility for the attack. Joseph Dudley wrote in late March to his fellow governor Fitz-John Winthrop (of Connecticut): "I am oppressed with the remembrance of my sleepy neighbours at Deerfeild, and that all that came to their assistance could not make out snow shoes to follow a drunken, loaden, tyred enemy, of whom they might have been masters to our honour." And, in a tone somewhat less bitter, Lord Cornbury (governor of New York) deplored "the negligence of the people [of Deerfield] who did not keep guard soe carefully as they should have done." Indeed, the issues of "negligence" and "keeping guard" were raised throughout the colonies. Government leaders in Maryland, for example, were described in late spring as being unwilling to send assistance to their northern neighbors, "for they are very apprehensive of their own danger from the Indians and French, especially since the cutting off of Dearfield."[7]

By then the news had crossed the ocean. Dudley sent a report to his superiors in London (the Council of Trade and Plantations). And the French governor, Vaudreuil, did the same for his superiors in Paris (the Ministry of the Marine). The tone of the French version was, of course, entirely different: Vaudreuil wrote proudly of "the success of a war party I sent over the ice into the region of the Boston government." (French officials tended to identify all Massachusetts— or even all New England—by reference to Boston alone.) It is probable that by year's end the widening circle of knowledge about the massacre had reached both the king of France and the queen of England.[8]

෴

INCREASINGLY, the focus shifted from satisfaction (on the French side) and recriminations (on the English one) to countermeasures. Church's attack on Maine and points north seemed to even the score:

Towns were laid waste, ships destroyed, prisoners taken from both the French and the Indians. And, practically from the start, there was the issue of prisoner return. As early as April 10 (and again in August), Dudley wrote to Vaudreuil demanding "considerate" treatment of all English captives. At the same time he raised the possibility of a one-for-one exchange.[9]

These letters, sent by means unknown, seem not to have reached their destination. But meanwhile other, less formal lines of communication were opening between the parties involved. In May 1704 John Williams succeeded in sending a letter southward with a traveling French priest; carried to the Iroquois town of Onondaga, it was then transferred to an Indian courier for eventual delivery to Peter Schuyler, merchant, mayor, and military leader in Albany. Soon thereafter Schuyler was to visit "Indian country" in person. While there he met with certain "French Indians" and "presented two belts of wompom, . . . desiring them to lay down the hatchet they had taken up against the Governments of New England"; they promised "answere in the fall." The source of this information was a merchant in Northampton, who also reported how "one of our owne Indians . . . did resolve to go to Canada and demand Mr. Williams of them, wch if they refus'd to deliver he would forsake their intrest and take up the hatchet agst them." Whether this particular "resolve" was actually carried out is not known; however, "going to Canada" would quickly become the heart of the story. With postal service so difficult and uncertain, there was no good alternative to personal communication.[10]

In fact, the succeeding months and years brought a remarkable series of efforts—some quite elaborate and official, others decidedly unofficial—to negotiate the return of captives. The wilderness corridor between Montreal and Albany, and the water-route from Boston to Quebec, fairly vibrated with activity. There was the usual lively trade in furs and imported European goods (as had been true for decades). There were sporadic acts of warfare. And now there were "embassies" back and forth: Englishmen enroute to Canada for discussions with the leadership there, Frenchmen bound for Boston on a similar errand.

At the end of September, Governor Dudley proposed to his Council that one Arthur Jeffrey, "being attended with two French prisoners of war, be sent . . . to Quebec, with letters to the governor, referring to the English prisoners there and to concert a method of exchange." But this proposal was soon superseded by another. Two men from Deerfield, John Sheldon and John Wells, "who both had relations in captivity," journeyed to Boston and begged in a "very urgent" way to "have license to travail thither [to Canada]." This pair was subsequently joined by Capt. John Livingston, a New Yorker "who had been several times there [and] was well acquainted in . . . the way thither from the upper towns of this province." The governor's council authorized a suitable appropriation to support the ambassadors.[11] And Dudley himself wrote a new letter to Vaudreuil declaring that "I have in my hands about 150 [French] prisoners," and offering specific suggestions for an exchange.[12]

Sheldon, Livingston, and Wells set out from Boston in late December, traveling first by way of Deerfield and Albany, thence northward through the wilderness to Montreal. The route, in midwinter, must have been difficult, and the method of travel (snowshoes and sled) unfamiliar, but the group arrived without mishap at the beginning of March. They would remain in Canada for approximately two months, pursuing a kind of double agenda: to locate and retrieve their immediate "relations" from captivity, and to advance the prospect of a general prisoner exchange. Wells must soon have received bitter news: His captive mother had been among those killed on the "march." Sheldon was luckier: His three children and daughter-in-law were still alive, though dispersed among different "masters" in various locations. Gradually he pieced together the details. From another captive he learned how his daughter, Mary, and his son's wife, Hannah, had survived "soe grat a iorney [journey] far behiend . . . expectations noing how Lame they was." His two young sons were "with the Indians"; he was unable at first to see them, for they were said to be "in the wodes a honten [hunting]." In April Sheldon managed to write to Hannah (then living with a French family in Montreal). The governor, he told her, had permitted John Williams to visit, and "I ded ingay [enjoy] his company about 3 wekes." Livingston had set out for Boston with letters of counter-proposal from Vaudreuil to Dudley, but was forced to return "by reson of the badnes of the ise." Sheldon himself expected to go to Montreal in May, and, in the meantime, Hannah must "doe as you can with your mistres that my children mite be redeemed from the Indanes."[13]

The negotiations with Vaudreuil and his colleagues were cordial in tone, but not very productive. In the end the French governor released five captives—including Sheldon's two sons, his daughter-in-law, and John Williams's daughter Esther—but the question of a general exchange was left unresolved. Vaudreuil did agree to send a deputy—an officer with the imposing name of Augustin Le Gardeur, Sieur de Courtemanche—back to Boston with the Sheldon party for a further round of discussions.[14] It appeared, in sum, that the mission had advanced Sheldon's personal goals far more than the general one. John Williams, too, could feel some particular gratification: one of his captive children was now free, and a second (son Stephen) had been suddenly ransomed from the Indians by the French governor—though not as yet allowed to go home.[15] The minister gave to the returning party a short letter for Mrs. Livingston, offering thanks for her "denyal of yourself the desirable company of your beloved consort for the sake of poor captives." Another letter to Mrs. Livingston, written by a Connecticut friend and dated May 31, 1705, recorded the receipt "this moment [of] the joyfull news of yor spouse and our frinds return from his noble interprise."[16] Within a few days more the returnees reached Boston, where Courtemanche laid the latest French proposals before Dudley and his Councillors.

From this point forward—until the summer of 1707—the process of negotiation was virtually continuous, encompassing no less than six face-to-face meetings between French and British officials. Prisoner exchange was the single most persistent point of concern, though occasionally discussion widened to embrace the possibility of a general "treaty." Warfare itself was for a time suspended, then sporadically resumed. Twice more did John Sheldon make the long journey through the wilderness to Canada; other "ambassadors" included William Dudley, son of the governor, and Samuel Appleton, a leading Boston merchant and Councillor. No pains were spared in these efforts to "redeem the poor captives," but progress was frustratingly slow—and incomplete. In fact, no agreements were ever actually signed by both parties; captives were released on a piecemeal basis—a handful here, a larger group there—in a series of "good faith" gestures. By this means some 200 to 300 were eventually repatriated, including virtually all the French held in New England.[17]

જ

IN DEERFIELD, in Boston, and in the surrounding communities, the negotiations were followed with the keenest interest. Solid information was scarce; every scrap was cherished and, doubtless, shared with neighbors. Initially it was not known for certain who had survived the massacre—or (more questionable still) who had survived the "march" to Canada. One result of the first Sheldon-Livingston mission was a count, perhaps even a list, of English prisoners in Canada. The total was nearly 200, including "about seventy . . . with the Indians."

(A majority were Deerfield residents; the rest had been taken earlier, from other places.) This "unexpected News"—as one contemporary described it—was "very reviving to the dejected Spirits of their mournful Friends, considering the many Deaths they escaped in their Captivity."[18]

Indeed, the negotiations became the chief line of contact between individual captives and their "friends" in New England. The negotiators themselves tried to visit as many captives as French authorities would allow; thus their time in Canada found them repeatedly on the move between Quebec and Montreal. John Sheldon's list of "Expenses upon ye Countrys accont in Canada" included items such as these:

> for a cariall to goe to See ye Captives
> att ye mohawk fort. . . . . 12 livres
> for a Cannoe and men to goe from Quebec
> to visit mr williams . . . . 6 livres
> for my 2nd visit of ye captives at ye
> mohawk fort . . . . 4 livres
> 8 sous

The results of such "visits" must have been fully communicated—and appreciated—when Sheldon returned home.[19]

In some cases, the negotiators carried personal correspondence to and from the captives. Thus, for example, in the summer of 1705 Cotton Mather gave William Dudley a letter for delivery to John Williams. The contents are a vivid reflection of the way both sides—captives and "friends"—would try to cope with the painful facts in front of them.[20]

> Boston, N. England
> 6 d. 5 m. in 1705

> My Dear Brother.
> You are carried into the Land of the Canadiens for your good. God has called you to glorify Him in that Land. Your patience, your constancy, your Resignation under your vast Afflictions, bring more glory to Him, than ye best Activity in any other Serviceableness. You visit Heaven with prayers, and are visited of Heaven with comfort. Our prayers unite with yours. You are continually and affectionately remembred in ye prayers of New England. The faithful, throughout ye country, remember you, publickly, privately, Secretly. The Supplications

will not be lost. An Answer is coming. Your Deliverance
will be part of ye Answer. We shall see you again, we
hope. Tis our Hope, that you may be preparing for a
more than Ordinary Usefulness yett before you Dy. Your
Calamities are useful in the meantime, even unto us the
ministers of N.E. They awaken us. They awaken our zeal
to carry on the Designs of Reformation. Since the fate of
Deerfield, great things have been done in several parts of
New England, upon those Holy Designs.

What shall we do, to be more particularly expressive
in our concern for you? One thing I took upon me as my
own more peculiar Charge: The expense of your Son
Eleazars Education. He often comes to me. You will have
a Blessing in Him. I have procured Subscriptions of about
12, or 13 lb. a year, to support him at ye Colledge. I shall
do what else I can for him. I was greatly beholden to two
worthy men, mr. Bromfield and mr. Bolt, (who would
be remembred to you and by you) for their Assistence in
that affayr of the Subscriptions.

I add no more; but with earnest cries to Heaven, that
you (and those with you, and especially yours) may be
Restored unto us, I subscribe,

Your Kinsman and Brother,
Co. Mather

Strikingly, these comments contain no trace of the remorseful tone
evident in the immediate aftermath of the massacre, no reference to
"the sins of a professing people." With the months of captivity stretch-
ing into years—and with individuals helpless to change things—
Mather took a different line. In fact, Puritans had long maintained
two different modes of understanding "affliction." One stressed punishment: God sending pain, in response to men's evildoing, for the
purpose of righting the moral order and promoting reform. The other
centered on "testing" and "trial": pain as a challenge to bring out the
best in the faithful and to present special opportunities for holiness.
Mather's letter is an affecting example of the second mode. What has
happened is *for your good* personally—and *useful* for New England as
a whole. Moreover, it will not continue indefinitely: *An Answer is
coming.* In the meantime, you are not out of sight, out of mind; to
the contrary, you are *remembered* here with prayerful affection. Finally, we—your kinsmen and friends—are doing what we can to help
your family. Thus, in brief summary, the leading themes of Mather's

letter: how simple, how direct, how warmly empathic. John Williams could only have been reassured.

Williams had other correspondents, including the redoubtable Sewall. In January 1706 and again in August, Sewall wrote breezily about the weather ("very pleasant"), the news from overseas (a "revival" of English fortunes in the war), and local doings ("Mr. Josiah Willard has left the College, and Mr. Whiting is chosen a Fellow, and takes the Freshmen."). Life goes on here in New England: another form of reassurance. Sewall, like Mather, showed a tender concern for the Williams children: "Your Son . . . dined at my house, and then went with my Son Joseph to Cambridge . . . I saw your Son again at Joseph's Chamber." And Sewall sent gifts to John Williams: a "Silk Handkerchief," a psalm book, plus "two Almanacks." (Something of an almanac buff, he asked for a return on this last: "If there be any Canada Almanacks, bring me one . . .")[21]

The "remembrance" of far-off captives took other forms as well. On July 5, 1704, Sewall, in his diary, described Commencement Day at Harvard: "Mr. Dudley made a good Oration," touching several topics including the "Captivity of Mr. Williams." Some months later Mather, writing in his diary, reflected on his "Prayers for our Captives in the Hands of the French and Indians." Sometimes he would "unaccountably . . . forgett to mention them; which makes me say to some of my Friends, I am afraid the Time of their full Deliverance will not yett come." Yet on other occasions, when "in our great Congregation pouring out Supplications for them . . . [as if] with a Mind irradiated from Heaven," he would feel an "Assurance" of their imminent return. Public and private "supplication," earnest conversation with friends, portents of things to come: Such were the outward manifestations of an abiding inner concern.[22]

There were acts of personal helpfulness—examples are scattered throughout the record. Mather's raising a "subscription" to cover the college fees of John Williams's son Eleazer (as noted above). Sewall's proposal to the Massachusetts Council "that a suit of cloaths might be made here for Mr. Williams." The Council's swift authorization of money to reimburse Williams for "considerable expenses" incurred in the care and "comfort" of his captive children. No doubt there were special opportunities of this sort whenever captives had newly returned home. Sewall wrote of one such group in August 1706: "They Landed well here the 2d Instt. I took the widow Hoit [a returned captive from Deerfield] into my House. It was a great pleasure to see Mr. Willard baptise Ebenezer Hinsdal and Sea-born Burt, two little sons Born [to Deerfield parents] in the passage."²³

"Landings" of returned captives would invariably elicit great public interest—and joy. The group to which Sewall here referred was some forty-five strong, much the largest so far. Cotton Mather, among others, threw himself into the matter of their "reception." He visited with "many of them, every Day." He prayed with them, individually and together, and "put Books into their Hands"—all in hopes "to do good unto them." He invited them to attend his church a scant week after their return, and they "agreed"; thus "we gave Thanks together, in the great Congregation, and I preached unto them a Sermon, on the great Things done by the Lord for them." The power and poignancy of such occasions would be hard to overestimate: the meetinghouse packed with expectant (and curious) parishioners; the returnees, perhaps still a little dazed from their months and years in "a sad Captivity"; the minister flushed with a special sense of "Opportunity [to] glorify the Lord."

In this case the opportunity continued beyond the meeting itself. "On the day following," Mather noted in his diary, "I composed a Collection of Memorables relating to the Captives." Its contents were something of a mishmash: stories of "Divine power and Goodness" as reported by the returnees, "edifying Poems written by some of them," and a "Pastoral Letter" prepared by John Williams (who was among those still detained). Mather supplied a title—*Good Fetch'd Out of Evil*—and arranged with a local printer for publication. The book was an instant sensation: 1,000 copies sold "in a week's time" (in a city of approximately 15,000 total population). Clearly, New Englanders were ready—indeed, hungry—for "edification" about the facts of captivity.²⁴

The excitement of these summertime events was soon eclipsed by the arrival of a second captive group, even larger than the first. On November 21, the brigantine *Hope* reached Boston Harbor with fifty-seven additional returnees—including John Williams and two of his remaining children.²⁵ Once again the people of Boston responded by opening their homes and their hearts (as John Williams would subsequently put it) "to give for our supplies in our needy state." The colony's General Court joined in the expansive spirit of these days, summoning all the captives for an official greeting and offering each of them a gift of twenty shillings. Moreover, the Court authorized a special appropriation of forty pounds for Rev. Williams if he would return to Deerfield and lead in the rebuilding of the still shattered town. There were social events as well—for example, a dinner hosted by Sewall, with Williams, the governor, and several Council-members among the guests.[26]

Most of the returned captives must have left Boston for their homes in Deerfield (or elsewhere) within a few days of their arrival. There were families to see, and lives to pick up; and, besides, the "charity" of Bostonians was not inexhaustible. John Williams stayed at least a month—Sewall reported him preaching at a private "meeting" on December 20—but surely Deerfield was on his mind, too. The Court's grant to him, and the arrival in Boston of a special three-man deputation from Deerfield "to treat with thair pastor . . . in regard to his resetl'g with them againe in ye work of ye ministry," must have underscored the choice confronting him. That he did have a choice—to return to his prewar home or not—there is little doubt. His Deerfield roots had been entirely severed; for the time being, no Williamses resided there. Moreover, several communities closer to Boston were apparently bidding for his services. Was he tempted to try another place? Perhaps the people of Deerfield thought so; certainly they offered what they could to make him comfortable. He would need a new house, and the town agreed to build him one "as big as Ens. Jno Sheldon's" (the biggest then standing). He would need money, and the town voted him an immediate allowance of twenty pounds. He would need help with his farmland, and the town ordered that "every male head of 16 years and upward [should give him] 1 day [of] work a piece and thos yt have teams [of oxen] a day with their teams for ye yere." John Williams was a celebrated public figure now, and little Deerfield would have to scramble to hold onto him.[27]

In fact, there is no evidence—from his side—that he seriously considered other alternatives. The *Boston News-letter*, in a dispatch from Hatfield dated January 9, reported the essentials of his return home: "The People of this County are fill'd with Joy, for the Arrival of the Captives; especially, for the Return of the Reverend and Pious Mr. John Williams, to Dearfield again, upon Saturday the 28th of December last: which is esteemed a general Blessing." Plans were drawn up for rebuilding the town "more Commodiously" than before, and for "regularly Fortifying of it." And on January 8, Deerfield held a special "Day of Thanksgiving," featuring an elaborate "religious exercise" in the church. John Williams presided, with two other Connecticut Valley ministers—his cousin William Williams and his father-in-law Solomon Stoddard—each "Preaching a Thanksgiving Sermon." Moreover, "sundry persons of Quality from other Towns" came over to join their Deerfield neighbors for the occasion. It was a time of great hope and prayerfulness, and even the heavens seemed supportive. A second *News-letter* dispatch described the appearance of a rainbow on the morning of December 28—the day of the pastor's return—"and some hoped it might be a Token, that God would not destroy Dearfield any more."[28]

ᢣ

EVEN AS HE NEGOTIATED his resettlement in Deerfield during those winter months of 1707, John Williams was beginning a new project. The memories of his captivity beckoned him to write—another chance to "edify" the faithful—and write he did. Within a matter of weeks he composed a "short account" of some 25,000 words, covering the entire period from the massacre to the time of his return. By the beginning of March he was back in Boston; on the 8th, Sewall reported that "Mr. Williams visits us . . . His Narrative is now in the Press." The narrative was published a month or two thereafter, under the synoptic title *The Redeemed Captive Returning to Zion: A Faithful History of Remarkable Occurrences in the Captivity and the Deliverance of Mr. John Williams, Minister of the Gospel, in Deerfield, Who, in the Desolation, which befell that Plantation, by an Incursion of the French and Indians, was by Them carried away, with his Family and his Neighborhood unto Canada.* The book would be issued in new editions no less than six times during the remainder of the eighteenth century, and an additional five during the nineteenth. It became in time a revered part of the literary canon of "Puritanism," and it remains to this day the fullest source by far on the Canadian side of the post-Deerfield captivities.[29]

Williams's March visit to Boston was prompted by at least one additional consideration. On the 6th he delivered, before "His Excellency [the governor] and General Assembly," an important sermon with another imposing title: *God in the Camp; or the Only Way for a People to Engage the Presence of God With Their Armies.* The occasion, it seems, was a meeting of colony officials to consider launching a major military offensive against Canada. The Williams sermon may have helped to decide the result; at any rate, an "expedition" was authorized and funds appropriated within a few days of its delivery.

When a considerable force of soldiers and sailors actually left New England in mid-May—for what became a miserably failed attempt on the French fortress at Port Royal—*God in the Camp* was not yet in print. By mid-summer the situation had changed; Sewall referred a correspondent to "the comon Stock for Mr. Williams's Sermon," and noted that "a Hundred of them [were] being sent to the Army at my Motion." Perhaps, then, the sermon was read and discussed by the campfires outside the Canadian fort. If so, its central theme, of armies defeated by home-front betrayal, must have seemed disturbingly prophetic.[30]

In late March, following a last dinner with the governor at Sewall's, John Williams returned to Deerfield and settled in.[31] His children, however, were still dispersed: son Stephen, "at school at Roxbury" and living with an uncle there; son Samuel, with another uncle in Charlestown; and daughter Esther, with Stoddard relatives in Northampton. Contact was maintained, as much as possible, through letters (and occasional visits). And, as parent, John Williams became the hub of a lively family correspondence. Some of his letters have survived; when read today, they present an affecting mix. Of information ("your Brs & sister were well last thirdsday" . . . "my house is shingled" . . . "the barn is almost finished and 20 load of hay in it"). Of advice ("be respectful to your uncles and Aunts" . . . "make such a proficiency in your Studys that you may be fitt for Colledge next year"). Of religious exhortation ("prepare for another world without any delay" . . . "labour after a thorough conversion"). Of fond concern ("I never forget you" . . . "I long to see you"). Each one concluded: "i am your loving father John Williams." There were letters among the siblings, too. Thus Esther, writing to Stephen in early September: "I would pray you to learn them verses that I sent cousen Elisbeth; them was the verses that my dear mother youste to singe." (The reference is to Eunice Williams, Sr., killed that "doleful day" on the march out of Deerfield three years earlier.) And Samuel to Stephen, a short while later: "By this I let you kno that being separated from you ye absence has Bene tedious . . ." (In this same letter Samuel asked his brother to send him "som things," including "an ointment . . . to kill lice and nits . . . [and] a lotion to make the hair Brite and longe.")[32]

This scattering of family, though "tedious" and painful, must have seemed necessary for a time. For one thing, the war continued, and Deerfield was scarcely less vulnerable than before. In May, Peter Schuyler wrote from Albany to Governor Dudley that "wee hear of two or three Partys which are Sett out [from Canada] against New England." In August, these warnings were sharpened on the basis of reports by certain "trusty Indians" recently back from Montreal; Schuyler urged that New Englanders "be upon their guard [lest they] . . . fall into ye hands of . . . bloody Salvages." Surely Deerfield was among the places to receive this ominous news; John Williams wrote to Stephen, at one point, that "we are full of fears." Moreover, the pastor had no proper home as yet; the fine house promised by the town was still a-building. Finally, he had no wife to provide the appropriate form of motherly care. Given all these circumstances, his children seemed well placed elsewhere.[33]

As summer passed, two of these deficiencies were made good. The house was finished, probably in July. And, at about the same time, Williams went courting. In late August, he wrote to Sewall of his plans to marry a Connecticut widow named Abigail Bissell. Sewall replied immediately, offering prayers for God's blessing "upon and with you in the resettlement of your family." However, there was also a problem (in Sewall's mind): The widow Bissell was first cousin to Williams's late wife, and "it is at least doubtful whether [such a marriage] be lawfull or no." At great length Sewall drew out Scriptural references to incest. Furthermore, he noted, the children of the second wife (by her first marriage) would become "Second Cousins" to Williams's own children, and "Mrs. Stoddard, that has been a long time your Mother [-in-law], will now become your Aunt"—an awkward result, to say the least. Williams, not surprisingly, disagreed. "I find it no where forbidden," he wrote of cousin-marriage; he hoped eventually to give his friend "full satisfaction that I am in this Matter directed of God." On September 11, Esther Williams wrote to Stephen (who was still "at school" in Roxbury) that "father is to be mared [i.e. married] nesct wek." And indeed he was. The children returned to Deerfield not long thereafter.[34]

If, then, we freeze the story of the Williamses near the end of the year 1707, the central motif is reconstitution and "resettlement." Back in Deerfield. Housing rebuilt, lands recultivated. Family restored to roughly its pre-massacre shape, with new wife and with children reclaimed from their interim homes. A set of lives, formerly interwoven, then ripped apart, now painstakingly restitched. The triumphant end to a four-year sequence of privation and suffering.

And yet the triumph was, at best, incomplete. The war raged on; for years to come, Deerfield would remain a leading target of French and Indian enemies. Each day was shadowed by "fears" and insecurity. Many times the Williamses must have wondered: Might they soon see a new round of violence?

Nor was the old round done. For there was Eunice, still "captivated" in Canada.

THREE

✧

MOST OF THE DEERFIELD CAPTIVES are beyond the reach of historians. We can discover their names (at the least). And, perhaps the barest outline of their experience as prisoners (where held, when—or whether—released). And, possibly a fact or two from their later years. In a few cases there is more: scattered bits of evidence that can, almost miraculously, be made to join, so as to yield the "thread" of a connected life. But in only one case is it possible to go further—to feel the twist of the thread, to catch the meaning of the experience. To know the thoughts and feelings behind the events.

Only one: John Williams. Which is all the more reason to take what Williams wrote and *study* it with the utmost care and patience. Williams, of course, was no more likely than the rest of us to say exactly what he felt. Or even to know exactly what he felt. His words are the words of his own time and place and people: strange to us, routine to him and them. His aim was hortatory, was rhetorical, while his method (sequence, diction, style) was conventional and formulaic. His writings conform, then, to "Puritan" type, and can be read as a standard piece of the larger canon.

And yet they can also be read another way, for they vibrate with Williams's actual experience. Restored to context, they show the personal side of a particular man, struggling to cope—with events, with people, with the inner world of the self. Again, one man only. But where experience was shared—the facts of captivity and "deliverance"—perhaps responses were also shared, at least in part. For now, John Williams may stand for his captive brothers and sisters at large.

THE WRITINGS have four parts—plus one. The four are, in chronological order: (1) the "pastoral letter" he wrote to those captives who returned home in August 1706; (2) a "lecture" he gave, days after his own return, in December; (3) his famous "narrative," written during the winter of 1706–7 (and published in April or May); and (4) his sermon *God in the Camp*, delivered before the governor and General Assembly, in early March. The order is important, as are the time and setting in which each one was composed. Individually and together, these products of Williams's experience reveal much of what captivity meant to him.

OCTOBER 1705: A PRISONER'S PLEA

But first, the "plus one"—a kind of prologue to the rest. As noted previously, the Massachusetts authorities voted money to compensate John Williams for charges incurred while he was still a captive. In doing so, they responded to a "petition" from Williams—which had been carried to Boston by William Dudley, following the Anglo-French negotiations (in Quebec) of autumn 1705. The petition is our prologue.[1]

It begins with a general statement of fact: "I have for a long time (well known to your selves) been in a sorrowful state of Captivity." From this it moves to a summary of Williams's "exercising trials"—and especially the trials of his children, "captivated . . . among the heathen where they were reduced to many straits." It cites the plight of young Stephen, who "came to me from the indians the 1st of May past without so much as a shirt upon him." In Stephen's case (and others as well), Williams had been "necessitated to be at considerable expences" for new clothing—"unless I would be unmercifully cruel and have hardened my heart to all unnaturalness." The money he needed had to be borrowed on the spot, and the resultant debts settled by Captain Samuel Vetch (skipper of the boat that had brought the Dudley group to Canada). It was, therefore, Vetch who required reimbursement now.

Straightforward enough so far. And—one would think—compelling enough to persuade the Court. But Williams concludes with a paragraph calculated not just to persuade but to make the Court members squirm. Please, he writes, be "so charitable" as to pay Vetch off in full; then he advances a disturbing line of comparison. "Our adversaries"—he is referring to Catholics, and especially to the Jesuits around him—"upbraid our religion that it falls so short of theirs in charity and good works." He has done his best to contradict them, but they remain unmoved in their sense of superiority. Now he has himself become an object of charity—and thus a test case. "I promise myself your charity to me in my affliction and want (having lost all I had at Deerfeild without any repining) will yet give me an occasion from my own experiences to refute their calumnyes." Then, a final hook: "Your charity herein will also be encouraging me still to keep my post (if God graciously return me) a post I lost without any default of mine."

Anger and frustration in the one who sends the petition; guilt for those who receive it. Captain Vetch was, we know, repaid in full. This would have squared the financial accounts between John Williams and his New England "friends." But what of the emotional ones?

MAY 1706: A PASTOR'S QUESTION

Picture the setting. Especially from the standpoint of John Williams.

For more than a year, his hopes of "deliverance" have been rising and falling in bitter sequence. When the first Sheldon-Livingston mission reached Canada, it "gave a revival to many and raised expectations of a return." When Dudley came a few months later, "great encouragements were given as to an exchange of all." But the actual results, in both cases, were disappointing. Now Sheldon has come again, and is again returning. And this time a large group of captives is returning, too. But the Deerfield pastor is not among them.[2]

The Jesuits are increasing the pressure on captives—especially young captives—to abandon their Protestant faith and accept rebaptism as Catholics. Indeed, earlier in the year, one of Williams's own sons was briefly induced to "turn" (which, the father will later recall, "occasioned grief and sorrow that I want words to utter"). With great effort and God's help he has apparently succeeded in reversing the boy's "abjuration." He feels that he ought to do as much for other captives similarly exposed (including two more of his children), yet he knows he cannot. He is simply without the resources to combat, singlehandedly, a widespread campaign "to seduce our young over to popery."[3]

A particular friend from Deerfield has recently died in captivity. And the Jesuits have used this death in an outrageous "strategem" of deception. The dead man, they say, has returned in spectral form to urge that other captives convert forthwith to Catholicism. Williams has done his best to refute this "popish lie," but it has already spread widely.[4]

There are ominous signs that the pace of warfare may now be quickening. Reports circulate of "an army of five hundred Mohawks and Indians" gathering in Montreal for an attack on the English towns to the south.[5]

Williams's personal circumstances as a captive have also been worsening. He is forbidden any longer "to go into the city" (of Quebec). His clothes are "ragged." And he has learned of a threat made by French authorities that if the pirate Baptiste remains imprisoned in Boston, they, in turn, will put Williams in prison and "lay [him] in irons."[6]

These things cause him to reflect. He is now "out of hopes of being returned before winter." He prays to God for a spirit of "holy submission" and "passive obedience" to His will. But to submit, to remain passive, is difficult. And so he decides to write to, and for, his "much Respected Friends that are in their Voyage from Quebeck for New England." This, at least, is something he can do.[7]

The result is no ordinary "letter." Surely, Williams imagines that it may be published—as, indeed, it subsequently is, in Cotton Mather's little compendium *Good Fetch'd Out of Evil*. It is long: some fifteen pages in print. It is carefully phrased. Its form is not unlike that of a sermon; there is "instruction" and "exhortation" and frequent resort to Scripture quotation. Yet its tone is decidedly personal; for Williams is deeply involved with those who will read his words.[8]

Writer and readers have, after all, shared an overwhelming set of experiences. But now they are to be separated—in both spatial and experiential terms. Sharing, followed by separation: this is the letter's central preoccupation, if not (in a sense) its motive. A single "we" has become "we" and "you," "us" and "them"—and the change is hard to bear.

The new boundary is acknowledged on the first page. Williams offers thanks to God for "opening a door of Return for you," and prays for "your Prosperity, for Soul and Body." You—the returning ones—must, for your own part, "continue to pray for us that are left behind, that God would preserve and recover us, and give us Grace to Glorify his Holy Name." It isn't easy—this glorifying of God—given our being "left behind." But if we succeed, "tho under fiery Trials, we shall be no losers . . . no matter what men say of us." (So: what *might* men say? That captives thus "left behind" must in some way have deserved their fate? The thought flickers in Williams's mind, then fades; it will come back.)⁹

"As for you . . . a few words of Counsel. . . ." (From this point forward, Williams puts the returnees at center stage.) "You have the World, as it were, to begin again." But such great opportunity means equally great responsibility—and "you will have many Temptations" to overcome. How, exactly, will you do, upon your return? Will you concentrate on "advancing the Glory and Honour of God, the highest, last, and most noble End Man was made for?" Or will you, instead, make it "your greatest design . . . to see your Friends so long separated from you; to Gain Estates, and recover your outward Losses; and to be free again to go and come as you list." If the former, then you will have "special and peculiar gain and profit"; if the latter, then "surely God has a worse Prison, than any you have yet been in." Captivity should, after all, prove a "purging and purifying" experience, one that leaves its victims like "Gold well refined; cleansed from all . . . filthiness." Specifically, in your case: "See to it after your Return that you be more lively, more exemplary, more self-denying, more tender, more holy in all your conversation, than before." Failing to be—and to act—this way, you will show that your time here was misspent, your opportunity wasted. Moreover, you will show that your release was unmerited. (And merit is truly the heart of the matter—for Williams and, presumably, for all the others remaining behind. Why— they cannot help asking, at least inwardly—why are you going, and we staying?)¹⁰

Again, there is the likelihood of "temptations." (Williams keeps reverting to this theme.) You can hardly avoid "thoughts [of] what to Eat, and what to Drink, and wherewith to be Cloathed." These are, of course, "Lawful Comforts"; yet, watch out lest they prompt an "Inordinacy of Desire." Comforts carry their own "soul exercising" risks and dangers. Indeed, "outward Prosperity has been more hurtful to the Children of God . . . than manifold trying Afflictions for a long time." (Possibly—just possibly—the remaining captives will be better positioned, in the long run, than those who return.)¹¹

Comforts, too, may erode memory—may promote "forgetting"— so beware. "Beware lest you forget your own judgment, whilest in Captivity, of the Preciousness" of freedom. "Don't forget the way God has led you in, to humble and prove you." And, finally—this not quite explicit, but almost—don't forget us, your former companions in captivity. "Oh, for the effectual pouring out of the Spirit from on high upon you that go, and upon us that stay here." (Again, that boundary, now a chasm: "us" and "you." And again, that question *why*.) "Pray for us that are so dull and slow of heart to do our Duty, and are therefore kept under the Rod." (Perhaps those left in captivity are not better off, in any sense. Perhaps they are more deserving of God's wrath, after all.)[12]

Thus the letter concludes, virtually where it began. A circle of religious cogitation, around a center of pain. And what of the addressees, those for whom it was specifically intended? How would they have received it? Did they pass it from one set of hands to another, as their boat sailed slowly homeward? Or was it read aloud to the entire group, perhaps in the course of Sabbath worship? Whichever: With Canada and captivity out of view, the pastor's words yet reverberated. Reassuring, unsettling, uplifting, depressing: The effect was mixed and contradictory. The "sheep" in John Williams's flock could only be grateful for his faith, his prayers, his continuing guidance. And doubtless they prayed for him. But they, too, must have felt the force of his question—about "us," and "you," and why—and searched their own hearts for the answer.

DECEMBER 1706: A CONQUEROR'S GLORY

Only six months have passed since John Williams composed his pastoral letter to returning captives. But his circumstances have changed entirely. Now he is himself among the returned. Reunited with his family (what is left of it). Cared for, indeed fawned over, by a bevy of "friends." Adored by strangers. Sought out by leaders from the governor on down. Lavished with the sort of material "comforts" lacking in his captivity. Many others have returned with him, and the atmosphere is one of extraordinary rejoicing. He is the leader of the returnees, of course, and thus the center of attention. Samuel Sewall captures the flavor of the moment with a short entry in his letter-book: "Mr. Williams returnd a Conquerour from Canada."[13]

December 5, exactly two weeks after the ship's arrival, is "lecture day" in Boston. This will bring John Williams's first public appearance—and his first public statement about his experiences in captivity. Cotton Mather has arranged it carefully. The site is Mather's own church. The congregation is the largest in Boston (1,500 strong), and on this occasion is swelled by additional worshippers from all around the Bay. When Williams rises to speak, there is a palpable feeling of—what to call it?—of restoration, of completion, and, yes, of conquest.[14]

Williams must have anticipated this moment from well before. The trip from Quebec was itself a time for thought and preparation and prayer: four weeks on the water, with fifty-six fellow captives, a ship's crew, a few "ambassadors"—and no regular agenda. Was it then that he found his theme, and an appropriate text: *"Return to thine own house, and shew how great things God hath done unto thee"* (Luke 8:39)? Perhaps, but likely, too, his thoughts took specific shape only after he had reached Boston. After his surroundings—the faces of the people, the very walls of the houses and the stones in the street—had proclaimed, in full measure, his extraordinary "return."

The gist of Williams's lecture is captured in the title under which it was subsequently printed: *Reports of Divine Kindness; or Remarkable Mercies should be faithfully published for the Praise of God the Giver.*[15] Publishing (in the old sense of making public) is, indeed, both its beginning and its end-point. Williams casts himself (and, by implication, his fellow captives) in the role of mouthpiece—loudspeakers for the Lord. What he (and they) must offer now is a matter of "reports," of "shewing to others what great things God has done for them." This, in turn, will "serve to advance the honour and glory of God in the world." For God's "design [in] . . . such things" (as captivity) is that of "advancing His own honour and glory." What's more: "God makes and disposeth all things"—not only captivity and similar "afflictions"—"for his own honour and glory." And still more: in "publishing" their experiences, mortal men are simply "answering that high and noble end we were made for . . . [to] glorify God." Glory, glory, glory, glory: the word and its variants appear almost forty times here. In fact, "publishing" proves to be a mere means to this self-evidently "noble end."[16]

To be sure, glorifying God was always a key point in Puritan worship and a staple of the sermon literature. That God cared only for glory, and that men were "made" to serve His needs: the rows of "auditors" spread out through the meetinghouse had heard all this before. Still, the December "lecture" seems unusual in its sustained devotion to theme. There were, moreover, other (equally standard) themes in the pastor's repertoire. He chose here—and, we must think, chose carefully. Captivity and "redemption" would indeed bring glory to God. But had they not also brought much glory to John Williams? More than he had ever known before? More than attached to any other person, just then, in all New England?

And: How did he feel about getting the glory? He was embarrassed—in fact, deeply troubled—by it. And he loved it. He sought to stop it, or at least to deflect it elsewhere. And he wanted to enjoy it—to roll it around in his mouth and drink deeply of it.

His lecture, read somewhat between the lines, consistently betrays this zig-zag reaction. For the theme of "glory" is not simply reiterated here. Its various parts—its tissues and fibers—are drawn out with the fondest possible care. God must have all the credit, of course, but the captives themselves remain squarely in the spotlight. Consider:

> We find . . . a person in a very doleful, distressed condition . . . forsaken of God . . . a dwelling place of evil spirits, deprived of all human comforts and delights, made to possess sorrow and pain to such a degree as to be a common subject or theme of discourse for all men to relate doleful things about.

This captive, evidently a prototype, is extreme in his suffering, so extreme that he is particularly noticed by "all men." But then: a striking change.

> afterward God, in very remarkable and wonderful works of power and mercy, not only gives release from his sorrowful possession . . . but he is sitting at the feet of Jesus.

A singular person, now occupying a special place. Not merely "returned," but raised to a great height. To be "sitting at the feet of Jesus" was to be well above other "mortal men."[7]

This paradigm—presuming, as it does, that captives hold great interest for both God and humankind—sets the tone for all that follows. "This man, for whom such great things have been done," then "petitions Christ that he may abide with Him." As "a subject of great mercy" and "a person spoken of," he receives "particular and special command from Christ, to be glorifying God." He answers with "obedience"—what else?—and for this "he is commended." Great, special, particular, glorious, *chosen*: The melody is loud and clear.[18]

But now the lecturer pulls back. In all this the captive is merely a recipient—or, at most, an instrument. "God is the bestower and giver of all our good things . . . Our mercies come to us . . . not by casualty or accident. Neither are they of our own procuring and purchasing . . . It is God who returns the captivity of Zion." And so on, for two solid pages. Back to ground level; the heights of specialness are too dangerous. Back among our fellow mortals, where "not one single mercy comes . . . without a commission from that God by whom our very hairs are numbered."[19]

From here the lecturer turns again to the duty of "publishing," and adduces a series of sermonic "reasons." He starts on a familiar track. Captives must publish, because God "aimed," in the "dealing out of these mercies," at increasing His glory; furthermore, as "our Lord and law giver, . . . he requires that we [glorify Him] by rehearsing His praise-worthy acts to the children of men." (As usual: God on high, all of "us" here below. But the remaining reasons reopen a distinction between captives and other "children of men.") Captives must publish, in order to "stir up others to bless God with them, and for them." (Note the two prepositions: not just "with," but also "for.") Captives must publish, in order to "put others in a capacity to be advising and telling us what temptations we may expect to meet with . . . and how to order our whole conversation so as God may have glory." (In short: captives become objects of special concern for "others"; strikingly, too, they need this because they undergo special "temptations.") Captives must publish, in order to "be instrumental to put others upon trusting God." (They will become examples for "others" to follow.) And: "What an honour to be instrumental to any soul's comfort." (A little "honour"—something short of full-blown "glory"—may be allowed to captives, after all.) Captives must publish "because the works of God towards them have been very wonderful." (A return here to the initial theme: captives as recipients of special mercies.) Captives must publish because this is "good evidence that they regarded . . . God . . . and would not forget his wonderful works toward them."[20]

"Reasons" explained; case complete. But whom is all this designed to persuade? The ostensible target is captives—all captives—as a group. Yet the persistent use of the pronoun "they" (never "you") suggests something else. In fact, John Williams was here talking about captives, to a large audience of "others"—and it is the others with whom he seems most directly concerned. This becomes quite clear when he concludes his list of "reasons," and declares: "it is very acceptable to God for Christians to entertain the report of the experiences of others [here alluding to captives], to excite their own hearts to glorify God." Indeed, God "lays the hearer under an obligation" to do so. Thus does Williams establish the legitimacy of "publishing," and demand his "hearers' " attention.[21]

Now, finally (fifteen pages into the printed version) comes the promised payoff. Williams will "now make a report of some of the great things God has done for those you have been putting up so many prayers to God for." (The audience is explicitly "you." And the captives are implicitly "we.") At last: some actual "experiences" of captivity. As expected, each one begins with a declaration of divine agency: "God has made," "God has upheld," "God has strengthened." But each one proceeds quickly to human "conditions" and circumstances. Here, briefly summarized and in the order given, is the full list. Indian captors showed surprising "pity" and "compassion" to those in their charge. And, as for the captives themselves: They (mostly) held to their (Protestant) faith, in spite of "all manner of disadvantages" and "painful endeavors used to seduce them" (to Catholicism). They found remarkable "strength" to endure "tedious journeys." They made of their religious beliefs "a little sanctuary" and received "refreshing favours from Heaven." They prayed regularly and to good effect, thus "making void the counsels of adversaries." They saw "their former Sabbath solemn attendances" and their "religious education" vindicated in their ability to withstand "practices . . . contrary to the precepts of God's holy word." They turned even the failures of a few among them—"falls to popery" and the like—into a "means for the recovery of others." They managed (some of them) to "welcome death . . . with a right Christian courage." They learned from their sufferings "to set an higher value upon the ordinances of Jesus Christ." They refused to bend their principles "not only . . . when threatened with all cruelties,. . . but when the hatchet has been lifted up."[22]

It makes, altogether, an arresting picture. Strong people. Steadfast in their faith. Tested by terrible adversity—thus stronger, more steadfast, at the end than the beginning. And yet: Their achievements owe everything to God's sustaining support; their personal credit is nil. This is the very point of John Williams's lecture.

At the end, Williams turns (as it were) and faces the captives—for the first time. In doing so, he implicates himself and lays bare the risks, the "temptations," to which their (and his) extraordinary experiences have left them (and him) open. What it comes down to is this: "Beware of all manner of pride." (Or—same thought, other words— "all vain ostentation.") The matter of "credit," God's and/or Man's, is again at the center.[23]

> Sometimes men's pride makes them so admire their own parts
> and contrivances, as to over-look the works of divine providence;
> they sacrifice to their own net, and burn incense to their own
> drag; and say they have so much learning and knowledge, that

they could easily answer arguments to seduce them to popery; and so do not see and acknowledge the goodness of God, in preserving and keeping them.

For "they" and "them" we might as well read "I" and "me." Certainly, the largest part of John Williams's own stay in captivity was a struggle to "answer arguments" by advocates of "popery": the reference is too personal to miss. And does he not feel the rest as well? The impulse to admire his own "parts and contrivances"? The wish to "sacrifice" and "burn incense" in his own name? With all of Boston sitting at his feet—for so it might have seemed, as he looked down from the pulpit that day—"pride" is hard to resist.

There is, however, one final check to pride: the remembrance of those captives who yet remain in Canada. Six months before, while captive himself, the pastor had warned other returnees not to forget those left behind. Now that he has come back to freedom, the warning holds for him as well. But how could he forget, with Eunice still among the missing? In fact, at three points in his lecture, he seems to refer (albeit indirectly) to his captive daughter. Early on, while affirming the power of God's providence, he comments: "It is he who takes away the captives of the mighty, the prey of the terrible; who contends with them that contend with us, and *saves our children*." (Emphasis added.) Much later, when describing the surprising "compassion" of the Indians toward captives, he recalls how "they [would] . . . carry on their shoulders, our little ones, unable to travel." Such, we know, was the experience of Eunice, during the long "march" to Canada. And, finally, this:

> Do not be discouraged, and say, your friends and relations have (being captivated when young) for a long time lived in popery, and therefore [there can be] no hopes of recovery; for God can make dry bones, very dry, to live, and can in ways unthought of by you, both recover them after they have fallen, and return them again.

Riding high, as he certainly was, on the wave of local adulation, John Williams here looked backward to his own years in captivity—and, simultaneously, toward Eunice. And, too, he looked ahead to another difficult time that would soon begin for him in Deerfield.[24]

"Beware of all manner of pride." And: "Do not be discouraged." The Boston lecture was a peak between two valleys in the jagged profile of his experience.

WINTER 1707: AN AUTHOR'S ACCOUNTING

There was one more lap in the conqueror's return: the 100 or so miles from Boston west to Deerfield. And (as noted already) he traveled this long-familiar route in late December, arriving on the 28th. At last, John Williams was home.

But home was not as he remembered it, years before. The outward wounds of the massacre were only partially healed; the inward ones were still raw and suppurating. Details can be pried out of various town petitions from the months immediately preceding:

the greatest Part of our Provision & stock of cattle [have been] plundered and destroyed. . . .

our crop of grain on wch we Depend for our livelihood was inconsiderable. . . .

the people being in a broken condition . . . most of us [are] very low in the world. . . .

Indeed, Deerfield would probably have been abandoned but for an explicit order to the contrary (by the Massachusetts authorities). The men of the town were "impressed" as "garrison souldiers," and the site was henceforth maintained as an outpost of frontier warfare.[25]

To be sure, the pastor's homecoming gave a great lift to local morale. Some who had "deserted ye Place quickly after ye Desolation" were encouraged now to return. But this process of reconnection—the shepherd with his shattered flock—was itself a heavy responsibility. Moreover, he had private burdens to bear. During those first days back in Deerfield, John Williams must have visited his wife's gravesite. Viewed the charred remnants of his pre-massacre house. Walked the paths and roadways with other survivors, sharing their bitter memories. No, this was not the Deerfield he knew—was not, and never would be.

It was at about this point—and perhaps in response to all he was feeling—that he began to compose his famous "narrative." No doubt the idea had been formed well before and encouraged by his friends in Boston. Captivity accounts were already a favored genre, and Williams was the most prominent captive so far. The opportunity—one might well say, the public necessity—was obvious to all.[26]

And yet: Here, too, the public mixed uneasily with the private and personal. By writing of his experience, John Williams would rethink it in fundamental ways—would sift the details and grope for their meaning. The words on the page would be part of his struggle to accept, to adjust, to understand. In the long run, his audience would be all New England—all America—but at first there was only himself.

These crisscrossings of agenda and audience created some untidiness of result. *The Redeemed Captive Returning to Zion* is an arresting book, but also an awkward one. Its structure is lopsided, its diction irregular, its tone erratic and wavering. It is more a compilation of events—and of "reflections" upon events—than a bona fide "narrative." To readers, then and now, it offers a distinctly bumpy ride.[27]

It begins, straightforwardly enough, with a prefatory dedication: "To His Excellency, Joseph Dudley, Esq., Captain-General and Governor-in-Chief." The point here is "thanks"—fulsomely reiterated thanks: to omit such would be "to the last degree criminal and unpardonable." All this is quite standard—even formulaic—in Puritan writings from the period. But even so, John Williams manages to strike a pose, and establish a mood, reflecting his particular experience. Thanks, dear Governor, for "your uncommon sympathy with us . . . expressed in all endearing methods of parental care and tenderness." And thanks, too, for "contriving to loose the bonds of your captivated children." The latter, of course, include "me, my family, and people"—objects, all, of "divine rebukes which the most holy God has seen meet in spotless sovereignty to dispense . . . in delivering us into the hands of those that hated us." The pastor writes as a chastened child; his thanks are crossed with his pain and sorrow. The up-side and the down: "recovery" and "redemption" after "tyranny and oppression." And which bulks larger in his mind? It isn't even close. The preface ends with a little prayer: "May heaven long preserve you at our helm, a blessing so necessary . . . in this dark and tempestuous season."[28]

And so to the narrative itself. At once, there are complications. The narrator's voice, for example—or rather the three voices alternately heard here, each expressing a different attitude. There is, first, the voice of a participant, communicating directly (and sometimes very powerfully) the immediacy of remembered experience.

> My feet were very sore, and each night I wrung blood out of my stockings when I pulled them off.[29]

> I answered, "Sir, if I thought your religion [Catholicism] to be true, I would embrace it freely . . . but so long as I believe it to be what it is, the offer of the whole world is of no more value to me than a blackberry."[30]

There is also the voice of a reporter, more distanced, more dispassionate:

> I am not able to give you an account of the number of the enemy slain, but I observed . . . many wounded persons.[31]

> On May sixteen arrived a canoe at Quebec that brought letters from Mississippi written May preceding giving an account that the plague was there.[32]

And, finally, the voice of a preacher, searching for lessons with which to instruct his audience:

> I mention it [the death of a remarkably pious young captive] to the end I may stir up all in their young days . . . to a giving then a holy boldness in the day of death.[33]

> And almost always before any remarkable favor I was brought to lie down at the foot of God and made to be willing that God should govern the world so as might be most for His own honor.[34]

The narrative swings repeatedly from one to another mode, reflecting the author's own ambivalence toward his material. Of course, he aims to preach: That is his lifelong "calling" (in Puritan terms) and his reason now for "publishing." And he apparently feels an obligation to report—especially on those parts of his experience that may have some military bearing. But the aspect of participation—his own—is what grips him most of all. Thus the central thrust of *The Redeemed Captive*: to review and evaluate "what had passed over me and what was to be expected."[35]

In part, this is a matter of re-experience—a going over, a doing again—to reach in the end a degree of mastery. One feels, thus, a kind of echo-effect as Williams remembers—especially his most difficult moments.

> My loss and the loss of my children [following the murder of Mrs. Williams] was great; our hearts were so filled with sorrow that nothing but the comfortable hopes of her being taken away in mercy to herself . . . could have kept us from sinking under at that time.[36]

> I mourned when I thought with myself that I had one child with the Mohawks, a second turned to popery, and a little child of six years of age in danger . . . to be instructed in popery.[37]

The pain in such passages is palpable; the narrator is as if recaptured—and again "overwhelmed." From such reliving he seeks a freedom made progressively more secure.

In part, too, the narrative is a process of sorting an otherwise jumbled succession of events. Nearly three years of captivity all told, under various "masters" and in several different sites, with an extraordinary cast of characters (English, French, and Indian): All this needs organizing to become finally comprehensible. Plus and minus, high and low, good and bad: in effect, an accounting procedure. There are villains to be remembered—and rebuked in print—especially the Jesuits with all their "diligence and wiles" and their "crafty designs." There are benefactors, too, some of them quite "surprising." Williams recalls with real appreciation how the Indians cared for his children en route to Canada, and how his own master "would always give me the best he had to eat." His encounters with individual Frenchmen and women—apart from the priests—were also disarmingly pleasant; indeed, "wherever we entered into houses, the French were very courteous." The French governor himself invited Williams into his home and was "charitable to admiration." There are heroes among the other captives: "an English girl" who "chose to be whipped" rather than wear a Catholic cross; "a maid of our town," forced into a nunnery and repeatedly beaten, who refused nonetheless to "turn"; "a very hopeful and pious young man" who, before his death, "carried himself . . . so as to edify several of the English and recover one fallen to popery taken the last war." There are exotics, like the French soldier who "came into my landlord's house barefoot and barelegged, going on a pilgrimage to Saint Anne." And, not least, there are strange hybrids: an Indian "savagess," who had once been an English prisoner "but was now proselyted to the Romish faith"; and "several poor [English] children" captured some years before and since become "very much like Indians and in manner . . . symbolizing with them." The latter group—the Indianized children—touch John Williams at an especially sensitive spot. His own daughter Eunice must now be like them, a "symbolizer" herself. She is "there still," he laments, "and has forgotten to speak English. Oh! That all who peruse this history would join in their fervent requests to God . . . that this poor child, and so many others of our children who.. are now outcast [and] ready to perish, might be gathered from their dispersions and receive sanctifying grace from God."[38]

Experience, too, must be sorted—which, in this case, meant

chopped apart and shaped into little episodes, each with its own front and back and interior structure. The extraordinary day, on the journey to Canada, when Williams was obliged to travel "forty or forty-five miles" without a break—and on badly injured feet. The time his prayers seemed to still a "boisterous" wind, enabling his captive-group to cross a large lake in safety. The afternoon when a priest composed "verses" mocking his captivity—even as, across the ocean, "the bishop of Canada with twenty [Catholic] ecclesiastics" was being "taken by the English." (A coincidence? Of course not. God evening the score.) Clearly, some experiences—indeed a great many—are omitted from the narrative and perhaps from the narrator's memory. Yet others are powerfully underscored. Connections among them are tenuously drawn; chronology serves to order the whole, but specific times are infrequently noticed and long periods are passed over entirely.[39]

The episodes are important also in another way. Read today, they are like playlets: brief, sharply rendered, often with pithy quotations from the featured characters. (This, in itself, suggests a revisionist project; no man's memory could possibly preserve such a plethora of actual detail.) The most featured character is, unsurprisingly, John Williams himself. And the theme, in virtually every case, is some sort of contest: typically, Williams versus one or another (or several) of his "Romish" adversaries. The issues—the stakes—are as one would expect. Fine points of theology and devotional practice. The present and future course of the Anglo-French war. "Offers" made—in effect, bribes to induce Williams to abandon his faith—and offers refused. Attempts by the pastor to reach, and support, his fellow captives, in the face of persistent "Jesuitical" opposition. And, finally, the campaign by the priests "to draw away the English to popery"—which Williams tries, in every way he can, to counteract. The most wounding of all these contests is the one around the "abjuration" of sixteen-year-old Samuel Williams. The pastor's account of his efforts for his son (including the verbatim transcription of several long letters) takes more than a quarter of the entire book.[40]

The tone of such passages is something less than triumphant. Usually Williams shows himself to good advantage—in effect, as winner of the argument—but he is not inclined to boast. He does not hide his anxiety, and sometimes he wonders about his strategy and motives. He recalls, for example, that once after being offered "a great and honorable pension" to turn Catholic, "I made an inquiry with myself whether I had by any action given encouragement for such a temptation." On another occasion, he prayed that "our friends in New England might . . . make a more thankful and fruitful improvement of means of grace than we had done, who by our neglects found ourselves out of God's sanctuary." And, on still another, he "found [in himself] a greater opposition to a patient, quiet, humble resignation to the will of God than I should otherwise have known." Doubts and questions like these are apparently unavoidable. Did I do the right, the moral, thing—given this or that set of circumstances? And did I feel as I ought (quite apart from my actions)? And why was I there, in the first place? Thus does the narrative strain to justify John Williams's experience: to himself, to his "friends," to the world at large.[41]

To re-experience (in the service of mastery), to organize (for the sake of coherence and comprehension), to justify (against persistent inner questioning): these, then, are the deeper currents—the motive ones—coursing through the narrative. Together they comprise the personal agenda of the "participant." The public agenda—of the "preacher" and "reporter"—remains in view, but is mostly overshadowed. To read *The Redeemed Captive* is to see the captive far more than the one redeemed. And behind the captive, another figure: the narrator himself, brooding at his desk, in a still "broken" town, during a "dark and tempestuous season."

MARCH 1707: A PREACHER'S REPROOF

Even as he put the final touches on his narrative, John Williams must have been looking ahead to another assignment: the sermon he had been invited to preach, in Boston, as the colony leaders considered a bold new attack on Canada. Prayerful preparation was standard on such occasions—and who better to take the lead here than the minister of Deerfield? As victim, as close-up observer, and (in a sense) as combatant, Williams had gained much front-line experience of the ongoing war. Who better to inspire the faithful, and invoke God's blessing, than he?

But the resultant sermon was hardly inspirational, nor was it an invocation. No fight-talk. No prayers. No goals defined or hopes raised. Instead Williams pointed his listeners toward a single question: how to get—in the words of the title—"God in the Camp."[42] His answer was simple, direct, and wholly consonant with local sermonic tradition. Repentance. And reformation. Thus, and thus alone, would God be drawn to the New England "camp."

His sermon-text was taken from the Book of Deuteronomy: "When the Host goeth forth against thine Enemies, then keep thee from every wicked thing." His opening paragraph notes "that which is supposed in the Text . . . That the People of God in a righteous Cause . . . are going forth in an Offensive War, against God's, and their Enemies." Both John Williams and his audience would surely suppose something more: that the "People of God" are themselves, that their enemies are the Catholic French, and that the proposed expedition to Canada will indeed be "an offensive war." Thus the implied, but obvious, connection to present circumstances.[43]

And what does an army—the "host" of the text—require for its success? First: "men of Courage and Activity . . . well accoutred, and every way prepared for Service." But this by itself is not enough, for "the gracious Presence of God with the Armies of His People is . . . absolutely needful for their Prosperity." God, in fact, is the source of those qualities and assets most essential to victory. "Wisdom and counsel for war are from the Lord," as are "strength and courage." "Valour" itself is "given or taken away, as pleaseth God." So it is, in the final result, that "the Lord . . . gives Success to which party He will."[44]

All this must have seemed entirely plausible and familiar—even comforting—to John Williams's many "auditors." What followed was also plausible, also familiar, but perhaps not so comforting. God's "presence," God's favor "in the battel," cannot be taken for granted, even by a "Covenant people." On the contrary: if they are "sinful," not to say "degenerate," they must expect "heavy, distressing Calamities of War." And now the preacher's main point, one he will repeat with steadily sharpening effect throughout the second half of the sermon: "The Sins of a People at Home do oftimes more against the Souldiery abroad, than the Sword of the Adversary." Thus does the focus shift: from the "People of God" versus their "Enemies," to the "People at Home" versus their "Souldiery."[45]

In fact, this declaration looks back toward past events rather than forward to the proposed "offensive." The war has been going poorly for New England, and the preacher asks (rhetorically): "How often has our Souldiery been unsuccessful, and Armies returned without any considerable annoyance of our Enemies?" Surely, there is meaning in this; at the very least "such disappointments should put us upon enquiries, Why God thus frowns." The inquiries heard to date—about "the Commanders of the forces employed . . . as tho' they wanted courage and were faint-hearted, or were not Persons of any conduct"— are misplaced. No, do not complain of commanders; instead, "let me ask you . . . Whither you hant reason to be turning some complaints against yourselves, *viz*. in taking courses to make God angry with the Land?"[46]

What is posed here as a question will soon become a thunderous attack, as the preacher extends the "uses" of his "doctrine" into the category of "reproof." To be sure, some reproof belongs with the soldiers themselves: their sins, especially their "unsatiable Tiplings [and] . . . delightful Debauching of themselves with Strong Drink" displease God and provoke Him "at least to say, That He won't honour them to do any great Service for Him, or His People." But the sharpest reproof by far is reserved for those "who tarry at home." Their wickedness is "blame-worthy" enough "at any time," but especially so "when their Armies are in the Field."[47]

Warming rapidly to his task, the preacher spreads out a broad bill of charges—in four major sections. First: "you act as tho' you had no Bowels of Charity to your Friends, Relations, and Neighbours [i.e. the soldiers in the field] and are doing of them the greatest injury." You blame the enemy for "Murdering so many," when actually it is "your ways and your doings [that] procure these things." Indeed, "the Sins of a Covenant People do more against their Armies & Frontiers, and slay more of their Friends, than their Enemies can do."[48]

Second: "You are thereby an occasion of a great deal of dishonour to the Holy God, and the Holy Religion you profess." Thanks to you "the Adversaries [i.e., Catholics, including the priests with whom John Williams has so recently tangled] reproach the true Religion as tho' God disown'd it because He frowns upon the Armies of them that profess it."[49]

Third: "You are dreadfully stupid under, & unaffected with, the Wrath of God that burns so against us." This remains true even though "God has brought such desolations . . . to give an occasion to say as to some of our own Plantations [i.e., Deerfield itself?], Go to my house [i.e., the preacher's own?] at Shiloh & See what I have done."[50]

Fourth: "You are very Presumptuous whilst you look for great Success to your Forces," while remaining yourselves "in such a way of unreformedness." Your prayers will not be heard, "so long as such idols are set up in your hearts." Instead, "you may expect that God will answer by Terrible Things."[51]

To repeat: uncharitable, dishonouring, stupid, presumptuous. And murderers, in effect, of those among your own people, who are serving in your own army, on your own frontiers. It makes, all in all, a devastating indictment.

From reproof to "exhortation," with scarcely a pause for breath.

Sounds better, but is it? In fact: more of the same. "God stands as it may be said, with his Drawn Sword in his hand to awaken you to a necessary Reformation." If, nonetheless, "you go on in your Unreformedness," you will oblige our soldiers "to meet the Enemy with the guilt of a backsliding People upon them." Moreover, you will "augment the fierce anger of God & bring a further decay upon Religion."[52]

He is almost done now. His concluding words are quieter, more restrained. As if he has exhausted his theme—and himself. "Let every one carefully in their place set themselves to Reform and amend": most especially, "those that are in Civil Authority . . . [those] that God has commissioned to Preach in his Name . . . and heads of families." Indeed: "All . . . should engage in a speedy and thorow care that we may be a holy People."[53]

God in the Camp can be read, on its face, as a specimen of the "jeremiad"—a long-standing sermon-type from early New England. At least since the middle of the preceding century, ministers had been using a "rhetoric of failure" to promote the goals of religious reform. Failure, of course, meant *sin*, and thus called forth a torrent of condemnation. The shapes and structures of human wickedness became, as a result, a regular part of the cultural landscape.[54]

Yet *God in the Camp* does not fit the type at every point. For one thing, John Williams barely refers to *specific* sins—within the general pattern of "unreformedness." For another, he does not raise the issue of "declension," of change over time. His interest is unreformedness *now*; unlike previous Jeremiahs, he offers no historical comparison (glorious past versus decayed present; virtuous "founders" versus sinful "rising generation"). Moreover, the particular linkage he stresses— sin among people "at home" causing death and defeat for soldiers "abroad"—is, at the least, unusual. His ostensible aim, his public aim, is defined by the current situation: how to reverse a string of failures in New England's war with New France.

But is there also a private aim, with which the public one coincides? Is the feeling expressed in such lengthy "reproofs" entirely ritualized and rhetorical? Where does Williams locate himself within the pattern described: on the home front or abroad with the "armies and frontiers"? Note his way of referring to the "home" group: first "we," then "they," and finally (when beginning the reproofs) "you." The "you" seems especially insistent—and accusatory. Thus is a distance established, a boundary drawn, with the preacher on one side and his auditors—"home" people, all—on the other.

Likely, too, at some level, this distance recalls others. Between

Canada and New England; between the suffering of captives and the "comforts" of their "friends" at home. Between Deerfield and Boston; between the meagerness of a frontier outpost and the splendor of a provincial capital. The "frontier" connection seems to hold a particular and lasting resonance for John Williams. His sermon explicitly joins "armies *and* frontiers" (emphasis added). And, following his death (more than twenty years later), his eulogist remembers this: "Mr. Williams would sometimes say, 'It was a dangerous thing to be set in the front of New England's Sins.' " *Set in the Front of?* Sins behind, enemies ahead, danger on the boundary in between. The echo of *God in the Camp* is too strong to miss.[55]

For the people who listen, that March day in the Boston church, John Williams is still a conqueror. Glory is still his, if he cares to claim it. But he doesn't; his own position has changed again, changed entirely. He has spent the previous two months in beleaguered little Deerfield. (Winter months, too, including a "massacre" anniversary.) He has written (and just completed) a narrative, and has thus been through a painful process of review and reliving. He has returned again to Boston across a key experiential boundary—from "we" to "they" to "you." He has felt the difference in his head and bones and belly. And now he re-experiences—without entirely remembering— another part of his captivity. Anger. No, a stronger feeling: rage. Perhaps it goes something like this:

> *Why was it I, and not you (who "tarried at home")? Did you do all you could to win my release? Or were you, instead, going along in sin, making God "angry with the land," and thus prolonging my torment? No wonder armies were defeated there. And frontiers laid waste. And captives left to languish, year after year.*

Impossible ever to say such things directly. But there is the sermon-invitation. Big audience; important occasion. A fine chance to voice God's wrath. He is the wrathful one, only He. And He must be heard. Go ahead. A "jeremiad" it is.

POSTSCRIPT: A CAPTIVE'S JOURNEY

He had traveled a long way these past months. From Quebec, to Boston, to Deerfield, and again to Boston. From the anguish of captivity, to the joy of freedom and the "pride" of "conquest" (with its accompanying "temptations"), to the sorrow and doubt of retrospective reliving, to the expression at last of a long-deferred rage. Both parts of the journey—the physical one, the psychological one—were deeply wrenching. He would never again be quite the same. Redeemed captive, captive redeemed: a badge, a brand, to carry for life.

And was it the same for other captives? Did their journeys follow a similar course? There is no way now to say for certain, but the presumption (at least) seems strong. The "frontiers" between New England and New France, between Protestantism and Catholicism, between Euro-American and Native American peoples: all were clearly drawn and carefully patrolled. To travel across them was costly and dangerous—and potentially transforming. Some who set out would not return.

For those who did return there was "redemption"—but with a difference. Certainly their contemporaries saw them as different, as marked by their captive experience. This, indeed, goes far toward explaining the extraordinary popularity of captivity narratives, from the last quarter of the seventeenth century to the beginning of the twentieth. Generation after generation of readers turned to such writings with a special—and intense—curiosity.[56]

> *What was it like for you, on the other side of the frontier? How much, and in what ways, were you changed? Were the changes personally compromising? Did you accept them willingly, or even seek them out? Can we trust you now?*

Such questions, running just below the surface of the page, presume difference. And also just below the surface: the captives' response. Or the one they struggled to find.

> *If we are different, we are better. Tested in the fires of adversity. Strengthened. Wiser and deeper than we were before.*

Two groups, inwardly set apart. Redeemed captives and others. Narrators and readers. "We" and "you."

And a third group, too, not yet accounted for: the captives still unredeemed. What about them?

FOUR

◈

THE CLOSING MONTHS of 1706 had brought a harvest of prisoner "redemptions." Two major missions to Canada—Sheldon's in late summer and Appleton's in the fall—had between them retrieved approximately 100 English captives; meanwhile, a similar number of Frenchmen had gone the opposite way. But there was still no government-to-government agreement about the process itself, and no assurance that it would continue. Some ninety English men, women, and children remained in Canada—so Governor Dudley reported to his Councillors in January 1707—with only a vague suggestion by French authorities of further repatriations "in the spring." Accordingly, Dudley proposed that Massachusetts have yet another "Person Ledger [i.e., ambassador] at Quebec to put forward that affair"—and, specifically, that "Mr. John Sheldon, who has been twice already, may be employed with a suitable retinue to undertake a journey thither."[1]

Sheldon and a "retinue" of three left Boston in mid-April. The trip was much more hazardous this time, because Indian war-parties were at large in the woods and the route followed was evidently unfamiliar. (Sheldon's expense account, submitted following his return, included payments "to an Indian to guide us into the way when bewildered.") Still, the "person Ledger" arrived without incident in early May. Then, new difficulties: Quebec was astir with excitement over the pending English expedition to Port Royal—and the visitors from Boston were placed under guard. But after the withdrawal of English forces (in June), the French relaxed these restrictions and Sheldon and his companions were free to travel about: to Montreal, to "Oso fort" (the Kahnawake mission-village where several captives, including Eunice Williams, where known to be held), and possibly to other places as well. Indeed, Vaudreuil claimed, in a subsequent letter to

Dudley, that he had allowed Sheldon "complete liberty to speak with all your prisoners, and to do whatever he could to induce them to go back with him." This permission had extended even to those "who are among the Indians." The results were admittedly meager—seven captives only "induced" to return—but there had been no lack of effort on any side. Moreover, wrote Vaudreuil—his tone shifting here from defensiveness to satisfaction—Sheldon was now a "witness himself of the firm resolution with which almost all your prisoners wish to remain with us."[2]

This outcome could hardly have been a surprise, however unwelcome in New England. In fact, the process of prisoner exchange had long been asymmetrical. In New England, captives were simply incarcerated—held in jails or other places of confinement. In New France, the situation was far more complicated. There was, first, an important distinction between those "in French hands" and others "among the Indians." And even the former category was not uniform. Some (but not very many) were imprisoned; others were more loosely held in "seminaries," nunneries, or hospitals; still others joined private households; and at least a few were left to shift entirely for themselves.[3] Joseph Kellogg of Deerfield, captured as a boy of twelve, wrote later that he had "travelled two & fro amongst the French and Indians . . . [and] . . . got into a very good way of business: So as . . . handsomely to support [himself] & was under no restraint at all." (Kellogg's travels took him as far west as the Mississippi Valley; he was, perhaps, the first New Englander to see that greatest of all North American rivers.)[4]

Another complication, bitterly remembered in John Williams's narrative, was the pressure on many captives to accept rebaptism as Catholics. And still another: a standing offer of naturalization—as French citizens—to any captives who wished. What inducements were used with them is impossible to say. But the bare facts—of both rebaptism and naturalization—are attested by numerous official "acts." For instance, this:

On Saturday, 25 April 1705 was baptized by me, [the] priest undersigned, . . . an English woman named Elizabeth who had previously abjured the Calvinistic heresy, who was born at Northampton in New England the 23d August 1683, . . . having been taken at Deerfield in New England the 11 March 1704 and brought to Canada, [and] is living with the Sisters of the Congregation at Ville-Marie.[5]

And this:

> Louis, by the grace of God, King of France and Navarre . . .
> [hereby grants] all the rights, privileges, and immunities enjoyed
> by our born subjects [to various English captives individually
> named], . . . all professing the catholic, apostolic, and roman
> religion . . . and desiring to end their days as our subjects . . .[6]

After rebaptism and naturalization, a further step—marriage:

> On Feb. 6, 1713 after one publication of the banns . . . I, the
> vicar of the parish of Ville-Marie, having received the mutual
> consent of Jean Daveluy, aged thirty-one, son of the late Paul
> Daveluy and of Elizabeth haquin, his wife, . . . and of Marie
> francoise french, aged twenty-one years, daughter of Thomas
> french and of Marie Cathaline of Dierfield in new england . . .
> married them and gave them the nuptial blessing, in presence of
> . . . several . . . relatives and friends of the parties.[7]

Any one of these events might be enough to fix a captive in his (or
her) Canadian setting; the combination of all three made such fixing
virtually certain. Within months of the massacre, Vaudreuil was writing to his superiors of English prisoners "who are become Catholics,
having resolved to establish themselves in this country." Already, he
said, they "are asking for letters of naturalization, if His Majesty will
permit it." Two years later, when reporting the return of "all the
English prisoners here in the hands of the French who wish to return,"
he described "many others, principally women, who have converted
to Catholicism and who are not willing to return." About the latter
group he added: "I have no doubt but that this will make trouble
between Mr. Dudley and myself."[8]

But the other major category of captives, those *parmi les sauvages*,
made greater trouble still. Even as the war began, both sides could
anticipate the probabilities. Indian neighbors had for decades played
a key part in French military operations. They would want prisoners,
as part of their "spoils of war," and prisoners they would have. Governor Dudley's first letter to Vaudreuil following the massacre demanded
that "you . . . withdraw all those Christian captives from the hands of
the savages and return them to me." His second was even more emphatic: "I cannot admit the pretext that the Indians have the right to
retain these prisoners, because I would never permit a savage to tell
me that any Christian prisoner is at his disposal." The personal phras-

ing chosen here—*I would never permit a savage to tell me*—reflects the governor's deep sense of affront. Savages must not be granted disposal of the lives of Christians: it was as simple—and, for Englishmen of the time, as morally compelling—as that.[9]

To Vaudreuil, of course, it seemed quite different. The Indians involved were actually Christians themselves; moreover, they were not French subjects but, rather, "allies." Hence the French governor could not order them around; instead, he must use "means of persuasion"—including money. Dudley bristled that captives should be "made a matter of trade between the savages and the subjects of your master [the King]"; such practice, he declared, "will be esteemed barbarous by all Europe." Vaudreuil, for his part, "knew no better way to retrieve the prisoners from Indian hands." *Dudley to Vaudreuil, 1705*: "I assure you sincerely that I will not give one cent for any prisoner under the pretext of money paid by you to the savages for ransom, because I cannot allow that Christians should be slaves of those wretches." Moreover, if Vaudreuil declined to resolve this matter promptly, French prisoners would be turned over to the New England Indians, "and your people . . . reduced to accommodate themselves to a savage life as well as mine." *Vaudreuil to Dudley, 1706*: "I am surprised, sir, that you speak to me still in your letter about prisoners who are in the hands of the Indians. I have written on this subject, and have told you that I would send only those who are in French hands, and that as for the others I would do the best I could to regain them, as we have always done." In fact, New Englanders should feel grateful for "the humanity shown by the people of this country in using their money to buy back [captives] and thus to end their servitude." And so it went: a running exchange of pleadings, threats, and accusations from the one side, for wounded (sometimes angry) rebuttals, on the other. If there was any middle ground between these positions, perhaps it was the one proposed in the abortive treaty negotiations of 1705: "In regard to the French or English prisoners who are in the hands of the Indians, the two aforesaid governors oblige themselves to do all in their power to withdraw them . . . and to send them back afterwards to their countries."[10]

The Indian approach to taking captives was a fluid mix of cultural inheritance, personal whim, and vigorous pursuit of the main chance. Some traditional practices had been gradually abandoned, at least among the Canadian tribes allied to the French. No longer were captives tortured to death (and cannibalized) to slake a thirst for revenge. (There were rare exceptions: for example, a New Hampshire man who in the summer of 1709 overpowered his Indian captor, escaped, was quickly retaken, and then was "Roasted to Death." Nor should we forget that John Williams himself was briefly marked for execution, while en route to Canada, to avenge the death of a Huron chief.)[11] On the other hand, "the ceremony of running ye Gauntlett" was retained in places like Kahnawake, as were various rites of public humiliation. One apparent eyewitness (an Englishman and an ex-captive himself) described this "damnable practise" as follows:

> They make a stope [upon reaching their home village], and strip their prisoners stark naked, and with their painting stuff red them all over, and sett them before the company that has been to warr, who have each of them a club in their hands, who, when the word is given, they run and their prisoners run, and what blows they can give them befor they get into the fort they have for to welcome them to their new habitation, and . . . there is att the entry of the fort gate a heap of squaws and childring who stand ready for to receive them with their sticks, clubbs, pols and fire-brands, who lay on with all the force and might till he getts into the wigwame where he is to live.

Nor was this necessarily the end. Newly arrived prisoners would sometimes be paraded here and there within the village, and forced to "dance" for their captors. (Most such "practise" was, however, reserved for adult men; female captives and children were treated much less harshly.)[12]

And there was the matter of "adoption"—of incorporating (some, not all) captives into particular Indian families. This, too, was an old practice among native peoples of the North American woodlands, and clearly it survived among the "French Indians" of Canada. The specific arrangements are difficult to trace from three centuries later in time, because they were not regularly put into writing. Still, baptismal and burial files of the mission Indians do mention individual cases, in passing.

> [Kahnawake, 1736] . . . Today I baptised with the rites of the church an adult woman about 23 years old . . . captured in war, whom Tsiorihoua has adopted as a daughter. . . .

> [Lac des Deux Montagnes, 1749] . . . Elizabeth Nimbs (Tewattokwas) [was buried today], an English woman adopted into the cabane of the chiefs of the family of the bear, after having been taken in the time of war, and aged about 48 years.

Moreover, there are at least two personal accounts of Kahnawake adoptions, one from the hand of a young Pennsylvania captive named James Smith, the other by Zadock Steele of Connecticut. Smith's experiences included an elaborate haircut, ear- and nose-piercing, painting of face and body, several changes of clothing, a ritual bath, and speeches by tribal elders—all of which supposedly meant that "every drop of white blood was washed out of your veins," and "you are adopted into a great family . . . in the room and place of a great man." Steele remembered similar features in "the ceremony of my own adoption, as well as that of many other of the prisoners."[13] Adoption was the strategy of choice especially, though not exclusively, in the case of captive children.[14]

But also: by (and even before) 1700, ransom had entered the calculus of Indian captivity. Governor Dudley's objections notwithstanding, the families of captives saw this as the single most efficacious means of redemption. Indeed, successful ransoms would typically produce petitions for "relief" to English officials—in whose records they can be rediscovered today. Sometimes the process was quite simple and straightforward: for instance, Benjamin Nason (Berwick, Maine), father of a girl redeemed in 1700, requesting reimbursement "for her ransom . . . £3—10s.—od.," and Richard Dollar (Exeter, New Hampshire) asking for help with his payment of £12—17s.—od., "to ye Indian captor at Canada."[15]

Occasionally, the Indians involved come into view, through these and similar writings. Susanna Johnson was pregnant when captured from her New Hampshire home in 1754. When subsequently she gave birth by the trail, her captor "clapped his hands with joy, crying 'two monies for me, two monies for me.' " Elizabeth Hanson, another New Hampshire woman "carried to Canada" (in 1724), was taken by her master "to the French, in order for a chapman [buyer] . . . he asked for me 800 livres. . . . But his chapman . . . put him in a great rage, offering him but 600; he said, in a great passion, if he could not have his demand, he would make a great fire and burn me and [my] babe." The chapman took this for the bluff it evidently was, and waited; the next day his offer was accepted. Meanwhile, a daughter of Mrs. Hanson had been taken to another Indian village—where her father subsequently visited "but could not obtain her Ransom, for the Indians would not consent to part with her on any terms."[16]

The Hanson story reveals the presence of the French as part of the redemption process. And, more often than not, French intermediaries were not only present but vital to success. To buy back (*racheter*)

English captives from Indians became a lively business for merchants in Montreal and Quebec; they, in turn, sought compensation from the families involved. Thus was established a line of exchange, which, by mid-century, became increasingly routinized. A letter from a Maine youth, captured by Abenakis in 1750, is illustrative:

> At Montreal, the 29 July 1751
>
> Honoured father
> This few Lines is to Let you know that I am in Good health, I live at Present with Mr. Gamelin at Saint Francois, he has Redeemed me from the Indians for 300 livers, I beg you Dear father to Redeem me as Soon as Possible you Can. I long much to Gitt home. . . . I Remain always your Dutiful Son
>
> Seth Webb[17]

Occasionally the line added extra segments. Edward Chandler's petition of October 1751 described how his son Joseph "was . . . Carryed to St. Francis & there sold to a Frenchman, who sold him to Mr. Cornelius Cuyler of Albany for £25 York Currency, & sd Cuyler . . . now detains him for ye paymt of sd Ransom money & Charges as by his Letter herewith Exhibited will appear." From the Indians, to the French, to the Albany Dutch, to the boy's New England father, to the Massachusetts General Court: five parties, four transactions, with (one suspects) profits to be made at most points along the way.[18]

Between them, adoption and repatriation-by-ransom covered the situation of many "Indian captives"—but not all. Some were held for longer or shorter periods without being adopted: to them the French word *esclave* (slave or servant) was occasionally applied. Their value lay principally in the work they performed. A captive from Ipswich was described in 1717 as being "somewhere about . . . Fort St. François [an Abenaki settlement east of Montreal] in the hands & Custody of an old Indian Squaw who hires him out to work." A boy from Northampton recalled later how he had "tended a piece of Corn, more than half An Acre" during a long summer of captivity.[19] A few captives were marked for marriage to the sons or daughters of their masters. Indeed, the circumstances of captivity were as varied as the numbers of people involved—on both sides.[20] One resourceful prisoner gained favor as an uncommonly swift runner and was matched in intertribal competitions; later he gained his freedom by agreeing to build his master "an English house."[21] Another resisted the violence of the gauntlet and subsequent attempts to humiliate him; in response, his admiring captors wished to make him a chief.[22] Indeed, several captives actually became chiefs—including two at Kahnawake, taken when young from their home in Massachusetts.[23]

Finally, there was the matter of escape—always a possibility, but usually a dangerous one, and not often tried. The chances of success were greatest soon after capture while still "on the march." In 1697 two Haverhill women, Hannah Dustin and Mary Neff, earned lasting fame by murdering ten of their captors in the course of a nighttime escape.[24] One of the Deerfield group got away undetected the evening after the massacre; others tried later and failed. In 1705 four young men from Deerfield, variously located among the French and Indians around Montreal, formed a daring plan to escape together. They reached home after a journey of some twenty-five days, half starved and virtually delirious; years later, one of them wrote down the grisly details in a letter sent to Stephen Williams "upon your desire."[25]

Stephen became, in time, a collector and guardian of captivity lore.[26] Among them the members of his family had personally known many of the experiences described above. Stephen himself had been used as a kind of servant by his Abenaki masters. Samuel had lived for two years with a French family, attended a French school, and been re-christened as a Catholic. His sister Esther had been "carefully tended in the hospital" through a period of illness and then sent back to New England with John Sheldon. His brother Warham was "redeemed by a gentlewoman in the city [Montreal] as the Indians passed by." (Subsequently, the same Indians thought better of their decision, and offered to trade "a man for the child, alleging that the child could not be profitable, . . . but the man would, for he was a weaver"; the "gentlewoman," however, declined.) All four of these Williamses—five, if we include their father—were objects of ransom.[27]

And the sixth, daughter Eunice, would have been ransomed had her captors agreed. But they didn't; John Williams was told (by one of the mission-priests) that "the Mohawks would as soon part with their hearts as my child." Eunice, we can be sure, was adopted into a Kahnawake family; she alone among the Williamses reached this last stage of formal acculturation.[28]

꒱

So, too, was Eunice the only Williams left in Canada after the exchanges of 1706. Her father had maintained at least occasional contact with her during the time of his own captivity: had seen her once at her Indian home and again "a few days after in the city [of Montreal]." Moreover, he had surely heard about her from time to time, through the French governor (who tried unsuccessfully to buy her freedom) and "his lady" (who "went over . . . [and] begged her from them, but all in vain"), not to mention fellow captives, "messengers," and assorted visitors to the mission-village. Now that he was himself redeemed, he was farther from her—much farther—and quite helpless to affect her fate. For the time being he would have to rely on others.[29]

The first news to reach him after his return came through Peter Schuyler of Albany, a merchant with extensive contacts among the northern Indians. Writing to Samuel Partridge (commander of frontier soldiers at Hatfield, Massachusetts) on February 18, 1707, Schuyler said:

> As to Mr. Williams Daughter, our spies which we sent to Canada are Returned, who as they were hunting, saw Mr. Williams Daughter wth ye Indian who ownes her, she is in good health but seemes unwilling to Returne, and the Indian not very willing to part wth her, she being (as he says) a pritty girll, but perhaps he may Exchange her if he can gett a very pritty Indian in her Rome, which he must first see, you may assure Mr. Williams I will do all that lays in my power to serve him, as I have formally wrott to him . . .

A puzzling—and disturbing—report. *Good health*: all right, thank God for that. *The Indian who owns her*: her master? her adoptive father? It just isn't clear. *Not very willing to part with her*: they'd heard as much already; still, painful to have it confirmed. *A pretty girl*: ambiguous qualifier. Clever? Skillful? Pleasing to look at? (All are acceptable eighteenth-century meanings.) *Perhaps he may exchange her*: an opening there, something to remember for the future. (Or is he simply leading them on?) *She seems unwilling to return*: that is new, and especially hard to bear. How can she? How dare she? . . . But, Schuyler will keep trying. And if anyone can bring it off, he can.[30]

A few weeks later, Partridge wrote back to Schuyler. A "Captive Boy" had recently returned, largely through Schuyler's efforts: "many thanks for yor kindness therein & [I] have Sent you . . . Seventeene pounds Nine shillings to make & Complete the dues for his Redemption." (The ransom line again.) As for the future: "Please to do what you can at all tymes to obtain mr Williams his daughter or any other Captives you may hear of within your Reach." This would become a familiar line in subsequent correspondence: *Mr Williams his daughter or any other captives.* Eunice out front—she has top rank here—the rest a bit behind.[31]

June 6: "att a Meeting of the Commissrs of the Indian affairs" in Albany. "Present": eight New Yorkers (including three Schuylers, Peter, David, and John), plus "Onnogharichson, Sachim of Canada." The sachem "Desires a belt of wampum to goe under the ground [i.e., be sent secretly] from hence to their [other Canadian] sachems, yt they should Shut up the Path of new England, yt their Indians Should not goe & Skulk there anymore, & yt ye govr of canada Should not know thereof." Said, and done: anything to avert further attacks by the French Indians on New England's battered frontier. Maybe Onnogharichson can persuade them this time. And one thing more, as long as he's going: "Likewise there is given To ye Sd. Sachim three small belts of wampum to Releace mr williams ye minister of dear feild his Doughter from ye Indians if She be possible to be gotten, for money, or Els to give an Indian girle for ye Same, which he promised to doe if it was in his Power." Ransom is still a possibility—isn't it? Or else that other plan: a captive-for-captive exchange.[32]

Onnogharichson agreed to "bring an answer himself in a Short time if his undertakeing has Success or not." Did he actually follow through? The records do not say. Sheldon, too, was in Montreal that summer, and visited the "Oso fort," and (as noted already) was allowed to "speak with all your prisoners."[33] Did he see Eunice? Again, the records are silent. But maybe something was changing; at any rate, the Williams clan took new hope. On August 4, Elisha Williams (son of John's brother, living in Hatfield) sent a letter "to his Loving cousen Stephen Williams in Roxbury." Family news, for the most part, including this: "A Post came from albany Last Saturday night [and] brought letters from Canada. [There] Is an letter yt came from Albany yt Saith yt ye Indian (Eunis's Master) saith he will bring her in with in two months."[34] In short: the most promising, the most specific report yet. Of course, one wishes for further details. Had the master himself been there in Albany? And what about that phrase *bring her in*: for a visit? or for a true release? Elisha does not say, and probably does not know.

In any case, it came to nothing. Her master did not bring her in. Nor did anyone else. There would be a gap of two years—two and a half—before the family heard of her again. (Correction: the gap, strictly speaking, is ours—and only maybe, not certainly, theirs. Two and a half years during which no single document now extant refers to Eunice.)

It was, all through, a dark time on the New England and Canadian frontier: a time of more war, and less talk, between the opposing sides. Sheldon's third "mission," in mid-1707, was also his last—and his least successful. And no other Englishman would appear in Canada, as "Person Ledger," until near the end of 1710. In fact, as early as 1706, Vaudreuil had "permitted several small parties of Indians to recommence hostilities" against New England; in succeeding years such "parties" were (or seemed to be) everywhere. The English responded with "garrisons" for their most-exposed towns, "patrols" in the countryside nearby, and "scouts" roaming far into the wilderness (to engage the enemy before he could reach their "settled habitations"). Governor Dudley explained to his superiors in London that warfare under such conditions was "very different from the wars in Europe." For "we have to do with very numerous barbarous salvages within our borders that decline to come to any fair open battle, but . . . [are] continually infesting us . . . [and] lying sculking under the covert of horrid thickets, woods, and bushes where it is impracticable to pursue 'em."[35]

It made, all in all, a fair approximation of modern guerrilla warfare, and the results could be devastating. Here are some highlights. *1708:* A French and Indian "expedition" ranges along the Massachusetts frontier and in late August makes a surprise attack on Haverhill. (From which: perhaps twenty English deaths and a like number among the attackers; massive destruction of property; about fifteen captives "carried to Canada.") Smaller "incursions" are experienced elsewhere: in Springfield, Brookfield, Northampton, Hatfield. *1709:* Deerfield is attacked again, but the townspeople are forewarned, and there is no repeat "massacre." (The toll this time: one dead, two captured, several wounded.) There are clashes, too, in other Valley towns—and farther east all the way to the Maine coast. *1710:* More of the same, especially in New Hampshire and Maine. By now, fear has infected daily life all through the New England backcountry.[36] John Williams's correspondence is sprinkled with comments like: "We are very much alarmed and full of fears," and "We are very often alarmed with the signs and sights of Indians."[37] At the same time, the English are attempting "invasions" on a much larger scale. A joint land-and-sea operation in summer 1709 has to be aborted because the expected "fleet" from England does not appear. However, in 1710, a similar plan brings success: the conquest of the French "fort" and trading station at Port Royal.

But these battlefield outcomes are far removed from actual experience. What was war like—how did it work—under such extraordinary conditions? Perhaps a "little story," within our larger story, will give some of the flavor. And will serve another purpose besides. . . .

Deerfield, April 11, 1709. A farmer named Mehuman Hinsdale is returning home with a cartload of apple trees from nearby Northampton. Hinsdale is thirty-six years old, a husband, a father of two small children. His Deerfield roots run deep: he was, indeed, the first English person born in the town. His father, his grandfather, and two of his uncles had all died in the "battle of Bloody Brook," during New England's first great Indian war three decades before. His infant son was killed in the massacre. He and his wife were taken captive and held in Canada for more than two years; they returned with the Sheldon party of 1706. Hinsdale knows danger, knows Indians, knows the countryside.[38]

On this particular morning he is not concerned. With spring barely begun—and the trees not yet leafed out—one can travel "without any fear of indians." Yet Indians are "skulking" in the Deerfield Valley; and, suddenly, two of them carry Hinsdale off "into ye west woods." From here the route stretches north through the wilderness to Canada; presumably, Hinsdale remembers it from his previous captivity. It takes eleven days this time; on the way his captors are "civil & courteous to him." They bring him to Kahnawake (evidently their home), and his luck changes. He must run a gauntlet of excited villagers "for near three quarters of a mile." Fortunately he is agile, and runs "so briskly as not to receive a blow" until almost the end; then he is "pull'd . . . down, and . . . struck by one fellow." Inside the walls of the fort, another "ceremony": Hinsdale must "sing and dance . . . In ye midst of a company." This goes well enough—maybe he is practiced, from before—except for his receiving a further "severe blow upon the naked back" from a youthful onlooker. Next he is "carid to the French Governour," who remembers him—and interrogates him about the "news . . . in his country." The governor suspects, quite correctly, that the English are organizing a major new "expedition" against Canada, and anxiously seeks details. Hinsdale succeeds for a time in concealing what he knows. But in June another English captive reaches Montreal and is more forthcoming. Whereupon Hinsdale is—for his evident deception—"put into ye dungeon."[39]

The English military plan is indeed large and menacing. General Francis Nicholson has organized an intercolonial army of some 1,500 men, including 600 warriors from the Five Nations Iroquois. Just now they are camped near the lower end of Lake Champlain, ready to strike toward the French fort at Chambly. This land operation will be coordinated with an assault by English naval forces, advancing from the east up the St. Lawrence Valley; however, at midsummer the latter have not been heard from.[40]

While he waits, Nicholson joins his Mohawk Indian allies in a "plot" to weaken the French side. The Mohawks will approach their "good brothers" at Kahnawake with secret proposals—in effect, an invitation—to "leave ye French & go over to Gen'll Nicholson." The man chosen to accomplish this delicate mission sets out sometime in July or early August. His message is favorably received; soon the Kahnawakes are concerting plans to move south and meet Nicholson's army. They would like, however, to find an English go-between—and they remember their erstwhile prisoner Hinsdale. Off to Quebec, where Hinsdale is languishing in "ye dungeon." A request to the Governor: might they "have Mr H to burn (pretending they should fight the better if they could burn an Englishman)?" Agreed; and soon Hinsdale is again "led away towards Montreal from Quebeck." At first, he is disconsolate—for he imagines "nothing but being sacrificed by them"—but then is "overjoyd" when told of their true intentions. So far all has been "kept private from the French." But now comes an unexpected reverse: "A certain Indian," falling sick, makes confession to a mission-priest and reveals at least some parts of the "plot." And the Kahnawakes decide to withdraw.[41]

Our source for events to this point is a captivity memoir, composed years later by Stephen Williams, perhaps from the words of Hinsdale himself. A second document, dated October 3, 1709, and found today among the colonial "state papers" in London, provides some specific confirmation:[42]

> The . . . prisoner . . . Named Mehumain Hindille belonging to Dearfield [was] brought to Muntryall by some Cannada Indians . . . and forced to rune the gauntlett, where they beat him as long as they would, and was given to the Governour . . . and examined . . . and put into prison att Quebec, and lying there about 6 weeks, the Indians was a going to warr . . . [and] they sent for him to be burnt, the Governour readily gave him. We have no news of him since.

But there is also a third source, presenting the same sequence as seen from the French side: a long dispatch prepared (in November) by Governor Vaudreuil for his superiors in Paris. Hinsdale is not mentioned; instead, the focus is "an Indian named Arousent, lately arrived from the enemy's camp."[43]

Arousent's intentions are not immediately clear; he has, however, been apprehended in Montreal and sent to Quebec for questioning. Once there he confirms for his "examiners" the English position to the south—and is soon released. As a direct result, Vaudreuil decides to reinforce Chambly, and to go there himself to take personal command. But while en route he receives a further message from his subordinates in Montreal, about "a Belt that Arousent had given in passing to the Indians of the Sault St. Louis [the French name for Kahnawake] on the part of the Mohawks." This sounds alarming, for "belts" are traditional instruments of Iroquois diplomacy; Vaudreuil feels obliged to investigate. And so to Kahnawake, for a meeting with the tribal leadership: what, he wants to know, was "the purport of that belt, and what were their sentiments?" The chiefs are quick to reassure him. It's true that "the Mohawks had sent . . . word by Arousent" of their (reluctant) involvement with Nicholson's forces. And true, as well, that the Mohawks had advised them to "retire" from supporting the French. But the chiefs have already decided to reject these overtures completely. Through Arousent they will send a return message, declaring their resolve "to live and to die with their father [the governor]" and their confidence that the French will ultimately prevail. Vaudreuil professes himself well satisfied with this response and urges them to "add that if [the English] caused the Mohawks too much regret they would always be very much welcomed by us."

It appears, in retrospect, that the French never learned the full extent of the maneuvers against them. Certainly, the Kahnawakes managed to conceal their own complicity during the initial phase and even to gain some credit with the governor. The military outcome was a virtual zero. The English warships were diverted elsewhere, Nicholson's army was disbanded, and the year ended without significant new engagements. But, taken as a whole, the sequence reveals something of the complexities of wilderness warfare and diplomacy. Poor communications, fragile alliances, "plots," and plain misunderstanding: all were part of this volatile mix.

And what became of the leading characters? Mehuman Hinsdale was "taken [back] from ye indians and again committd to prison." And (later) "sent to France in a man of war . . . and after a while

. . . ship'd at Saint Meloes [St. Malo] for London." And (still later) "order'd . . . on board one of the Queen's Ships . . . [and] brought . . . to Rhode island, whence [he] got home in safty . . . after [he] had been absent from his family ab't three years and a half." All that for misjudging the risks of travel on a spring day outside Deerfield![44]

And, finally, Arousent? When the plot was discovered—according to Stephen Williams's memoir—"the fellow yt was the projector of it . . . had timely notice, so as to escape to Shamble [Chambly]." There he "putt a trick" on the officer-in-charge so as to obtain food and weapons for the journey home, then outmaneuvered a band of "pursuers." Back among the Mohawks he disappears from view—but we shall meet him again. A star player in this "little story," Arousent has a role, too, in what follows.[45]

✧

HOW MUCH of the little story was known in Deerfield at the time? Probably nothing, after Hinsdale's disappearance and presumed capture. A team of horses and a load of apple trees found unattended in the roadway: the townspeople would know what to think. But of their neighbor's up-and-down experiences in Canada, of Arousent and the Mohawk belts and the Kahnawakes, of the "plot" and its discovery and Vaudreuil's meeting with the chiefs: of all this they would remain at least temporarily unaware.

The following winter did, however, bring one small opening to the captives in Canada. A local man named John Arms, one of two prisoners taken in the French-and-Indian attack of 1709, reappeared near the end of February at his home. He had been sent back by Vaudreuil as part of a proposed exchange for a French officer held in Massachusetts.[46] The news he brought of his fellow captives was eagerly received in Deerfield—and quickly communicated elsewhere. Among those who saw him was Esther Williams, eldest daughter of John (and, of course, an ex-captive herself). At once she wrote to Stephen, then an undergraduate at Harvard. "Dear brother," she began, "these lins are to inform you that Joh arms is come hum from cannada and by him we have news from many of our captivs."

For example, news of Eunice: "goodman Clesson [another Deerfield man, taken along with Arms] see sister but he was not able to tallk with her." Even so,

> we are in grate hops of her redemtion for colnol sciler sent to her master to come down to live at albany. he sends word that he

would onely he is afeard that they will tacke her away. one of the
family is come down and ses that he thinks they will tack an indian
girl for her and they have sent him back to perswade them to
come as far as the lack [i.e. Lake Champlain] if not further.

These few lines are packed with valuable information. The Schuylers
are working hard for Eunice's redemption and are in direct touch with
members of her Indian family. Her master worries that she will simply
be taken—retaken—from him, if he brings her as far as Albany. The
idea of a one-for-one exchange is still alive, and the Schuylers propose
a meeting—presumably to discuss it further. *Great hopes*, greater,
certainly, than any in a long time.

From Eunice, Esther's summary moves on to other captives. "Eb-
nezer nims is marreed to Sarah hoite . . . mrs wainrights dafter
[daughter] siulaer is tacken in to thear church . . . mr whellrites dafter
is with child by an indian . . . freedom french and mata wight [write]
to thir father they would come hum if it was not for the sake of ther
soules." And so on, through a long list—all in the same breathless
tone of excitement. This is fact—and gossip—of the greatest local
interest. Esther must have enjoyed writing it down, and Stephen, for
his part, surely was glad to receive it.[47]

But then, another hiatus. There is no further word of Eunice, and
no sign either of progress in captive-related negotiations. On the New
England side, Dudley reiterates his resolve "never to set up an Algiers
trade" by ransoming captives from their masters. "I always pity a
prisoner in Indian hands" he writes in February 1710, "but no consideration of that nature has yet altered my resolution never to buy a
prisoner of an Indian, lest we make a market for our poor women and
children in the frontiers."[48]

Winter, spring, summer, fall: no movement, no real change. Then
in October comes the surprising English triumph at Port Royal. The
leaders move quickly to press what they see as a major advantage.
General Nicholson, again in command of New England's forces, prepares a stiff letter of demands for Vaudreuil. One part refers to "a
great many Brittish prisoners, either imediately in the hands of the
French, or your Indians; particularly a Young Gentlewoman, daughter to the Reverend Mr. Williams, Minister at Dear field." These must
be returned as soon as possible; "otherwise you must expect that the
like number of the Chiefe inhabitants of this country [the area around
Port Royal] shall in the same manner be made slaves amongst our

Indians." The process of "restitution" should, moreover, include all English prisoners "in whose hands soever they be French or Indians."[49] The letter is signed by Nicholson and other members of New England's "Council of War," and carried by Major John Livingston, himself a veteran of previous captive negotiations. Livingston is obliged to travel by water and foot through a particularly wild stretch of eastern Canada; the journey is a mix of weather extremes, near starvation, canoeing accidents ("I fell in over head and ears and wet me through; being gott out my cloaths immediately froze stiff on my back"), and encounters with unfriendly Indians ("one of them flew at me with his hatchett, and taking hold of my collar was about to murder me, but . . ."). Eventually he reaches Quebec, where the governor receives him "with all imaginable marks of civility." He lodges in the governor's own house. He buys new clothes, since he had lost most of his belongings when his canoe was "oversett," and the "shirt . . . I had on I had worn 44 [consecutive] days." He is guest of honor at a succession of dinners for "Gentlemen and Ladies of ye town," with "great plenty" and "musick and dancing and . . . drums . . . at my door." From famine to feast (quite literally): all part of the strange counterpoint of life—and war—in the American wilderness.[50]

Livingston describes his "entertainment" at length in his diary and notes, too, his visits with various captives. ("This being our New Year's Day, ye English prisoners came to see me, and wish me a merry new year, I knew their meaning and gave them money.") He hardly mentions official business, except to say that "I demanded of ye Governor Mr Williams daughter, [but] he told me it was not in his power to gett her; she was among the Indians." When at last he leaves (a little reluctantly?), he takes letters from Vaudreuil to both Nicholson and Dudley: familiar replies to familiar demands. To Nicholson, the governor reiterates the distinction between captives in French and captives in Indian hands. Over the latter he has no control; the *sauvages* are bound to the French in friendship, "but they are not dependent on us to the point that we could make them change their habits and customs." (Was this an oblique reference to their "custom" of adoption?) And as for the one captive the Council has mentioned by name: "Mr. Williams, minister of Deerfield, whose daughter you demand from me yet again, knows as well as anyone how impossible it has been to see this young girl, and how hard I have tried . . . Time alone can faciliatate this affair for us." To Dudley, Vaudreuil declares that he will permit the return of any captives who wish it, but as for "those who prefer of their own will to remain here, I will not force them to go back."[51]

These replies must have seemed virtually to foreclose further redemptions, since captives held by Indians and captives unwilling to leave covered almost the entire lot. Eunice Williams was, evidently, irretrievable on both counts. Thus in 1711, the Massachusetts leadership began to consider another—and tougher—approach to the problem of her continuing captivity. Twice that year, and once a year later, proposals surfaced for a more coercive form of exchange. In April, Samuel Vetch, the newly appointed English commander at Port Royal, reported the taking of a certain "Father Justinian, a French Priest," as a "lawfull prisoner of War." Vetch ordered the priest held "with design to obtain Mr. Williams' daughter in exchange for him," and asked the Massachusetts Council to approve of this (and pay for it). The Council "advised that the sd. Priest be kept to be exchanged accordingly." Moreover, the very same meeting approved a separate— but similar—plan. An "Indian woman" and her two young children had recently been captured in a campaign "against the enemy Eastward." And the governor proposed "sending [her] . . . with a Letter directed to Maxis the Eastern Indian Sagamore, importing that if he will procure Mr. Williams daughter from her Indian Master at Canada . . . then this squaw & her son & daughter (who are to be detained as hostage for her return again) shall be sett at liberty and returned home."[52]

Two proposals—one with French, the other with Indian, bait. In fact, the records do not refer again to the first, but the second was definitely pursued. The "squaw" appeared in Montreal some two months later, as noted in the following letter by an English-speaking priest there.

Montreal, June 26, 1711

Sir:

Since you are gone, a squaw of the nation of the Abnakis is come in from Boston . . . She goes about getting a little girl daughter of Mr. John Williams.

The Lord Marquis of Vaudreuil helps her as he can. The business is very hard because the girl belongs to Indians of another sort, and the master of the English girl is now at Albany . . . The same Lord chief Governor of Canada has insured me in case he may not prevail with the Mohoggs for Eunice Williams, he shall send home

four English persons in his power for an Exchange in the
Room of the two Indian children.

Tantalizing, to say the least. Did the Williamses know of this curious
initiative? Perhaps—but, unfortunately, none of their surviving correspondence dates from these months. Did the "squaw" succeed? Yes
and no. Yes, she succeeded in regaining her freedom and that of her
children. But, no, the exchange was not for Eunice Williams. (A
subsequent note in the Council Records mentions only "some English
prisoners procured . . . for that purpose.") Probably the "hard business" of crossing tribal lines—of persuading Kahnawakes to yield for
the sake of Abenakis—was simply too hard to resolve. But other
English families, not to mention the squaw's own Indian kin, must
have been gladdened as a result.[53]

These maneuvers could only have heightened public concern over
Eunice Williams's fate. Cotton Mather, for example, mentioned her
twice in his diary that summer. "I have a poor Kinswoman," he began
on July 31, "who has been six or seven years a Captive, in the hands
of the French Popish Indians. I am afraid I have not considered the
miserable Condition of that Child, with such a frequency and fervency
of Supplication, as I should have done." And again, a month later:
"As I have often pray'd for her Deliverance, I would now grow in
the Importunity of my frequent Supplications for her; every Day
constantly remember her and mention her." John Williams was himself
in Boston at midsummer, and perhaps his presence drew further attention to Eunice. Mather's diary noted a special resolution to "make
her condition an Argument in Discourses with my own children, for
Thankfulness and Piety." Already something of an exemplary figure,
Eunice would in subsequent years become "an Argument in Discourses" among people all across New England.[54]

The summer of 1711 also took John Williams back toward Canada
for the first time since his own redemption. He accepted appointment
as chaplain to the latest, and largest, in the annual series of military
expeditions against New France. Alas for the English, the ships carrying their attack force went aground and broke up near the mouth of
the St. Lawrence, with much loss of life and weaponry.[55] How the
chaplain personally experienced these events is not known. Back in
Deerfield weeks later, he and his family awaited another winter with
mingled hope and apprehension. "No news from Albany," he wrote
to Stephen in early December.[56]

Spring brought plans for renewed activity, on both the military and the diplomatic front. In April, a force of 30 men left Deerfield to "scout" for Indians in the upper Connecticut Valley; Samuel Williams, John's eldest son now grown to manhood, was its "lieutenant." After days of fruitless "tracking," a small group of Indians was surprised in canoes "on ye water": by "firing briskly on them . . . we did kill 9." Among the dead, wrote Samuel's brother Stephen some while later, was "my old master Wottanommon." (Did Stephen feel gratified by this? Or perhaps a twinge of regret? He gives us no hint.) For Wottanommon's scalp (and the others) scout-members received £30 compensation from the colony's General Court.[57]

And then: back to diplomacy. Vaudreuil had sent a letter with fresh proposals for prisoner exchange, and Dudley was glad to respond. A small number of French captives were marked for return, and "messengers" chosen to accompany them north. Samuel Williams "who hath the Frentch tongue" was appointed group leader—this "with the consent of his ffather." The journey took ten weeks from start to finish, and proved at least a modest success. A manuscript diary of Samuel's shows various details of the route: "Our canows proving very leaky we spent a great part of the day mending of them. . . ." And: "we lay by and made shelters, it rained all day. . . ." And: "we judgd we went this day nere fifty miles." And, too, the days spent in Canada—the point of it all:

> July 30 we came this day into Shamble [Chambly, the French fort east of Montreal] . . . where we continued until the 4 of august, then the governor sent for me to morial, the rest of the men continued at Chamble until 23 august then the governor sent for them to moreall where we all Continued until 28 august, then the governor delivered 9 captives to me and we set out. . . .

The essential facts, the bare bones of experience: nothing more. Three weeks back in Montreal, site of his own captivity years before—and here is all he says. Did he visit his still-captive sister, across the river in "Oso"? Likely not: that he would have mentioned. Did he consider such a visit, discuss it with the governor, or even send a request to the mission-priests? Yes, probably, and perhaps; but this is guesswork only, for we have no firm evidence at all.[58]

By now, overseas, diplomats from the major European powers were slowly negotiating an end to the war. In August 1712, came agreement on a "cessation of armes"—to be applied also in the colonies involved, around the world. The news reached Boston two months later and produced a formal "proclamation" there on October 29. Signing of the final treaties was another several months away, but the fighting was over in North America. Still, the issue of captives remained, and New England's leaders were deeply concerned. Even before the cease-fire they sent to London "a memorial relating to the English prisoners in Canada." Some prisoners had been carried by the Indians "into ye woods" and kept there as "slaves." "It is fear'd that a Peace will not extend to the redemption of these captives; it is therefore humbly propos'd that the King of France be moved to send an order to the Governor of Canada to release 'em." This, and perhaps only this, would shake the resolve of Indian captors, "who depend on the French, and dare not refuse, when they know it is the pleasure of the King of France."[59]

Additional letters passed between Dudley and Vaudreuil through the autumn. On November 12, Dudley stated his "readiness to send every French prisoner from hence," and demanded—yet again—that the French take a similar position for "all in your hands." He concluded, emphatically, "upon my honour I will detayn none," but then added this postscript, "I have here in my keeping one Indian sachem of Quebeck [and] one other sachem of your Indians near in blood & kindred to the woman that has Mr. Williams daughter which I will exchange for her, or otherwise I will never set them free." Apparently, for Dudley, Indians and Frenchmen now formed separate categories of prisoners—to be treated in different ways. Perhaps, in his mind, this separation mirrored the one which Vaudreuil had long insisted on—between English captives "in French hands" and those "in the hands of the Indians." Perhaps, too, the next phase of "exchange" might specifically embrace the least favored categories on each side: Indians (held in New England) and English people held by Indians (in Canada). Certainly this latest proposal regarding Eunice was aimed primarily at her Indian captors. The French, in effect, would be out of it, except as a line of communication. From now on, dealings for Eunice—and for other captives comparably situated—must go to the source, as directly as possible.[60]

New strategy; new hope? Perhaps so; a letter written by Peter Schuyler (in Albany) to Dudley several weeks later suggests hope—and even a specific expectation.[61]

> as to what your Excellency mentions Relating to Mr. Williams
> his doghter, the squaw nor she is not come here yet nor have I
> heard anything of her Coming altho I shall be very glad to see
> them and do assure your Excellency If they come together or be

it ye squaw alone I shall use all possible meanes to get the child exchanged Either as your Excellency proposes or what other way the squaw will be most willing to Comply with. In the meantime shall Inform my Selfe by all opportunities whether the said Squaw & Child be coming here or if they be anywhere near by. Your Excellency may depend that whatever I can do for ye obtaining of ye sd Child shall at no time be wanting.

The squaw? Not the Abenaki woman who had previously tried to swap Eunice for her own captive children; that business had by now been concluded. This must be another squaw: presumably, *the woman that has Mr Williams daughter*, the one *near in blood and kindred* to the *sachem* held captive in Massachusetts (as mentioned in Dudley's November letter). In short: Eunice's owner, her *mistress*, her adoptive mother. At last they were reaching the source.

Or were they? There is no record of further dealings here, no sign that the "squaw" in question actually appeared at Albany, with or without Eunice. Dudley must have heard something, somewhere, to prompt this alert to Schuyler; but it came to nothing.

And then, a further disappointment, the worst one yet. In fact, so grave, so wounding, that at first our informants do not call it by its name. Here is Cotton Mather, writing in his diary on March 18, 1713:

> The dark Dispensation of Providence, which detains my poor Kinswoman in her Indian Captivity, calls upon me to address her nearest Relatives, with the best Consolations I can study for them.

A *dark dispensation* calling for *the best consolations*: what can this be?[62]

Here is Sewall, writing in his diary, on March 26:

> Mr. Saml Danforth visits us in the evening. Has hopes of Mr. Jno. Williams's daughter at Canada; may be as when Samson married a Philistin.

Has hopes? Hopes for what? And why the Biblical allusion: Samson marrying a Philistine? Does he mean to suggest that . . . ?[63]

Here is Elisha Williams, writing to his cousin Stephen, on March 29:

> I Conclude you had before Us The Melancholy News Concerning Cousen Eunice Which I hope We have still Grounds to hope is Not True, & Must Still pray In faith for her redemption, May I Not Say as Was said to Monica The Mother of Augustine, That

a Child of So Many Prayers Cant be Lost, There is Still a Way
for her recovery should she be Embodied wth ym (Which Words
I can't Write wthout Tears) . . .

What *melancholy news*?[64]
They just cannot face it, cannot quite write the words *without tears*.
But they know. And they grieve. For Eunice, their Eunice—a *young*
gentlewoman, daughter to the Reverend Mr. Williams, minister at
Deerfield, and *child of so many prayers*—has just been married. And
her husband is a "Philistine" indeed.
   An Indian.
   A Catholic.
   A *savage*.

FIVE

੭

HOW JOHN WILLIAMS took the "melancholy news" of Eunice's marriage in Canada is not known, for no single writing of his survives from the relevant period. Surely he was distressed, perhaps even devastated; probably, though, he was not altogether surprised. The "strategems" of the Jesuits, he had noted in his famous narrative years before, included efforts "to get [captives] . . . married among them."[1] And Eunice had reached an age when most girls (among the Canadian Indians) had already taken a husband. Still, he continued to pray—and to work—for her redemption. Indeed, the ensuing year brought the most determined efforts yet to reach Eunice—efforts in which her father was both directly and indirectly involved.

Governor Dudley, for his part, continued to press the French for a full exchange of prisoners. In December 1712 he had sent to Quebec "a coppy of the cessation of armes" and his personal assurance for the return of "all such prisoners of the French nation that have fallen into my hands." He confided to his superiors overseas his worry about the numerous English captives yet remaining in Canada, "severall of them . . . thrust . . . into nunerys and religious houses, and many more left in the barbarous hands of the Indians, some of them gentlemen's daughters, to be made heathen and wives to the Maquas [i.e., Mohawks]." (This last seems an uncanny—because prophetic—reference to the fate of Eunice Williams, which would not become known in New England until some weeks later.) Dudley hoped that "the French King's orders to his Governours [would] . . . command" the return of all captives, and urged that "some gentlemen from hence . . . be allow'd to go to Quebec, Montreal, and other parts . . . to search and find them out."[2]

This strategy would soon take specific effect, but by way of Albany rather than Boston. In fact, as the war simmered down, it was the fur-traders of New York—and of French Canada—who first succeeded in resuming normal relations. As early as May 1712, a delegation of Kahnawake Indians had come to Albany "to take the hatchet out of the hands of those that were kild," and to request "that the path be open and free for us as formerly." By the following year, experienced New York traders were once again traveling north on a regular basis.[3]

Among these were the several Schuylers, Peter, David, John, and Myndert; it is John who concerns us here. Sometime in the early spring (of 1713), he began a "Journey to and from Canada." Probably he had personal affairs to look after (the renewal of commercial contacts?), but he seems to have had official business as well. The general business of prisoner exchange: in this he would act on behalf of Dudley. And the particular business of Eunice Williams, "upon the instant and earnest desire of her ffather now Minister at Dearfield."[4]

The phrasing is part of a summary—a "true and perfect Memoriall"—of Schuyler's "proceedings in behalf of Margaret Williams," sent to Dudley following his return in June. (*Margaret* Williams? That, it appears, was Eunice's second baptismal name, the one she took upon being rechristened as a Catholic.) Whether or not the memorial is "perfect," it has the look of being "true." And it is deeply, irresistibly affecting.[5]

I arrived from Albany at Mont Reall on ye 15th of Aprill . . . Where I understood yt Monsr de Vaudruille Governr and Chief of Canada was expected then every day from Quebeck, Upon which I thought proper not to mention any thing touching the aforesaid Captive, untill his Excellency should be here himself. . . .

Because this is a particularly important—and sensitive—matter, Schuyler decides to wait for the governor's arrival, rather than deal with subordinates. Vaudreuil, after all, has previously seemed to favor Eunice's redemption. And Vaudreuil's position gives him supreme authority over all the colony's external relations, including war and peace and prisoner exchange.[6]

and accordingly when he arrived here; I proposed the matter to him. . . .

Presumably their meeting takes place at the official residence of Claude de Ramezay, governor of the city of Montreal: a large and sprawling stone mansion—fortress-like—more imposing by far than any public building in New York or New England.⁷ Vaudreuil and Schuyler greet each other with words of mutual respect. Still, Schuyler is the petitioner here and he plays the role carefully. He thanks the governor for previous efforts on behalf of the captives. He recounts the details of Eunice's plight, her father's unceasing prayers for her, the concern felt throughout the English colonies.

> [He] gave me all the Encouragemt I could immagine for her to go home, he also permitted me, to go to her at the ffort where she was, to prepare if I could persuade her to go home, Moreover his Excellancy said that wth all his heart, he would give a hundred Crowns out of his own pockett, if that she might be persuaded to go to her Native Countrey. . . .

Vaudreuil responds, then, with extraordinary protestations of understanding and sympathy. He has the highest personal regard for Mr. Williams. He has long regretted Eunice's captivity, and has tried repeatedly to arrange a solution. He cannot force the girl's release, but will help however he can. Schuyler has his consent to visit her Indian home—and has, too, his wishes for success.

> I observing all this, then was in hopes I should prevail with her to go home. Accordingly I went to the ffort of Caghenewaga [Kahnawake] being accompanied by one of the Kings officers and a ffrench Interpreter [and] likewise another of the Indian Language . . .

The escort the governor provides is a clear sign of his personal interest in the matter. Eunice, he knows, has long since forgotten the language of her birth. Thus two interpreters will be needed: one to translate Schuyler's English into French, the second to go from French to Mohawk—which, presumably, is all she knows.

> Being upon the 26 Day of May entring at the Indian ffort. . . .

The approach, of course, is from the river. By boat, with a crew of Indian oarsmen. Not a long ride, but an arduous and—in springtime—a potentially dangerous one. Kahnawake is at the head of a notorious rapid, which announces itself, as the Jesuits remark, with the sound of a "roar." The little craft carrying Schuyler and his companions flings wildly about; then, at last, slices through—and out. The passengers see the line of palisades surrounding the village, somewhat old and decayed now, but a mark of its exposed position. And, beyond the line, the villagers' fields, brimming with new plants—corn, beans, pumpkins, melons, sunflowers. And, in the fields, the scattered shapes of village women, bending to their appointed tasks.[8] The boat lands at a small stone wharf. A gate admits the visitors inside the fence. Immediately to the east, on a small height of land, stands the mission-church—with wooden frame and bark covering—the most elaborate single building in the village. Beside it is the house of the resident priests and, nearby, the barracks for a little garrison of French soldiers. Behind this cluster of "civilized" influence stretch the *cabanes* of the Indians: low, windowless, rectangular dwellings, bark-covered and with roof-holes that discharge smoke from the firepits inside. On some of the roofs are small piles of beads and corn and animal parts—offerings, it is said, to the sun. Other immediately noticeable features here? To the south, one larger structure, with the look of a traditional Iroquois "longhouse," perhaps a council site. To the west, a public bake-oven, itself the size of a small cabin. By the waterside, a gristmill for the villagers' corn. And, also near the shore, three large cannons for their defense.[9]

From the height near the church, Schuyler can see the full extent. Fifty or sixty buildings all told, within a space of perhaps a quarter-mile in any direction. Compact, coherent, complete. Even with the mission-complex, there is the feeling of a unified whole.

> I thought fitt first to apply mySelf to the priests; As I did, Being two in Company. . . .

The priests serve, in effect, as gatekeepers for the indigenous community. Who are they? Pierre Cholonec holds the title, at present, of "superior." A man past seventy, born in Brittany, but a part of the Canadian missions through his entire adult life, Cholonec has been with this particular group (at Kahnawake) in every stage of its development. He was, years ago, a personal confidant of the famed Iroquois convert Kateri Tekakwitha, and is now her biographer; this gives him a particular cachet. Julien Garnier is his colleague: also a septuagenarian, also a Breton by birth, and no less remarkable for his missionary labors. For thirty years, Garnier has worked right on the front line, as a resident priest in the Iroquois heartland. He knows each of the Five Nations firsthand: knows their languages (plus Huron and some Algonquin), knows their customs and traditions as well as any European alive.[10]

Cholonec and Garnier: only "two in company," but full of the authority conveyed by age, experience, and evident accomplishment.

Their attitude—Schuyler must know—could well decide the result of his "proceedings" about Eunice.

> And [as I] was informed before that this infant (As I may say) was married to a young Indian, I therefore proposed to know the Reason why this poor captive should be Married to an Indian being a Christian born (tho neerly taken from the Mothers Breast and such like Instances &c). . . .

Schuyler has learned, either before leaving Albany or after his arrival in Montreal, of Eunice's recent marriage. He sees this as a key to the question of her return, and, too, as a weak spot for the Jesuits. Eunice is, after all, a birthright Christian, and is still so young. And is "pitiable," and vulnerable, by reason of her continuing captivity. Her marriage, under such circumstances, seems morally questionable—to say the least.

> Whereupon the priest Sett forth to me Such good Reasons, wth Witnesses that [neither] my Self, or any other person (as I believe) could fairly make Objection against their Marriage; (First sd he they came to me to Marry them) very often wch I always refus'd wth good words and persuasions to the Contrary, But both continuing in their former resolutions to Such a Degree, that I was constrained to be absent from ye ffort three Severall times, because not Satisfyed mySelf in their Marriage

Which priest, first of all? Probably Cholonec—in his position as "superior," and as the one with longer tenure at the mission. So he, too, finds their marriage questionable. He has tried, he says, to dissuade them; and failing in that, to avoid them. All to no avail. This is clearly their own idea—no sign of families involved—and their persistence is itself impressive. But is the priest being truthful? Well, he has "witnesses," and Schuyler is inclined to believe him.

> Untill [at] last, after Some days past they both came to me, and sd that they were Joined together, And if he would not marry them they matter'd not, for they were resolved never to leave one the other But [to] live together heathen like; Upon wch I thought proper to Join them in Matrimony and Such like Reasons as aforesaid the priest did plainly Sett (forth). . . .

A striking admission here: the limits of the priest's own authority. They will have what they want, this young Indian and his English-born sweetheart. They would rather be "joined" in the Christian way;

but if that is denied them, never mind. Indeed, they feel joined already, joined forever: a love-match, it seems. What could the priest then do? And what can Schuyler do now?

> and after some further discourse, I desired the priest to let me see her at his house, ffor I knew not where to find her. . . .

Time, Schuyler decides, to confront her directly. And better to do that at the priest's residence than in her own *cabane* (or elsewhere in the village). He must, at this point, feel great curiosity. No one, from the English side, has seen Eunice since her father was here almost a decade ago.

> upon which he sent for her, who prsently came with the Indian She was Married to both together She looking very poor in body, bashfull in the face, but proved harder than Steel in her breast. . . .

Perhaps Schuyler was hoping to see her alone. If so, he is disappointed; they come as a pair. And how does she seem? Her physical appearance is disconcerting. Presumably, she wears the ordinary clothing of a Kahnawake woman: loosely fitted, sleeveless tunic on top, simple skirt hanging to the knees, leggings ornamented with moosehair and held together by porcupine quills, leather moccasins for her feet. Perhaps, too, she has a bead necklace and earrings. Her hair would be heavily greased, and pulled back behind her head with a ribbon of eelskin. (The grease gives off a distinct odor, unpleasant to Europeans.) Probably there are dabs of vermilion (paint) on her cheeks and forehead. Serviceable enough, all in all, and suitably "modest" (as the priests would say), but hardly fashionable by "civilized" standards.[11] Indeed, her appearance announces her loyalty to other standards—which Schuyler can only regard as "poor." And then, too, her demeanor: the set of her jaw, the look in her eyes. He feels—how to say it?—something chilly there. And faintly uncomfortable, a little embarrassed. Implicitly she puts a distance between herself and the visitor from New York. As for the "steel in her breast," that will be evident when conversation begins.

> at her first Entrance into the Room I desired her to sitt down, wch she did. . . .

Schuyler and Eunice at the center; husband nearby; priests and "witnesses" on the edge. The moment has arrived.

I first Spoak to her in English, Upon wch she did not Answr me;
And I believe She did not understand me, she being very Young
when she was taken, And liveing always amongst the Indians
afterwards . . .

Schuyler has heard as much already, so perhaps he is testing her now.
All right, the test confirms her loss of her native tongue.

I Imployed my Indian Languister to talk to her; informing him
first by the ffrench Interpretor who understood the English Language, What he should tell her, and what Questions he should
Ask her, Accordingly he did I understood amost all what he said
to her; And found that he Spoak according to my Order. . . .

The translation system goes into effect: English to French to Mohawk,
just as planned. Moreover, Schuyler himself has a working knowledge
of Mohawk, so he can check on the results.

but could not gett one word from her. . . .

Now the real problem: she will not respond—will not so much as
open her mouth—even when, clearly, she does understand. Schuyler
makes his case anyway. He tells her, he asks her, he implores her. The
war is over now; many captives have returned already, others will be
returning soon. Her family longs for her: her father, the beloved pastor
of Deerfield; her sisters and brothers, growing older now; her new
half-siblings; her grandparents, uncles, aunts, cousins, and countless
other "friends." All awaiting—prayerfully awaiting—her eventual redemption. Must she still disappoint them? Does she not belong with
them? *Come back with me, child, come back to your home.* But still
she sits there: impassive, silent. No single sign that she is moved by
any of this. No flicker of warmth or even of interest.

Upon which I advised the priest to Speak to her. . . .

He must try another approach. She will not answer him, it seems; but
perhaps Cholonec will have better luck.

And if I could not prevail wth her to go home to Stay there, that
She might only go to see her ffather, And directly return hither
again. . . .

Another proposal, too: more limited, a compromise. Let her try a
visit—and then make up her mind.

The priest made a long Speech to her and endeavoured to persuade her to go, but after almost half an hour's discourse—could not get one word from her . . .

Cholonec is doing his best. To Schuyler's arguments he adds some of his own. The charity she has learned in his church. The honor of her adoptive community. She dare not resist such reasonable proposals. But the steel holds tight; her silence continues.

And afterwards when he found She did not Speak, he again Endeavoured to persuade her to go and see her ffather, And I seeing She continued inpersuadable to speak; I promised upon my Word and honour, if she would go only to see her ffather, I would convey her to New England, and give her Assureance of liberty to return if she pleased—the priest asked her Severall times for answer upon my earnest request, And fair offers. . . .

They are virtually begging her now. The terms of the offer will protect her fully; what more could she possibly ask? At least they must have her answer. Some answer. Any answer. And finally they do.

wch was after long Solicitations (Jaghte oghte) which words being translated into the English Tongue their Signification (is) maybe not but the meaning thereof amongst the Indians is a plaine denyall. . . .

There it is. Two Mohawk words. *Jaghte oghte. Peut-etre que non. Maybe not.* It comes to the same thing: one word really. A word the Indians would rather soften. But, to be blunt about it: *no.* Not to stay, not for a visit either. Eunice won't go.

and these two words were all we could gett from her; in allmost two hours time that we talked with her, Upon this my eyes being almost filled with tears, I said to her mySelf, had I made such proposalls and prayings to the worst of Indians I did not doubt but [that I would] have had a reasonable Answere and consent to what I have sd. . . .

One last-ditch appeal, baldly based on shame: Eunice is worse than the worst, her behavior wholly unreasonable. Or is this simply a bitter thrust—an attack—born of Schuyler's mounting frustration? Appeal *and* attack: probably a little of both.

Upon wch her husband seeing that I was so much concerned about her replyed had her ffather not Married againe, She would have gone and Seen him long Ere this time But gave no further reason. . . .

Wait. The steel bends open, if only a crack. This is the Indian talking, but he must know her thoughts. A reason of sorts—her father's remarriage—a scrap to take home. But how to understand it? Schuyler doesn't know.

> and the time growing late and I being very Sorrowfull, that I could not prevail upon nor get one word more from her I took her by the hand and left her in the priest's house.

Frustration, fury, sorrow: Schuyler feels them all. Evening is coming: time to get back in the boat and return to Montreal. A clasp of her hand—he insists on that much—and he is gone.

✧

WE WHO READ this "memoriall" almost three centuries later can easily understand the feelings of its author. But what about its subject, the unredeemed captive herself? What were *her* feelings—held tight, though they were, behind the "steel in her breast"? Her husband gives us a clue, with his reference to her father's remarriage. And there is, as well, a certain logic in her situation. Otherwise we can only speculate—only imagine—but that much, at least, we must try.

> *So the trader would be here, this very afternoon. She had talked with the headmen, with the priests, with her family: all had assured her that she would be kept safe. Her husband would be with her the whole time; a priest would see the trader first and explain her position. Her home now was the village; her people were the Kahnawake. She would not go back to her English father, not now, not ever.*
>
> *Her English father: what claim could he possibly make on her anyway? With a clarity born of old bitterness, she remembered the last times she had seen him.*
>
> *She remembered his coming to the village when she was still a small child—feeling scared and strange, and gripped inside by the ties of her old life. She had begged him then to take her away, but he had failed her utterly. A prayer; some empty words of comfort; a sorrowful good-bye. In her mind's eye she could still see the back of his bowed head, the heaviness in his step, as he trudged off toward the river.*

She remembered the long journey through the forest, up from Deerfield. At first, she had clung to him tightly, as a squirrel clings to a tree; but weak as he was, and clumsy on his snowshoes, he could not walk for the two of them. Then a kind, strong man from the village—a man she knew now as her uncle Hatironta—had swept her up and set her atop his own broad shoulders. And in that position she had traveled almost the entire route to Montreal. When, from time to time, she had turned her head for a glimpse to the rear, she had seen her father lurching heavily through the drifts, falling back, gasping, calling out for rest. The Kahnawake had laughed and joked about him. This tall man with the fine clothes and finer words, this great leader of the "Bastonnais," this favorite of God: how he had been brought low! Her sorrow for him had turned to pity, and finally to shame.

And there was more. The journey had begun with a terror so extreme that her memory could not sort out the details. But strangely disconnected images remained—images that included herself as though seen by someone else. Herself shocked from sleep, and flung out of bed, in a pitch-dark room—as intruders smashed in the door. Herself squeezed with her English brothers and sisters (shadowy figures now) beneath a bench against a wooden wall. Herself amidst a disordered throng in the meetinghouse, prisoners awaiting an unknown fate. Herself frozen on a trail by a winding river—what trail? what river?—as her mother—what mother? was led off to be killed. Her father was there, too: there in the dark room, struggling vainly to fire his gun; there in the meetinghouse, eyes raised toward an apparently indifferent God; there by the riverside, helplessly bidding her mother good-bye. (Had he really taken another wife, so soon after his return?) Faithless, forgetful father: protector who could not protect, comforter who would not comfort, caretaker who did not care.

All that was behind her now, far behind. Yet the trader's coming had brought it back, like the embers of an old fire stirred to life beneath the ash. The priests said she must see him, must give him a hearing. All right: she would see, she would hear. But they couldn't make her speak. Silence would be her reply; its meaning would be clear enough.

Schuyler's memorial leaves us also with a different question. Who was Eunice's Indian husband, this man who stood by her—and, at least briefly, spoke for her—during the meeting in the priest's residence? Again, no firm answer is possible. But again, there are grounds for speculation.

Nearly a century ago, a priest at Kahnawake solved the mystery of the husband's name. By painstaking study of entries in the mission register, he first "found" Eunice (concealed behind her several acquired names, both French and Iroquois), and then her spouse.[12] There he was, and there he is now for any who wish to examine the register: François Xavier Arosen. To begin with, his baptismal name—one that linked him with the saint to whom the mission itself was dedicated (Mission de St. François Xavier du Sault St. Louis). Then, Arosen—his Mohawk name, meaning "squirrel." Does it have a familiar look and sound? In the story (from a preceding chapter) of Mehuman Hinsdale's capture and the Kahnawake "plot" to abandon the French alliance, a key figure was a Mohawk "spy" named Arousent.[13] Arosen and Arousent: same sound, slightly different spellings. But, in fact, the differences wash out with the peculiarities of Iroquois orthography. (For example: "o" and "ou" are two ways of rendering a single Iroquois vowel-sound, which is precisely captured by neither.) So this is one name only. And did it refer—in eighteenth-century Kahnawake—to one man only? Was Arousent, the Mohawk spy of 1709, also Arosen, the husband subsequently of the captive Eunice Williams?

The answer turns, in part, on Iroquois naming practice—which was so complex as virtually to foreclose the chance that two individuals might carry the same name at the same point in time. No Smiths or Joneses, no Johns or Marys, among the Mohawks: everyone had his (or her) distinctive names. The mission-register at Kahnawake—to take the most obvious, and pertinent, example—shows no sign whatsoever of the nominal repetition that is immediately apparent in English sources from the period.[14]

Another consideration: the man chosen to convey secret proposals from the Mohawks to their Kahnawake "brothers" would, presumably, have been someone prepared for the task by prior experience. Someone who knew the route, knew the place, knew the people on the other end. Someone who had been to Kahnawake before, perhaps quite often. Someone who may even have had family there (as was the case with not a few of the New York Mohawks). Someone, in short, for whom it is plausible to imagine an actual removal, from the Mohawk Valley to the Canadian mission, a few years later—when the war had ended, and families were being reshuffled on both sides.

In addition, the ages look right, or at least not palpably wrong. If we make Arosen a young man—say, in his early twenties when chosen for the spying trip—he becomes twenty-five or twenty-six three and a half years later, at the time of Eunice's marriage. And she was then sixteen. These ages, his and hers, would both fall a little on the high side of average for Kahnawakes (men and women) at first marriage.[15] But only a little. Moreover, the gap between them would be quite common, indeed customary.

And one last thought—more tentative than the rest—about their status, their relation to the local community. Each was, though in different senses, an outsider: Eunice as a captive-and-adoptee from New England; Arosen as a newcomer from the valley to the south. Perhaps this, too, was part of their "joining together."

To summarize: here is Eunice, coming of age in her adoptive community, secure, and increasingly well integrated, yet still a trifle "strange" given her unusual origins. And here is Arosen, known to her from childhood as a visitor to the village: an outsider, yes, but also a tribal "brother," and with blood-kin resident nearby. As Eunice matures, and reaches the age appropriate for marriage—just then Arosen returns to the mission for good. More familiarity. Growing interest. "Resolutions"—that's the priest's word—"resolutions" to marry. The priest tries to dissuade them, but cannot. They know their minds, and will have what they want. They have reached this point from radically different directions and refuse now to turn back. Marriage will bind them here—to each other and to the place they have made their own.

·~·

SCHUYLER'S MEMORIAL was enclosed in a letter to Governor Dudley, dated June 10 in Albany. He had arrived the day before from Montreal, having "waded through many Difficulties in ye way." Nine captives had returned with him—but these, of course, did not include the one who was most on the minds of New Englanders. Of her, Schuyler wrote simply: "My indefatigueable Pains therein came to no purpose." By June 26, the news, both good and bad, had reached Boston. Sewall's diary for that day noted a visit from John Williams, the arrival of the returned captives, and the fact that "Mr. Schyler could not prevail with Mr. Williams's daughter to come away." Eight days later, another entry: "Tis known that Lt Saml Williams died at Derefield last Tuesday night to the great grief of his Father." Samuel's activities of the preceding year—"scouting" against the Indians, and leading a team of negotiators to Canada—had held the promise of an illustrious future. Now he was dead, at twenty-four. And Eunice might as well be dead. The father's grief was doubly compounded.[16]

Schuyler's trip to Montreal also prompted a fresh exchange of letters between the French and English governors. Vaudreuil wrote first, taking credit for the "nine of yor prisoners who askt to return." Schuyler, he said, could testify "that I retain noe body here by force." And, as for Eunice Williams, Schuyler "will . . . tell you . . . how he could never oblige her to promise him even to go and see her father as soon as peace should be declared." Vaudreuil professed hurt "at the little justice you doe me . . . about the marriage of that girle with an Indian." He had never approved their match, "but not being able to foresee it, 'twas impossible for me to prevent it." He felt "more chagrin" than Dudley himself, "on account of her father, for whom I have the greatest esteem." Why, if the King ("my master") should make inquiry, Vaudreuil could easily give "my reasons, . . . which you will not hear."[17]

Dudley replied almost immediately. The nine returning captives were "far short of the number I justly expected"; surely, more would have come "had they been allowed to do so." In particular, "I have no satisfactory Answer to my Complaint of the Treatment of mr. Williams's Daughter . . . [in] her marriage to a Salvage." She was, after all, "carryed away early in her infancy before she had discretion to judge of things for her own good"; even now "she is to be considered as a minor within the age of consent to make choice for herself." Vaudreuil must use his authority "to free her from the impositions made on her tender years," and to end her continuing "detention." Dudley was confident that the French king would indeed call his governor to account, and order the release of all the remaining captives. "Reasons" rejected; "complaint" renewed. *Status quo ante.*[18]

Dudley's hopes of breaking this impasse were pinned, more and more, to Louis XIV. In August, he wrote to London of "having sent away out of these Goverments every French man prisoner, or others"—and of his continued "hope [that] I shall obtain the English prisoners yet remayning in French hands, so soon as I have the French King's orders to Mr. Voderil to send with Commissioners from hence to receive them." Shortly thereafter he received something that answered his purpose—unfortunately the document itself does not survive—and began to prepare a further step. Sewall's diary for October 21 notes this: "Govr speaks of sending Mr Williams and Mr Stoddard to Canada." A few days later the Council authorized money for such a "commission" and Dudley wrote a new letter for delivery to Vaudreuil. The plan he proposed was simple enough on its surface: the captives should first be "assembled" in some convenient place, then "I will send a ship early in the spring up Canada river for their transportation home." But the process of negotiating this result—or, more accurately, of negotiating toward it—proved enormously complex and difficult.[19]

The difficulties are detailed in another remarkable journal, kept by Captain John Stoddard, one of the two designated "commissioners."[20] Stoddard was a young "gentleman" of Northampton, much respected for his contributions to public—especially military—affairs. He was also the son of the Reverend Solomon Stoddard—and, from that connection, an uncle of Eunice Williams. The second commissioner was John Williams himself. There were, moreover, three "attendants," Captain Thomas Baker, Eleazer Warner, and Jonathan Smith, plus an "interpreter," Martin Kellogg. Baker, Warner, and Kellogg were all Deerfield men, and former captives, too. Taken together, this was a team of formidable skills, long experience, and much direct interest in the project at hand.

Thence to Canada, yet again. They will follow the familiar route, up the Hudson, across Lakes George and Champlain, down the Richelieu River, past Fort Chambly, to Montreal. At the outset they are delayed in Albany by poor weather and travel conditions. They improve the time by hiring Indian guides and a local chief reputed to have "great influence on the Caghnawaga [Kahnawake] Indians" and willing to "improve his interest for the deliverance of our English prisoners." Eventually, on January 22, they start northward; their first night's lodging is at "Col. John Schuyler's farm" (he of the "commission" immediately preceding). The journey is uneventful: "We travelled down Wood Creek [by canoe] . . . We passed Fort Anne four miles. . . . We lay still, it having snowed most of the day before. . . . We marched in snowshoes, eighteen miles. . . ." In just over two weeks they reach Chambly, where they transfer to a "carryall" (sleigh) supplied by French officials. They stop briefly in Montreal, then push on over the snow to Quebec, arriving on February 16.[21]

Immediately they "wait on" the French governor, present their credentials, deliver the letters they are carrying, and stake out their ground for the negotiations to come. The war is "happily terminated" and peace restored "between these two Crowns." The articles of peace direct that prisoners should be returned from both sides "without distinction"; Stoddard and Williams have come with specific orders "to demand all prisoners whomsoever." Vaudreuil receives the commissioners with "honor and respect." He promises that "all prisoners should have free liberty to return—and that those that would go should have his blessing." Is there an agreement on terms? "All prisoners whomsoever" *versus* "those that would go": different phrasings with apparently different meanings. The issue between them is that of choice; according to Vaudreuil, each captive must exercise his (or her) "liberty" to go or to stay.[22]

Vaudreuil has a clear advantage here—because he has the prisoners—and the commissioners do not challenge the principle of individual choice. But they do try to limit its application. Under-age prisoners, for example, "should be compelled to return." And those with Canadian spouses and/or children should not be held back by family considerations. There is, moreover, the problem of captives held by Indians: their "liberty" will need special protection. Vaudreuil counters with "reservations" of his own. "A considerable number of English people" have recently been naturalized as French citizens; they must be excluded from this process altogether.[23]

And another problem: what to do about the intervention of various third parties? Williams and Stoddard are especially vexed with the Jesuits, "who, not being content with the endeavors they have used with the prisoners for many years, . . . do now make it their business to go from house to house to solicit our people to tarry in this country." When they protest to Vaudreuil, he replies "that he could as easily alter the course of the waters as prevent the priests endeavors." There are "laity"—even some "French gentlemen"—who work toward the same end. Moreover, there is persistent infighting within the administrative hierarchy of New France, which keeps the governor "from acting your own inclination." (Or so the commissioners believe.)[24]

The discussions grow increasingly bitter, as the days become weeks and months. In March, the site shifts to Montreal—better, perhaps, for the commissioners, since they are closer to most of the captives. Talk is supplemented by long "letters" (in effect, position papers). Dispatches of various kinds move overland to Massachusetts and overseas to France and England. Captain Baker leaves to confer in person with Dudley and returns many weeks later. John Williams describes the situation for his family; echoes (only) survive to the present. "You don't tell me," writes Elisha Williams in early April to his kinsman

Stephen, "whether Uncle sais Any thing of Cousn Eunice's Marriage."[25]

In fact, to this point there has been no contact with Eunice at all. Surely, she has been much on her father's mind; and several of the leading points in the negotiations—age and family status, for example—bear directly on her case. But Stoddard's journal does not mention her, until mid-May. At that point the commissioners begin to stress "the ill circumstances of our poor people with the Indians." Perhaps they have come to realize that this group will be particularly hard to reach; the journal records their demand "that care might be taken that [such prisoners] . . . might be brought out of the woods." Vaudreuil himself acknowledges a difficulty, since some of the Indians involved have "already taken the precaution to make them [i.e., the prisoners] go into the woods upon receiving word that English [emissaries] would be sent here to take them away." (In short: prisoners are kept in hiding.)[26] Still, the governor will do what he can to help— and on May 14 he takes an important step. By his personal order a French officer goes to Kahnawake, with this result:

> Mr. Junceur . . . discoursed with Mr. Williams' daughter, and with her Indian relations, who said they would leave her to act her liberty respecting her return. The Governor promised that if her relations would consent he would compel her to return.

It is hard to know now exactly what happened. The officer did talk with Eunice, but the journal gives no hint of her reply. (Might she have again presented her "steel" curtain of silence?) He talked as well with her captors—no, her Indian "relations"—and they say it's up to her. The governor, for his part, will force her to return if they (the relations) agree. Is this, in sum, an advance on the previous position (as known from Schuyler's visit the year before)? Not an advance, but not a retreat either. If only she can be brought around, the Indians will "consent," and the governor will then see to it that she goes.[27]

There is one more card to play: a visit from the commissioners themselves, a meeting of Eunice with her father. And two weeks later they try it. "29th [May], We went to Cagnawaga [Kahnawake], to visit the natives and the prisoners with them, which we found rather worse than the Indians."[28] That is all the journal says; fortunately, there is a letter from John Williams (to Samuel Sewall) which adds a few details.[29] The date of the letter is June 1, three days after the event; here is its key paragraph:

it is the pleasure of an holy God to exercise me with sorrow upon sorrow. It was not till Hartford election-day that I could see my child. And she is yet obstinatly resolved to live and dye here, and will not so much as give me one pleasant look. It's beyond my ability, in the contents of a letter, to make you understand how ours here are besotted. We are like to be very unsuccessful. We take all the best methods we can, and put on all the patience we have; but the English are so naturalized to the customs and manners of the French and Indians, and have forgotten the English tongue, and are so many of them married, or gotten into nunneries, &c., that I think it would be far easier to gain twice the number of French and Indians to go with us than English . . . We need all your prayers.

Only a sentence speaks directly of Eunice. But clearly the rest applies to her, along with others of *ours here*. Perhaps for John Williams the sorrow is easier to bear when framed in general terms. Eunice is one of several—in fact, dozens—won over to alien ways, and unable any longer to speak English, and bound by new ties of marriage and family. These *naturalized* persons are a kind of outrage: how to find the words? Schuyler, the year before, had rated Eunice below *the worst of Indians*. Stoddard's journal uses similar language: *the prisoners, . . . which we found rather worse than the Indians*. And John Williams thinks it would be *far easier* to reason with Indians than with the captives. In the depths of their apostasy—their betrayal—they have sunk even lower than their "savage" captors.

But still the commissioners will not give up. For, on the day following their visit to the mission, they arrange to meet with "some of the chiefs of Cagnawaga," at the governor's residence in Montreal. The mission-priests are present, too, together with "divers other gentlemen": in short, a major gathering. First, the governor speaks "to encourage them to restore us our people." Then, their response: "the chief speaker . . . rose up and said that those taken by them were adopted into families, and not held as prisoners, but as children; and it was not their custom to compel any to return, but should leave them to their own liberty." At this point the commissioners ask to talk with the chiefs alone "at our chamber." There they can press their case without constraint or contradiction. (Perhaps they are especially eager to exclude the Jesuits.)[30]

Their argument has several parts. It is "the custom of all nations in Europe to compel all persons in minority," since "such persons had not discretion to know what was for their good." (Hold them to civilized standards.) Besides, "it could be of no benefit to them to detain such children." (Show them their true interest.) Surely they must know "that their [i.e., the captives'] parents and friends were much exercised about them." (Appeal to their basic sympathy.) Moreover, "were they under the like circumstances, they would desire the like of us." (Remind them that someday these positions could be reversed.) Finally, "if they would deliver [the prisoners] to us, it would be pleasing to the Queen of Great Britain and the King of France, to the Governor of Boston and the Governor of Canada." (Overawe them with the power of authority.) And yet: it doesn't work. "After all [we] said, they were sensible that it was difficult with . . . [the captives'] friends at home, yet they could do no otherwise than they had said before." The Indians will not force Eunice—or the others in their care—to return.[31]

Perhaps, then, the governor will? Williams and Stoddard try again, and this is truly their last hope. *June 3* (the day after their futile meeting with the chiefs): they write to Vaudreuil. "We demand, whether the Indians in this country, who have English prisoners in their hands, are subjects to the King of France, or whether we must treat with them as a free people. . . . If they are subjects, we demand that all prisoners in minority, that are in their hands (of which there are many) might be compelled to return." *June 7:* they write again. Because the governor "has very often manifested an earnest desire for the deliverance of our children out of the Indians' hands," they offer now a specific proposal. A "considerable number of those children" would like to go home, but are too frightened to say so openly; moreover, "some of the Indians, at least" see the "justice" of their wish. On the other side stand "the clergy" and "some [French] gentlemen" and (presumably) most of the children's Indian "masters." The governor could personally tip the scale: thus "we desire of your Lordship . . . that you would, by a letter to the chiefs of Cagnawaga, . . . as their father, signify your sincere desire that they would deliver our people to us."[32]

In the meantime, the commissioners plan "another journey to Cagnawaga." A chief in the village has just agreed to "deliver an English boy . . . in case the Governor would give order for it." This, quite likely, served to inspire the commissioners' second letter to Vaudreuil—by furnishing a model of strategic intervention. But it, like so much else, comes to nothing. The governor is not ready to "give order" at all. And the local bishop, during a recent visit to Kahnawake, has "thanked the natives for not delivering our people." And the Jesuits have been preaching "that if they delivered [the captive children] to us. . . . Christ would be angry with them." Faced with such broad resistance, Williams and Stoddard conclude that "it [would be] to no purpose" to revisit the village themselves.[33]

By now it is mid-June. The commissioners have been in Canada, and about their task, through four full months. The result of their efforts so far is deeply disappointing: three or four captives released and returned (by land), a few others promised, others seen but not promised, and many not seen even once. They decide to go back to Quebec—where a ship from Boston, sent to carry the whole group home, is expected any day. They reassert the general principle of access to all captives, and demand that "all . . . be assembled at Quebec, there to give answer whether they will return or not." They have occasional, small successes. A Frenchwoman from Montreal brings them "two English boys, which she had bought of the Indians at Cagnawaga." (Vaudreuil, moreover, has reportedly "bought a girl . . . with his own money.") There are other questions, less easily resolved. A captive woman, the widow of a Frenchman, is allowed to leave but refused the right to take her children and property with her. A captive boy says he wants to return, but is subsequently talked out of it by a local priest. A captive family—husband, wife, and young son—decide to leave and are strongly opposed by "a great number" of their Indian "relations."[34]

Increasingly, general issues give way to individual cases like these. The commissioners reduce their demands: now they would see only the captives held in Quebec and "places adjoining." Vaudreuil agrees, and most (though still not all) of those affected are brought together and given the choice of returning. Their responses are mixed: some yes, some no. In the meantime the ship from Boston—a brigantine called the *Leopard*—has finally reached Quebec. There is a last flurry of discussion and "dispute." On August 23, a group of Indians brings in an English child but refuses to release him "without a ransom of one hundred and sixty livres"; this is reluctantly paid, "the one half by Governor Vaudreuil, the other by Mr. Williams." The following day the ship raises anchor and begins its return journey with the commissioners, their attendants, and twenty-six prisoners. Measured against the group yet remaining in Canada, this is a success rate of one in six or seven.[35]

In New England expectations run high. Stephen Williams—by now a "schoolmaster at Hadley"—is informed by a Boston cousin of "news that unkel [uncle] is a-coming with one hundred and fifty captives &

that we may look for them everry day." That is from a letter dated September 9. On September 21, the *Leopard* reaches port, and the actual results become known. There is no sign of any general rejoicing this time. Surely some individual households are gladdened, but for a great many more there is sorrow—and a continuing sense of "affliction." John Williams and the members of his household are, of course, among the afflicted. "I greive with you," writes Elisha Williams to Stephen (in mid-October), "at ye Disappointment of Uncle Relating to Cousen Eunice."[36]

There is, apparently, nothing further to be done. *We take all the best methods we can, and put on all the patience we have*: that was how John Williams had put it, in writing to Sewall, months before. Yet Eunice remains *obstinately resolved to live and die* where she is.

Has he abandoned hope? Not if prayer implies hope. Years later it was said that "he was scarcely ever known to utter a prayer, however short, of which some petitions did not make a part, in behalf of his beloved and unfortunate daughter Eunice, who was in captivity among the Indians."[37]

But he would never talk to her, never see her, again.

SIX

∿

To the French—those leaders and functionaries who wrote about them—they were *les Iroquois du Sault*.

To the Jesuit fathers, they were *nos pauvres sauvages*.

At Deerfield, and elsewhere through the English settlements of Massachusetts Bay, they were "the French Mohawks."

In New York, wrote one who had seen them close up, "they are now commonly known . . . by the name of the Praying Indians, it being customary for them to go thro' the streets of Montreal with their Beads, praying & begging alms."[1]

The Abenakis, their Indian neighbors to the east (and fellow Christians), addressed them as "praying Iroquois."

And the non-Christian Iroquois to the south, their cultural (sometimes blood) kin, called them "our brethren at Canada."

To themselves, they were simply the Kahnawake (pronounced, roughly, Gah-nah-WAH-geh).

This varied nomenclature directly reflects the ambiguity of their cultural, and geographical, placement—and the extraordinary complexity of their history. Mohawk, Iroquois, Indian, in ascending order of generality; Christian, to a degree; French, in a limited sense; "brethren" to some, allies of others, and, of course, enemies of still others: the Kahnawake were all these, and more. Less than four decades old when Eunice Williams came to them, their community was already known—some said "renowned"—on both sides of the imperial border, and across the ocean as well.

Its beginnings are shrouded in legend. The keepers, the originators, of this particular legend have always been the Jesuits.

The time of the wars between the French and the Iroquois being passed, we saw the prophecy of Isaiah literally fulfilled: "the bears and the lions shall dwell with the lambs." We saw the Iroquois come to seek the friendship of the French; we saw the French go on missions to the country of the Iroquois.

The tone itself is seductive. And the substance has been, through many generations now, warmly compelling.[2]

Beginning in 1667, a priest named Rafeix undertook to develop a vacant "tract" on the south side of the St. Lawrence, opposite the French settlement at Mont Royale (Montreal). Bestowed on the Jesuits by a royal grant some years earlier, this new place was called LaPrairie, because of its fair and open prospect. Through the spring and summer a small cadre of French farmers prepared it for regular habitation: at the same time "God was inviting some Indians [*sauvages*] to come."[3] Specifically: seven people from the Oneida tribe—one of the Iroquois "Five Nations"—began a journey to Canada. They would protect, and guide, a French missionary who had been serving among them. In addition, their leader, a Christian convert named Tonsahoten, would try to obtain "remedies" (medicine) that could not be found in his homeland.[4]

In due course they reached the St. Lawrence, "over the ice." They met Father Rafeix and were induced by him "to go upon his lands." And they visited Montreal—with overwhelming results. "These poor barbarians, . . . having entered the church, were so greatly delighted . . . that they no longer thought of the Iroquois whence they came."[5] Tonsahoten's wife, Gandeaktuea, was "especially" delighted, and persuaded her husband to remain at LaPrairie. Meanwhile, other Indian people, hunting nearby, encountered Tonsahoten's group and also fell under the sway of Rafeix. In sum: "There . . . one saw anew what had happened at Jerusalem, when the church was formed out of all the assembled nations."[6]

By such means, through several succeeding years, the little community grew: the Indian community and, alongside it, the French. Two groups, two "villages," separate yet joined; and the Jesuits, Rafeix and an assistant, presided over both. Mass was said in a "little board cabin, which was common for the French and the savages." Although their numbers were few, "they nevertheless held prayers, evening and morning."[7] Indeed, the dominant strain of village life—according, still, to the legend—was a truly extraordinary piety. To the regular masses and prayer meetings were added a broad array of saints' days and festivals, baptisms and confirmations. On such occasions, the priests noted, the "savages" typically outdid the French.[8]

Their detachment from their own indigenous traditions seemed especially noteworthy. Almost overnight they abandoned "so many evil customs," to embrace the church. They scarcely mentioned the "superstitions" of their native country—except to "accuse themselves for even having thought of them."[9] Two "evils," most of all, they resolved to exclude: drunkenness and sexual license. These were tangibly represented by a pair of trees set near the entrance of the village, on which new recruits were supposed to "hang" (discard) their sinful proclivities. Thus, "among the Iroquois, this saying became a proverb: 'I am off to LaPrairie'—that is to say, I give up drink and polygamy."[10]

The success of the mission was broadcast throughout the Iroquois homeland by converts returning for visits with relatives or simply for the annual hunt. "The Christians who left LaPrairie . . . to hunt beasts went also to hunt men"; and, on returning, "the hunters always brought back some of their kinsmen or acquaintances." The latter, with "God touching their hearts," would typically take instruction from the priests—and, in due course, would themselves join the church. In one remarkable instance a "famous warrior" sought and received baptism—and subsequently persuaded forty others, in his Mohawk village of origin, to go with him to the mission.[11]

The same success was widely reported among the French as well; and LaPrairie became something of a religious showcase. Priests en route to and from their stations farther afield frequently stopped there. The Bishop of Quebec made an especially elaborate visit in the spring of 1675, and was followed weeks later by the *intendant* (a civil officer with powers nearly equivalent to those of the governor), the mayor and *curé* of Montreal, and "over fifty of the most notable persons of the country." Typically, these events were accompanied by special services in the church, parades, "feasts," and "rejoicing" on all sides.[12]

᠅

THE LEGEND, as noted, was the cherished creation of the Jesuits; hence it reflects their viewpoint, their interests. But in some respects it is incomplete, in others simply inaccurate. Historians must try to peel back its surface and touch the more complicated reality behind.

Take, for example, the matter of motive. If we follow the legend, and only the legend, we must conclude that Indians came to LaPrairie for deeply religious reasons. Yet were there not other reasons, too? A single Jesuit source invites us to look further, to think harder.

> Some of them come here with but little disposition to embrace our Faith; others, in still greater numbers, in a state of complete indifference—rather through complaisance or necessity than from inclination; and many even with quite contrary dispositions, and fully determined not to believe and not to listen on this point to the Fathers who instruct them.[13]

What, then, might "complaisance and necessity" have meant in the lives of these migrants? Lacking any answer—any hint of an answer—that would come directly from them, we can only speculate. But there are some suggestive clues.

Timing is one sort of clue. The year 1667 was critical in the history of the Iroquois: a year of peace, following decades of intertribal and intercolonial warfare, a year of recovery from the devastation inflicted by a French invading army (the preceding autumn). The country between the Mohawk Valley, the Great Lakes, and the lower St. Lawrence lay open, once again, to travel and commerce. And, especially for refugees from burned-out Mohawk villages, there was incentive to get away.[14]

Place is also a clue. LaPrairie lay within the limits of territory which Iroquoian peoples had traditionally counted as their own. To range northward through these forests, to this river, would not have seemed unusual; Tonsahoten's group was crossing familiar ground. Too, it was valuable ground, fertile ground, since the recent wars had interrupted regular patterns of use. Free of hunting parties, animals had flourished there; free of farming, the earth had replenished itself. Where better to look for new prospects—and make a new home? Trade was also part of the prospects. With French merchants close by, with the ever-widening European demand for "beavers" (furs), Indians could use their knowledge of the country to good advantage. In years to come this trade would prove vital to the Kahnawake, and its possibilities must have been apparent from the start.[15]

And, then, the people: the individual migrants themselves. Tonsahoten, we know, came to LaPrairie from the Oneidas. But he had been born a Huron, and presumably became a captive, or refugee, in one or another of the Iroquoian wars. His wife, Gandeaktuea, was originally an Erie—another tribe "destroyed by the Iroquois"—and had subsequently been made a "slave." Neither one, in short, was native to Oneida; both had come there under some sort of duress. Other early arrivals at LaPrairie were also notable for the complexity of their origins. "They . . . are all coming from different Iroquois nations," wrote one eyewitness, "and [are] either natives of that country, or dwellers there as prisoners." A human flotsam, extruded from Iroquoia in the turbulent aftermath of war. "Many who were not naturalized Iroquois resolved to steal away and come to LaPrairie," said another source. Marginal people—and, on that account, likely to remove.[16]

To speculate about secular pressures on the migrants is not to discount religious ones altogether. Many of the Iroquois "prisoners," especially those from the Huron country, had previously been baptized by French missionaries; Tonsahoten was a case in point. Moreover, some among the "natives" had quite recently come under Catholic influence. By the late 1660s, French missionaries to Iroquoia were intensifying their "quest for souls"—against the resistance of tradition-minded "elders." There was much bitterness and bloodshed in the result. Some of the LaPrairie settlers were driven from their villages in disgrace; others confronted angry demands to stay. Either way, religion seemed to multiply their difficulties at home—and to suggest a route of escape elsewhere.[17]

Mixed motives, then. Religion. And personal safety. And opportunity. And planful pursuit of the main chance. And who knows what special considerations, in each individual case? The result, of course, was the same. *We will go to LaPrairie. And, if it suits us, we will stay.*

꒕

THE LEGEND stresses the social "harmony" achieved at LaPrairie. Somehow this "mixed multitude" of tribes and races—including the French—is supposed to have "acted as one body." But even within the legend there are, on this point, hints to the contrary.[18]

Until 1671, the missionaries "took all the cares" of governance upon themselves. But then "it became necessary to elect captains who should have jurisdiction over the village"; in effect, responsibility—and power—passed to the Indians. A few years more, and a single structure of authority became three: separate captains, now called chiefs, would henceforth serve each of the largest constituent groups, Mohawks, Hurons, and Onondagas. Immediately, however, "dissension arose in one faction": the Hurons, instead of simply choosing their leader, "were long in consultation." Finally, "feeling piqued"—it's not clear why—a number of them "separated themselves, and went to start a new mission beyond the river." That these transitions were managed without stress seems implausible. About the Huron separation, the legend is unusually direct: "this . . . was painful, and did not fail to keep their minds at variance," at least for a time.[19]

About the French at LaPrairie, and their relations to the Indians, the record is mostly opaque. One does glimpse them here and there in Jesuit accounts: beginning to "apply themselves in good earnest to the trade," for example, or lined up as a greeting party for the bishop's visit.[20] But clearly the priests' main interest, at least for publication, was the care of their "savage" charges. This is unfortunate for historians, because LaPrairie in its early days made a unique experiment in bicultural living. We should like to know just how bicultural—and in what specific ways. Certainly, their dwellings were separate: each group in its own village (with a few hundred yards in between). Probably, too, their planting fields were separate: the French to the east and south, the Indians to the north abreast the river. Even the church was "divided into two apartments, one for the French and the other for the savages." Yet they frequently interacted; the priests remarked on "the visits and the little services that they rendered one another."[21]

Moreover, they traded. Animal skins for "strouds" (European cloth). Moosemeat and venison for cookware and guns. And brandy: soon to become a pivotal element in the life of the mission. The pledge taken by new recruits, the temptations they "hung" on the liquor tree: such measures did not always hold. Jesuit sources are vague here and shift the blame away from the Indians. "This mingling" with the French, they say, gave an opening to Satan "to tempt the savages." In 1672, a tavern was opened at LaPrairie, and Indians were among its customers. But "divine providence . . . [intervened] to destroy this demon"—which is to say that the priests persuaded the colonial governor to forbid trading in liquors there. A year later, however, the governor's protection was withdrawn, and local Frenchmen once again "introduced drink at LaPrairie." The priests, supported by the village chiefs, fought back and the situation improved—at least temporarily. In fact, the same sequence would repeat itself time after time: the demon came, and went, and came again. At one point, matters reached such a crisis that a large group of "sober" Indians left the community for good, saying "they found themselves as greatly annoyed by drunkards as they were in their own country."[22]

Even early on, the demon of drink had helped to split the original settlement at LaPrairie. In 1676, all the Indians there, together with two priests, removed to a new site three miles upriver. The priests had come to think that separation from—not mingling with—the French would best advance the interests of the mission, especially in the matter of "brandy." For the Indians there was an added—and central—consideration: their steadily worsening "poverty."[23]

This last was compounded of several factors. From the start the farmland assigned to the Indians had been too low and damp for good results with their corn. Moreover, the demands placed upon it were great: the settlers had to provide not only for themselves, but also for hundreds of transient Iroquois who came each summer "after the hunt." Their own traditions of hospitality demanded a bounteous welcome, and the visitors, "after having eaten much corn . . . carried off a great deal [more] for their provisions." Under such pressures the soil itself was steadily depleted; harvests shrank and "left the village destitute in . . . winter and at planting time." The same problem, with minor variations, had long been familiar to Iroquois peoples; and resettlement was, in fact, a familiar response. Thus, in moving from LaPrairie, the mission was following native—not European— precedents.[24]

There is little doubt that the "savage" villagers were eager to go— and perhaps not only for material reasons. For, once they had moved, they asserted themselves much more vigorously than before. The French referred to the new site as Sault St. Louis, after the adjacent (and fearsome) river rapids. But the Indians called it Kahnawake— the first time they had used this name—and remembered thereby an important old "castle" in their homeland.[25]

The changes went deeper as well. Governance was now firmly in the hands of the Indian "captains," whose authority embraced all aspects of secular life and was sometimes extended outside the mission itself. For example: "some among the most zealous savages" were regularly appointed to keep watch at Montreal during the big seasonal trade fairs, when mission residents were most at risk of succumbing to drink; there, wrote an observer in evident admiration, "they employ . . . even force, sometimes with their own people, sometimes with the French."[26]

Religious practice, as well, showed a strengthening of native influence. Formerly, Indian parishioners had been "merely present at mass and at vespers, which were sung by the French, but now they do everything themselves in their chapel." Henceforth, key parts of the service were said "in their language"; a priest referred also to "their psalms" (in contrast to "ours") and "their prayers . . . set to the principal modes of Church Music." Moreover, "they" took special pride in building the chapel at the new site—and then in rebuilding it, piece by laborious piece, some years later after a damaging windstorm. And they gave it their own look inside, by using as decorations "their robes, . . . their collars, . . . their porcelain bracelets, . . . shields which the women wear to adorn their hair, and . . . belts, which are the savages' pearls." Finally, Indian converts became leaders of the faith, principally in the role of *dogique*. Men who held this position assisted the regular priest: sang the psalms and chants, and occasionally preached the sermon. "Savage boys" served as acolytes and adults formed the choir.[27]

These developments, all following close on the move from La-Prairie, helped to generate a marked demographic spurt. New migrants poured into the mission from native "castles" to the south; two hundred were said to have come in 1679 alone. In 1676, immediately after the move, the village contained twenty-two "cabins" and a population of perhaps 200; six years later, both numbers had tripled. Over the same span, the annual total of baptisms at the mission rose from 17 to more than 60.[28]

But beneath these numbers and matters of form lay profound change of another sort. Briefly put: the nascent Kahnawake mission underwent a revolution in spirituality itself. The story has become a cornerstone of the Jesuit legend; even today it is well known to Catholics throughout Canada and around the world.[29]

It starts near Christmastime in 1676, among a small group of the mission's women. Inspired—so the sources say—by the example of French nuns in Montreal, these native "sisters" adopted a variety of penitential disciplines. Indeed, they wished to found "a sort of convent" of their own, but were prevented by their priests (who "did not think that the time had yet come for this"). So the women directed their efforts, instead, to "exercises" of self-mortification. They appeared naked in wintertime "at the foot of a large cross that stands beside our cemetery." They dug holes in the river ice—also "in the depth of winter"—and flung themselves into the freezing water. They beat each other with whips made from thorn branches, fashioned iron girdles to wear, and fasted for days at a time. They mixed ashes and dirt with their food, and put "glowing coals between their toes," and "disfigured themselves by cutting off their hair." In short: "they did all the harm they could do to the body, which they call their greatest enemy." There were lesser "austerities" as well: vows of chastity, and promises "never to put on their gala dress"; long, impromptu prayer-sessions "in the woods"; tearful confessional meetings; rosaries said at the rate of twenty times per day.[30]

The priests responded to all this, first with wary (perhaps envious?) fascination, and then with mounting alarm. Some thought that Satan himself, enraged by the conversion of so many Indians, "drove them on." At the very least, steps must be taken to "prevent their fervor from proceeding to excesses that might greatly injure their health." Details are lacking just here, but gradually—over the course of four or five years—the "excesses" slackened.[31]

Perhaps the pace of events was moderated by the death of a key participant. Kateri Tekakwitha had come to the mission from her home in the Mohawk Valley barely three years before. She was twenty years old, sickly, partially blind, and utterly single-minded in her pursuit of God's grace. Quickly she moved to the front of the building spiritual ferment. She rejected proposals of marriage, "avoided company as much as she could," and renounced everyday "amusements"; instead, "prayers, toil, [and] spiritual conversation [became] . . . her sole occupation." Then she "fell into a dangerous disease," and presently died; thereafter "the example of her most holy life" gave rise to "a kind of cultus" in her name. Almost at once her fellow penitents began to pray at her grave, and soon pilgrims "flocked from all parts of Canada [to see] . . . the miracles wrought there." Known to history as "the Lily of the Mohawks," she has, in the late twentieth century, been accorded beatification by her church—and may yet be canonized as its first Native American saint.[32]

It remains to wonder—also in the late twentieth century—what lay behind the intense spiritual outpouring which Kateri so exemplified. Was this perhaps an indigenous "revitalization movement" in the anthropologists' sense of the term?[33] A movement of recovery from progressive cultural trauma? A recasting of old ways and values, in the guise of something new? Key elements of the usual sequence do appear: the destruction of material life, in the preceding French wars; the erosion of cultural life, by insistent (Catholic) proselytizing; the transformation of ecological life, through contact with external (European) markets. Plus physical removal, and the timely appearance of a charismatic "prophet"—or, in this case, a prophet*ess*.

Furthermore: beneath the outer layer of ostensibly Christian forms, one feels a distinctly "native" spirit. Some of the physical "torments" that the penitents inflicted on themselves were curiously similar to practices traditionally used in Iroquois torture ceremonies. (In one of the Jesuit accounts, Kateri is said to have "burned her feet, as is done to prisoners.") Clearly, these violated the priests' sense of religious propriety—and were, from their standpoint, a dangerous innovation. But again: probably not from the standpoint of the converts themselves. People of Iroquoian stock had long regarded ecstatic states as key to spiritual experience. Some would find these in a "vision quest" (complete with its own forms of self-denial), some in dreaming, some in the rigors of the "sweat-house," and some in the rapid ingestion of alcohol. The converts had forsworn, more or less, all such traditional methods; but now they found another. The excitement at Kahnawake in the late 1670s expressed, at bottom, a special and "savage" version of Christianity.[34]

At some level, surely, the Jesuits understood this. For their writings gravitate repeatedly to a single theme: their own cultural and religious ways versus those of the "savages"; the adjustments and compromises they feel obliged to accept, and the core of "essentials" they must vigilantly defend. Some elements of native cultures they could easily admire—for example, the emphasis on sharing and mutual concern. This, wrote one of the mission priests, extended "even to the point that they possessed nothing individually."[35]

But drunkenness and sexual promiscuity were—as noted already— different matters; likewise divorce and "pagan" burial rites. Divorce, the priests wrote, had become an "infrequent occurrence"; in fact, in the two decades after the mission's founding "one would not find twenty husbands who have left their wives." (But is this really such a low number, given the small size of the original pool? Evidence from a somewhat later period of Kahnawake history shows a high rate of marital failure, at least by European standards of the time.) About burials they gave a similarly cheerful verdict. According to Iroquois tradition, the dead should be interred with food, jewelry, clothes, and other personal effects—and commemorated with lengthy "feasts" and lavish gifts to mourning relatives. The Jesuits advocated a more restrained approach—without "cries and lamentations"—and urged, in particular, that the property of the deceased be distributed among the village poor. Mostly, they claimed to have won their case—although mourning feasts were continued at Kahnawake for many years.[36]

Indeed, there were numerous examples of compromise between the two systems. Presumably, the Indians' special pleasure in church singing reflected their previous experience; so, too, their insistence that new priests be "adopted" into one or another of their traditional clans. And consider the following "heroic exercise"—clearly the Indians' own idea—described by a priest in 1694:

> It was called *hotounongannandi*, that is to say 'public penance', because it was done in the name of all. The men, gathered together according to the savage custom—that is, at a feast—expressed their destestation of the drunkenness which mastered them. This was done as follows: after agreeing together as to what they could do to give satisfaction to God . . . each spoke as the spirit of penance moved him; and some did so more eloquently by the tears that flowed in abundance from their eyes, than by their voices broken by sobs. . . .

In sum: a Christian ceremony, animated by love of the Christian God, yet intermingled with "savage custom," and called by a savage name. Even the issue at hand—drunkenness—can be seen as a cultural bridge. "Brandy," produced by Europeans, was traded into Indian communities. But there it was received, and used, in a specifically native context as a quick and powerful stimulant to spiritual experience. However, it "mastered them"—which is to say that its effects were complicated and ultimately destructive. Thus some Indians turned to Christianity, as a means (in part) of warding off "this demon." Yet their practice of the new religion retained many of their old ways. From such crisscrossings came an elaborate, and unmistakable, "syncretism."[37]

There was one additional point of sharing between the Kahnawake "savages" and their Jesuit mentors. Together they created, in the early years of the mission, a local tradition of martyrdom. The Jesuits had their own long experience of this—personal experience in the tribal heartlands. Jean de Brebeuf, Isaac Jogues, Charles Garnier, Gabriel Lalemant (among others): revered names, all, of men who had given their lives to the cause of God's work in America. Now the Indians at "the Sault" would be called to make a parallel contribution. Kateri was one sort of martyr. And there were other sorts, as well. Some converts endured "painful persecution" simply for declaring their intent to go to Kahnawake; at least one was murdered because his fellow tribesmen could "not suffer any one . . . to prefer . . . [Christian] society to that of the real Iroquois, [feeling] that it was a slur on the whole nation." Others underwent agonizing, sometimes fatal, tortures after being captured and returned to their home villages. Such experiences were described, to the last appalling detail, again and again in Jesuit writings. "We count three or four martyrs here," began one of their annual reports. "She died a true martyr, in the fire," concluded a second. "People in the town still speak of her edifying death," stated yet a third. To the priests' way of thinking, these were supreme proofs of the success of their mission.[38]

The frame was explicitly Christian; the Jesuits, to repeat, had their own roll of martyrs. But the Indians were not mere imitators of an alien model; their culture, their history, their values contributed strongly to the evolving pattern. War captives in Iroquois society had always been objects of ritual torture: objects, and subjects, too, for their response was no less a part of the tableau. Courage in the face of pain and death was a prized virtue—to be remembered, almost gratefully, by the torturers themselves. And such courage could be easily transposed to the new situation of captives who were also converts (and became targets on that very account).[39]

꒳

PIETY, martyrdom, spiritual innovation and "excess": thus the public face of Kahnawake during its early years. But at roughly the same time, and largely out of view, the life of the community was developing along other tracks as well.

None would prove more important in the long run than participation in the intercolonial fur trade. From small, ad hoc beginnings this enterprise grew to become the mainstay of the local economy. Because it was outside the law—French law—and because our sources today are entirely French and English, we cannot follow its course as closely as we might wish. But its outlines, and its inner dynamic, are clear enough.[40]

Most of what we can see reflects the viewpoint of French officialdom. As early as 1681, the governor—the Count de Frontenac—was writing to the king of "certain individuals . . . conveying beaver to Orange, . . . and bringing back money and merchandise." This, the count continued, "would cause serious injury to Your Majesty's treasury, if not promptly remedied." Orange was the original (Dutch) name for the Hudson River town now called Albany; it belonged, of course, to the English colony of New York. French law restricted some branches of trade across imperial boundaries, and entirely forbade others. Furs, in particular, were reserved for one or another merchant "company," officially chartered by the Crown and obliged to collect a royal duty (*le droit du quart*) in return. In short: the trade with "Orange" was a smugglers' operation, through and through.[41]

And Kahnawake was right in the middle of it—was, indeed, its geographical center. Frontenac's memorandum of 1681 spoke of the mission-village as the "entrepot for this traffic," and similar comments echoed through official correspondence far into the eighteenth century. To a limited extent the Kahnawake obtained furs in their own annual hunt; but, much more often, they served as carriers (*porteurs*) for merchandise originating elsewhere. Some traded on their own account, while many others worked in the direct employ of French merchants. Typically, the merchants arranged an initial purchase at the source (in the rich, fur-bearing regions far to the north). When brought down to the St. Lawrence Valley, the goods were stashed in hideouts around Montreal; from there they could be transferred to Kahnawake itself. Of this crucial linkage, one French official wrote as follows: "I am informed that the squaws who visited Montreal carried away beaver in their baskets; they went with it to the Sault, whence it was eventually exported." The *porteurs* in the subsequent leg of the trade were also Kahnawake, men as well as women. The Richelieu River, Lake Champlain, the Hudson, with some short portages in between: such was their usual route. Often they traveled in small groups of two or three canoes; but at least occasionally they combined to form "convoys" of fifty or sixty. Upon reaching Albany, they met with traders appointed to receive the cargo; these, in fact, were mostly men of Dutch extraction. From Albany, the furs would continue down the Hudson—now in other hands—to New York, and thence across the ocean to England.[42]

Individual *porteurs* can be glimpsed from time to time in the account books of the merchants involved. There they appear with names and some additional bits of description:

Gaingoton, sauvage du Sault [Indian of the Sault]

un sauvage qui s'appele Harris d'un extraction Anglais [an Indian named Harris of English extraction]

la sauvagesse [the Indian woman] Agnesse

Marie Magdalaine, qui a un impediment a un de ses oeiul [who is blind in one eye]

Ashareiake, ein Canidaien Jonghen wilt blanche [a young Canadian white Indian]

ein maquas wont in Canada [a Mohawk living in Canada], Dwaerhoeseeraghqua[43]

They were paid per trip; moreover, they customarily "skimmed" a few furs for their personal profit, dousing the remainder with water to conceal the lost weight. Each journey took five or six weeks (to and from). The "season" as a whole lasted from April to October.[44]

What made this "illicit traffic" so tempting were the vastly different returns available in Albany, as compared with Montreal: fully twice the value during some periods. Moreover, the quality of goods offered in exchange seemed better: English strouds, in particular, were sturdier in construction and more attractive in design than their French equivalents. Strouds were necessary to begin the next round of trade; Indians sought these above all other articles. At the same time, return cargoes included a broad range of European goods: rum and brandy; finished clothing (shirts, coats, stockings, shoes); knives, copperware, and other household utensils; beads; axes, kettles, gimlets, hatchets; guns and gunpowder; tobacco and smoking pipes—to mention only the more common entries in the account books.[45]

French leaders, one after another, fretted and fumed about the trade. Repeatedly they urged—or begged—the Indians to comply with official regulations. Occasionally they attempted direct measures: searches of local housing, as well as "interdiction" of movement on the rivers south. But none of this came to very much. Indians insisted on their "liberty" to trade as they wished—certainly with their own goods, and, implicitly, with whatever the Montreal merchants placed in their hands. In fact, the French were constrained by a fear that the Indians might simply leave, "to return to their brethren among the Iroquois," if trade restrictions were fully enforced. The Kahnawake, for their part, understood this advantage well, and refused "subordination" to French policy. The result was—again, in the eyes of the French— that "Sault St. Louis . . . has become a sort of republic . . . [where] foreign trade is carried on." Worse yet: because of this trade, "almost all the people . . . have English hearts, as the Indians express it."[46]

In fact, however, the English had their own reasons for concern. The profits from smuggling were confined on their side to two groups, the Dutch merchants of Albany and their partners in New York; other colonists benefited hardly at all. And, from an imperial standpoint the trade seemed wrong in all its effects. "French Indians" were supplied with weapons, for example, and these could easily be turned back against English foes; French merchants, meanwhile, gained new channels of wealth. When the trade continued during periods of war, as was frequently the case, it bordered on treason.[47]

Moreover, there was the further problem of population loss. As long as fur-smuggling remained so strikingly advantageous, people in the Iroquois heartland would be drawn northward away from English influence. Initially, the English seemed unable (or disinclined) to recognize the roots of this pattern. At conferences with their "Five Nations" allies, they would often bemoan the "subtil insinuations" used by Jesuit missionaries to entice migrants away and the "severities" practiced by French authorities to prevent repatriation. But the Indians themselves knew better. "You demand the reason why our Indians go to Canada," said one Iroquois sachem to the governor of New York in 1702. "That is easily answered, for . . . ye elk and moose skins are a better commodity there than here."[48]

Eventually, English perceptions—and policy—came to grips with the true situation. In 1727, a report by New York's Commissioners for Indian Affairs referred to the Kahnawake as "those Indians [who] have . . . continually been imployed to carry on the Stroud Trade between the Inhabitants of this place and the French of Canada." Indeed, "the said trade . . . is their chief Livelihood . . . [and] was also a motive for them to settle in Canada." At about this time New York authorities made their own first attempts to outlaw the trade with Montreal, in the frank expectation that "these Indians must [then] remove" to their original homeland.[49]

༆

TRADE WAS, for the Kahnawake, a point of entry into the larger world of the European colonizers; and, once begun, it led rapidly to other involvements. Above all, there was warfare—virtually continuous warfare—spanning almost three decades. The conflict known to Europeans as the War of the League of Augsburg (1688–97) would be fought in British America as King William's War; similarly, the War of the Spanish Succession (1702–14) became, for the colonists, Queen Anne's War.

The Kahnawake were drawn in immediately, on the French side. Indeed, as early as 1687, they joined a large invasion force against the Seneca (westernmost of the Iroquois nations and staunch ally of the British). This prompted fears of retaliation, to which "the Sault," with its southerly exposure, might be especially vulnerable. The French stationed a small force of soldiers at the mission, and offered the resident Indians "presents" and "supplies . . . for their subsistence . . . [because] they have been unable to hunt this year." Two years later, with enemy raiding parties all around the St. Lawrence, French leaders pleaded with the King to furnish additional support for the Kahnawake and also "some ammunition"; otherwise "it is to be feared they will alter their inclinations and join the Iroquois from whom they separated." That summer French troops were described as "transporting the corn of the Indians at the Sault mission and building them a fort."[50]

But immediately thereafter the French reached a more drastic decision: to evacuate the mission entirely and invite its people inside the gates of Montreal. This was meant as a temporary expedient, based—said the governor—on a report "that the enemy had resolved to seize them." The "exile" of the mission lasted nearly a year, and apparently was uncomfortable for all concerned. Both the priests and colonial officials worried lest close contact with ordinary Frenchmen ensnare the Indians in "drunkenness" and "bring about [their] destruction." In fact, wrote one contemporary, their stay in Montreal left them "unrecognizable, both as regards morals and piety."[51]

Whatever the substance behind such allegations, the mission was successfully relocated in autumn 1691. Its new site was a few miles west of the previous one, alongside the most turbulent stretch of the river; its new name, Kahnawakon, meant (in Mohawk) "in the rapids." Here, behind newly built "stone redoubts," it could better repulse an enemy attack. Here, too, it could avail itself of fresh farmland and escape the hardship threatened by exhausted soils.[52]

In the meantime, the level of war-related violence reached new heights. The Iroquois raids of 1689 were followed in 1690 by a series of devastating counter-strikes. Combined units of Frenchmen and "domiciled" Indians carried the fighting back to Iroquoia—and to English New York. Their most sensational single campaign occurred in midwinter (when it was least expected); its target was Schenectady, a thinly guarded settlement above Albany. The result appears, in hindsight, a rehearsal for Deerfield, complete with nighttime onset, wholesale burning and pillage, the death of several dozen residents, and the capture of many more. Kahnawake contributed a large contingent of warriors, and its war captain—one Athasata, also known as "Kryn, the Great Mohawk"—played a leadership role.[53]

The mission was no less involved in other battles, large and small, throughout the succeeding months. For all this it paid a severe price in lives lost—"more than sixty of their warriors," according to one source—and property destroyed, and routines disrupted. Among the latter was the Albany fur trade, described in 1696 as "now decay'd by reason of the Warr." Appreciative colonial officials would subsequently urge their superiors in Paris "to remember the services which the Colonies of the Iroquois Christians established in New France have rendered" and to "cause some marks of the King's bounty to be conferred on them."[54]

Yet not all French officials were appreciative. Indeed, Governor Frontenac himself grew increasingly suspicious of his allies at the Sault. Relations within the military command were far from smooth; in some cases Indian units declined, or evaded, orders from the French. Even worse, from the governor's standpoint, were the continued contacts between Kahnawake residents and the Iroquois enemy to the south. Some of this, no doubt, reflected old ties of blood and friendship; and some involved commerce. But there was, too, a persistent effort—within both Indian groups—to settle the differences between them. Negotiating "belts" traveled back and forth through the intervening valleys; visiting "ambassadors" came and went. The initiative lay largely with the New York Iroquois, who pressed on their Canadian "brethren" the idea not only of peace but also of repatriation. The Kahnawake responded warily, but would not reject such overtures outright. Moreover, they insisted—against strong French objections—on their rights of communication through enemy lines.[55]

Peace came, in stages, after 1697; its culmination, in the colonies, was the famous Montreal Treaty of 1701 between the French (with their native allies) and the entire Five Nations. A key provision guaranteed Iroquois neutrality in any future Anglo-French conflict. But there was no similar clause for Canadian Indians. In fact, England and France were again at war within the year: in Europe (alongside other Continental powers), and in America as well. Hence the "border raids" on New England of autumn 1703; hence Deerfield in February 1704. The Kahnawake, we well know, were centrally involved.[56]

And yet, as the struggle continued through another eight years, old complexities reappeared. The Indians of the Sault fought hard, and successfully, on some occasions—but half-heartedly, or not at all, on others. In one notorious instance, they began by joining a major campaign to the south, then withdrew en route "pretending" (so the French said) an outbreak of illness within their ranks. The English tried periodically to detach them altogether from their French alliance, with more "belts," some sent "underground" (i.e., in secret), and more "ambassadors," chiefly New York Mohawks—causing more suspicion among the French. The wilderness corridor between Albany and Montreal remained neutral ground, since the Iroquois were no longer cast as belligerents. The smuggling of furs continued apace, and may even have increased. The French protested, and so did the English—especially those Massachusetts residents who bore the brunt of violence. Decades later they would still recall how "the French Indians [were offered] ammunition for their skins, . . . [and then] went directly from Albany to murther in a most cruel and barbarous manner the People of New England."[57]

Warfare would continue to color the history of Kahnawake for another half century. Three times more the Indians of the Sault were called to join their French neighbors in fighting against the English: in Father Rasle's War (a bloody border conflict in the mid-1720s), King George's War (1744–48), and the French and Indian War (1754–63). Moreover, they were similarly called to French campaigns against other native groups: for example, the Fox in 1728 and the Chickasaws in 1739. They answered with their usual mix of enthusiasm and diffidence. On some occasions they would fight "ferociously," on others they held back or "retired." French governors and generals were grateful and exasperated, by turns. But the larger point became ever more clear: the Indians were "faithful" (*fidèles*) to French interests—or not—as it suited them.[58]

The impact of these many wars must have been profound. In human terms, there was both loss and gain: fighting men died, captives were taken. The infusion of new blood into the village pool, through the captives, was especially important: English blood, and Dutch, and Indian (of several sorts), a veritable mélange. The results are manifest to the present day in the enormously varied appearance of native Kahnawake: more than a few are fair-skinned and blue-eyed.[59] Moreover, expeditions and battles, and captives, too, left a lasting cultural impress—in effect, a "warrior tradition." The *esprit* of the village and the pride of its people were forged, from the start, in the fires of its war councils.[60]

⌇

IN FOLLOWING the track of warfare, this historical account of early Kahnawake has gotten somewhat ahead of itself. There are other tracks to pick up now, if only briefly.

Demography, for example. Having reached a total of nearly 700 in the mid-1680s, the population fell off sharply during the period of King William's War; a census for 1695 gives the figure 485. However, with the return of peace came a sharp jump—presumably from renewed Iroquoian migration. At the start of the new century the total was approximately 800. From then on, the numbers moved more gradually, reaching perhaps 1,000 by 1730, and 1,200 by 1760. This made Kahnawake one of the largest Indian settlements in New France—indeed, in all of eastern North America. It was larger, too, than the great majority of colonial settlements, French and English.[61]

Geography, as well. LaPrairie, we know, had yielded to Kahnawake within a few years, and then to Kahnawakon in the midst of the Iroquoian wars. In 1696, came another "removal"—a few miles farther west, but still flush on the river. The new site was called Kanatak-wenke, a Mohawk term meaning "from where one sets out." (The French, to be sure, identified all these sites as Sault St. Louis. And the Indians retained Kahnawake for referring to themselves as a people.) It was here that the Deerfield captives were brought in 1704; here that John Sheldon and other English emissaries came soon thereafter; here that John Schuyler held his fateful interview with Eunice Williams in 1713; and here, in the following year, that John Williams himself saw his daughter for the last time.[62]

The village remained at Kanatakwenke for twenty years, then was moved a fourth time. In this case the process can be followed quite closely, through petitions sent by the priests to the *conseil* in Paris. The reasons for the change were just as before: "the soil was exhausted and the woods too far away." Because—the priests explained—the villagers "cultivate nothing but Indian corn, which greatly impoverishes the soil, their lands cannot last them long." They had picked out a new site "two leagues farther up on the river." They proposed to clear "two arpents" (a little less than two acres) of land for building "about 100 cabins"; in addition, they would need a new church, a "residence of stone" for the missionaries, a "fort" (also of stone), and a wall to enclose the whole. The costs would be high, and the priests asked urgently for government support. "It is absolutely necessary to begin work there," they wrote in 1716, "in order to induce the savages not to settle among the five Iroquois nations." The latter "have done all they could this year, either by presents or threats, to attract the savages of the Sault [back] to them." This was, by now, a familiar tactic: give us what we want, or we will simply decamp. But it worked, yet again.[63]

꒰

THE 1716 REMOVAL was also their last. Kahnawake—with its original name restored—has remained a fixed place from that day to this. The church burned in 1846 (and was quickly replaced); the missionaries' "residence" still stands. The Indian "cabins" are long gone (and also replaced), but parts of the wall survive. The river flows past, though altered by a "Seaway" development. The profile of modern Montreal looms large to the east. But the sky overhead is blue as ever.

SEVEN

ᔓ

ABOUT EUNICE WILLIAMS inside this strangely positioned community we know only a very few, very bare facts. But because Kahnawake was so often described by visitors, it is possible to reconstruct at least the outlines of her experience there.

Indeed, the visitors are a remarkable resource. They include the Jesuits who were present from the start—and composed a famous set of "relations" (written reports) for their superiors overseas. And French leaders and functionaries who sought to exert some degree of authority over their *sauvages domiciliés*. And itinerant traders, military spies, political informants, "ambassadors," repatriated prisoners, and, during the last years of Eunice's life, Protestant missionaries from the English colonies to the south.

One of the visitors deserves our particular attention—and appreciation. Joseph François Lafitau was a resident priest at Kahnawake from 1712 to 1717. While there he gathered evidence for a massive and magisterial study, which he would publish in France some years later under the title *Moeurs des Sauvages Amériquains Comparées aux Moeurs des Premiers Temps*. (The currently standard English translation makes it: *Customs of the American Indians Compared with the Customs of Primitive Times*.)[1] This work contains a trove of information on the people whom Lafitau called "our Indians"—and it does seem clear that Kahnawake was his chief point of observation. The *Moeurs des Sauvages* is strikingly modern and scientific: in method, in tone, in the very shape of its inquiry. As a result, Lafitau is sometimes identified today as "the first ethnographer," or even "the first anthropologist."[2]

With his help and the help of others, the bare facts of Eunice Williams's "savage" life can be richly contextualized. In the pages that follow, the facts appear, separately and sequentially, with attached "ethnographic" discussion.

FACT: *Sometime after her arrival at Kahnawake, Eunice Williams was given an Indian name, variously spelled in the mission records as A'ongote, 8aongot, Gonaongote, 8ahongote.*[3]

Like most names at Kahnawake, this one was Mohawk Iroquois. And Mohawk Iroquois people had, by 1704, emerged as the leading part of the community. The initial wave of immigrants was mixed, including some from each of the Iroquois "Five Nations," a substantial contingent of Hurons, and a scattering of Canadian Algonquians. But the Hurons left early on, and Mohawks predominated among the later recruits. Geography itself was decisive here: The traditional Mohawk "castles" (fortified villages) lay due south and were easily accessible through the Hudson and Champlain Valleys. Indeed, this current of migrants was so strong that eventually more Mohawks would live in Kahnawake than anywhere else, including their original homeland.[4]

Mohawks, like other Iroquoian groups, attached a singular importance to names: thus "each family preserves a certain number of them, which they make use of by turns." Deceased relatives were remembered and "requickened" when their names were transferred to the living. As Lafitau noted, the force of this transfer was "in some manner . . . [to] resuscitate . . . those who, issuing from that family, have made it illustrious," and the recipient was expected to carry on "their qualities, virtues, and deeds." Implicit in "requickening," then, was the idea of replacement: the new carriers—of old names and "qualities"—would fill particular gaps in the ranks of the local community.[5]

These practices were regularly extended to captives and other new recruits from outside. Even the French priests at Kahnawake were subject to name transfers. Lafitau, for one, agreed to "revive the Indian name of the late Father Bruyas" (an admired predecessor); subsequently, the Indians "treated me . . . as they would have him himself, because I had entered into all his rights." And Father Luc Nau was given a welcoming "banquet," where he took the name "Hateriata [which] in Iroquois means 'the Brave', . . . [and] enrolled in the bear clan."[6]

Above all, these ceremonies signaled a crossing of cultural boundaries and incorporation into the Kahnawake community. And, in Eunice Williams's case, the process was delicately invoked by her name

itself. A'ongote means, literally, "she has been planted as a person."
Or, more freely: "They took her and placed her as a member of their
tribe."[7]

Whether the same name had belonged to another before Eunice—
presumably another captive—we have no way of knowing. But with
or without the replacement motif, such "plantings" took deep root.
Lafitau described the warmth, and fullness, of the standard sequence.
"If the captive is a man who requickens an Ancient, . . . he becomes
important himself and has authority in the village." And: "if the captive is a girl, given to a household where there is nobody of her sex in
a position to sustain the lineage . . . all the hope of the family is placed
in [her]." A certain Captain Franquet, who visited Kahnawake in
1752, noted the presence of "many English children taken prisoner in
the last war whom they have adopted. . . . [They] are raised in the
manner of . . . savages . . . and when they are grown, they never
dream of returning to their homes."[8]

In fact, the same result could have been observed at any point
during the preceding half-century. Eunice Williams was one of at least
a dozen Deerfield children who came to Kahnawake as captives in
Queen Anne's War. Five of these, all girls between the ages of six and
eleven, would remain for the rest of their lives—would marry and
bear children, would become fully integrated and "Indianized." Four
others may also have remained permanently (though the evidence is
uncertain). Still others stayed for periods of varying duration, some
for as long as twenty-five years. And additional English children, not
from Deerfield, were similarly "placed" in Kahnawake.[9]

There is no way now to discover how much, or even whether, these
young captives identified with one another as a group. But perhaps
they played together, or prayed together (when out of sight of the resident Jesuits). And perhaps in the early, most difficult phase of their
acculturation they could take comfort in knowing that it was shared.

FACT: *The still extant records are sprinkled with references to Eunice
Williams's closest Indian connections: particularly, to "her master"
(also called "the Indian who owns her") and "the woman that has
Mr. Williams's daughter."*[10]

For most captives acculturation included adoption into one or another family. And the references noted above point, almost certainly,
to Eunice's adoptive parents.

But family at Kahnawake and family at Deerfield were markedly different things. New Englanders of the time lived in households of a generalized "European" type. Their form was "nuclear": the residential unit was typically husband, wife, and "natural" children. (Occasional, usually temporary, add-ons might include a servant or two, an apprentice, or an elderly grandparent.) Property descended through the male line, and authority, too, was centered in men. Children were raised in accordance with "Puritan" norms and values—were subject to careful discipline, and were obliged, most especially, to curtail their expression of personal "will."[11]

The Kahnawake Indians diverged from this pattern at virtually every point. Take, for example, the point of residence. Traditionally, Iroquoian people had lived in vast multifamily "longhouses"; some reports from the early seventeenth century described as many as a dozen nuclear units—comprising fifty or sixty individual persons—assembled under a single roof. The Kahnawake reduced these dimensions substantially, but not all the way to the European norm. "There are sixty houses," wrote one of the priests in 1682, "which is to say 120 to 150 families, as there are at least two in each house." And a map of Kahnawake, drawn in the middle of the next century, suggests a similar distribution: seventy-eight houses, to shelter a total population of roughly 1,200. The average of fifteen to sixteen persons per household was more than twice what obtained in English communities of the time.*[12]

Moreover, the principles that governed membership in these households were extraordinary by European standards. In traditional Iroquoian practice, wrote Lafitau, "the husband and wife do not leave their family and lodge to set up a family and residence apart." Instead, each "remains at [his or her] home, and the children born of these marriages . . . are counted as being of the wife's lodge and family, not the husband's." The presence at Kahnawake of this "matrilocal" system was confirmed in specific cases by the priests: for example, a reference by Father Cholonec to a certain "good old woman and three of her daughters—all married and living in the same house with her."[13]

Alongside "matrilocal," two more anthropological terms suggest themselves: "matrilineal" and "matrifocal." Kinship and family "line" were measured by reference to women. Marriage was based on a principle of "exogamy": partners must be chosen outside the mother's household. Lafitau recalled an interesting case "when one of our mis-

*The map in question implies, without making definite, that most Kahnawake houses were indeed two-family units. A few, however, are drawn so as to suggest the co-residence of four families.

sionaries proposed the marriage of a captive to some member of the lodge to which she had been given . . . [and] the Indians rejected the proposal with horror." From this he deduced both the strength of the maternal connection and the fullness of the adoption process.[14]

In fact, wrote Lafitau, "the father's household is foreign, as it were, to the children." And another early visitor commented that "in general, the children are regarded as belonging more to the mother than the father." Moreover, said a third, for the father himself "his mother and his sisters are more dear than his wife." Kahnawake men would always retain "the right to be fed" in their mother's household, where "care was taken to guard their portion"—and where they would "ordinarily spend most of the day."[15]

Indian people, and Iroquoians in particular, were notorious among Europeans for indulging—indeed "spoiling"—their young. "We may justly reproach them with the way in which they bring up their children," wrote Pierre Charlevoix in an early-eighteenth-century travel journal; "they do not so much as know what it is to correct them." And another traveler commented, just a few years later, that "the [Indian] child is not troubled in any way; they leave him to do entirely as he wishes." Toddlers and younger children were typically left "naked in the lodge"; mothers would "let them do everything that they like . . . under the pretext that they are not yet at the age of reason." Lafitau was especially struck by their playfulness: "One sees them jostling each other with kicks and punches." Older children were given little chores—"they follow their mothers and work for the family"— but through suggestion, not firm discipline. Moreover: "No one . . . would dare to strike and punish them."[16]

In short, the "savage" child experienced a notably mild regimen— at least by European standards. And this seems to have been true for captive children as well. Franquet explained the reluctance of captives to return home by "the liberty and licentiousness with which they are raised," and described an Englishman, introduced to him at Kahna-wake, as a clear case in point. Deerfield's own Joseph Kellogg, taken in the massacre but subsequently repatriated, confronted the parallel question of why so many had willingly accepted Catholicism. His answer was as follows: "The Indians indulge the english boys abundantly [and] let them have the Liberty they will . . . and so an easy way of life and libertinism is more prevailing with them than any affection they have to religion." These outcomes of captivity seemed to underscore the differences between English and Indian childrearing.[17]

Equally different were the physical surroundings of domestic life.

From framed wooden dwellings, of square or rectangular shape and replete with English "appurtenances," captives moved to homes of Iroquoian design. The latter were built "in the form of a vault or arbor," with rough posts at the sides and bent saplings to create an arched roof; these, in turn, were covered with elm-bark. Traditional Iroquois longhouses extended to as much as 100 feet, with a lengthwise alignment of hearths (*feux*) down the center and smoke-holes overhead. Kahnawake dwellings, like Kahnawake families, were far smaller: A single hearth was perhaps the norm, and two or three the maximum. Indeed, by the 1750s (according to Franquet) "these savages [were developing] . . . the taste for building houses French style, in square frames, or even in masonry." Still, their "ordinary cabins" (the great majority) followed the old model. A drawing from mid-century shows Kahnawake as an array of "arbor"-like structures.[18]

Typically, their interiors were simple—and very functional. Longhouse construction had always included open "platforms" along each side (for lounging and sleeping), and roughly the same pattern was retained at Kahnawake. Franquet speaks of side "cots," assembled from "planks, . . . elevated about two feet above the ground [and] covered with mats of rushes or straw." The "place of honor," he said, was near the door and was customarily reserved for the *chef de la cabane*.[19]

Europeans found these arrangements uncomfortably close and disorderly; Franquet called them a virtual "pell-mell." Lafitau, though less fastidious than most, deplored the "fleas and bedbugs" of the houses in summertime—and the way they "stink . . . when the Indians dry their fish." In winter there was cold so penetrating that "I do not know how they can survive . . . as little covered as they are, especially those who sleep far from the fires." Worst of all, in any season, was the smoke—which Lafitau called "unendurable . . . when one is standing erect," and which another priest found "so dense that I fail to understand how they do not lose their sight."[20]

For Eunice Williams, the changes may have been especially abrupt—more so even than for other captives. Her Deerfield family was, after all, an accentuated version of the main English type. Her house itself was more spacious and elaborate than most—as befitted the Williamses' high status. There were "chambers" of several sorts, and furnishings well beyond the average for a frontier settlement, and books, and other accoutrements of "civilized" life.[21] Her father's eminence in the local community must have translated into special, even "patriarchal," prerogatives at home. Certainly, in later years, he showed himself to be an active, forceful parent. He tells us, in his famous narrative, that Eunice "could read very well," and had learned her catechism. And perhaps she was, more generally, a precocious example of "Puritan" childhood. The training, the discipline, she experienced would surely have been firm—and carefully channeled.[22]

From this to . . . a new family, a different family, in utterly "savage" surroundings. An Indian "cabin" of essentially a single room, with hearth instead of chimney, rude "cots" instead of proper beds, straw mats instead of rugs and blankets, and a far simpler technology of domestic life. Adoptive parents: a father who was not a strong presence, a mother whose ministrations were probably diffused among other female relatives. (The Mohawk word for "mother" applied to aunts as well.) A relaxed, even carefree, style of life, in which children were left to express themselves as they pleased, and training was by example only.

Different it was, very different. And yet, within a relatively short time, it took. By 1707, Eunice was reported to be "unwilling to return." And the Indians—including, one presumes, her new family—"would as soon part with their hearts" as with this successfully "planted" child.[23]

FACT: *Within two years—perhaps less—of her arrival in Kahnawake, Eunice Williams had "forgot [how] to speak English."*[24]

This change seemed especially shocking to Eunice's Deerfield family. The phrasing quoted above is from a letter of consolation written to John Williams by his friend Sewall; presumably, it answered one from Williams himself. *The Redeemed Captive* touched poignantly on the same theme.

The process of such forgetting can only be imagined now. Quite possibly it included coercive measures. Joseph Kellogg would remember of his own stay in Kahnawake that "the Indians prohibited the [captive] children speaking together in the English tongue; if we did speak, it must be in the Macqua [Mohawk] language."*[25] And the children in question presumably included Eunice. Moreover, psychology could well have played in here. The trauma of capture—including, as it did, the deaths of mother and siblings—might call forth its

---

*Eunice's brother Stephen reported the following about his own stay among a nearby group of Abenaki: "While I lived there I observed that some English children . . . when alone . . . would talk familiarly with me in English about their own country, etc., whereas, when before the Indians, they would pretend that they could not speak English."

own "repression"; forgetting everything would be a kind of defense. Whatever the actual sources of change, the result was deeply significant. From now on Eunice could communicate only with her new people, in her new place, within a new set of customary forms. Language was the pivot and symbol of her personal acculturation.

The culture revealed itself, first of all, by way of appearances: dress and coiffure, for example. Most visitors agreed that Kahnawake clothing was a curious blend of native and European styles. Lafitau grasped its organizing principle in this comment: "At present, most of the Indians who are in contact with the Europeans have changed only the material of their clothing, keeping their former style." Thus, instead of fur robes, they wore wraparound blankets imported from France. And leggings of wool or linen, not leather. They added to their decorative repertoire European lace and ribbons (chiefly as garment borders), while also retaining such traditional elements as moose hair, porcupine quills, and bird feathers. For footwear some used "moccasins of smoke-dried deer-skin," others "shoes of French make with silver buckles." They took special pride in their hair: visitors reported elaborate combing and braiding (especially among the women), cutting and shaping (among the men), and greasing (both sexes); in addition, beads, eelskin, and feathers were frequently applied. Both men and women used jewelry: earrings, necklaces, bracelets, pendants of many shapes and materials. Both men and women put paint on their faces. Lafitau noted that personal ornamentation was principally for the young, and "the moment this age has gone by, [they turn to] living in quite the opposite way." A middle- or old-aged person sought to show thereby that "his mind is on serious things."[26]

For captives the combined effect of these sartorial practices must have been strong. New Englanders of the colonial era were not as austere as we used to imagine; still, their presentation was far less flamboyant than the prevalent mode at Kahnawake. Moreover, captive children had no choice in these matters; just as they were forced to accept the native language of their captors, so, too, were they obliged to adopt a native appearance. Sometimes the change was ritualized as part of the adoption process. Titus King, captured by Canadian Abenakis in the 1750s, was made to exchange his "shurt . . . and Sleve buttons" for "an old shurt of theres that stand with Indian Sweet [sweat]"; at the same time his captors "put wonpon in my neck [and] painted my Face." As a result, "I began to think I was an Indian." If the captives themselves were thus persuaded, so also were other Europeans who might subsequently encounter them. Thomas Hutchinson, governor of Massachusetts, recalled meeting one who "had so much the appearance of an Indian, not only in his dress, but in his behavior, and also his complexion, that nobody had any suspicion to the contrary."[27]

Other elements of Indian appearance were harder to specify. Some observers admired their posture—and their very physique. "The savages are of better build than the French," wrote Father Nau after his arrival at Kahnawake in 1735. "Nearly all the men of our mission are nearer six feet in height than five. Their countenance is in keeping with their stature, and their features are regular." Lafitau noted their propensity for lounging "tranquilly" when not engaged in productive activity: "The Indian, wherever he may be . . . is always seated or lying down." Moreover, "they are . . . surprised to see the Europeans continually pace to and fro." Comments like these hint at distinctive modes of body language (as we would say), itself a form of cultural display.[28]

Also on the visible surface: the material objects, the "things" of Indian life. For travel: canoes (those at Kahnawake were made of elm-bark), and snowshoes, and sleds, and "packs," and tumplines. For hunting: traps of various kinds (depending on the target animal). For storage: leather "casks," and bags made from basswood bark, and splint and straw baskets. In other respects they had, by 1700, given up their "traditional" technology and borrowed heavily from Europeans. No more clay pots; iron kettles instead. Steel, instead of stone, axes. And, most especially, guns instead of bows, arrows, and spears. (War "hatchets" they did, however, retain.) A series of excavations at the Kanatakwenke site, in the 1950s, produced a bewildering mélange of remains. European nails, knives, hinges, fish-hooks, pins, and assorted tools. Indian beads, amulets, pipe bowls and stems, and clam-shell spoons. As usual, Lafitau saw the complexities of cultural change. He described, for example, the way the Kahnawake used their newly acquired axes of sharpened steel to continue their old practice of girdling—not directly felling—nearby trees. And he noted, too, their preservation of a few "ancient" ax-heads (in stone) as "a precious heritage for the children."[29]

Less directly seen, though hardly invisible, was the prevailing pattern of social relations. European visitors remarked a certain formality, even ceremonialism, among their Kahnawake hosts. When Captain Franquet arrived at the village in 1752, he was greeted by "20 or 25 [men], the big chief at their head." Next came a round of pipe-smoking, then speech-making, then gift exchanges, then more pipe-smoking, then a final, solemn "shaking of the hands." Franquet was struck by the elaborate costumes of the headmen and by the way they "speak only figuratively." Actual diplomacy was more formal still—with specially designated orators, and ritual salutations, and the giving of wampum-belts.[30]

"Feasts" had long been central to the social world of Iroquoians—and continued to be central at Kahnawake. The priests, in their *Relations*, described many such occasions: some organized to repair a social breach, others as a form of "public penance," still others to announce a conversion to Christianity. There were war feasts, too, where dogs were boiled and eaten, hatchets "lifted up," dances danced, songs sung. "Each warrior had a tomahawk, spear, or war-mallet in his hand," wrote James Smith about one of these, "and they all moved regularly towards the east, or the way they intended to go to war." The protocol was elaborate and disciplined; Lafitau described numerous details, evidently from personal observation. In some cases the traditional Iroquoian "eat all" principle obtained: "participants . . . [would] have to eat everything set before them . . . from morning until evening."[31]

On private and personal relations our sources are less specific. But most Kahnawake visitors noticed a kind of decorum—a pervasive spirit of "gentleness" and "respect." "Excesses" of emotion and behavior were rare, and "their language is chaste."[32] Indeed, wrote Lafitau, "they have . . . an admirable composure, and do not know what it is to burst out into insults. I do not remember ever seeing any one of them angry."[33]

Differences of age and gender counted for much. Young people treated their elders with "the greatest deference." The categories of "Old Men" and "Young Men" held deep significance, especially in political affairs, and something similar obtained among women as well. Men and women were separated in various public situations: for example, in religious worship and in most kinds of work. "Young girls would carefully avoid stopping . . . to talk with persons of a different sex." And young men "maintain certain reserves, in public." Yet this etiquette of distance may also have promoted a certain competitiveness. "Old Men" and "Young Men" were notoriously at odds over decisions on warfare—the latter preferring bold action, the former urging caution and restraint. And men and women contested for preeminence in religion. "The women . . . learned the prayers sooner than the men," noted one priest; indeed, the piety of Kahnawake women, especially in the group around Kateri, was celebrated throughout Canada. The men, for their part, sought a similar distinction, since "they will not let themselves be outdone."[34]

Officially, however, competition was disapproved, and the local culture expressed at many points an ethic of reciprocity. "Charity united them," wrote one early missionary of his Kahnawake charges, "among whom sociability, visits, hospitality, feasts, and mutual sharing are much in vogue." Even outsiders would be included here. Smith was taught, while living with his captor's "band" in the 1750s, that "when strangers come to our camp, we ought always to give them the best that we have."[35] The priests were repeatedly impressed—and dismayed by the implied rebuke to their own people. Father Claude Chauchetière spoke for many:

> We see in these savages the fine roots of human nature, which are entirely corrupted in civilized nations. . . . Living in common, without disputes, content with little, guiltless of avarice . . . it is impossible to find people more patient, more hospitable, more affable, more liberal, more moderate in their language. In fine, all our fathers and the French who have lived with the savages consider that life flows on more gently among them than with us.[36]

But other elements of "savage" morality seemed more problematic. Iroquoians, for example, displayed an absolute "love of liberty," a "toleration and impunity . . . in which everyone does what seems good in his own eyes." The priests viewed this as "a very great disorder." And French colonial officials expressed similar opinions; their authority would count for little among "people who possess no subordination" and are "opposed to all constraint."[37]

An additional cluster of Iroquoian values referred, more or less directly, to their warrior tradition. Personal "honor" and "the glory of the nation" were, according to Charlevoix, "the chief movers in all enterprises." James Smith was exhorted by his adoptive clansmen always to "do great things and never be found in any . . . little actions." When wronged or slighted, a man must seek redress; otherwise he would lose respect. Personal courage and endurance in the face of pain were also greatly prized—and for women no less than men. Lafitau described "one woman two of whose nails were torn off in my presence . . . who did not utter a cry nor a sigh, and I noticed only a slight expression of pain on her face." Youngsters were trained for feats of courage "from the tenderest age." Parents gave instruction in the "heroism" of their ancestors, and children responded by creating their own tests of endurance, such as "putting burning coals" against their bare arms "and challenging each other as to who would hold out with most firmness."[38]

How these unfamiliar patterns of belief and value conveyed themselves to captives—especially young captives—is impossible to say. But the early stages of captivity itself must have served as a kind of initiation. Certainly the captives knew pain: in the assault on their homes, and the loss of their loved ones, and the rigors of the "march" that followed. The march, indeed, was a kind of torture, which they must somehow endure, or die. And if they endured, they saw vivid instances of the Indians' commitment to equality and sharing. Food was scrupulously divided, even in periods of extreme scarcity. Differences were negotiated. Help was given, and received, as needed. Presumably, then, when they reached Canada, captives had already begun to learn an important set of cultural lessons.[39]

FACT: *By 1713, and probably several years before, Eunice Williams had acquired a new Christian name: Marguerite.*[40] *This was the official mark of her rebaptism and entry into the Catholic Church.*

The conversion of English captives was, of course, a primary goal of the Jesuits and other priests throughout Canada. One source (only) describes this process in detail: Joseph Kellogg's remembrance of his own time at Kahnawake. According to Kellogg, the priests began by isolating their younger prisoners from "all the grown persons"; then "they used all their art to make us in love with their religion." They scoffed at "our [Protestant] bibles," and "told us the Rise of our Religion was King Henries the eight Wickedness, [and] that he killed two Wives and married his own Daughter." They particularly inveighed against "Luther's and Calvin's apostasie"; of Luther they said that "he had eaten a bushel of salt with the Divel." (And so on, at very great length.) Kellogg's account is one of unrelenting pressure, and it may have been self-serving. For Kellogg did yield to "their insinuations to be a Roman Catholick"—at least for a time—and was anxious to explain himself upon returning to New England. Still, even allowing for exaggeration, we can glimpse some kernels of reality here. There is, in fact, convergent and corroborating evidence in the experience of other captives as well.[41]

The Jesuits themselves afford occasional views of the same process from the other side. In 1699, Father Jacques Bigot wrote of young captives at another mission near Kahnawake: "At first I find them greatly prejudiced against us, but they gradually allow themselves to be persuaded by the devotion of our Abenakis [the local Indians] and their zeal for prayer—which they do not find, they say, in their [own] colony." This experience would, evidently, take deep hold: dozens of English children had recently refused repatriation. And religion was, according to Bigot, a key element in their decisions. "I shall be lost," one boy reportedly told his Indian captors; "keep me with you, so that I may not be damned." About the "persuasion" of Eunice herself we know only a little. "They force me to say some prayers in Latin," she told her father when he first visited her at Kahnawake, "but I don't understand one word of them. I hope it won't do me any harm." Harmful or not, she became a Catholic when still a child: this, too, was part of her ongoing transformation.[42]

The center of Kahnawake Catholicism was, of course, the mission itself. And the mission was visibly symbolized by the Church of St. François Xavier: the largest building in the entire community, steepled, altogether impressive. Alongside and joined to it by an enclosed passageway was the priests' residence. Nearby stood a guardhouse (in which, from time to time, a small contingent of French soldiers might be stationed). And a store run by three French merchant ladies, "the sisters Desauniers." And assorted stables, sheds, gardens, and animal yards. The whole was designed to constitute a "fort"; but the high stone walls, originally planned for all sides, in fact enclosed only two. The parts facing the river (north) and the Indian village (east) remained open, until at least the 1750s.[43]

Within these borders the priests sought to maintain (what one called) "a fully organized church." They delighted in describing their regular routine. There were morning and evening prayers, sometimes with a special sunrise round "for those who have to go out to the fields to work." There was "our everyday mass" with hymns appropriate to the season. There were special "recitations" for the children, and catechism classes for unbaptized adults. There were hours spent in the village, "going about visiting the sick and . . . deciding disputes which may have arisen." On Sundays there were confessions to hear, and high mass, and (in the afternoon) the singing of vespers. And on saints' days there were special worship "exercises." There were meetings as well of "two associations . . . the sodality and the holy family"—composed of the "really devout souls."[44]

To all this, insisted the Jesuits, the Indians responded with extraordinary devotion, so much so that visitors from outside were sometimes moved to tears. And the effects spilled over to the wider community around Montreal. French men and women, no less than Indians, made "pilgrimages" to Kateri Tekakwitha's grave: "to cure the diseases that ordinary medicines cannot relieve, they swallow in water or in broth a little dust from her tomb." Moreover, "festivals" were held annually, throughout the Montreal region, in honor of Kateri and three other "martyrs" from Kahnawake.[45]

Such, then, was the spirituality of converts like Eunice Williams. And yet (as noted previously) it was not defined entirely in French Catholic terms. The wampum "collars" decorating the mission church, the warriors' costumes sometimes worn to mass, the special "feasts" of penance, the self-mortification of Kateri herself (and her followers) bespoke a blended, or syncretic, influence.[46] Moreover, out in the village—where most Jesuits could not, or would not, see—a native spirituality survived. Fortunately for us, Lafitau did see—and was frank to write about it.

For example, he saw shamans. (Other Frenchmen called them "jugglers"; we might say "witch-doctors.") He remembered especially the way they went "visibly into that state of ecstasy, which binds all the senses and keeps them suspended." He thought it "heroic . . . [even] among Christianized Iroquois . . . when, in illnesses, one does not have recourse to shamans."[47]

He saw charms and fetishes—such as "little bundles of twisted hair, bones of serpents or extraordinary animals, pieces of iron or bronze, figures of dough or corn husks," believed to promote good health or good luck. He knew "several Indians . . . [who] said to me often, speaking of their illnesses, that they knew very well secrets for curing them."[48]

He saw divination by dreams. "This principle," long powerful for Iroquoians, and "still widespread among our Indians, gives them an obstinate respect for their dreams passing all imagination." Indeed, he apparently witnessed an annual ceremony called "the Feast of Dreams or Desires," when "all the village goes into a kind of frenzy."[49]

He saw individual villagers perform gestures of libation: "throwing small morsels of food served them on the ground or in the fire, or pouring out drops of liquor given them." And he watched large groups conduct animal sacrifice: "they pray to the Sun to accept this offering, to lead them and give them victory over their enemies; to make the wheat grow in their fields, to cause them to have good hunting or good fishing."[50]

Finally, he saw elaborate "round dances," sometimes ordered by shamans "as a religious rite," sometimes "used [as] . . . an exercise for amusement." About these he allowed himself a rare opinion: "I have not felt . . . pleasure . . . at our Indian festivals." The music and dancing he found "barbarous" and "revolting." But the villagers themselves were "mad with enthusiasm about feasts of this sort," some of which would continue "whole days and nights." Indeed, these events were "so noisy that they [would] make the entire village tremble."[51]

We have a second witness to this complex, two-track spirituality: not a "visitor," but the young Pennsylvania captive James Smith. Smith's impressions were heavily influenced by one Tecaughretanego, an admired "brother" in his adoptive family and a man who still adhered to "the Indians' old religion." From Tecaughretanego Smith learned the rudiments of that system: the benevolent oversight of the Great Spirit "that rules and governs the universe," the "great numbers of inferior deities," and the ceaseless activity of "demons." He watched a shaman "conjuring" in the moonlight, supposedly to counter an enemy threat. He helped Tecaughretanego build a "sweat house," in order to "purify himself before he would address the Supreme Being." And he concluded that Kahnawake spiritual life defied easy summary. While some rejected Catholicism outright, others were (in Tecaughretanego's words) "a kind of half Roman Catholics." And still others "profess to be Roman Catholics, but even these retain many of the notions of their ancestors."[52]

Catholic, half-Catholic, devotees of an "ancestral" religion: thus, too—we must surely imagine—the famed "unredeemed captive" from Deerfield. Her names tell the story. Except to her blood-relatives in New England, she was Eunice no more. Instead—in Kahnawake—she was both Marguerite and A'ongote. And so she would long remain.

FACT: *In the opening months of 1713, or possibly a little before, Eunice Williams married an Indian man identified in the mission records as François Xavier Arosen. (He apparently had an additional name variously spelled as Tairagie, Turroger, and DeRoguers.)*[53]

Of Arosen's life at Kahnawake very little is definitely known. Indeed, apart from his connection to Eunice, there is only one certain datum about Arosen: the record of his death "at an advanced age" (*d'un age avancé*) on 22 January 1765. He was buried the following day.*[54]

Much can be learned, however, about general patterns of courtship and marriage-making among the Kahnawake: from Lafitau, from captives like James Smith, and even from demographic information contained in the mission archives. The archives permit us, for example, to discover when marriage most commonly took place. When, in the annual cycle of the seasons? midsummer, June and July, and midwinter, January and February. (This pattern contrasted sharply with European preferences of the time; French Canadians, and New Englanders, too, married in hugely disproportionate numbers during the late fall.) And: when, in the life cycles of the people involved? Fourteen and a half years was the average age of marriage for Kahnawake females; by eighteen fewer than twenty percent remained unmarried. For males, the average was twenty-one. (Again, these figures differed dramatically from European norms; twenty-two and twenty-seven were the comparable averages among French Canadians.[55])

The process of courtship, the personal experiences leading up to marriage, were no less different. In general, thought Lafitau, "marriages are regulated rather by interest and mutual respect than by the inclination of the contractants." Indeed, matchmaking was viewed as a project of entire households, with the "matrons" (senior women) typically in charge. The project included an appraisal of other households: some were avoided because of their small size, others because they included "personalities difficult to live with." The potential spouse's personal qualities were also important: "what is sought in a young man is that he be brave, a good hunter and warrior; in a girl that she be of good reputation, hard working, and of a docile personality."[56]

An initial approach would come from the household of the young man: "when the matrons have determined the choice of a wife, . . . they go to make the proposal to the girl's relatives." The latter would then hold their own "council" before making a response. And the future husband and wife would have to give their consent. If the proposal was accepted all around, presents were exchanged ("wampum belts, skins, fur covers"), and the husband would go to the wife's *cabane*, "accompanied by all his relatives," to receive there a "nuptial

---

*An attempt has been made, in a previous chapter, to explore his possible involvement in a complex plot between the Kahnawake and their "brethren" in the Mohawk Valley during the middle years of Queen Anne's War. But this was, and remains, speculative.

bowl" of corn soup. "And that," said Lafitau, "is the whole ceremony."[57]

Once the marriage was made, "these allied households [would] con-
tract new obligations towards each other." Not only must the wife
prepare food for her husband and provisions for his travels (when
hunting and making war); she would also "help the people of her
husband's maternal household" by giving labor in their fields and
supplying wood to their cabin. The husband, for his part, must give
"all his hunt . . . during the first year of marriage" to his wife's family;
thereafter he "must share it with them." Sexual fidelity within marriage
was expected, but not always achieved. Men, for example, occasionally
took "concubines . . . when in the field." And the mission registers
identify a considerable numbers of births as *illegitime*—nearly twenty
percent of all those recorded.[58]

Some marriages failed—for a variety of reasons common everywhere—and when that happened, there was ready acceptance of
"separation" (in effect, a divorce). James Smith wrote that spouses
"are under no legal obligation to live together, if they are both willing
to part." Separating husbands would frequently try to claim their
sons, but the wives, "looking upon themselves always as mistresses,"
could usually prevent that. The children, since they were "always
brought up under their mother's wing," were inclined to side with
her.[59]

Only at a few small points can we connect this generalized portrait
with the actual experiences of Eunice (Marguerite A'ongote) Williams
and François Xavier Arosen. Eunice's age at the time of their wedding—sixteen—was within the usual range. And their timing apparently conformed to the regular midwinter peak in Kahnawake
marriages. Had their respective households negotiated the terms of
their union? It appears that some village families did apply the traditional courtship standards—and did play a supervisory role—with
their captive children. However, with Eunice the case may have been
different; so, at least, John Schuyler's account of his 1713 interview
implies. The mission priests told Schuyler that Eunice and Arosen
had presented themselves to be married, evidently without families;
that they felt "joined together" and had "resolved never to leave one
the other"; and that, if denied the usual ceremony, "they mattered not
. . . but [they would] live together heathen-like" anyway.[60] With them
"the inclination of the contractants" (in Lafitau's rather stiff phrase)
may, after all, have proved decisive.

FACT: *Eunice and Arosen had children—whose arrival, in two in-stances, was specifically noted in the mission records. Their daughter Catherine was born 4 August 1736, and baptized the following day. Another daughter, Marie, was baptized 23 September 1739, following her birth "recently" before. In addition, they almost certainly had a son—apparently named John, and born at a time and place which cannot now be determined.*[61]

This is surely no more than a piece of Eunice's childbearing history: two children, probably her last two, born as she reached and passed the age of forty, plus a third whose existence can barely be docu-mented. There must have been others—as fragmentary evidence strongly implies. An early-nineteenth-century source (which cannot be verified) speaks of her "eight children," only two of whom "lived to grow up." And, more reliably, her brother Stephen's diary includes the following entry for 27 July 1722: "This day I also saw J. Kellogue who is come from Canada. He brings bad news [from] thence. My poor sister lives with her Indian husband; has had two children, one is living, the other not."[62]

Unfortunately, the mission registers do not survive from any year before 1735; otherwise we would, very likely, find hard evidence of additional children born to Eunice and Arosen. But the same registers permit inferences about average Kahnawake experience with childbearing.

Two patterns seem noteworthy. The first was a surprisingly low rate of fertility overall—which, in turn, reflected long spacing between births (to the same mother). Three years was the most commonly experienced "birth interval" for Kahnawake mothers—whereas, in European populations of the same era, two years was typical. Lafitau noticed these differences and attributed them to "a kind of sterility." Indian women, he wrote, "although of a strong and robust constitu-tion, have not the fecundity seen elsewhere, especially in northern Europe." In fact, there was another, more likely cause, which Lafitau also noticed but did not understand: the contraceptive effect of lacta-tion. "They breast-feed their children as long as they can, weaning them only when it becomes necessary." (Other visitors put the usual age of weaning at "three years running" or "three to four years"; and one believed that "custom" enjoined nursing women from all sexual contact with their husbands.)[63]

Lafitau also felt that Kahnawake women "take very little care of themselves during . . . pregnancy." They would continue with their regular work until virtually the time of delivery—would "go into the fields," and even "carry heavy burdens." Childbirth itself they managed with "ease," and sometimes entirely alone. Subsequently, "they return to their lodge as if nothing has happened, and from that very day they seem capable of their usual duties." If perchance they should "suffer" in the delivery, "they conquer their pains by an admirable force of will, and abstain . . . from giving the least sign of weakness." Lafitau recalled, in this regard, an exception which helped to show the rule: "In our mission, when a woman had shown too much sensitiveness to pain some years ago, the old people were heard discussing this phenomenon and concluding very solemnly that she must not have any more children because she would not be able to bring into the world anything except cowards."[64]

Visitors to Kahnawake were invariably struck by the prevalent style of infant care. Lafitau noted its "real, solid, and lasting . . . tenderness," and Charlevoix called it "beyond all expression." Its most remarkable aspect, from a European standpoint, was the use of a cradleboard, "which enables the mothers to carry [their infants] everywhere with them." Lafitau described the delicacy—and ingenuity—of cradleboard construction and the "the bracelets . . . and trinkets . . . which [when suitably attached] serve as . . . playthings to divert the child." (A number of early Kahnawake cradleboards, elaborately carved and decorated, can be seen in Canadian museums today.) Swaddled in "good furs," resting on a bed of down, and gently rocked by the motion of his mother's body, an infant could only feel "content."[65]

For all that, his health—and his very life—were frequently imperiled. This is not something on which the visitors much commented, but the mission registers make it plain enough. Infants in Kahnawake died at an inordinately high rate: in one twenty-year period, half of all deaths in the village were of children under three years old. Translated into rates of "age-specific mortality" (as demographers would say), this meant an almost one-in-three chance of dying in the first year of life, and approximately one-in-six in the second year. (The comparable rates for most eighteenth-century European populations were less by half.) The causes of this mortality cannot now be discovered, but infectious disease was almost certainly crucial. The totals of infant death varied markedly from year to year—the lowest was five, the highest twenty-nine—which suggests the periodic appearance of contagious pathogens. Little wonder that Kahnawake mothers were such tender caregivers.[66]

There remains the recurrent question of connecting Eunice Williams's individual experience to these larger patterns. The three-year spacing between her two known daughters looks right, for one thing. And if we imagine similar spacing during the preceding twenty-three years of her marriage, the sum of her childbearing would indeed reach eight (the number given in that early but unverifiable source). It seems virtually certain, however, that no others of her children (besides the last two) survived to adulthood. And this can be seen as an extreme case of the generally stark life-chances for the young.

Two final points about Kahnawake childhood. Infants were ordinarily taken, within days of their birth, to be baptized in the mission church—and to receive a Christian name. This was specifically true for the daughters born to Eunice in the late 1730s. But a Kahnawake child would also receive another name—an Indian name—apparently in a traditional ceremony "performed at a feast" when (s)he reached the age of three or four years. Here, too, Eunice's daughters seem to have conformed to type. Catherine would be identified as Gassinontie (translates to "flying leg") and Marie as Skentsiese ("newfish") when mentioned later in the mission records. Like their mother, they were chartered in two worlds.[67]

FACT: *At some (undetermined) point in her life, Eunice Williams acquired a second Indian name. This was "Gannenstenhawi," which can be roughly translated "she brings in corn."*[68]

We have no full account of Kahnawake naming practices, but their flexibility—one could well say their fluidity—is immediately apparent. A Christian name and an Indian name: the minimum for each person. And, in many cases, two (or more?) Indian names. "They even sometimes change them as they grow older," wrote Pierre Charlevoix. "There are some which cannot be used after a certain age." It is tempting to think that "A'ongote" was Eunice Williams's childhood name—referring, as it did, to her beginnings in the community. And that "Gannenstenhawi" was her specifically adult name—pointing to the responsibilities of a mature woman.[69]

In fact, every Kahnawake woman was involved with "bringing in corn." But this deceptively simple phrase compressed a large variety of separate activities. There was planting and tending corn fields. And harvesting the fully grown corn crop. And braiding the husks together so as to form corn shocks. And drying the bound shocks on large wooden frames. And shelling the dried ears (usually not till wintertime) for storage in large casks made of elm bark. And grinding the stored kernels (as needed) in wooden mortars; and sifting the product (corn flour) through small trays of interwoven branches; and leaching the sifted flour on hot ashes, and boiling it in water over a cook-fire; and serving the finished "stew"—known throughout Canada by the name *sagamité*—in "as many little pots or plates . . . as there are people in the lodge." And carefully guarding a few bits for the next season's planting. An ever-turning, endlessly repeated cycle: women bringing in corn.[70]

Visitors to the woodland cultures of northeastern North America were struck by one practice, above all: Women go into the fields. In England, and throughout western Europe, it was never so; farm work, as "heavy work," belonged to men. Certainly this was true of grain agriculture: women shouldn't do it. What to make, then, of Indian women? Said the visitors, almost as one: They are no better than slaves.[71]

There was, moreover, another piece to this assessment: Indian men are parasites—and tyrants. They make hardly any contribution to the sustenance of their families and communities; for the most part, they are "idle." True, from time to time they "go on a hunt"—but this is largely "sport" and "pastime." Otherwise they are fed and flattered by their "squaws." They act the part of a leisured aristocracy—an aristocracy of gender—and it is wrong.[72]

The visitors did not, perhaps could not, understand. Gender was indeed an organizing principle here, but not in the way they conceived it. The boundaries, the human ecology of gender, were different, to be sure. Indian women, including Kahnawake women, were farmers par excellence. They raised the corn and much else besides: beans, said Lafitau, and "pumpkins of a species different from those of France," and watermelons, and sunflowers. Much of this work they did together, in "bands according to the different quarters where they have their fields"; typically, they "pass from one field to the other, helping each other." In spring, just before planting time, they took sap from the maple trees; in summer they gathered roots and berries. And, in all seasons, they cut and hauled wood from the forest for cook-fires. The Kahnawakes extended the traditional range of Iroquoian agriculture in one important way: by adding domestic animals. Wrote one of the priests in 1735: "They raise horses, pigs, and poultry . . . as do our own people." Caring for these also fell to women.[73]

It made, all in all, an imposing list of "duties." Lafitau thought the men "lazy" by contrast—indeed, "they consider their laziness a distinction"—but himself provided evidence to the contrary. Their "hardest work," he wrote, included "the building or repairing of their houses," and of protective palisade-fences; making household furniture; preparing "the skins of which their clothing is fashioned," plus "their war equipment" and "gear for hunting and fishing"; and "adorning themselves and putting themselves into trim shape." This, too, made quite a list—and it comprised only what men would do in the village. Surely, a key point is all they did elsewhere: in the forest, and on the rivers, hunting, fishing, making war.[74]

Every winter "the hunt"—principally for deer and beaver, but also for bear, moose, raccoon, and fox—sent most Kahnawake men ranging far into the wilderness. "The men leave us about the end of September," wrote Father Nau, "nor do they return to the village before the month of February." Sometimes, the hunt extended even into March, and was merged with fishing runs as spring unlocked the ice on Canadian rivers. It is true that at least a few women accompanied these hunting parties—to cook, and to help with drying and transporting animal skins back to the village. But clearly the men were in charge here.[75]

Expeditions of war were usually reserved for the summertime (Deerfield being a conspicuous exception). These, too, could be very prolonged; three to four months "on the trail" was not uncommon. Of course, such expeditions were less regular than the hunt: in some years they might not happen at all, in others they would involve only small "parties" of warriors.[76] Still, most Kahnawake men, in most years, probably spent more time away from the village than at home in their "lodges." And the time away was arduous—with long "marches," direct exposure to extremes of weather, and (often enough) meager supplies of food. It was dangerous, too: Men died on the hunt and, most of all, men died in battle. One set of demographic information from the early eighteenth century shows an appalling imbalance between the sexes: only about 100 adult men at Kahnawake, alongside nearly 300 women.*[77]

*Interestingly, there is no such imbalance in the younger age-cohorts. Its causes, then, can only be death or out-migration (specific to the category of adult males). And, given the recurrent warfare of the early eighteenth century, death seems the more likely explanation.

Perhaps, then, the apparent "laziness" of men when inside the village is understandable—as a sort of release following the difficulties and dangers of their exertions elsewhere. One source spoke of the numerous "occasions for drunkenness . . . [when they] return from the hunt"; another described a period of merriment, of "going from house to house, eating, smoking, and playing at a game resembling dice."[78]

What all this particularly underscores is a pervasive separation of men's and women's lives. Gender boundaries were drawn deeply enough in European communities of the time, but were deeper still in the native cultures of the American northeast. Deeper and, of course, different: this, too, was part of the learning process every captive must undergo. James Smith remembered testing the boundary while visiting a cornfield "to see the squaws at work." He decided "to take a hoe . . . and hoed for some time." The women "applauded me" (perhaps derisively?), but when he "returned to the town, the old men, hearing of what I had done, chid me, and said that I was adopted in the place of a great man, and must not hoe corn like a squaw." Never thereafter would he do "anything like this again."[79]

Back to. . . . Gannenstenhawi, "she brings in corn." And the puzzle of her multiple names. A'ongote, we have already speculated, may well have been her first name, her childhood name, and Gannenstenhawi its adult counterpart. But perhaps, just perhaps, the change had another significance as well. A'ongote was a singular name—a name that identified its bearer as someone special, coming (initially) from the outside. Gannenstenhawi was, in its meaning, the opposite of singular, and might easily have been given to any Kahnawake woman. Perhaps, then, this second name was a kind of salute—and a mark of inclusion. Perhaps it implied: You are one of us now.

FACT: *Four times Eunice Williams, a.k.a. Marguerite A'ongote Gannenstenhawi, appears in the mission records as godparent to newly baptized members of her community.*

Interestingly, the first two of these baptisms involved adult women from outside: one, a "captive in war" of "about 20 years old," the other, "an Iroquois woman . . . of 27 years, [previously] baptized by the English." To both she gave her own Christian name, Marguerite. The third and fourth cases were more typical: "a girl born recently," and "a girl born today"—named Cecilia and Marguerite, respectively.[80]

Godparenting was, of course, a traditional Christian (and European) way of building connections across the lines of kin. And so it also developed in the lives of the Catholic Kahnawake. Especially with firstborn children, a godparent would likely be someone in the father's household: an uncle, an aunt, a cousin.[81] Such choices served to strengthen the ties between "lodges"—ties that were already in place, but that may well have seemed tenuous or shaky. The father's divided loyalty to both households was a particular point of strain; hence his relatives became both a problem and a strategic opportunity. Bind them in, with this official (Church-sponsored) device, and the strain might lessen.

There were, as well, other forms of connection between households. The traditional Iroquoian clan system was especially important this way. All of Kahnawake, like all the old "castles" in the Mohawk heartland, was divided into three clan-groups, each identified with a totem animal—the bear, the wolf, and the turtle. (Sometime before 1738, wrote one of the missionaries in that year, the turtle family became so numerous that it was subdivided "into the great and the little turtle.") Moreover, "all newcomers are made members of one of these clans."[82]

Clan affiliation conferred broadly defined rights and obligations on all individual members. For example, hospitality: fellow clanspeople must be generously received—sheltered and fed—when in need. And the settlement of disputes. And the suppression, and punishment, of criminal actions. And collective vengeance in cases of injury at the hands of outsiders. According to one source, residential space within Kahnawake reflected clan organization: "The most numerous family takes one side of the village, and the other two have the rest."[83]

Yet another kind of linkage involved "particular friends" (as the visitors usually put it). This "very ancient" feature of Iroquoian culture tied pairs of men (not women) together on a lifelong basis. As a result, wrote Lafitau, "the two become companions in hunting, warfare, and good or bad fortune"; moreover, "they are entitled to food and shelter in each other's lodging." The missionaries cast a dubious eye on these "unions," fearing "abuses . . . from them." But the pattern seems, nonetheless, to have survived at Kahnawake: a visitor in about 1720 reported that "everyone has his own" particular friend.[84]

Considered overall, then, Kahnawake was a place of much social complexity. The individual household, or "maternal family" (in ethnographic language), was everywhere the primary unit. But such households were building blocks for the much larger clans. And clans, in turn, were crisscrossed with links formed by marriage, godparenthood, and "particular friends." Outsiders, including captives, were absorbed at each overlapping level. The details in Eunice Williams's case are mostly unknown; but we can be sure that she was, in the fullest possible sense, supported, protected, taken in.

FACT: *Eunice Williams's two youngest daughters—apparently the only ones to survive to adulthood—married Indian men from the village. The husband of the first (Catherine Gassinontie) was named Onnasategen, and was identified in the records as "grand chief of the village." The husband of the second (Marie Skentsiese) was Louis Sategaieton, also a locally prominent figure.*[85]

That Eunice's daughters should have married so "well" is itself a suggestive datum. Were they accorded some implicitly high standing—perhaps in dim recognition of her own pre-captive origins?

The matter of social standing was itself of much interest to Kahnawake's visitors. On the one hand, they were struck by the spirit of "equality," and respect for individual "dignity," that pervaded all social experience. On the other, they sensed subtle gradations of rank and prestige. Lafitau, for example, noted a group of families carrying "the great female names—that is, the noble families." Conversely, "some [other] households are shunned"—especially in the matter of marriage-making—"because they are . . . poor and held in small esteem."[86]

It was, apparently, from the "noble" families that village leaders were drawn. Each clan had its "civil chief," and a "war chief" (to lead in military affairs) as well. The clans remained separately responsible for their own internal doings and made independent judgments about diplomacy and war. In 1744, for example, a Dutch trader at Albany reported the following "intelligence" from Kahnawake about the possibility of renewed warfare against the English: "The French governor has Gave them the hatset [hatchet] to take up, which the tribe of the Wolf has taken up, but not the Turtle and the bare." One of the three clan chiefs was acknowledged as "grand chief of the village." (Lafitau speculated about the basis for this "preeminence"—whether family connections, or character, or some additional factor—but confessed that "I cannot always . . . decide which one it is.")[87]

Chiefs at every level were extremely careful in exercising their authority, seeking always to build consensus and avoid "any trace of absolutism." They had "neither . . . crown, nor sceptre, nor guards,

nor consular axes to differentiate them from the common people."
Their opinions carried much weight, however, and their "commands,
given as requests," were usually followed. Chiefs were seconded by
deputies called "agoianders," and after these came the Council of
Elders (which some termed a "senate"). This body discussed, and
decided, all matters of general concern to the village. Visitors were
fascinated by its measured tone and the evident "wisdom" of its delib-
erations. The chiefs spoke through "orators," men of great "natural
eloquence." On the whole, thought Lafitau, "they treat affairs of state
with as much coolness and gravity as the Junta of Spain or the Council
of the Sages at Venice."[88]

In all this, said the traveler Bacqueville, "the women only listen,
and the men deliberate." But others, like Lafitau, who lived in the
village for extended periods, formed a different opinion. Women, for
one thing, played a central role in choosing the clan chiefs. Typically,
the "matron" of the household, in which a chiefdom was "perpetual
and hereditary," decided who among her kinsmen was "best fitted, by
his good qualities, to hold this rank." In addition, there were regular
women's councils, which "are always the first to deliberate . . . on
private or community matters"; these would "advise the chiefs on
matters on the mat, so that the latter may deliberate on them in their
turn." On some "matters" women had both the first and the final say:
on the disposition of captives, for example, and on initiating wars of
revenge.[89]

Considered together, the various rights and responsibilities of
women led Lafitau to a sweeping conclusion. "Nothing is more real,"
he wrote, "than the women's superiority." For:

It is they who really maintain the tribe, the nobility of blood, the
genealogical tree, the order of generations, and conservation of
the families. In them resides all the real authority: the lands,
fields, and all their harvest belong to them; they are the soul of
the councils, the arbiters of peace and war; they hold the taxes
and the public treasure; it is to them that the slaves are entrusted;
they arrange the marriages; the children are under their authority;
and the order of succession is founded on their blood. The men,
on the contrary, are entirely isolated and limited to themselves.
Their children are strangers to them. Everything perishes with
them.[90]

This assessment, with the supporting evidence presented here and
there throughout the *Moeurs des Sauvages*, established the theme of

"matriarchy" as an essential key to Iroquoian culture. Elaborated (and complicated) by Lewis Henry Morgan in the nineteenth century, and given wide prominence through the theoretical writings of Marx and Engels, the workings of Iroquois matriarchy continue to preoccupy anthropologists today.[91] In truth, many of the latter now regard Lafitau's view as overdrawn. But few would deny that Iroquoian women possessed "real authority": in family life, as producers of essential resources (including food), and even in some aspects of governance.[92]

There remains, finally, the matter of comparison and contrast: between the women of Iroquoia (including Kahnawake) and the women of Euro-American "colonial" society. Was the situation of one or the other group clearly preferable? Many Europeans of the time—especially European men—continued to insist on the subordination and "slavery" of all Indian women. But how, then, to explain the large number of captive women who chose to remain with their captors—larger by far than the number of similarly choosing men?[93]

Eunice Williams was, of course, a celebrated example of this choice—and of these women. The mission records identify her simply as "the mother-in-law of Onnasategen, the grand chief." But was she not also a woman of authority in her own right? Like Kahnawake women in general?

FACT: *There are no more known facts about Eunice Williams's life among the Kahnawake—except one, which is reserved for a later chapter.*[94]

Eight

ॐ

JOHN WILLIAMS had visited his daughter in Kahnawake at least twice, but there is no evidence that he reflected carefully on her life there. None of his still extant writings offer so much as a comment on the ways of the mission Indians. They were Catholics: that much he knew. But the rest was screened behind stock imagery of "savages."

His son Stephen had, of course, been through a full experience of living with Indian people. But Stephen, too, seems to have flattened that memory into stereotypes. An entry in his diary, for November 5, 1718, declares his general attitude.[1] Some "eastern Indians" had been visiting near his home, and:

> toward night I went up to. . . . [their] wigwams, & there had opportunity to observe how wretchedly ye poor creatures livd. They are to be pityd. Oh, what reason have I to bless them who deliverd me from ye Indians wth whom I was a prisoner & who was very desirous to have brought me up wth them. Oh, what shall I render to ye Lord for this so great mercy.

How wretchedly they live. How fortunate am I to have escaped their clutches. And, by implication at least: how unfortunate my poor captive sister. Not for him the sharp-eyed curiosity of a Lafitau.

Indeed, all comment by Williamses on Eunice and her Indians was narrowed to a single track: Could she, would she, yet be "redeemed"? Her father's disappointment on seeing her in May 1714 had markedly cooled their hopes. They had no choice left but to wait.

Echoes of concern are sprinkled through their personal writings. Thus Stephen, in his diary, 12 April 1716: "This day I heard that my Father had a letter lately from Albany, but no comfortable news concerning my sister." (Albany continued to be the most likely conduit for "news.") And John to Stephen, 14 May 1718: "If you hear from your sister, send me word." From time to time a rumor floated. In January 1717, Samuel Sewall wrote to John Williams of meeting "Mr. Thos. Oakes in the street . . . as I was coming home. He told me your Daughter was come out of Captivity with two Children; her husband Dead." But, continued Sewall, "I fear the Report was groundless"; at least "it quickens the Remembrance of her in Prayer." Two years later, John Williams wrote to Stephen of "news from Boston that the Regent of ffrance has promised to send home all our captives, willing or unwilling." But this, too, proved without foundation.[2]

In fact, governments on both sides of the colonial border remained intermittently concerned with the problem of captives. A letter from the Massachusetts authorities to Governor Vaudreuil in April 1717 stressed "the mutuall stipulations for restoring the Captives taken on both sides in the time of the war," and urged him to act on behalf of those "who are so injuriously detained in the French or Indians hands." And a similar appeal was sent, through the same channels, in September 1721. The issue was pressed with the Ministry of the Marine in Paris, by a certain "Mr. Sutton, plenipotentiary of the King of England." The authorities there responded by reviewing all Anglo-French negotiations since 1712, especially those touching the right of captives "voluntarily" to decline repatriation. "It is definite," said an official summary of the Ministry's position, "that those who are actually in New France . . . remain there by choice and have the same freedom as the French themselves." The summary traced Sutton's "complaint" to a specific source: "a minister established in New England whose daughter converted to Catholicism and who has never been willing to go back to her father no matter what pleadings were made to her."[3]

There were also personal initiatives on behalf of captives, some officially sponsored by colonial authorities, others organized informally and known only through passing references in family correspondence. For example, this from John Williams to Stephen in August 1717: "Goodman Beamond has been gone for Canada a fortnight." And this, by the same route, in November 1718: "Jonathan Small is come from Canada. . . . He says he did not see Eunice, [but] that Deacon ffrench his daughter among the macquas [e.g. Mohawks] & one, if not both, of the Kellogues have a mind to come home."[4] (Actually, the final word of this sentence was written "hope," not "home"—a touching slip that reveals the underlying drift of the writer's thoughts.)

The Kelloggs mentioned here were living at Kahnawake. And members of their family would play a long role in the history of captivity, some of it specifically touching Eunice. They, too, had been major sufferers in the Deerfield massacre: a boy killed, the father (Martin, Sr.) and four other children (Martin, Jr., Joseph, Joanna, and Rebecca) taken prisoner, the mother "escaped." Martin, Sr., returned to New England in one of the first prisoner exchanges. Martin, Jr. fled (apparently from Kahnawake) with three other boys in 1705 and made his way back to Deerfield—only to be recaptured, and repatriated for good, in 1708. After the peace of 1713, he returned to Canada to retrieve his brother Joseph. And Joseph would subsequently undertake the same errand—several times—on behalf of his captive sisters. The latter, however, chose to remain; Joanna, indeed, would subsequently marry a Kahnawake chief.[5]

One of Joseph Kellogg's return trips was made during the spring of 1722, in company with two other ex-captives, Thomas and Christine Baker. Goodwife Baker had previously sent a "memorial" to the Governor's Council, expressing her wish to recover her children still in captivity and to "be Useful to persuade many others in the Hands of the French Indians to return to their Countrey & Religion"; the Council responded by granting her an "allowance" of £20.[6] It was the Kellogg-Baker venture which verified (as noted in Stephen Williams's diary) that Eunice lived on in Kahnawake "with her Indian husband." This "bad news" started new ripples of sorrow among the family members. Stephen heard a few weeks later from one: "I sympathize in the dark loss of your poor captivated sister." There is even some evidence of Stephen's wishing to become more actively involved. A letter from his father, in March 1719, contained the following: "There can be no thought of encouraging your going to Canada . . . for I cant perceive that the publick will in certainty give any encouragement, but only if they gain any [captives]." (What John Williams meant by "publick . . . encouragement" was, quite simply, money. The Council had grown chary of committing funds for projects of captive repatriation in advance of actual success.)[7]

These events, and non-events, were played out against a backdrop of increasing intercolonial exchange. The treaty of 1713 began the first considerable period of peace, in Anglo-French relations, for at least a generation. And with the Indians, too, there was peace—for a time. Old trade routes reopened, not least the smugglers' route between Montreal and Albany. Indians reappeared, in friendly postures, at frontier stops like Deerfield, and occasionally ventured even to the colonial capitals. The visitors included a number of participants in the

1704 "massacre." John Williams himself wrote to Stephen, in May 1718, that "My Indian Master has been to see me several times, [and] is [now] here about." Presumably, this "master" was the man responsible for holding Williams during the long "march" to Canada. Four years later a group of Mohawks, invited to Boston for "a Conference with the General Assembly," provided lively entertainment as well. According to a local newspaper, "they have several times diverted themselves and great Numbers of Spectators by their own manner of Dancing." Moreover, "on Friday last . . . they kill'd an Ox with their Bows and Arrows, and boil'd him in the Common, where they continu'd dancing till late in the Evening."[8]

Another such group, consisting of "twenty-two French Mohawks" (probably from Kahnawake), was boarded at public expense by a Boston tavern keeper. Joseph Kellogg stayed with them—also at public expense—apparently to serve as an interpreter. The tavern keeper's bill included the following charges:

> 19 days victualling and lodging
> 2 Dinners and suppers for the Eastern Indians which they invited
>   and liquour for Ditto
> wine, rhum, beer, and Cyder each day as they had it
> 4 Gross of London Pipes broken & carried away
> 39 dozen of Tobacco
> breaking two Tables Sundry Chairs & Sundry Knives
> breaking & carrying away 14 mugs & cups & 6 Glasses
> Dr. Williams bill [Dr. *Williams*? apparently no kin] and nursing
>   and attendance for sundry of them . . . by the Doctor's order
> damage done to the House and furniture [such] as daubing walls,
>   tables, chairs, breaking windows, etc.

Was it only, or mostly, a Big Party? How did the Bostonians feel about the conduct of their guests? And how, for that matter, did the Indians feel? One imagines a mix of impressions on both sides: curiosity, puzzlement, hilarity, embarrassment, fear.[9]

But the peace itself was not to last. The Abenaki Indians of (what is today) northern New England grew increasingly alarmed by the advance of colonial settlement, and by 1723 native warriors were again found "skulking" near the frontier. Three years of intermittent violence followed—a sequence known at the time as both Father Rasle's War and Grey Lock's War. (Father Rasle was a Jesuit missionary to the Abenakis; Grey Lock was one of their chiefs.) Indian war parties of varying composition—including some men from Kahnawake—opposed English forces assembled by Massachusetts, Connecticut, and New Hampshire. The fighting, as before, was guerrilla-style: ambush and escape, stealth and surprise.[10] Deerfield was among the places most directly affected; the town was again "garrisoned," and served, too, as a base for operations farther north. A letter from Colonel Samuel Partridge, dated July 1724, described the general plight of the frontier towns. "We have been much distressed with lurking enemies," declared Partridge—before detailing a series of attacks in and around Deerfield. "So, being in the midst of our harvest, we are forced to go 30 or 40 men in a day with their arms and a guard, to accompany and work together." A few weeks later he wrote, simply, that "we wait in peril of our lives."[11]

Gradually, in 1725 and '26, the war simmered down. A meeting of English officers and Kahnawake chiefs at Albany produced a "covenant" of renewed friendship. An English victory over the "eastern" Abenakis (of Maine) led to an imposed peace in that quarter, while farther west, Grey Lock and his warriors seemed to fade into the forest. Deerfield, and its neighbor towns, were again relieved of their imminent "peril."[12]

As for the Williamses: a personal backdrop as well. In October 1716, Stephen Williams was ordained and began a sixty-five-year tenure as minister at Longmeadow, Massachusetts. His father stage-managed the "installation": "your uncle [Solomon] Williams will preach the . . . sermon"; your "father [actually grandfather] Stoddard hopes to be there"; "it's time to write to the churches you intend to send for"; and so on. Two years later Stephen married; his bride was Abigail Davenport, daughter of the Reverend James Davenport of New Haven. Again John Williams was present—and in charge. Shortly thereafter Stephen visited his father's old friend Sewall in Boston. The latter made him a gift of two silver spoons, each inscribed with a date of great personal significance: *February 29, 1704*, the date of his capture (following the "massacre"); and *July 3, 1718*, his wedding day. The point, said Sewall, was "to shew how God sets Adversity and Prosperity one over against another."[13]

༤

JOHN WILLIAMS, while very much a frontier clergyman, remained closely attuned to the world beyond Deerfield. He fretted when in wintertime "the providence of God . . . prevented much travelling . . . so that we hear seldom from Boston." He asked his sons: "if you have any late prints or news, pray send [them] by the first opportunity." He was known to others as unusually "publick spirited"; a colleague remarked "how careful was he to inform himself of the Transactions and Affairs of Europe, and to understand the State and Circumstances of this Province, that he might Calculate his Prayers accordingly." He traveled with some regularity to Boston—his visits are noted in Sewall's journal—and was frequently invited to preach before the governor, magistrates, and deputies on the colony's annual "election" days. He was also interested in science and scholarship. His "commonplace book" from the 1720s contained careful notes on a broad range of topics: "Of mists and Fogs . . . Of ye Earth . . . Of Beasts, Fowls, and Fishes . . . The Drunkard Described . . . Antidotes for ye Sting of a Scorpion." (And so on, for dozens of pages.)[14]

Of course, too, there was his work as a pastor: the recurrent rounds of preaching, of public and private prayer, of baptisms and burials, of visits to individual parishioners, of participation in clergy "consociations," and of countless informal services to the local community.[15] No other part of his life was more visible—or more central. And he was followed in his "holy calling" by each of his three eldest sons: Eleazer, minister at Mansfield, Connecticut; Stephen; and Warham, minister at Watertown, Massachusetts. Moreover, his daughter Esther married a clergyman, the Reverend Joseph Meacham of Coventry, Connecticut.

Of all these younger Williamses, Stephen is most fully approachable now—thanks to his years of assiduous diary-keeping. Into this extraordinary project (which today yields some 4,000 pages of typescript) Stephen poured the manifold contents of his everyday experience. Above all, his intense, often agonized spirituality: "I wd be humbled before God, for my sin, my Baseness & ingratitude, my Stupidity, my incorrigibleness under judgmts." But also his domestic affairs: "This day Tom [his black slave] was taken cold and a violent pain in his Breast & Head; I put him to Bed & followd him with Tan-water that caus'd him to Sweat freely, & in ye Evening he was Easy." His social experience: "This day I Pceive Some uneasiness in Some of my neighbours (Occasiond by Some Stories raisd groundlessly) wth me; ye Ld be pleasd to fergive those yt wrong me & Give me wisdom & grace to cary inoffensively." His financial arrangements; "I have been to ye Town & ovr ye River, to gather Some money & to pay Debts." His efforts in hunting: "This day I killd a Stately wild turkey in my lot; thus God gives us ye fowl of ye air fer our Nourishmt & Support."

His fidelity to Puritan traditions: "December 25: Call'd Christmass, and kept as a day of carousing & frolicking by Some; I bless God yt I have learnt better." And even the anniversaries of his childhood captivity: "This day, 28 years ago I was taken captive by ye Indian enemy—a day to be remembered; oh, ye truble and distress I and my Father's family & our neighbours were therein."[16] Much else could be added to this picture of life among the New England Williamses in the early eighteenth century. But, for now, perhaps one further detail may suffice. In each of the families of John's four adult children (Eleazer, Esther, Stephen, and Warham) was found a daughter . . . named Eunice. Herein lay a double remembrance: of their martyred mother, taken in the "massacre" and slain on the "march" that followed; and also of their "captivated" sister, now living as an Indian woman far to the north in Canada.

And then, another turning-point—for the family and for our story itself. . . .

On Monday, July 9, 1729, Stephen Williams arose in his Longmeadow home after a "restless" night. His youngest daughter was ill, and he went at once to fetch a nurse. A little before noontime a family friend arrived from Deerfield—with "heavy news of my Father being seiz'd with [an] Apoplectick fitt ye last night." Stephen left immediately and reached his father's side that evening after a grueling seven-hour ride. ("I was so fatigu'd . . . [that] I was like to have fainted.") John Williams was by now "in great distress, incapable of speaking & incapable of stirring one side"; apparently he had suffered a paralyzing stroke. The following day he seemed marginally better: "he opened his Eyes and look'd steadfastly upon me, & was much affected and sd 'my son.' " But on Wednesday he "grew insensible" (lapsed into a coma), and "at 35 minutes after 12 of ye clock at night he Breathd out his precious Soul into ye Hands of ye Lord."[17]

His survivors were left to ponder his death "& ye awefull circumstances of it." They were troubled "especially [by] his not being able to speak to us," and speculated that this "may intimate ye displeasure of Heaven agst us for not observing ye counsell & instructions & reproofs given to us heretofore." Relatives and neighbors gathered in the house amidst "great Lamentation and mourning"; Stephen would describe himself "like one . . . crushed." Friday was "ye day of ye funeral . . . dark & melancholy." The Reverend Isaac Chauncy, pastor in the neighboring town of Hadley, presided "before a great & affected auditory."[18] The sermon was a lengthy paean to the virtues of the deceased—"He was valiant and courageous . . . patient under afflictions . . . hospitable . . . charitable . . . obliging . . . modest . . . [and] temperate"—with much affecting detail.[19]

The news of Williams's death reached Boston within a few days, and prompted additional forms of response. *The Boston News-letter* and *The New England Weekly Journal* printed fulsome obituaries. The *Journal* specifically remembered, in a list of his personal "afflictions," his daughter "living . . . in a doleful Captivity . . . for whom may the prayers of God's people be yet offer'd up to him." A week later the pastor of the First Church of Boston presented a "lecture" entitled *Eli, the Priest Dying Suddenly*—this "Upon Occasion of the Sudden Death of the Reverend Mr. John Williams . . ."[20]

Moreover, his friends wished to create a printed "memorial" of John Williams's ministry. Hence, within weeks of his death, there appeared in Boston a small volume entitled *A Serious Word to the Posterity of Holy Men, Calling upon Them to Exalt Their Father's God*. It contained, according to the printer, "An Abstract of a Number of Sermons Preached by John Williams, M.A., Pastor of the Church of Christ in Deerfield."[21] Its quality as "abstract" was unusual; perhaps it offered a distillation of comments on a favorite theme. Perhaps, too, it was something of a last testament.

In one sense the theme was entirely familiar and conventional. Declension: the loss of piety, the failure of spiritual nerve, over the span of recent "generations"; the absolute necessity of reform; the certainty of God's punishment if reform were not achieved. Williams, and his auditors and readers, had been through all this before. *God in the Camp*, for example—his "publick" sermon to the General Court in 1707—had played one variant on declension. Now he presented another, and again infused it with meaning drawn from his own life.

The rather vague and generalized phrasing of the title became, on an inside page, something sharper; the subtitle reads, "The Privilege and Duty of the Children of Godly Parents." From "posterity" to "children," from "holy men" to "godly parents": the reference grew decidedly more personal. It is, declared John Williams, "an exceeding great Favour and Privilege to be born of godly Parents." The children involved are "dignify'd and distinguishd" in various ways; their lives begin with "peculiar Opportunities, Advantages, and Helps." Their parents' "covenant relation to God" affords them the presumption of a similar status. Moreover, they have "the advantage of many Prayers put up for them," especially the prayers of their parents. "We may well think that believing Parents lay out their strongest Faith and

Fervour in wrestling with God for . . . Graces and Blessings . . . to be dispensed to their dear Children." Alongside the prayers, they have other forms of "high Privilege": they are "early devoted to God"; they "have a pious Education bestowd upon them"; they "have the Spirit early striving with them." (Was he remembering his past experience—his prayers, his spirit strivings, his teaching of personal piety—with his own children long ago?) Such parental efforts, he noted, should yield "Encouragement of hope" even to children "surrounded with Dangers." (Was he thinking of one child in particular, who had lived for many years amid extraordinary dangers?)[22]

However, "peculiar Advantages" impose "peculiar Obligations." Indeed "God expects more" from the children of godly parents "than from others not so favour'd as they." Parents expect more, too: "To exalt God is the best way to please their pious Parents, if living, and to Honour their Memory, if dead." (Did he hope, while yet living, to be pleased by all his children? And does he refer here, however obliquely, to their other parent, long since dead but ever deserving of honor?) Children who fail in these obligations must be roundly condemned. They show, thereby, "a very disobedient, stubborn, and ungrateful spirit." They have, in effect, "cast off their first Faith . . . [and] have drank in very loose and hurtful Notions of Religion, if not damnable Heresies." (For example, popery?) Implicitly, they cast "base Reflections on their Fathers themselves," and especially "upon the Choice [the fathers] made of God for their Ruler and Portion." (Choice for the parents; choice, too, for the children.) God himself will respond "with the utmost Indignation." These ungrateful children "shall be to Him as the Children of Ethiopians, the very filth of the World, the most despicable of Mankind," indeed "as very children of the Devil." (He didn't say Indians, but: a dark-skinned people, despised by their betters, who live in filth and worship the devil.)[23]

In his concluding pages John Williams framed a direct appeal; the children of godly parents, previously "they," now became "you." Consider, he urged, "from whence you are fallen. . . . Consider, and turn again." (The phrasing recalled his famous narrative: "turning" as an image for religious change—for "apostasy," for "recantation.") "O, the vile ingratitude you are guilty of." (Ingratitude remained, for him, a core element.) "We trust your case is not yet desperate. For God . . . invites even backsliding Children to return." (He had never lost all hope for her redemption.) If, however, you resist these entreaties, "your godly Parents will be loud witnesses against you in the day of reckoning; their Examples, Prayers, Counsels, and Warnings will

rise up in Judgment against you." (How hard he had tried! And
how bitter he felt about the result!) Moreover, "you will be eternally
separated from your holy Parents." (Her isolation from him, initially
measured in human time, would then become forever.) And: "You
[will] . . . bring down the Judgments of Heaven, not only on your
selves, but on your Families too (if you have any.)" (Was a "savage"
family really a family at all?) "How doleful and terrible a thing will it
be, if you are found in the number of them that help on the Ruin and
Destruction of New England, by provoking God to depart from us!"
(The stakes were very high, and the prospects dark indeed.) Beware,
then, lest you "take a Course to have Sword and Famine and Pestilence
employ'd, to the emptying [of] Families and Towns, and laying waste
a pleasant Land." (He knew all this personally: war, death; a town
abandoned, its land destroyed. Deerfield, 1704.)[24]

༄

WITH THE FUNERAL OVER, the obituaries written and read, the
"abstract" of his sermons prepared for the printer, John Williams's
spiritual estate could be considered settled. There remained, however,
his temporal estate—which was in itself no small matter. Curiously,
he had not left a will, so the local probate court was obliged to take
charge. The court appointed his widow and son Stephen as administra-
tors; they, in turn, prepared the required "inventory" of properties.
The list was completed and returned to the court on November 26;
its length and complexity gave some idea of the ampleness of his
life.[25] Though he had remained a resident of a remote village and
had repeatedly complained of "want," his possessions included: "fine
shirts" and "silk muslain handkerchiefs"; a large array of "checkerd"
and "flower'd" coverlets, calico quilts, "china" curtains and bedding,
"Holland towels . . . and pillow cases"; some thirty chairs, a half-
dozen tables, assorted beds and chests; a variety of brass kitchenware,
silver spoons, cups, and tankards, and "twelve pewter plates." Plus
fifteen cows, ten horses, twenty-one sheep, and—listed right after his
livestock—"the black boy Kedar" and "the mulatto boy Mesech." (In
short, his slaves.) Plus eleven separate plots of land, and numerous
debts and "legacies." Plus the contents of his large library. (Judging
from their titles, his books ran a familiar gamut for the Puritan clergy.
Most were religious treatises of one sort or another. But a few may
have reflected his captivity experience: a "French dictionary," for
instance, and a "French history," and several additional "French

books"; and one that was entitled *Tryall of the Romish Clergy*, and another called *Indian Converts*.) The total value of the estate was more than £2,300, a very large sum for the time.[26]

The court turned next to the estate's "distribution" among his various heirs. About a third went to the "relict" (widow), with the remainder "to be divided to & amongst the Children . . . in Equal parts." The latter were identified one by one: males first, then females, in order of age. And they specifically included "Eunice the Second Daughter"; her share, like all the others, would be "two hundred & twenty pounds & Eight pence." The court declared, in this way, its insistence that she was still a member of her Deerfield family and community. It showed, as well, an unwillingness to recognize her Indian family connections: she remained "Eunice" while her married elder sister was officially "Esther Meacham." Moreover, her inheritance would go to her directly, whereas Esther's would be "paid . . . to Mr. Joseph Meacham in Right of His wife." It was standard practice, in all colonial courts, to treat women as "covered" by the legal person of their husbands. But that would not extend to *Indian* husbands—like François Xavier Arosen.[27]

The estate settlement seems, in retrospect, a kind of enticement to the unredeemed captive—seems to say, "Come back, Eunice Williams, and make your life with us, after all, instead of your Indian captors." And, just possibly, it was communicated somehow. At any rate, we must now ask this question: Was it sheer coincidence that later in the very summer of John Williams's death Eunice appeared on the outskirts of New England for the first time since her capture? Here is the relevant note from Stephen's diary:

> [August] 28: this day we had Some news yt my Sister Eunice had been at Albany & was like to be there again in 8br [October] & yt there was Some Hope She might be pswadd [persuaded] to come down & See us. I have [been] discoursing with Some Dutch Gentlemen at allbany. I pray to God to appear for our help & yet return my poor Banish'd Sister if it may consist wth his will, by reason of my going to see those Dutch Gentlemen.

To summarize and paraphrase: she had recently traveled to Albany and would soon be coming again. She had apparently talked with local residents and had shown interest in meeting her New England relatives. Stephen had been developing his own Albany contacts and was considering a visit there to improve the chances of her "return." New hope, cautiously expressed.[28]

But it wouldn't be realized for some while yet. If Eunice came back to Albany in October, the fact was not known to Stephen (or at least was not mentioned in his diary). And he himself did not travel that way.

Then a year later, the same sequence began again. This time its parts were fully revealed—in a long letter addressed to Stephen (at Longmeadow) by his cousin Ebenezer Hinsdale (of Deerfield). Hinsdale had spoken to one "Mr. Corse," a trader with extensive intercolonial connections. (Their meeting had occurred "in Pursuance of your Request.") Corse had seen Eunice's husband not long before—indeed had traveled "with him to Albany [from Canada]." The husband had expressed "a willingness to Come to New England to see her friends, was Eunice willing." But Eunice, for her part, "says she is Exceedingly afraid of ye English & Endeavors to avoid ym as much as she can when at Albany." (Afraid of what? Perhaps of recapture? He left that inference, but didn't specifically say.)²⁹

The husband "was very Desirous of sending you a letter by Mr. Corse," but was thwarted by circumstances. He trusted only the Albany "commissioners" or the merchant Cornelius Cuyler "to write him one"—and they were not available. Never mind: "ye Indian said he should be their again [in] about 6 weeks with Eunice, when he would get Mr. Cuyler to write to you, that you might have an opportunity to See her." Furthermore: "Mr. Corse discoursed with ye Indian about Coming to Deerfield or to ye fort [an English military post higher in the valley] when he came again & told him, if he would bring Eunice, . . . he would Give him a good blanket & Incouraged him by [describing] other presents he thought would be made to ym." (Their strategy was clear: get the husband pulled in. They believed, too, that "presents" were especially persuasive with Indians.)³⁰

And one more thing: "If her friends pretended to Detain her against yr wills, he [Corse] would Do what Lay in his power to Steal her away for him." (He was responding, in short, to Eunice's fear of being taken again. But, of course, she would have to trust him.) "Ye Indian Promised he would Come to one of the places or Write to you from Albany when they were both their." (Yes, that was a promise. If only one could believe what they said.) Finally: "Mr. Corse saw her [Eunice] at Canady, but thinks it needless to say anything of yt, only yt she Was Well." (But: why not say more? Perhaps he assumed that the Williamses would shortly be able to see for themselves.)³¹

Hinsdale's letter parts a curtain that till now has obscured key parts of the story. It reveals, for example, the full importance of (what might be called) the Albany channel. Dutch traders, with a base there, moving back and forth to "Canady." Indians traveling the same route. Arosen and Eunice personally involved. (Their appearances in Albany have the look of regularity. Were they, perhaps, traders themselves? Or, at least, *porteurs* for the merchants of Montreal?) The letter also shows that Stephen Williams had linked himself to this channel. He knew about, and was known to, some of its leading promoters: Corse, for example, and Cornelius Cuyler, and probably the "commissioners" as well. If both sides wished to use the channel—and, admittedly, that could not be assumed—communication was reasonably direct and secure. The letter implies, finally, a growing receptiveness on the other side to visiting New England. At least Arosen seemed receptive; Eunice still had her fears. But apparently they were discussing it, and exploring its terms and conditions.

But as often as the channel opened up, so, too, did it then close down. There was no more news of Eunice in the summer and fall of 1730. And, in summer 1731, only this: "20 [September]: this day I heard yt Mr. Wendle & ye other Gentlemen yt have been to Allbany & were returned . . . bring no comfortable tidings concerning my poor Sister. I desire to refer her case to ye Ld, praying he wd be pleasd to appear fer her relief & yet restore her."[32]

However, it is possible that important communications from about this time have been lost. In March 1732, Stephen "was sent for . . . to See Mr. Lydius who is going to Canada—hy whom I have sent [a letter?] to my poor Sister." (Lydius, another Dutch merchant, was also part of the Albany channel.) And, the following September: "Mr. Lydius and Mr. Livingstone were here at meeting [in Longmeadow]." From them Stephen learned "that the earthquake we had here last November was very great at Canada," but nothing new (so far as his diary reveals) about Eunice. There may, even so, have been additional contact—originating at her end. A Deerfield historian of the late nineteenth century described "a silver cup among the plunder [of the massacre] that came into the possession of Eunice . . . [and] in 1732 . . . was by her given to her brother Warham." Supposedly, it remained thereafter "in the hands of his descendants. It is marked 'Feb. 29, E.W. Obt., 1st March 1703–4. June 10, 1732, E.W. to W.W.'" This apparent gift (which cannot be authenticated today) may have come back with Lydius that same summer. And it does suggest a reaching out toward the New England Williamses.[33]

In December 1733, Stephen once again saw Lydius—and sought "to project some measures respecting my poor sister at Canada." And several months earlier there had been this comment in a letter received from brother Warham:[34]

> If you hear anything from Canada concerning Sister Eunice, I hope you will communicate it, & as to what part of her Estate is in our hands, I should think it very proper & advisable if you would consult such who are good judges in matters of that nature. If that affair could be finished, I believe it would be well for us. As it lies at present I fear it will lay a foundation for Difficulties and Uneasiness hereafter.

Her estate? Of course: her inheritance from John Williams, as ordered by the court three years previous. Evidently it was still unclaimed—or at least unpaid. *Project measures? Matters of that nature? Difficulties and uneasiness hereafter?* The language of the law—and of property. Details are now opaque, but this much seems clear: As Eunice and her Williams relatives maneuvered, bit by bit, toward some sort of reconnection, money was both a motive and a worry.

In February 1734, more news: the most hopeful—and worrisome—yet. Eleazer Williams wrote from his home in Mansfield, Connecticut, to brother Stephen:[35]

> When I came Home from your house my wife told mee she had heard that thir was a woman lately come to Newport, and she sayd she came from Canada and yt hir name was Williams. . . .
>
> Just now Mr. John Hatch comes in and informs mee that he saw her and she says she was taken at Deerfield & her father was a minister and yt ye Indians killed her mother and yt her Indian Husband is dead and hir children by him and, as he understood, she [now] married to a frenchman. . . .
>
> and also . . . I have a letter from mr Beal who is at Newport, and he writes . . . yt she cannot talk any English (except a few words) but he talked with her by a French woman . . . and she came from Canada about a year agoe. . . .
>
> By what I have heard I am prone to think she may be some English Captive if not sister, and I should be glad [if] you would come down here and let us consult [about] what may be proper to be done. . . .

On the backside of this letter, as it survives today, are some scribbled notes in Stephen's hand, evidently the draft of a message sent soon after to a third brother (probably Elijah). Eleazer, Stephen wrote, "would have me go to mansfield & so to Newport," but "I cant think ye person there is Sister"; at this point "I don't know what is best to be done." He enclosed Eleazer's letter and asked that it "be sent along to capt. Kellog [in order] yt we may have his thot." Stephen sounded perplexed and troubled; something had raised his suspicions about "the person there" who claimed to be Eunice.[36]

On February 14, "ye affair," as he called it, entered his diary: "I am Satisfyd the Pson is a cheat, but pray fer Divine Direction." February 15: "Ye Story about ye woman at Rhodeisland Seems to increase. I am at a loss what to do." February 16: "Some whose tho'ts I value, Pticularly Mr. R. & Capt. J.C., advise going to Rhodeisland." February 18: "this day I went to Mansfield (tho it was a Stormy day) in order to go to N-port to See ye woman yt pretends to be my Sister Eunice. I pray God to preserve & direct me." February 22: "I went to Rhodeisland; lodg'd at Capt. Ebry." February 23: "I went to look after ye poor woman, who was very Shie of me, but at length I came to Speak wth her. I found her to be a meer cheat, a vile wick'd woman yt had followd ye army fer a great while. She was very Brazen & impudent." February 24: "Sabbath. I preached in ye [church] Service . . . God grant yt my comeing to Newport may be of Some Service to Some poor Soul." February 25: "this day I left N.P. (after haveing receivd a great deal of Kindness & civility, for which I bless God)." February 28: "this day I returnd home in Safety, & found my family well . . . Oh Lord, pity poor captives, I do beseech thee, & let us See them in comfort, tho we have been so often disappointd."[37]

Disappointed again; disappointed indeed. Now a *mere cheat* could set the family to scurrying; they must be more careful another time. In fact, six months later a similar sequence was played out in the Connecticut town of New London. A diarist there reported the arrival of "a french woman . . . that says She was the Daughter of . . . Rev. Mr. Williams of Deerfield, taken by the French & Indians from thence When that Town was Taken 30 years ago." Stephen seems not to have become involved on this occasion, but his elderly uncle Ebenezer Williams of Stonington (adjacent to New London) did "Come to see" the visitor—and, presumably, dismissed her as another "cheat." Taken together, the two episodes showed a growing danger that outright impostors might claim the identity—not to mention the patrimony—of the (still) "unredeemed captive."[38]

Stephen's diary would not so much as mention Eunice through the entire span of the next two years. But he did begin a new round of contacts with Indians. The Massachusetts authorities were attempting to organize a "mission" in western New England, and Stephen became directly involved. In July 1734, he received a visitor sent to Longmeadow for the sake of "pressing upon me the undertaking [of] ye Indian mission. . . . I can't think I have a Call thereto, tho I am a well wisher to ye design." A week later he noted that his "thots are much taken up about ye Indian affairs." And the succeeding months brought meetings with other concerned clergy, days spent "writing to Boston about ye Indians," and then (beginning in February 1735) repeated intervals when he received young Indians to "be instructd & taught" in his home. This, in turn, was part of a larger program to "christian-ize" the remaining native people—indeed to "civilize" them by chang-ing their "whole habit of thinking and acting . . . [and] raising them as far as possible into the condition of an . . . industrious, and polish'd people." (The words were those of the Reverend John Sargeant, Ste-phen's friend and kinsman by marriage, and future minister to the mission settlement at Stockbridge.)[39]

References to his Indian charges are dotted through Stephen's diary from the late 1730s and early '40s. Thus: "Three of ye Indian lads are come . . . to dwell with us, to go to school; I desire it may be fer their benefit & advantage that they are come. . . ." And: "this day two of ye Indian Boys left us, being Sent for upon ye account of ye sickness of their mothers. . . ." And: "one of ye Indian youths seems to be touchy and out of frame." Did he recognize his work with these boarder/pupils for the turnabout it transparently was? Did he remem-ber anew his own boyhood experience with Indians, who taught him to hunt and fish "after their own manner," who cut his hair "like an Indian's, one side long and the other short," and who were, in general, "very desirous to have brought me up with them"? His diary gives no sign that he made the connection, none whatsoever. But perhaps, at some level, his interest in this "civilizing" project touched long-buried feelings about his own captivity.[40]

The authorities were aiming, too, for better trade and diplomatic relations with the "western"—and northern—Indians. And, in August 1735, they organized an elaborate "conference" at Deerfield.[41] Stephen was there as spectator and, to some extent, as participant; his diary speaks of "a great Hurlyburly indeed."[42] The Kahnawake were there, too: the "grand chief" Ountaussoogoe, and others representing each of the village clans, and their wives ("who we always want with us"), and several of their neighbors from the St. Francis mission—the "whole [delegation] being Twenty-seven." Massachusetts Governor Jonathan Belcher presided, "at a large Table under a spacious Tent," accompanied by several members of his Council, the General Court, "and a great Number of Gentlemen and other Spectators." Joseph Kellogg served as a "Sworn Interpreter."[43]

There were flowery speeches of welcome. *Governor Belcher:* "It is a great pleasure to me that we have the Opportunity of refreshing our Faces with the sight of each other." *Auountauresaunkee*, "Indian speaker" from Kahnawake: "Our desire is that all Tears may be wiped from Your Excellency's Eyes." There were elaborate gift exchanges: "a parcel of Deer skins," "a large Belt of Wampum doubled," "provisions" of various kinds. And there were bibulous "salutations": to "King George's Health" and "the Health and Prosperity of the Tribes." The conference stretched through an entire week, with the various Indian groups shuttled into—and out of—the governor's presence. Finally, at his third meeting with the "french Mohawk" chiefs, Belcher got to the point. At Fort Dummer—a newly created outpost on the Connecticut River above Deerfield, "where Captain Kellogg commands"—a "Father" (minister) had been appointed to teach Indian children "to Read and Write, and . . . the Principles of Our Religion." In return, the governor expected that "if there should happen a War between King George and the French King . . . your Interest will hold you to Peace with us." Moreover: "you will be always honestly dealt with by Capt. Kellogg at the Truck House, where you may have such things as you need, at a cheaper rate than any others . . . will let you have them." He made, however, no reference to captives. And, when the Kahnawake had finished their speeches, Stephen Williams noted (in his diary) only this: "nothing extraordinary appear'd, in my opinion, from them."[44]

Increasingly, Stephen was pulled to the center of the proceedings. The Housatonic Indians, for whom the Stockbridge mission was principally designed, "desir'd me to be present with them to draw [up] their Speach." In short, he helped to compose—and to write down—what this second group would say to the governor; moreover, when the time came, he read it for them. On the Sunday when the conference concluded, before "a very numerous Assembly . . . both of English and Indians," John Sargeant was formally ordained "to ye work of ye ministry . . . among ye Heathen"; Stephen was one of five clergymen in charge. His part was to extend "the Right Hand of Fellowship," and to offer a sermon. "In the afternoon," wrote another diarist, "the Revd Mr. Williams . . . preach'd from 2 Is[aiah]: 4: 'And he shall judge among the nations & shall rebuke many peoples: and they shall beat their swords into ploughshares, & their Spears into Pruning Hooks.' " No further record of his words survives, but one can easily imagine. *Judgment, rebuke, swords, spears*: he had seen these himself and felt their bitter sting. *Ploughshares* and *pruning hooks*: a promise for the future? And after these—though perhaps the thought remained unsaid—*redemption*.[45]

꙳

THE KAHNAWAKE had urged that "the Path may be clear and open, and no Difficulty in the way." And events did seem to be moving in that direction. Travel and trade, north and south through the Champlain Valley, were flourishing as never before. Fur smuggling, in particular, had become the despair of French officials—as evidenced in repeated exchanges between Quebec, Montreal, and the ministries in Paris. When Gilles Hocquart assumed the post of *intendant* in 1731, he immediately heard "reports from many sources that people are using the Indian route to carry . . . to Orange [Albany] their beaver which they trade their for cloth." A year later, he visited Kahnawake and was "distressed to see nearly all the Indians clothed in blankets and fabrics of English make." He concluded, however, that "the country is so vast and the profits to be made so great that it isn't possible to suppress [this trade] entirely."[46]

Hocquart and his colleagues in colonial administration decided, instead, to limit "the evil" by attacking its external supports. The trader Lydius—the same man who would subsequently assist Stephen Williams in efforts to contact Eunice—was temporarily "banished" from Montreal for "carrying on illegal trade with New England . . . [through] Indians whom he has tried to win over with gifts and feasts."[47] Inside Kahnawake itself, the authorities sought to remove the Desauniers sisters, whose "store" was widely seen as a hive of illicit activity. The missionaries were pressed to join in official "remonstrances" with their Indian charges. (However, one among them was himself suspected of participating in the trade.)[48] French officers at Fort St. Frederic—midway down the route to Albany—were offered full value on any goods seized "in the woods" from Indian smugglers— this to stimulate greater efforts at enforcement. And, in 1738, the ministry resurrected its old scheme of posting an armed "garrison" at the mission.[49]

These counter-measures threatened, in turn, the "attachment" of the Indians to French interests. "It is necessary," wrote Governor Beauharnois, in opposing the garrison plan, "to avoid every occasion of resentment among the domesticated Indians." They "consider themselves free"—and they remained, after all, valuable allies in French efforts of war and diplomacy. The possibility of their "absconding" to the English side could not be ruled out. Their participation in the Deerfield conference of 1735 was itself an alarming portent, and by the end of the decade there were rumors of new overtures "in secret" between New England and "the Indians at the Sault."[50]

In this climate of growing Anglo-Indian contact and heightened Franco-Indian tension, English captives felt increasingly inclined to visit their original homes. The "path" was, in several senses, wide "open," the "difficulty" much less than before. Perhaps, too, the inducements—curiosity, adventure, property, and money—seemed particularly strong. And so they went, as individuals and in family groups. Their footprints (figuratively speaking) remain to this day scattered through the diaries, and other contemporaneous writings, of various New Englanders. In October 1736, for example, Stephen Williams met with John Carter, "who is lately come from Canada after a captivity of above 32 years."[51] The story of this man and his family, which must have been well known to Stephen (among others), is one of the most gripping in the entire Deerfield saga.

Carter had belonged to the original captive cohort, along with his stepmother and five siblings. (The father was away on the night of the massacre; upon returning, he found only an empty house and the body of a murdered son lying in the doorway.) The stepmother and two more of the children were killed on the first, second, and fifth days of the "march"; the remaining four reached Canada. One was ransomed and returned to Deerfield three years later. Another was drowned, as a young man, while crossing the St. Lawrence River. A third (a girl named Mary) married an Indian and lived on in Kahnawake. And John, only eight at the time of his capture, was transferred to the French community, raised there, and married to a Frenchwoman. Subsequently he appeared as Jean Chartier, *habitant*, in the records of several different Canadian villages. When his father died in 1728, John/Jean was left a £500 estate, if—and only if—he would come to live permanently in New England. (A similar bequest to daughter Mary was conditioned on *her* return, with her Indian family, for a period of at least ten years.)[52]

When John/Jean appeared in Longmeadow (in 1736), he was en route to visit his one surviving brother in Norwalk, Connecticut. He had a guide, provided by two merchants in Albany ("for [the] Reason we was afraid . . . [he] should Lost himself . . . for he knew not the road"). Stephen Williams received him eagerly, and their conversation

inspired new hope. According to Stephen's diary, Carter "gives En-
couragemt yt he will Stay here, & Send for his family." And this, in
turn, yielded further "encouragement": that others among "our poor
friends . . . may be returnd." The words continued in a kind of rush:
"I desire to wait upon & hope in prayer hearing God—on behalf of
my poor Sister—yet in Canada—oh yt God—would graciously hear
prayers for her & others—& yet deliver—& Save us."[53]

But: three more winters passed, and two summers, without additional news of Eunice. Then, in March 1739, a new pair of visitors:
"this morning [the 19th] I was sent for . . . to See some prisoners
come from Canada, who belong to the Fort where my Sister Dwells.
Ye men had been there above 30 years & are marid to Indians, but
are come to visitt yr Brethren: They Give me Some acct of my poor
Sister. Oh, yt God would yet open a Door for her return."[54] This time
the feeling of contact was stronger still. John Carter, after all, had
returned from the French community; but the "prisoners" described
here were fellow villagers of Eunice's. They knew her; they could
speak of her life and doings from immediate knowledge.

Who were they? Stephen doesn't bother to name them, but clearly
(from other evidence) they were brothers born long ago to the Tarbell
family of Groton. They had been captured as young boys, during one
of the numerous summertime raids of Queen Anne's War; legend has
it that they were surprised while picking cherries behind the family
barn. "Carried" to Kahnawake, they were raised there, took Indian
wives, and prospered (evidently) in the fur trade. Some years later a
Massachusetts merchant saw one of them at Albany, and remarked
both "his Indian dress and . . . his Indian complexion (for by means
of grease and paints but little difference could be discerned)."[55]

The Tarbells had journeyed with an English guide and interpreter
named William Rogers, Jr. (who subsequently billed the Massachusetts government for their food and other costs and his own "trouble
for bringing [them] . . . here"). And Rogers, too, made an appearance
in Stephen Williams's diary. April 30, 1739: "This morning I went
up to speak with Mr Rogers who is going to Canada; he says he can
bring my Sister down to Albany. God grant it may be so, & yt we
may be allowd to see her."[56]

Closer. Still closer. John Carter; the Tarbell brothers; William
Rogers. But again the summer passed, and the following winter and
spring.

And then, on August 9, 1740: "This day I have a letter from Allbany, informing me yt my Sister Eunice is Expect'd at Allbany next

week & I am desir'd to go thither. I rejoyce to hear of any prospect to See my Sister & I pray God to direct in this affair in Every Step & yt my poor Sister may be Enlighten'd & taught of God & yet be brot home."⁵⁷

But how, he must have wondered, could they be sure? There had been other hopes, even a "promise," before. Once he had traveled right across New England—a two-week round trip, in midwinter—to find a "meer cheat" masquerading as his sister. His caution shaped the phrasing in his diary. Passive voice: "I am desir'd to go thither [to Albany]"; not "I desire to go. . . ." And stilted tone: "I rejoice to hear of any prospect to See my Sister. . . ."

For all that, he must respond. The "prospect" seemed sharper, more definite, this time: "My Sister . . . is Expect'd . . . next week." Was there possibly a message sent forward from Eunice herself?

Two days later (August 11): "I have wrote to my Br at M [my brother at Mansfield] giveing him an acct of what I have heard from Albany, & wait this day to See whether he'll come. Oh yt God wd direct & help us all in this weighty affair."⁵⁸

His brother (Eleazer) must have arrived almost immediately, and also his brother-in-law (Joseph Meacham). For, on August 12, the three of them "Set out fer Allbany" together. Three days more, and they had "Got to Allbany River"; the town was on the other side.

Maybe here.
Maybe now.
At last.

NINE

ↄ

ALBANY. In their approach, from across the river, they would have seen . . .

A crooked line of shacks and sheds and little jetties, stretched low along the water's edge. And boats, darting this way and that. "Yachts" with commodious passenger cabins. Slim dugout canoes. Flat-bottomed cargo vessels (commonly called *bateaux*).[1]

Just beyond: the mass of the town itself, its rutted streets climbing a gentle slope. And rows of gray townhouses, their gabled ends set to the front, their roof-lines cut in stepped sequence—the whole expressing, as another visitor said, "the old Dutch Gothic style."

One street (Staats, or State) wider and longer than the rest. At its near end, the new three-storied town hall. Further up, the "ancient" (circa 1640) Dutch church: square, stone-built, with arched windows, and bell tower on top. Behind that, the covered market, and then the "English church" (smaller, less prepossessing than the first). Finally, set on a hill high above, the straggling walls and turrets of the "fort."

And people everywhere. The Dutch, most especially: descendants of the founders; in look, in speech, in manner, all very Dutch. But English people, too. And Germans. And African slaves. And, of course, Indians—themselves a striking mix. Local "river Indians." The "Six Nations" Iroquois. Some from the "far nations" to the west. Others from the "praying tribes" of Canada.[2]

For the visitors from New England it must have been strange (to say the least). Indeed, for New Englanders at large, Albany had long seemed a dangerous, even infamous, place. "The avarice and selfishness of the inhabitants . . . are very well-known throughout all North America," wrote Peter Kalm (a Swedish traveler) in 1742. Worse yet, in the midst of the Anglo-French wars "the people of Albany remained neutral, and carried on a great trade with the very Indians who mur-

dered the inhabitants of New England." Avarice, selfishness, and treason: a deeply malignant combination. As a result, concluded Kalm,
"nobody comes to this place without the most pressing necessity."[3]

Of course, the Williams trio had exactly that. They had contacts,
too—the merchants, and others, with whom Stephen corresponded.
Cornelius Cuyler, the trader Lydius, the erstwhile "Mr. Corse": any,
or all, of these might well have afforded them a greeting. Or even a
place to stay.

In fact, we know nothing of how they managed their wait. But wait
they did; they arrived on the 15th, and found no sign of . . . her. One
week passed, another began. Were they inclined to lose hope? The
documents do not say.

Then, finally, the documents do say: "on [the] 27th . . . we had
ye joyfull, Sorrowfull meeting of our poor Sister yt we had been
Sepratd from fer above 36 years."[4]

The words are Stephen's, and they leave much to our imagination.
Where, for example, did the meeting take place? And who else was
present, besides the principals? And what was said, and felt—and not
said, and not felt—on both sides?

Perhaps it went something like this:

*The message comes at dusk, as the three of them—guests, these
several days, of Mr. Cuyler—are together at prayer. A young
Indian, pausing by their open window, says simply: "She has
come now; you will see her tomorrow at our house outside the
walls." Our house? He must mean the "Indian house," kept by
the people of Albany for the use of native traders.*

*Their prayers resume, more fervently than before. Their supper
comes and goes, scarcely remembered, and the night passes without sleep. They pray again in the early dawn.*

*After breakfast Cuyler leads them up the hill. Past the streetside
shops, shutters opening to the new day. Through the herd of milling
cattle, bound for pasture beyond the fort. Out the guarded gate.
While the sun climbs, hot and hazy, above the river to the east.*

*The Indian house comes in view. A strange architectural hybrid,
it is part Iroquoian longhouse (with arched roof and bark covering), part European farmhouse (frame along the bottom, plank
doors, casement windows).*

*Cuyler gives the traditional greeting (in Mohawk), and they are
admitted inside. Smoke from the firepit stings their eyes. Voices*

float indistinctly toward them from the far walls. Human forms, a dozen or more, loom in the murk: squatting, lounging, bent to one or another little task.

Slowly, one of the forms—no, two—move forward: a woman slightly ahead, then a man. The woman draws very near, her eyes searching the three strange faces in front of her. Stephen turns briefly toward Cuyler, as if to ask a question; Cuyler nods. Turning back, Stephen makes a little bow, and says: "I am your brother. I rejoice to see you. Thanks be to God." Eunice returns the bow, and looks warily, almost beseechingly, into his eyes. Then, on an unspoken cue, they embrace: rather formally, a kiss on each cheek. "And this," says Stephen a moment later, "is your Brother Eleazer, and this your sister's husband Joseph." More bows. More embraces.

Eunice, of course, has not understood a word. And Cuyler moves now to translate. Quietly, she listens, her face barely tracing a smile. Then, from behind her steps Arosen, to begin a new round of greetings and introductions.

Stephen is overcome; his eyes glisten. Arosen motions him to a small chair; Eunice sits on the ground alongside. They are silent for a time. Arosen lights a pipe from the fire, puts it to his mouth, inhales deeply, and passes it to Stephen; around the circle it goes. Stephen asks them to lower their heads, and—his voice thick— begins a prayer. "Lord, we seek thy blessing on all this company, and especially on our poor lost sister, now come from a long captivity in Canada. We pray that she may yet be redeemed, and stay among us, in full reach of thy mercies and care." Cuyler translates this as well. Eunice and Arosen follow, without expression.

Presently Eunice rises, and again embraces her visitors. They sense that their time with her is over, for today. But they will come again tomorrow, to press for further communication—and for her return to the land of her birth.

This, of course, is no more than conjecture. What Stephen actually tells us is something of the emotional impact. It was, he says, "a joyfull, sorrowfull meeting." The words stand right together, in stark contradiction: divided meaning, divided feelings. Of course, it was also momentous, as measured by the time elapsed—"above 36 years"—which was most of his lifetime, and of hers. Note, too, the phrasing: not "whom we had not seen," but rather "yt we had been

Seprated from." Joined, at first (long ago); then, separated; now, joined again. The end, so it seemed, of one very long chapter. And perhaps the start of another?

> August 28: ye next day, we got her, and her Husband's promise to go wth us to my house & tarry wth us 4 days.

Another very spare notation for what must, again, have been a pregnant encounter. *We got her*: he implies a real discussion, perhaps a kind of negotiation, with terms and conditions carefully worked out. *To my house*: their destination, then, was Longmeadow, and the two of them would be Stephen's personal guests. *Tarry with us 4 days:* a short visit only. Stephen had surely hoped for more, but Eunice was proceeding cautiously, still fearful of possible recapture.[5]

> We prepard fer our Journey, & Set [out] Aug:29.

They were traveling together now: Stephen, Eleazer, Joseph Meacham, Eunice, Arosen, and perhaps a small escort of "friends" and guides. The route, most likely, was south along the river (or on it), then east through a region of what Peter Kalm called "vast woods and uninhabited grounds" to the Massachusetts border. And then, one suspects, to Stockbridge, site of the Indian mission-settlement that Stephen had helped to found a few years before. There they could well have made an overnight stop with the Reverend John Sargeant. There, too, they would have encountered additional Williamses: Sargeant's bride (of the year before) Abigail, and her father (one of four English householders in town) Ephraim. Stockbridge might, in fact, have reminded the travelers of Kahnawake: with its mixed population, its religious motive, and its vividly bicultural appearance (native wigwams alongside traditional "English houses"). From here a rough road had been cut, barely five years before, through a series of frontier townships—Great Barrington, Monterey, Otis, Blandford—to Westfield; the latter was but a half day's ride from Longmeadow.[6]

> Thro ye Good hand of God upon us . . . [we] got Safely to my house on ye 2d of Sept. at night, & ye whole place Seemd to be greatly movd at our comeing.

The atmosphere of public excitement must, indeed, have been extreme; searching for parallels, Stephen invoked a Biblical passage (as noted in his diary), "Ruth 1–19." The reference was to the story of Naomi, who had left her native Bethlehem with her husband and young sons for a "sojourn" of many years in the country of Moab.

Eventually, husband and sons all died, and she decided to go back to her own people, accompanied by her daughter-in-law Ruth. "So they two went until they came to Bethlehem. And it came to pass, when they were come to Bethlehem, that all the city was moved about them, and they said, is this Naomi?" So, also, at Longmeadow that September evening in 1740: a populace "greatly moved" with hope and wonder. And the obviously parallel question: Is this Eunice?[7]

Naomi's was a story of return and reconnection; somehow she must come to belong again to the land of her birth. Fortunately, a "kinsman" of her husband remained there. And this man would, in due course, marry their daughter-in-law Ruth. And so the family "line" continued at Bethlehem—and Naomi, in effect, was "redeemed." Thus, for the people of Longmeadow, a second question, more powerful than the first: Will she stay and belong here again?

৯

WE MUST DRAW BACK A LITTLE, to set the scene. Longmeadow in 1740 was a community nearly a century old. Initially established in 1645 as part of the township of Springfield, it had achieved a separate "precinct" status in 1713. At that point, too, its residential center had moved, from the lush lowlands beside the Connecticut River—lush but repeatedly subject to springtime flooding—to the crest of a gentle ridge line about a mile farther east. There its houses had spread, north and south, along a spacious "main street." Wood lots, meadows, swamps, and ponds stretched back toward the river; five small streams cut the street at irregular intervals. With so much water close at hand, there were fine opportunities for milling; a corn mill sat near the northern boundary, a sawmill and gristmill lay somewhat to the south. The prospect, as a whole, was open and abundant; indeed, Longmeadow ranked with the most fortunate of all Massachusetts farm villages.[8]

The town's linear orientation was broken only at its center. There a small "highway" pointed off toward the east, with a "burying ground" along one side. There, too, the street itself widened to a full 100 yards, so as to enclose a small "green." There the meetinghouse rose, its clapboard walls, shingled roof, and bell chamber visible from every direction. And there stood the "parsonage," the minister's residence and home for many years of Stephen Williams.[9]

Where Eunice would be welcomed as guest. Her arrival on September 2 was evidently anticipated: thus the greeting offered by "ye whole place"; thus, too, the appearance of Joseph Kellogg "yt [same] evening." Kellogg had been her fellow captive long ago, and (following his return) had repeatedly put his knowledge of Indian languages at the service of other New Englanders. He lived now in Suffield, across the border in Connecticut, and by coming to Longmeadow he meant to act as interpreter.[10]

But language was only one part of the culture gap dramatized by Eunice's visit. Physical appearance—clothing, coiffure, personal adornment—was another. A long-standing local "tradition" describes her Longmeadow relatives pressing Eunice to "to put off her Indian blankets" and adopt "English dress." And a parallel tradition reports her unwillingness to lodge inside her brother's home. Instead—so the story goes—she and Arosen "camped out" in an orchard nearby.[11]

These preferences cannot have made for easy communication. And the press of public curiosity was also complicating. An eyewitness "remembrance" describes "the attentions and largesses of a crowd of friends and visitants, who flocked from Deerfield, Mansfield, Lebanon, and all the towns in this vicinity." Indeed, Stephen's diary for the period of the visit is a virtual roster of comings and goings. For example: Wednesday, September 3, "my brother E.W. [Eleazer Williams] and Br. M. [Joseph Meacham] went home. Capt. Kellogue's Sister came to us & cousin Thos Hunt and ye neighbours come in & shew Great kindness & Mr. Edwards of N.H. [the famous revivalist Jonathan Edwards of Northampton] came to visitt us."[12]

Thursday "we gain'd a promise from my Sister & Husband to tarry wth us till Monday night"—in short, an extension of the original agreement—while Friday was "clutter'd & full of care & company; joyfull & Sorrow, hope & fear." Thus does the diary hint at moment-to-moment strains. Each step was subject to careful (and bilingual) negotiation, with "Capt. Kellogue" in the middle. Every day brought mixed possibilities and widely variable feelings.[13]

The "Sabboth" (September 7) was a kind of culmination: "My poor Sister attendd ye publick worship wth us both parts of ye day . . . oh, yt this might be as a pledge yt she may return to the house and ordinances of God from wch she has been so long Sepratd." The setting of the meetinghouse must have sharpened the focus and intensified all the excitement. Here, within the confines of a thirty-eight-foot square building, were gathered the 300-odd residents of Longmeadow: married couples arranged in "pews" on the ground floor, facing the pulpit and "deacon's bench" along the north wall; others in the "gallery" above, with separate sections for "singers," "bachelors," "maids," "large boys," "large girls," "small boys," "small girls," and "negroes."

Some years previous, the congregation had voted "that the middle pew
. . . at the lower end of the body of the meetinghouse [should] be for
the use of the Revnd Mr. Williams family, and . . . be raised five or
six inches from the floor." It was probably in this place—central,
elevated, altogether conspicuous—that Eunice and Arosen sat, on the
Sunday following their return.[14]

Almost certainly there were prayers for the visitors. Likely, too, the
sermon was directed toward them. But Stephen's diary does not provide details; instead it moves out of the church to another part of the
day.

> In ye Evening we (Collnll S. assisting & directing) had a Set
> discourse wth my Sister & her Husband.

A *set discourse*: the phrase is immediately evocative. The principals
are drawn together, in a kind of official conference, with a locally
eminent figure—Colonel John Stoddard—acting as moderator. (This
is the same John Stoddard who, decades before, had traveled to Canada with Eunice's father in the cause of prisoner redemption.)

> And tho' we could not obtain of ym to tarry with us now. . . .

Here, of course is the main issue: how to make them *tarry with us*.

> Yet they have promisd us that now the way is open they will
> certainly come and make a visitt & spend a winter in ye country
> among yr friends.

Now the way is open: an Indian voice, her voice (and Arosen's), is
heard in the diary.

> They Seemd in Earnestt, & Say they wont be divertd unless it be
> Something very Extraordinary.

The meeting ends on a note of assurance: They mean what they say,
about coming again. And, more generally, they seem open, trustwor-
thy, *in earnest*.[15]

The following day (Monday, September 8) was their last in Longmeadow, and

> many friends & Neighbours came to visitt us.

Moreover, the neighbors

> sent in plentifully to us [meaning food and drink] and came to
> assist us; so that we had Even a Feast.

They are building, all of them, toward a grand farewell: *even a feast*, on the potluck principle.

> Our Sister & family Dind in ye room wth ye company.

Dined in ye room: Is this unusual? The phrasing suggests that Eunice and Arosen have been keeping their distance at mealtimes, heretofore.

> Sister M. [Esther Meacham] and I Sat at ye table wth them.

There is real sharing here, and a kind of cementing, too: sister, brother, sister, brother-in-law, sitting to eat *at ye table* together.

> At evening our young people Sang melodiously, [and] that was very Gratefull to my Sister & company.

From a feast, to a concert. It is all for her benefit, and she does seem *very grateful*.

> I hope we are Something Endeard to her. She Says it will hurt her to part wth us.

Thus the immediate goal: to make her feel, as she leaves, *something endeared* toward the Williamses and their various "friends." Her words about the pain of parting give ground at least for *hope*.[16]
Tuesday, September 9:

> my Sister & company left my house. I accompanyd them beyond Westfield, about a mile.

In short, he escorts them on their way—*beyond Westfield* means a good dozen miles from Longmeadow—and this itself is a mark of caring.

> And when I took leave of her I do think her affections were movd.

Again, he is looking hard for evidence of *her affections*. (He says nothing, directly, of his own.)

> She repeatd her promise of comeing & Spending a long time with us if God Spard their lives.

This is the compromise to which both sides have agreed: not (yet) her permanent return, but at least another visit—and that for *a long time*.

> Ye Lord be pleased to confirm & Strengthen this resolution.

Events have moved out of his hands again, and for the first time in a week the diary turns to prayer: *Ye Lord be pleased to . . .*

My son John is gone with them to Allbany.

A further escort. And perhaps they need a guide on the unfamiliar route *to Allbany*.

The Lord be wth & bless them all & Give them a prosperous journey.

Another prayer, which puts a kind of period to the week's extraordinary events. Farewell, my sister, and amen.[17]
The following day (Wednesday) brought an inevitable, and painful, letdown. The last of their guests departed, "so that now [we] are left together [in] our own family, after a great cluttr." Stephen struggled to settle his thoughts and feelings. "If reall Good redounds to my poor Sister I shall think all my pains & cost well bestowd." His ultimate recourse remained, as always, God's over-ruling providence: "I desire to . . . cast all my care & Burden upon him." On Thursday the letdown deepened and reality itself seemed temporarily in question: "We are now still & quiet in ye House." And: "I Seem as if I had been in a Sleep or Dream." (Had she actually been here at all?) By Friday, these feelings had taken physical form: "We are Some of us not well, but blessd be God we are not down Sick." On Saturday, they were steadied by news from elsewhere "of Some more captives returnd to their friends . . . Oh, that there may be many of these Exiles returnd and resettld in their native country." Then came Sunday, which Stephen would spend "in quiet at Home." (Was he feeling too depleted to reassume his pastoral duties right away?) In any case, he wished to "bless God fer his Sabboth opportunities . . . and . . . to prize & improve them aright." And he added a pointed afterthought: "Ye Lord pity those destitute of Such advantages."[18]
The next week brought a gradual resumption of regular business. On Tuesday, he "went into ye woods to hunt Bears." On Wednesday, he "rejoiced" in a visit from a clerical colleague. On Thursday, he led a church meeting "as usuall, before the Sacrament." On Friday, "my Son John returnd from Allbany, . . . [and] tells me that his Aunt & Husband were well pleasd wth thier visitt, and went away cheerfull." And on Saturday, he prepared for the coming "Sabboth & Sacrament" with a long session of prayer and soul-searching—which included his specific concerns for Eunice. "Oh Lord," he wrote in his diary that day, "be pleasd to pity & Save & return my poor Exil'd Sister & Lord be pleasd to reveal thyself in thy Son to her and hers." Briefly thereafter he seemed to "feel well," but within another week a sense of "disqui-

etment" had returned. "I seem unfitt for Study," he noted with obvious frustration; "I pray God to calm and compose my mind & thoughts." And, the Sunday following: "a fine day . . . but how cold and lifeless am I." The aftermath of Eunice's visit was proving no easier to "compose" than its long and suspenseful anticipation.[19]

One question of which the diary does not speak is the reason—the motives—for the visit. Did Stephen not think to ask his sister directly about this? Perhaps, indeed, her motives seemed unimportant to him. Or perhaps they were simply assumed: Of course, she would (eventually) choose to come back—to the land of her birth, of "civility," and of "true religion."

Whichever: we must wonder, for ourselves. And the possibilities, as suggested by historical hindsight, are several. For example, pressure by others. A manuscript account, written roughly a hundred years after the fact, stresses the role of two colonial officials—and of her own fellow Indians. Supposedly, the governor of Massachusetts persuaded the governor of New York to urge some Kahnawake chiefs (at a meeting in Albany, in summer 1739) to press Eunice to make a visit. The Kahnawake were moved—or, rather, shamed—into compliance by appeals to their personal honor. ("It is ungenerous, brothers, for you to keep poor and weak females from seeing their friends.") And they, in turn, used similar tactics with her. ("They told her that she must remember the charge that was alleged against them, viz. of awing their women so as to make them fear to visit their friends.") Subsequently, the matter prompted widespread "conversation, for months, within the village." As the object of this long chain of influence, Eunice was obliged to agree—albeit reluctantly.[20]

The chain is not, to be sure, supported by hard (and contemporaneous) evidence; it may well be fanciful. A softer version of the same sequence would stress ready opportunity for a visit. Kahnawake leaders were meeting that summer with chiefs of the Iroquois and the "Indian Commissioners" of New York. The site was Albany, and the timing was virtually the same as Eunice and Arosen's visit; perhaps, indeed, they all had traveled in a single party. There was, in addition, the example of others. The Tarbells, we know, had visited New England the year before, and now—also in August 1740—came two more captives, Silas and Timothy Rice (formerly of Westborough, Massachusetts). Not only was "the path [from Canada to New York and New England] open and smooth"; the gates of Kahnawake itself were swinging wide.[21]

Other possible motives (in Eunice) are purely conjectural. Did she perhaps feel some curiosity about the country—and people—of her origin? The records we have do not say. And might she have wished, even at this late date, to claim the property left to her in her father's will? This seems a stronger possibility—given the previously noted correspondence among her New England brothers—but there is no clear evidence to confirm it. Thus, when we take it all around, her side of the sequence remains largely in the shadows. She had made a visit after an interval of "above 36 years"; she had gone home to Canada; she had promised to come again. Perhaps that was all Stephen and her other Williams relatives really knew. And perhaps it is all we can know now.

⌇

THE MONTHS following her visit are also in the shadows. Stephen's life in Longmeadow went on as before—and so, presumably, did hers in Kahnawake. That communication between them may have continued (in some form) is hinted by a single document. "I rejoice," wrote Joseph Sewall (son of Samuel) to Stephen in January 1741, "to hear that your pious & brotherly Endeavours to Recover your Sister have been so far encouragd and succeeded by God. . . . May that God, wth whom all things are possible, deliver her from the strong delusions of the Romish Idolatry, & Enlighten her wth the Saving Knowledge of ye Gospel of Christ." It is known, as well, that Stephen was exchanging letters with Cornelius Cuyler, his chief friend and ally in Albany. On April 25 he wrote (in his diary) that "Capt: C. C. . . . informs me yt my Sister's husband was at Allbany in ye winter & Gives acct they all are well, & yt they are resolvd next August to come down with thier family & live with us at least a year." Two months later he sent off "twenty one pistoles & twenty shillings York money to be transmitted to Capt. Cornelius Cuyler at Allbany"—possibly to cover costs linked to Eunice.[22]

In the meanwhile, New England was beginning to feel the intense religious revival known to later generations as the Great Awakening. The itinerant English preacher, George Whitefield, had visited Boston in the fall; on September 23 Stephen noted that "his preaching is well approv'd." By January, the excitement was palpably increasing. Sewall's letter to Stephen, quoted above, described how "it has pleased God . . . to awaken considerable Numbers by ye fervent Preaching of the Revd Mr. Whitefield; and since [Whitefield left] of the Revd Mr. [Gilbert] Tennent . . . Several have been with me under Concern about their Spiritual State. O, that All may issue in a saving Conversion to God!"[23]

Then, in summertime, the "fire" of spiritual enthusiasm leaped out toward the Connecticut Valley; Stephen's diary provides a gripping, ground-level view of its progress. On July 7, he visited Suffield, Connecticut, and immediately "heard of ye remarkable outpouring of ye Spirit of God . . . [such] that on ye Sabboath there were 95 Psons add'd to ye church." That same afternoon, he watched his brother Eleazer and his brother-in-law Joseph Meacham lead a religious meeting—outdoors, "on ye Meeting-House Hill"—with a "congregation remarkably attentive & Grave." In the evening, Meacham preached again, "and there was considerable Crying among ye people in one part of ye House or another." Next morning: more preaching "& many cryd out." After lunch, Stephen and his "friends" traveled to Enfield, where they heard "Dear Mr. Edwards" preach in a "most awakening" way.[24]

This last, in fact, is a unique eyewitness reference to one of the most famous sermons in all of American history: Edwards's depiction of "Sinners in the Hands of an Angry God." And it continues: "Before ye sermon was done there was a great moaning & crying out throughout ye whole House." Stricken parishioners called repeatedly to one another: "What shall I do to be saved?" and "Oh, I am going to Hell!" and "Oh, what shall I do for Christ?" Their "shreiks and crys" became so "piercing and amazing" that Edwards was, for a time, "obligd to desist." Stephen and several other clergymen were sitting behind the preacher, and at the end they "descendd from the pulpitt" together. Additional, more personal consultations followed, "some in one place & Some in another." And, all in all, "amazing & Astonishing . . . power [of] God was Seen, & Severall Souls were hopfully wrought upon that night." The following morning, when Stephen awoke, he was full of hope "that God would give me to see at L-M [Longmeadow] what I had seen at Enfield." He felt deeply "affected & movd, ready to dissolve in Tears, but cant well tell why."[25]

He returned home and found his family "in a Different posture from what was usuall." His brother and brother-in-law were still with him—the three of them had become, in fact, a traveling team—and that afternoon they "went to meeting . . . [where] a great Assembly of people were got together." The awakening was about to ignite within his own congregation. "Mr. M. preachd from Matthew 24:40 & Mr. W. from Job 27:8. There were considerable shakeing & trembling before ye revive was finishd." Immediately thereafter, a group of

"concernd & woundd [parishioners] were Directd to go to my House."
Stephen, however, was called away to another place, where one man
"had been carid in Great destress . . . and [others] Seemd Smitten
and struck Down in ye time of prayr." Returning later to his own
home, he "found the concern had increasd, & many were crying out
in Destress." The evening passed in a frenzy of spiritual excitement,
with Stephen and his fellow ministers shuttling repeatedly between
households. Some of the most "affected" worshippers were gripped
by an "anguish . . . that was allmost too much for ye human frame to
Bear."[26]

Soon the conflagration enveloped Stephen's immediate family. His
son Warham was among those in acute "destress," and also his black
servant Phyllis. Presently, he "heard a crying out in ye yard," and
found "my own son John Speaking freely, Boldly, & Earnestly to ye
people & warning of them agst Damnation." Stephen was alarmed;
John seemed "distracted . . . and beyond himself." With difficulty
"we persuadd him [to come] into ye house where . . . he Seemd weak
& faint."[27]

The succeeding days brought recurrent periods of anguish, excitement, and—for some at least—a sense of ultimate "blessing." At one
point, Abigail Williams (Stephen's wife) became "much affectd . . .
[and] Spoke in an unusuall & (to me) Surprizeing manr of Divine
things . . . [She] kept herSelf awake a great part of ye night & me
[also] very considrably." For Stephen himself the experience was complicated—and unsettling. On some days, he was moved to "rejoice
. . . [that] God is showing his Great powr." On others, he "felt weak
& Spent . . . yet kept about . . . & Spoke more than I was wont to
do." He prayed for help in "doing my duty . . . and skill & prudence
to deal with Souls aright." He was worried when one of his parishioners
seemed "over born all most. I fear whether his nature will bear [such
strain]. Oh, Lord, keep him from distraction & Give him relieve as
to Bodily & Soul Difficulties." But, perhaps most of all, he worried
about himself. Surrounded as he was by a host of "enlarged" souls, he
found his own to be pathetically small. "Oh, Lord, I am nothing. I
can do nothing," he wrote at one point. And, at another, he begged
God "in very deed [to] own & bless & succeed me, a poor worthless
worm." On a Sabbath, when he had preached from the Book of Ezekiel
about "ye vision of ye Dry Bones," he drew its meaning directly to
himself: "Lord, make me Sensible of my Leanness, and . . . fer thy
name's Sake, pity and help me. . . . Come, oh Breath, and Breathe
upon these Dry Bones."[28]

The entries in Stephen's diary, throughout the first part of July, are unusually long and detailed. And every line reflects his preoccupation with the Awakening. But into this supercharged atmosphere a new element was about to be introduced. On July 20, he received a letter from his friend Cuyler (in Albany) reporting that "some indians from Canada Give him acct yt my Sister & family design to be wth us this Sumer." His hopes shot up, yet again: "Oh, yt God wd bring them to us, & reveal himself in his Son in a saving manr to them." On Sunday the 26th, he preached in Suffield, and that evening "came a messengr to me . . . bringing me an acct [that] my Sister was come to Westfield from Canada." He rushed home the following morning, and "found my Sister & her husband & two children" waiting.[29]

Their stay this time would be very brief, since Stephen worried lest they "take ye infection of ye meazells" which had recently appeared in a neighbor's family. He noted, and appreciated, their "easy" spirits. Arosen "went ovr to Capt. Kellogue's"—who, in turn, sent back "an acct [of] what their Sentiments are." This refueled the old dream that "they may be prevaild with to come & tarry in ye country."[30]

However, the central scenes of their second visit would be set not in Longmeadow, but in the Connecticut towns of Coventry and Mansfield. The former was the home of Eunice's sister Esther Meacham, the latter of her brother Eleazer. To Coventry, noted Stephen in his diary, "my Sister & company are gone" the morning of July 29. And, by August 4, they had moved on to Mansfield. That day—a Tuesday—would be a memorable one: for Eunice, for her Williams relatives, and, presumably, too, for hundreds of ordinary Connecticut townspeople.[31]

The Awakening had, by this point, spread throughout the countryside east of the Connecticut Valley. Word of Eunice's arrival had also spread; one minister, several towns distant, noted in his journal, "Mr. Williams's sister, Sannup [a colloquial term for an Indian man], & children at Mansfield." Now, the two events came together in the context of an extraordinary religious "exercise." The site was the Mansfield meetinghouse, the preacher Eunice's cousin Solomon Williams (pastor at Lebanon, Connecticut).[32]

The title page of Solomon Williams's sermon (as subsequently published in Boston) noted the special circumstances of its delivery: "at a Time set apart for Prayer for the *Revival of Religion*; and on the Behalf of Mrs. *Eunice*, the Daughter of the Reverend Mr. *John Williams* (formerly Pastor of Deerfield), who was then on a Visit *there*, from Canada; where she has been in a long *Captivity*." The text mentions "a numerous Audience . . . brought . . . together . . . [by] this strange, unusual Occasion." A later account claimed that "people at the distance of twenty miles repaired thither"—in fact, so many people that "only a small portion" could be seated inside. For the sake of others who remained "without," the windows were raised, "and the preacher was so placed as to face, and be heard by, both [groups]."[33]

And where were Eunice, her "sannup," and children amidst this expectant throng? One imagines them down near the front, perhaps in another Williams family "pew," decked out in their Indian blankets, and clearly the center of attention. The other worshippers might well have construed their presence—coincident with the Awakening—as a mark of "Divine providence." (In fact, those words appear in the first sentence of Solomon Williams's sermon.) Perhaps the coming of the famed "unredeemed captive" would itself enhance the revival process. Perhaps, too, the atmosphere of spiritual "enlargement" would improve the chances of her permanent return.

The sermon's title was emblematic: *The Power and Efficacy of the prayers of the people of God, when rightly offered to him; and the obligation and encouragement thence arising to be much in prayer*. Its point, throughout, was indeed prayer: prayer to God, and—reading a bit between the lines—prayer to "Mrs. Eunice" herself. Clearly, her situation had prompted much prayer over many long years. The question the sermon addressed was one that could also have been put to her: under what conditions will prayer be heard—and answered?[34]

According to the preacher's "doctrine," prayer begins from a condition of perplexity—and it seeks, first of all, understanding. This requires that "you . . . Submit to [God's] Will as your Maker . . . and then you may humbly ask him about the most dark and difficult Events and Passages of his Providence towards you, and his Designs therein." (*The most dark and difficult events*: for example, those dramatized by the visitor of the day?) Once understanding is achieved, prayer itself may follow. But it must, in every case, meet certain "qualifications": adherence to "God's Word" (as revealed in scripture); mediation by Christ; and "fervent and continual" repetition. With all this in place, the "efficacy" of prayer is certain; numerous scriptural "examples," not to mention repeated "promises of God," show that He "will answer . . . when rightly addressed." Moreover, there are good "reasons [for] . . . the efficacy and prevalency of the Prayers of God's People." Prayer is consistent with His own "spirit," with Christ's "intercession" and sacrifice, and with the terms of the revealed covenant.[35]

From doctrine the preacher turned to the "use and improvement" of his subject. "Use I" was simply this: "Let Godly people never grow weary in offering up their Prayers rightly to God." And here, addressing the congregation directly, he drew the obvious link:

> You may well think I have all along had some special Eye to the uncommon Occasion of Prayer at this Time: that Person . . . present with us, who has been for a *long time* in a *miserable* Captivity with a barbarous and heathen People . . .[36]

One imagines a sharpening of interest—and a general turning in her direction—as the preacher continued.

> Some of you know well, as I am sure I do, how long she has been the Subject of Prayer; what numberless Prayers have been put up to God for her by many holy Souls now in Heaven, as well as many who yet remain on Earth.[37]

Among the holy souls in Heaven, one seemed especially worthy of mention.

> How many Groans and fervent Prayers can these Ears witness to have been uttered, and breathed forth, with a sort of burning and unquenchable Ardor . . . [by] her dear Father now with God? I know not that ever I heard him pray after his own return from Captivity, without a Remembrance of her.[38]

It was true that God had not allowed her father to "see the Performance" of his wishes for her. Instead, she had been "left . . . in the Same State, to try the Faith and call forth the Prayers of his People" even to the present day. Still, her readiness "of her own Accord, to make a Visit to her Friends" was itself a positive sign, in which "we . . . see some Dawnings towards this Deliverance." With additional "constant, unceasing, & earnest Prayers" there would be ground to hope for "one extraordinary Conviction more."

As he proceeded, the preacher adopted an increasingly monitory—and passionate—tone.

> Oh, give not over; cry mightily to the Lord, in this Day of great Grace . . . for her who is a Child of the Covenant . . . with the most raised Expectations and Assurance. . . . Believe me, the more you pray, the more you will have Occasion to praise God. I will not tell you what Assurance I have . . . of this Truth, but this I will say for myself, that when I believe God will not answer the right Prayers of his People, I will then believe there is no

Covenant of Grace, no Promises, no Truth, nor Savior, and no God.[39]

And no God? This last was a remarkable admission, a kind of going-to-extremes, which showed the depth of their anguish about Eunice's continuing "captivity." If their prayers for her "deliverance" should go unanswered, they faced an abyss of spiritual despair. At stake in the outcome was nothing less than faith itself.

The second "use" of the preacher's doctrine was different, but not— so it proved—unrelated. Prayer was needed, too, for the progress of the Awakening. "An uncommon spirit of prayer" would necessarily precede—and in a sense predict—any "extraordinary Work of Conversion"; moreover, prayer would be a "Means of [its] Accomplishment." But this line of reasoning quickly became an arrow of "reproof."

> Do not your Hearts convince you of great Want of Zeal, and Life, and Fervency in your Prayers for these Things? Be you not more earnest for Temporal, and outward Prosperity, than for the Glory of Christ in the Advancement of his Kingdom of Grace in the World?

To be sure: "There is some Revival of Religion among you; some are inquiring the Way to Zion." Still, it was necessary to ask "why is there no more Good done by all the Advantages you enjoy."[40]

While that question reverberated, the preacher moved to "Use III"—which was "to learn the miserable Condition of poor prayerless and christless Sinners." He deplored the "great Numbers here present that are in an unconverted, unrenewed, unpardoned State," and pulled attention back to Eunice. How is it, he wondered, that "you now look with great Pity and Compassion on that poor Captive," without, at the same time, being moved "to inquire into . . . your own Condition?" In fact, "is your state . . . not worse . . . than hers?" She, after all, had been living "in the Thickness of popish Darkness & Superstition"; hence "her own misery is unfelt & unseen by her." But "you have enjoyed . . . the Means of Grace . . . all your days." And "if you die [in an unconverted state] . . . your Misery will be aggravated inconceivably beyond [hers]."[41]

Inconceivably beyond hers. These thoughts, this comparison, led straight to a scathing summation.

> When you think with Pity on the Slavery, Captivity, and mean State of this Person, whom you see here . . . remember that if you are without Christ you are in a State of Slavery to Sin,

led about by divers Lusts; and under the reigning Power and Dominion of those Corruptions which debase your Souls, and bring them down . . . to the vilest, most shameful and cursed Bondage.[42]

And again:

With all your Freedom, ye are in the worst Slavery, and Enemies of God & Christ . . . And you are opposing all the Means of your own Deliverance and Salvation; the Offers of Grace, the Allurements and Invitations of the Gospel . . . have all been ineffectual to perswade you to accept of Deliverance from a Slavery you are now willingly held in.[43]

You are worse than Eunice, your "captivity" is deeper—more reprehensible—than hers: Thus was her experience used to drive home the familiar themes of sin, retribution, and repentance. Yet it would be a mistake to read this sermon simply as standard-issue revivalism. Eunice's presence was, on its own terms, galvanizing; some of the questions raised here spoke powerfully to her own situation. And one question, surely, loomed over all others: Why had she, so far, refused their offer of "redemption"? Why, in the language of the sermon itself, had so many *allurements and invitations . . . all been ineffectual to persuade you* [read: her] *to accept of deliverance from a slavery you* [she] *are now willingly held in?* The sermon's topic was prayer, including *constant, unceasing, and earnest prayers* for Eunice. But besides prayers *for*, there had been many prayers *to*. Indeed the theme of her whole visit—and of the previous one as well—had been prayer in the second sense. And she had not *answered*.

For this they would deeply resent her—not to say, feel furious with her. But, of course, they could not show their fury, lest they frighten her away, and thus destroy any chance of her future "deliverance." Instead, they must continue their prayer—for, as well as to—and stifle the pressure of their feelings. Actually, some of their feelings were not so much stifled as diverted elsewhere. The preacher's bitter comparison between their own spiritual "state" and Eunice's invited them, in effect, to turn their anger on themselves. We are "the vilest, most shameful" ones, while she—in her "darkness and ignorance"—is innocent. If our prayers have not succeeded, the fault is our own.

Solomon Williams's sermon was, in sum, a deeply resonant response to all the disappointment with and about Eunice. It engaged the listeners directly, at their current emotional flashpoint: exposing but deflecting their anger, sustaining their hope, softening their despair.

It acknowledged their sense of urgency about the outcome. And it transmitted a message with several underlying parts. First: She is not herself to blame, for she does not understand what she has done. This made her continuing "captivity"—and, after thirty-seven years, they still insisted on that word—more bearable, because it was not knowingly and "willingly" chosen. She had never, in short, truly rejected them. Second: We must keep on praying—more fervently and earnestly than before. Perhaps there was special comfort in thinking that they might improve the "qualifications" of their prayer. They had not, as yet, mounted their own best effort; they could, and would, do better. Third: Our continued perseverance—our faith, our hope—will eventually be rewarded. As the preacher said, with reassuring finality, "If you have long waited for an Answer of Prayer . . . it will come at last."[44]

The Mansfield "exercise" was a high point in Eunice's second visit to New England. Unfortunately, other points lie out of view. Stephen's diary remains our best available source; but this time its value is limited because the visitors did not return to Longmeadow. The diary does show a variety of comings and goings directly related to Eunice. In mid-August there was a family gathering in Coventry—presumably at the Meachams' home. On the 12th, Stephen's brother Warham (pastor at Watertown) and a cousin reached Longmeadow, en route "to See Sister E."; two days later "they Set away for Coventry." The same afternoon a half-brother and brother-in-law "came hither" (to Stephen's house), then "went away to Coventry." Stephen himself stayed put, but hoped that "the Lord [would] be pleasd to Grant yt the meeting of So many friends may be fer ye benefit of themslves & of our Sister." Otherwise, he continued to track the course of the Awakening—noting, at one point, that "we See & hear many unusuall, strange things"; and, at another, that "there is still a concern yt is considerable among this people, & in Pticular in my own family."[45]

On September 3, he caught a parting glimpse of Eunice.

> This day I went to Westfd, to meet my Sister & Family (who are upon their return to Canada). Tis pleasnt to See her, but Grievous to part wth [her]. Ye Lord mrcifully over rule that she may yet return & dwell wth us.

His son John again accompanied them to Albany. And Stephen added a prayer that God "be with, bless, and preserve" the entire party. A few days later, as he made his regular Sabbath preparations, Eunice remained much in his thoughts. "Oh, Lord," he wrote in his diary, "be pleasd to bless my poor Sister Eunice & graciously bring her & hers home to thyself . . . & cause [that] She may long to return to us."⁴⁶

For him then, for us now, the shadows lengthen again.

ᗒ

T H E P A R T of Stephen's diary treating the next two years has been lost; we have only some "excerpts" (made by a copyist in the nineteenth century) to help us find our way.⁴⁷ But one of the excerpts does deserve a mention. On November 1, 1742, Stephen heard from his old friend Cornelius Cuyler,

> that my sister's Husband & son have been at Albany, & Says that the reason why my sister has not been with us this summer is that their old Mother is yet alive & sick, and could not be left & that they hold their resolution to come again & see us.

An interesting, tantalizing fragment. Arosen appears again as a visitor to Albany; his presumed connection to the infamous "Canada trade" looks increasingly firm. But whose is "their old mother," his or hers? And what—we must continue to ask—lies behind "their resolution" to come once more to New England?⁴⁸

In any case, they did come—almost ten months later.

> Sept. 4, 1743. Lord's day Even[ing]. Betwixt meetings my Sister Eunice & her Husband came thither from Canada. Thus our thoughts turned anew; the Lord graciously direct us & help us. Oh, that her coming may be in mercy to her soul & the souls of hers.

There was the usual gathering of the clan. On the 14th, "Brother & sister Hinsdell & Brother Elijah" arrived from Deerfield. On the 19th, "Brother Meacham came thither" (from Mansfield). On the 27th, "Capt. Kellogg visited us" (presumably to act as interpreter). On the night of the 29th, "we had no less than 28 persons to take care of." Meanwhile, too, the news spread beyond the family. John Sargeant wrote from Stockbridge to "congratulate you on this third visit from your poor captive Sister" and added his "hope [that] she will now be persuaded to stay with you." And another clergyman-friend of Stephen's wrote to a third: "I conclude you have Heard that Mr. Williams's Sister Eunice is Now with Him, wth Her Husband & Two Children, & yt they Purpose to Spend the Winter in the Country."⁴⁹

Their "purpose to spend the winter in the country" would make this latest visit quite different from the preceding two. And it sparked renewed hope that they might "now be persuaded to stay." Did they themselves intend, possibly, to use the ensuing months as a kind of trial run? And if so, what might their "friends" do to strengthen the case for their permanent return?

September passed with no apparent sign of decisions. At least the visitors and their hosts had more time together than before, and perhaps they forged new patterns of accommodation. Probably, too, they were planning further steps—including further travels—that might eventually yield decisions. On October 5, Eunice, Arosen, their children, Stephen's son John, and some additional "company" left Longmeadow and "went towards Boston." Their first destination likely was Waltham—where the youngest of the Williams siblings, Warham, served as pastor. Their progress en route had something of the flavor of a grand tour. According to later accounts, "the history of her father's captivity being generally known, and her own fate . . . [having] excited a great commiseration, wherever she stopped she was received . . . with much kindness"; in Waltham itself "she was visited by a crowd of strangers." When she moved on to Boston, she was (supposedly) "entertained with great hospitality" by leading members of the clergy, by the congregation of King's Chapel, and even by Governor Jonathan Belcher.[50]

In truth, many of these particulars are hard to confirm now, but one indisputable datum leaps out from the pages of the Massachusetts legislative records. On October 21, in the colony's Great and General Court, it was

> Voted that the Sum of twelve pounds, ten shillings be allowed to be paid out of the publick Treasury to Tarragie (an Indian of the Cagnawaga Tribe who hath married an English Woman), His Wife, and Children, now in Town, as a Present.

> And that the further Sum of Seven Pounds, ten shillings of the Bills aforesaid be allowed Annually to the said Tarragie and Wife during their natural Lives, provided they with their Children come & Settle and constantly reside Among the English Inhabts within this Province. And behave themselves peaceably and as dutiful Subjects to His Majesty.

Tarragie. Also known as François Xavier Arosen? Of course; there he is, with *his wife and children, now in town*, at the end of a long journey from Canada, via Albany and Longmeadow—and the object, that day, of a considerable offer by the highest legislative authority of the Commonwealth. He was to receive *a present*—an outright gift—of twelve and one-half pounds. (The process of conversion to today's values is inexact, to say the least; but perhaps $2,000 would be a very rough equivalent.) In addition, he was to have a somewhat lesser amount as an annual stipend—this to depend on his (and her) willingness to *come and settle and constantly reside within this province*.[51]

Shall we call it a bribe? Whatever, it was extraordinary. If other captives—and spouses of captives—were similarly favored, the evidence is hard to find. Moreover, the evidence here is peculiar; one catches a whiff of embarrassment right in the record itself. The offer is made to *an Indian of the Cagnawaga Tribe* and to his wife, *an English woman*. As if the representatives, and the public generally, did not know exactly who these people were? In fact, few other spousal pairs—from any corner of colonial America—would have been as easily recognized.

The "present," presumably, was theirs to take; the stipend would have to wait. Stephen Williams, on receiving the news a few days later, was full of appreciation—though he, too, was coy about details.

> October 28: Saw abundance of the goodness of God in the kindness of friends to me & to my poor Sister *Eunice*, and hope & pray that she may return & settle in this her native Country, [with] all her family, etc. My father's friends seemed greatly rejoiced. Oh, that God would hear the many prayers offered up . . . for this poor Excile.

The goodness of God in the kindness of friends: an oblique way of acknowledging this act of official largesse. Note, too, that the kindness is *to me*, as well as *my poor sister Eunice*. And that *my father's friends rejoiced*. The representatives' vote was, in short, a gesture of healing on behalf of the entire family—and even of the wider community.[52]

After this, Eunice "and company" drop out of sight for more than a month. (An educated guess might put them in Connecticut, visiting other Williams relatives.) Then, on November 30, they arrived in Longmeadow for a further, three-week stay. And now, for the first time, there would be trouble between hosts and visitors. On December 12, according to Stephen's diary, Arosen "went to Suffield"—presumably to see, and converse with, Joseph Kellogg. "And upon his return [he] fell into the River & was remarkably preserved." Ever alert to the meaning of such events, Stephen hoped that "the providence may suitably affect him." In fact, Stephen might well have hoped—just then—for any sort of providential intervention. His next words were: "I perceive by the Letter which Capt. Kellogg sends me, he [Arosen] is out of frame especially with my son John." *Out of frame?* Upset, resentful, angry (as we would say). The following day Stephen expressed the "fear [that] I am too much perplexed about Tarragie's being out of frame." *Too much perplexed?* Confusion, puzzlement, and plain misunderstanding were, no doubt, a major part of it. And Stephen fell back, yet again, on his "desire to cast this & all my cares upon the Lord."[53]

However, the situation seems only to have worsened, so he decided to ask for help from his friend Kellogg.

LM December 16, 1743

Respected Sir:

This is earnestly to request of you to come over to my house with this bearer—to interpret to my Sister and her Husband, in an affair of importance relateing to their Giveing a power of Attorney—some account of which the bearer (I sopose) can give you, etc. I myself want likewise to have you here—that we may endeavour to remove the wrong Notion yt Tairagie has receivd concerning my son; who has been so far from being a master to them that he has been a Servant & even Slave to them etc. Pray fail not of comeing, if your Health will possibly allow it, & youd add to the many obligations you have allready laid me under. My service to madm etc.

from, Sir, your obligd humble Servant
Stephn Williams[54]

The letter does not entirely explain itself, but clearly they were much at odds. Their trouble seems to have had at least two parts. One was *an affair of importance relating to their giving a power of attorney.* There is no way now to know specifically what this was, but—something about property? And the law? Perhaps it even looked back to the matter of Eunice's inheritance from her father (a sum far greater, after all, than the "present" offered two months earlier by the Massachusetts General Court). The other part was personal: a breach between the visitors and Stephen's son John. Arosen (Tarragie) had formed a *wrong notion* that John was intent on *being a master to them*—when the truth (according to Stephen) was that he had *been a servant, even a slave to them.* The issue, then, was power and preference: Had John exploited his position (as host) to lord it over the visitors?

Certainly there had been close involvement all along. John had escorted them each time they left Longmeadow. Just recently he and they had traveled together on a lengthy tour through eastern New England; no doubt their cultural differences were fully exposed en route. The Iroquoians' code of personal "honor" and "independence" (what Lafitau called their "lofty and proud hearts") and the English penchant for construing relationships in hierarchical terms ("betters" and "inferiors"): to rub these tightly against each other was awkward and potentially explosive. Words and gestures might easily be misunderstood. Helpfulness itself could seem a form of "mastery" (or "servitude") and true reciprocity an unattainable ideal. Of course, we cannot view the actual points of the rub, but the possibilities are clear enough. The distress they caused is also clear; Stephen's letter of the 16th carried an unusual tone of urgency. His *request* was *earnestly* made: Could Kellogg please *come over with this bearer* (that is, immediately)? *Pray fail not, if your health will possibly allow it.* And so on.

However, the next entry in Stephen's diary is very different.

> December 19 Capt. Kellogg is here & we had a free discourse with my sister & especially her husband respecting his uneasiness manifested at Suffield last week, & [he] is sorry, he says, for what he said, & is, I hope, now quite easy.

If we are to believe this, the turnabout was virtually complete. *A free discourse*: in short, an open, unconstrained airing of views. And: Arosen *is sorry for what he said*. If only we could watch how that was managed. At any rate, he is *now quite easy*: comfortable, composed, not *out of frame*. (But Stephen does add a qualifier there: *I hope*.)[55]

The following day "my sister & family went up the country accompanied by my son John." *Up the country?* This meant north through the Connecticut Valley. In fact, at other points in the diary it specifically meant to Deerfield. And, local "tradition" places Eunice in Deerfield at about this time. Moreover, there were other Williams relatives there. And the graves of her parents. And, as a later writer put it, the "scenes of her childhood." In sum: The likelihood is strong that she "and family" did visit Deerfield that winter—a full forty years after she had been "carried away."[56]

On February 6, Stephen received word that the visitors "design to be here sooner than was expected"; apparently, "they grow uneasy at their long stay." Stephen felt that a time of decision might be approaching and reverted to his old refrain: "I do pray God to touch their hearts & incline them to settle in this country." But February passed with no further sign of them. It was only on March 2 that Stephen "heard my sister . . . and family are got back as far as Northampton & design to be here next week." On March 6, their design was fulfilled: "My sister Eunice & family are come again."[57]

Events were moving now toward some sort of climax. Winter was ending, and the visitors' thoughts were turning toward home; time for one more push—an intense, familywide effort of pressure and persuasion. On March 20, "Brother Warham Williams came thither." On the 21st, other "friends came in, viz. Brother & Sister Meacham & Capt. Kellogg." On the 22nd, "brother E. [probably Eleazer] and Mr. E. [possibly Jonathan Edwards] are yet Behind," though obviously expected. On the 23rd, "Brother Hinsdell came, at which we rejoice." Thus "the family are coming together. Oh, that God would be wth us & direct us what to do wth & for my sister." *With and for*: the one as much as the other.[58]

And so to March 24, the day toward which the entire sequence had been pointing. With a dozen or more Williams relatives now on hand. And Captain Kellogg there to perform his customary role as interpreter.

> This day we made our set & concluding speech to my sister & family. Things look dark. But God has all hearts in his hands. With him I desire to leave the affair.

A *set and concluding speech*: their last, best arguments to convince her to stay. Stephen does not identify these, but they are easy enough to guess. Faith and "true religion." Blood and kinship. Love and friendship. Comfort and property. (The government's "present" and promise of an annual stipend. And was her paternal inheritance still to be claimed?)[59]

But they did not succeed, so *things look dark* indeed. Remembering her interview with Schuyler three decades before, we are bound to wonder how fully she replied. And since we cannot hear her reasons directly, we are left to gather impressions from a considerably later time. Stephen Williams's successor in the Longmeadow pastorate wrote, in a letter dated April 1811, that "Eunice could by no considerations be persuaded . . . [And] the only reason which she offered . . . was that living among heretics would endanger her and her children's salvation." A grandniece, writing in 1836, made a similar declaration:

"She positively refused, on the ground that it would endanger her soul." Among nineteenth-century Williamses, it was also said that "she preferred the Indian mode of life, and the haunts of the Indians, to the unutterable grief of her father and friends." If we pull all this together, it reduces to two things: her feeling for the life and culture of her fellow Kahnawakes, and her allegiance to the Catholic church. Or, in the charged language of her New England contemporaries: "savagery" and "popery." The battle had been lost on both fronts.[60]

TEN

ॐ

ON MARCH 28, EUNICE and Arosen made their farewells to Longmeadow.

On March 29, England declared war on France.

These two events, so distant in circumstance and setting, may not have been entirely unrelated. And they serve, in any case, to shift the focus of our story. The *petite histoire* of particular households and villages yields to the *grande histoire* of colonies, kingdoms, empires. Increasingly, the characters on our "stage" respond to forces beyond their sight or control.

Intercolonial and international tension had been building for at least five years. In 1739, the conflicting commercial interests of England and Spain had produced the picturesquely named War of Jenkins' Ear. (The unfortunate Captain Jenkins did, in fact, lose an ear to Spanish coast guards; carefully preserved in a pickle, it would subsequently rouse the fighting spirit of the British.) Meanwhile, in the heart of the European Continent, a dynastic clash sparked by the death of the Hapsburg emperor Charles VI led to the War of the Austrian Succession, and then to a series of territorial struggles known as the First and Second Silesian Wars. France and England were not officially enemies until 1744, but their ships had fought, in various maritime theaters, for some years before.

In the Americas, too, there was an unmistakable sense of sliding toward war. The leaders of New France, New York, and New England competed, throughout the early 1740s, for the allegiance of nearby Indians, and the Indians themselves prepared for renewed violence. In places like Kahnawake there was steadily mounting concern. How long would the trading path south to Albany (and points beyond) remain "open and free"? And would their "father," the French governor, again force the mission warriors to "take up the Hatchet" against their Mohawk "brethren" in the land "below"? In places like Deerfield, the townspeople turned, for the first time in decades, to questions of local defense. Might the old "palisade" fences be refurbished and restored to some effectiveness? Should a new system of "mounts"—strategically placed towers for the use of armed sentries—be immediately installed?[1]

Eunice Williams and her family, traveling from one town to another in the New England countryside, cannot have been oblivious to these concerns. In February, Stephen noted in his diary, that "they grow uneasy at their long stay." And a nineteenth-century chronicler, referring to the same part of the visit, mentioned their anxiety "in consequence of the increasing difficulty between the French and British governments." Moreover, when they finally left, Stephen could not—or anyway, did not—look ahead to the future. Twice before, at similar moments, he had consoled himself with hopes of additional visits—and Eunice had encouraged such hopes. Now he wondered bleakly "whether I shall ever see her again."[2]

Fighting began that spring in Nova Scotia, even before news of the English (and French) declarations of war had crossed the ocean. But it did not immediately involve the chief settlements. Visitors continued to pass, for some while longer, between the two sides: for example, Eunice's fellow captive (and fellow Kahnawake tribeswoman) Mary Harris. In October, Harris appeared with her two sons at a "blockhouse" below Lake Champlain kept by the trader John Henry Lydius. By December, the sons (though not the mother) had reached Connecticut and were staying in Suffield with Joseph Kellogg.[3]

Lydius and Kellogg would subsequently report on these visits to the Massachusetts authorities, and much of their information concerned Kahnawake. The French governor was pressing to reaffirm the tribal alliances; recently he had "sent his officer and Interpreter, which ordered five Cattle to be killed at Cahnowauga [Kahnawake] In order to hang on the Kittle of Warr against the English." The Indians, for their part, were reluctant (according to Kellogg) or divided (according to Lydius). In any case, they had not yet given a full response. At the same time, the English "commissioners" at Albany made overtures of their own, urging the "Canada Mohawk" chiefs to "come and Smoak a pipe [of peace]."[4]

In fact, the summer passed without further hostilities. Winter, too, came and went, with all sides in a state of anxious anticipation. Then, in April 1745, a large force left New England to attack the French fort at Louisburg (on the eastern shore of Cape Breton). After a seven-week siege the fort surrendered, and, from that point onward, the struggle was fully joined. The French, with their "domiciled" Indians, counterattacked to the south and west. One of their initial strikes, aimed deep into New York at the town of Saratoga, brought a Deerfield-like result: approximately thirty inhabitants killed, another 100 taken captive, housing and fields burned to the ground. In New England, too, there were murderous "raids," though on a smaller scale.[5]

The pattern of 1745 was repeated in each of the next three summers: sudden, surprise "appearances" by French and Indian invaders; belated replies by English defenders; bloodshed and "scalping," fire and pillage, all along the settlement frontier. By 1748, the frontier itself had moved well back to the south. Most of the English forts in the upper Connecticut Valley had been abandoned, and there were no "white" residents left in (what is today) the territory of Vermont.[6]

The experience of all this—up close and on the ground—mixed sorrow and fury with recurrent terror; some of it can be glimpsed in personal correspondence and diaries. A Massachusetts militia officer described one assault (in April 1747) as follows: "They seemed every Minute as though they were going to swallow us up, using all the threatening Language they could possibly invent, with shouting & firing as if the heavens & earth were coming together." In another case, an eyewitness reported two of his friends "most Barbarously murdered, haveing their Eyes plucked out, their heart taken out, the Crown of their head taken off, and most Inhumanely mangled an butchered." An incident near Deerfield began when "a number of Indians came upon our men at work, killed and scalped Samuel Allen, Eleazer Hawks, and one of Capt. Holson's soldiers, and . . . [took] captive . . . two of widow Amsden's children . . . [and] one boy of Samuel Allen's, and chopped a hatchet into the brains of one of his girls."[7]

Farther from the front, Stephen Williams recorded the dismal news as and when it arrived. For example: "[July 30, 1746] I hear a man is taken by ye Indians at colerain; thus we are still distressd & disruptd." And: "[October 6, 1747] this day I hear yt ye brave Capt. Eastman is killd by ye Indians; a great loss."[8] But Stephen had also been close to the war, while serving as a regimental chaplain in the Louisburg campaign. His journal offers a graphic picture of events there: of the siege, and the moment of victory, and the long grinding occupation that followed. Stephen was daily involved with comforting the wounded and the sick and conducting "burialls." Eventually he himself was taken "dangerously sick" and evacuated to Boston, where he underwent a slow convalescence. He did not return home to Longmeadow until nine months after he had left.[9]

It is possible, as well, to see some parts of the same sequence from the other—the French and Indian—side. An official "abstract of the different movements at Montreal, on occasion of the war," includes entries like the following: "April 20th [1746] . . . Theganacoeiessin, an Iroquois of the Sault, left with 20 Indians of that village, to go to war near Boston; they returned with 2 prisoners and some scalps."[10] This, indeed, was one of four such departures—all from Kahnawake—in a single day. And it was only the beginning. The total for the months of April, May, and June, 1746, was seventeen separate parties, involving more than 250 men. (Some, apparently, were repeaters; one of the June parties was expected to "return where they have already struck a blow.") The results are not always indicated, but in most cases there were "scalps" taken—and, in some, a prisoner or two.[11]

The impact on Kahnawake itself must have been extreme. Many, perhaps most, of the village's adult men were on the warpath, and thus were at risk of injury or death. Moreover, the English and their Indian allies (principally Mohawks) managed to launch damaging counter-strikes. The French authorities noted that "the enemy has frequently made his appearance . . . near the village of Sault St. Louis." On one occasion, in 1747, a woman was killed "and [her] husband . . . scalped, though he is not dead, notwithstanding he received several wounds as well on his head as on other parts of his body." The killing, the maiming, the terror extended, quite impartially, to both sides.[12]

Despite the efforts of its warriors, Kahnawake's involvement in King George's War (so-called throughout North America) was complex—and deeply ambivalent. There is evidence that its leaders tried initially to prevent, or limit, the outbreak of hostilities. Kellogg's report of his "intelligence" from the Harris brothers described how, at one point, "the sachems . . . took the hatchit and Carried it back to the Gouenour again." Obviously, this position was not sustained. But French officials, throughout the war, remained intermittently suspicious of their Kahnawake allies. In May 1747, when the governor was organizing the defense of Montreal against Mohawk raiders, "it was not thought proper to invite the Iroquois of the Saut, as 'twas feared . . . that they are treacherous and favor the Mohawks in their incursions on our settlements." Indeed, "they are even suspected of giving the enemy notice when we are in pursuit of them, by firing three shots when the detachments are approaching their camp." These suspicions led eventually to an open confrontation—at "a council" held in Montreal, "when they [the village chiefs] gave very lame excuses, and presented a War belt, . . . promising to behave better in the future." As before, the Kahnawake were caught in the middle: compelled to please their French allies and patrons, but reluctant to attack their fellow Mohawks from the south, and wishing always to preserve the lines of their very lucrative trade.[13]

And what of Eunice during this turbulent time? Clearly, there could be no thought of revisiting her New England kin. Stephen's diary does not so much as mention her for a good half-dozen years: no correspondence, no third-party news, not even the occasional prayer. And the mission records are equally silent. Presumably, she had much to think about: the usual women's round of farming and domestic care, the rearing of her children, the special danger posed by enemy raiders—and perhaps, too, the danger to her husband in his own activities outside the village.

For Arosen does make one appearance in the record of this time. In October 1745, near a small "stockade" on the upper Connecticut River, an English farmer named Nehemiah How was surprised while cutting wood by "twelve or thirteen Indians with red painted heads." Easily captured and "pinioned," How was then taken to the French encampment at Crown Point (on Lake Champlain). There he was made to "sing and dance," following the usual practice with captives. There, too, he met an Indian "whom . . . I knew, named Pealtomy." This man, in turn,

> brought to me another Indian, named Amrusus, husband to her who was Eunice Williams, daughter of the late Rev. John Williams of Deerfield; he was glad to see me, and I to see him. He asked me about his wife's relations, and showed a great deal of respect to me.[14]

Amrusus? A corruption, surely, of Arosen. (And one that would stick for at least a century.) He *asked me about his wife's relations.* The interest, the sense of connection, was still very much in evidence. He *showed me a great deal of respect*: this to a captive, bound and pushed about, and headed (within a few more weeks) for prison in Quebec. Arosen's feeling for the Williamses overrode the meaning of the war.

But why was he there in the first place? It is hard not to think that he had, himself, a part in the war. Crown Point was a center of military operations; How had noted, upon arriving, that "the people, both French and Indian, were very thick by the waterside." Many of the war parties, traveling from Canada "in the direction of Boston," would stop at the Point for refreshment and resupply. And, most likely, Arosen belonged to one of them.

Did he know—could he even imagine—how many of "his wife's relations" were engaged on the opposite side? Here is a probably incomplete list. Captain Elijah Williams of Deerfield (son of the Reverend John by his second marriage) had charge of scouting parties sent to search the woods for enemy "tracks." Major Israel Williams of Hatfield was second-in-command of all the forces on the western frontier. Colonel Ephraim Williams of Stockbridge was leader of the local militia, while his son, Captain Ephraim Williams, Jr., commanded a company of Massachusetts volunteers. Colonel William Williams supervised the rebuilding and defense of Fort Massachusetts in the upper Connecticut Valley. Dr. Thomas Williams of Deerfield was appointed to the post of surgeon general. Reverend Elisha Williams of Wethersfield was chaplain, then commander, of a Connecticut unit. And Stephen Williams, of course, was a chaplain, too.[15]

Officially, the war ended in autumn 1748 with the signing by the various European powers of the treaty of Aix-la-Chapelle. The terms stipulated that all territories and borders in North America should resume their pre-war shape. What this principally meant was the return to France of Louisburg (a somewhat bitter pill for the people of New England). In fact, peace was only gradually, and partially, achieved in the frontier regions. In summer 1749, parties of Canadian Indians were reported to be again "abroad" and menacing English settlements; occasional isolated clashes might still shed blood—and yield a captive or two. Stephen Williams's diary reflected a continuing apprehension. In October, he noted a report (which proved false) "yt ye indians on ye Cape Sable are haughty & turbulent & yt war is proclaimed agst ym." And in December, following a particularly bloody incident on the coast of Maine, he expressed his concern "lest we have a new indian war" and the concurrent wish "yt God wd awaken us to repentence."[16]

But even in these uncertain circumstances trade and travel across the wilderness border were cautiously renewed. And the early spring of 1750 brought a sharp surprise to Longmeadow. As Stephen wrote, with typical understatement:

[March] 25 & Sabboth. Toward night my Sister Eunices Husband came hither from Canada, an unexpectd visitant.

The situation was immediately different from each of the previous visits. This time there was no foreknowledge: no letters from Albany, no greeting party, no escorts. And this time Arosen came without family.[17]

The following day (the 26th):

> Capt: Kellogg & my brother Elijah are here; Auresa tells us his business. I do pray God to direct us & show us our duty with respect to him.

Kellogg had come, as usual, from Suffield (probably answering a specific request), while Elijah rode down from Deerfield. And *Auresa* (another corruption of Arosen) was able—with Kellogg interpreting— to announce *his business*. Apparently, he had something quite specific to say.[18]

Then came the 27th:

> a stormy day—Capt: Kellogg and Auresa are here—they told indian stories. Oh, if God would direct and bless us.

How fascinating and (for us) frustrating: if only we could hear a few of those *Indian stories*. But, the ease, the comfort, the sense of familiarity are evident, in any case—and are themselves important. The ex-captive Kellogg and the Indian "visitant" Arosen shared, if not a culture, at least a traditional lore. Stephen, for his part, seemed to be wondering about the future—and again asked God for guidance.[19]

On the 28th:

> Br. Elijah & Auresa went to deerfield and my son Samuel went to Westborough; ye Lord [illeg. word] overrule all our concerns to his own honour & Glory & be pleasd to keep us from sin & all Evill.

The meaning of these departures is not made clear, but almost certainly they involved Arosen's *business*. Deerfield was still, in a sense, the Williams family seat. And Westborough was another town with much experience of captivity, and of ex-captive "visitants."[20]

For two days thereafter (March 29 and 30) the diary treats other matters. Then, on the 31st, it says this:

> I pray God to calm ye Spirits of people who are uneasy upon account of ye money & I pray God to prepare me for his own day

&c. This aftern my Son Samll returnd home from Westborough & my brother Elijah & Auresa returnd from deerfield & people are ready to say we have a cumfutable prospect. I do pray God to direct—oh Ld, thou hast all hearts in their [sic] hand.

Again the surface seems clear, while the center is opaque. The travelers had *returned home* from their respective errands. Property—that is, *ye money*—was somehow at issue. Certain of the people involved were *uneasy* about the direction of events, but others felt assured of *a comfortable prospect*. Stephen wished to identify himself with the more hopeful viewpoint—but closed with another appeal to God's providence.

Two days more (April 1 and 2) passed without comment on Arosen's business. But on the 3rd came—so it seems—the climax:

> This day ye Company I expected came hither, i.e., mr. Rice of Sudbury, capt: Kellogg & my brother E.W. Esq., Auresa, etc. We are at trouble & expense. But I thank God we are able to manage so well. We had severall conferences & proposalls & Auresa was plesant & Good humourd.

The roster of participants—*ye company I expected*—looks significant. Two Williamses: Stephen and Elijah. (Elijah had become, by this time, a man of much wealth, a family leader, and a leader, too, within the regional aristocracy of "River Gods.") Joseph Kellogg: interpreter and—one presumes—skilled negotiator. And "Mr." Edmund Rice of Sudbury: also a town leader, whose two sons (born Silas and Timothy) were now Kahnawakes. That others were present is suggested by the *etc.*; altogether, then, this was a *company* of some size and distinction.[21]

Moreover, they held *several conferences* and considered various *proposals*. The substance of the latter is not indicated, but Stephen speaks of *trouble and expense*. Evidently, they were negotiating terms: perhaps for a settlement of Eunice's inheritance? If so, they must have offered concessions, as a result of which Arosen seemed *pleasant and good-humored*. (At a comparable moment, several years before, he had been *out of frame*.)

The result, as a whole, was a satisfied feeling—at least for Stephen; he was grateful that they had been *able to manage so well*. On the day following their "conferences" he noted that

> ye company dispersd—& my Son John accompanyd Auresa to Westfield.

And he added a concluding comment:

> I desire ye effect of this visit may be ye restoration of my Sister and family.

His phrasing invites a further thought. Previously the favored terms for their project with Eunice were "redemption" or, simply, "return"; *restoration* is unique to this passage. Perhaps, more than the others, it suggests a deal—not exactly a ransom, but something bought and paid for.[22]

However: There was no sign in the months that followed of any actual—or impending—restoration. Stephen's diary from that summer shows him again immersed in his everyday concerns—and again fearful of renewed war. On July 31, he reported a "post from Allbany" with "news of 200 Indians come out to seek revenge," and prayed that "God wd Give us help from trouble." He was then on a preaching tour in Northampton—from which he "went along to Deerfield." There he looked for, but missed, his sister and brother-in-law—they "not being at Home." About the next day he wrote simply: "Spent at Deerfield—a melancholy place to me."[23]

Deerfield, his childhood, the massacre, and its *sequelae* were irrevocably linked in his memory. And his diary is studded with anniversary remembrances. In his early years, these were relatively brief and formulaic. For example:

> [1730: February] 28. This day 26 years ago I was captivatd by ye indians; ye Lord be pleasd to affect me wth his Frowns and mercies.[24]

But as he aged, they would lengthen—and deepen. Thus:

> [1772: March] 11. This day Sixty Eight year ago I was taken captive by ye Indians (a memorable day indeed). God preservd me when wth ye indians, deliverd me out of yr Hands, brot me to my Native country & has Given me to See many days . . . This day I read my Father's Narrative of his captivity—and desire to bear upon my mind God's mercies and afflictions.[25]

He could not, would not—and certainly did not—forget.

⌇

THE DECADE of the 1750s is especially problematic for our story. The elements of *grande histoire* loom overwhelmingly large, while those of *petite histoire*—of the Williamses, of Eunice and Arosen—practically fade from view. Great events were indeed in progress and rolling toward lasting conclusions. The rush, by both the French and the English, for positions of advantage in the Ohio Valley (late 1740s and early '50s); a new round of English-Abenaki tensions in the frontier northeast (1750–53); the youthful George Washington leading colonial militiamen in a first, violent challenge to the French at Fort Duquesne (1754); the mounting of a much bigger challenge under General Braddock, and its rapid, catastrophic defeat (1755); a long string of subsequent French victories, at Fort Frederic, Fort Oswego, Fort Edward, and Fort William Henry (1755–57); the tide-turning British success, for a second time, at Louisburg (1758); the eventual, immortal battle between the armies of Montcalm and Wolfe on the Plains of Abraham above Quebec (1759); the final surrender by the French of almost their entire North American empire (effective in 1760, but not officially ratified until the Treaty of Paris in February 1763): headlines, all, in an agonizing, death-dealing struggle for continental supremacy known to later generations as the French and Indian War. (The concurrent fighting in Europe was called the Seven Years War.) The result would alter the landscape, and shape the future, for generations to come.

How was it viewed at the local level? Longmeadow was too far from the front to be itself a target, but individual townsmen were called to fight in one or another of the English campaigns. And news of the war was anxiously received. Stephen Williams composed a memoir of separate Indian "depradations" along the Massachusetts frontier, to a total of sixteen. The particulars were, by this time, familiar enough: farmers attacked while "at work in the meadow"; militiamen slain "and their bodies horribly mangled"; women and children "captivated" (or, if lucky, "escaped"); "cattle killed and houses burnt."[26]

Deerfield, some thirty miles north, was much closer to the fighting; indeed, the town served as a center of operations for English forces all through the contested borderlands. Weapons and other supplies were stockpiled there; "patrols" left and returned on a virtually continuous basis. The town erected new "garrisons" (fortified houses) and organized a rotating system of "guards." Remembering the massacre of a half-century before, the military command stationed a special detail of soldiers inside the minister's house. Still, the townspeople felt grievously vulnerable to surprise attack. As Elijah Williams wrote in August 1755: "we at Deerfield [are] so reduced by many of our people being gone into the service . . . that we have but 70 men left in the town &

how we shall be able to keep up our stock, and seed our ground, I know not."[27]

The view from Kahnawake was different in some respects, but—one must assume—no less distressing. As the war began, the mission chiefs had briefly held back, but by 1755 they stood together with their traditional French and Abenaki allies. Warriors from "the Sault" seem to have participated in most of the Canadian campaigns against New England. The extent of their losses cannot be determined, but probably it was substantial. At the same time, they took numerous enemy prisoners, some of whom would eventually return home to recount "great hardships while in captivity." For all this, questions were raised yet again about their fidelity to French interests—and their allegedly "English hearts." Moreover, their wartime experience was complicated by a split within their own ranks. In 1754, some thirty families left the mission to settle a new village upriver, called by the French St. Regis (and, by the residents themselves, Ak-wasesne). The leaders of the seceding group were the brothers Tarbell, captives (long ago) from Groton, Massachusetts.[28]

The Williams family had, as before, its own prominent part to play in the war. Elijah held a commission as "major" in the English forces, and several of his cousins were similarly placed. Stephen once again served as a regimental chaplain: first, during the spring of 1755, in a bloody campaign at Crown Point "when our camp was attacked by the french indians," and again, the following year, in an expedition to Lake George. He was by now past sixty years of age, but his commitment to the cause remained strong.[29] Indeed, a crumbling folder of his sermon notes, dating from the period between his two chaplaincies, shows an extraordinary ardor—one might well say, venom—against "papists" and their supporters. The ostensible theme was this: "Let no man deceive you by any means." (Had not his captive sister been deceived exactly so?) But the substance was a furious diatribe against Catholicism. "There was never such an apostasy from Christianity since it had being in Christ," he declared. The Roman Church "is a society and succession of men where ye Sodomy, blasphemy, incest, Adulteries, Sorceries, murders, Treasons, etc. etc. are not only commitd but countenancd." But worst of all were the "tragedies" and "massacres" (*massacres?*) which the Church inflicted on its opponents. According to Stephen, the latter were routinely "burnt . . . and most miserably harrassd & abusd & tormentd & rackd." He wrote out a long list of "particular incidents":

at one time 80 of their babes were found dead in yr cradles dismemberd . . . women with child were ript up . . . some were burnd by fires, others torn in pieces with red hot tongs . . . infants [were] torn out of yr mothers bellies [and] cutt to pieces . . . some [were] coverd with pitch & burnd, some strippd naked & draggd about the streets, some strangld.

And so on, for ten unbroken pages. He made no specific mention of Canadian Catholics, but it is hard not to feel their presence here. Some of the cruelest "massacres" he attributed to persons "set on by priests and friars."[30]

Stephen's participation in the war was ended by illness—what he termed "the diarrhoea difficulty, Jaundice, etc."—contracted at Lake George.[31] Returning to Longmeadow, he resumed his pastoral and familial duties. Among the latter were the probate arrangements for the estate of his stepmother Abigail (second wife, and widow, of John Williams). She had died, at Deerfield, in June 1754, and her property was to be divided among her "Several Heirs Surviving." The latter would include "Mrs. Eunice Williams," whose share was both a cash disbursement and some carefully identified lands ("at the west end of the [family] homelot" and "on the South Side of the Lot in the Great Meadow"). One might imagine, from these provisions, that Eunice lived just around the corner.[32]

In fact, the family had no direct contact with her during the entire decade of the '50s. The closest they came was the following, as reported in Stephen's diary:

[1752: July] 29. I hear from Allbany yt my Sister's children have been there Lately & yt Mary is marrid to a young man whose mother was an English woman. I cant but observe how it has been orderd yt they shd marry (both of ye children) to Such as are one party English as well as ymselves. I wish it may be overruld for yr real Good. Oh, yt God wd pity ym all, & reveal himSelf in his Son in a Saveing manr to them.

Otherwise there was only a single report, received in March 1755, that (in Stephen's words) "my poor sister was alive at Canada last january."[33]

This evidence, scanty as it is, needs also to be considered for what it reveals of Eunice's experience before and during the war years. The marriages of her daughters, for example: Both had been wed by the summer of 1752, when their ages were thirteen and sixteen respectively. (Evidently, they were following the usual Kahnawake pattern of early marriage for women.) Both, according to Stephen's information, had taken husbands one of whose parents was English. (Does this suggest a certain affinity among the families of captives?) Neither, as events would subsequently prove, was at all prolific. Catherine (Gassinontie), the older daughter, seems not to have borne any children of her own—though she did, later on, adopt at least two. Mary (Skentsiese), the younger, bore a son baptized Thomas (and also given the Iroquoian name Thorakwaneken) in January 1759; he would be Eunice's only surviving grandchild. There is, too, the shadowy figure of her son John, about whom "tradition" says that "he died childless at Lake George in 1758." Possibly, he was a casualty of war. Arosen himself may have had some part in the war; one much later source mentions his "being seen" in 1755 in the upper Connecticut Valley— though he would by then have been old for actual combat.[34]

☞

WITH THE DECADE ENDED, and the war as well, Eunice came back into view from New England. In autumn 1760, Stephen received a succession of reports on her welfare.[35] On October 2, from a visiting army officer: "I hear yt my poor Sister at Canada is liveing & yt She is Sick herself, but her family well." On October 21, by letter from his friend Cuyler in Albany: "I have receivd . . . an acct yt my Sister & Family at Canada are liveing." On November 21: "A young man . . . [who] has been a prisoner in Canada fer four years . . . Gives me Such an account of my Sister yt I am ready to think She is alive & her Daughters [too], & yet She has been ill, but was got about. Ye Lord be pleasd to help her & direct [me] what course to take respecting her." On December 11, by letter from another "valuable" friend: "I have . . . an acct of my poor Sister at Canada, who is liveing & her children . . . I pray God to direct me, with respect to my Sister & family."

The borders had reopened—and soldiers, ex-prisoners, and letters were flowing through. And, for Stephen, old concerns reasserted themselves. The substantive news was mostly reassuring. First, Eunice and family *are living*. Each time he began with that; evidently, it had been a source of much worry. Second, she herself *has been ill*, but now *was got about* (i.e., was recovering). So this left the further, entirely familiar question: *what course to take respecting her?* And his typically prayerful response *that God would direct me*, and Himself *be pleased to help her.* He was not yet done with hoping—nor with trying.

Six months later, Eunice left Kahnawake for another visit to her blood-kin and "friends" in New England—her fourth overall, but her first in nearly twenty years. An entry in the journal of the Reverend John Ballantine, minister at Westfield, gives a kind of snapshot of her progress en route:

> [June 30, 1761] Mrs. Williams, daughter of the Rev. Mr. Williams of Deerfield, taken captive when about 4 years of age, has contin-ued with them ever since, is a Catholic, is married to an Indian. She, with her husband and daughter and daughter's husband and child, being on a visit to Rev. Mr. Williams of Springfield, breakfasted with us as they went along on their journey.

The picture is an attractive one, and it suggests the ease with which Eunice might now travel in New England. (But, one cannot help wondering: did Ballantine speak Mohawk? And if not, how did they all communicate, that morning over the parson's breakfast table?)[36] Later the same day, the travelers reached Longmeadow. Stephen's diary specifically identifies them as: Eunice, Arosen, their daughter Catherine and her husband Onnasategen, and their two-year-old grandchild (by their other daughter) Thomas. They would stay for a mere ten days—a much shorter period than previously—but the shape of the visit was largely the same. Repeating the language he had used for their initial meeting (at Albany in 1740), Stephen called it a "joy-full, Sorrowful occasion." In fact, his diary expressed little joy—and a great deal of anxiety. "I am in concern," "my cares increase," "I am weaird & fatigued": Thus did he describe his own feelings from one day to the next. Initially, they had "no interpreter & So can't Say what her intentions & professions are." (Joseph Kellogg had died several years before.) Three days into the visit an interpreter arrived from Sunderland, "Sent by Sister Wms of deerfield," but it appeared that "he does not understand ye Language very well."[37]

In the meantime, Stephen sought yet again to muster the ranks of the family. "I am Sending hither & thither to my children & friends," he wrote at one point, "and I pray to God to bring ym together, yt we may have a comfortable, profitable meeting." On July 4: "My daughter Eunice [namesake of . . .] & Martha are now here wth me." On July 6: "My children John & his wife & Stephen, wth one Mr. Dodge an intrpreter, are come hither; our company and care increases." Meanwhile, too, the neighbors were crowding in. After a regular

Thursday "lecture" (in church) "people came in Great numbers to See my Sister." Stephen worried about her reaction to all this: "I am fearfull yt it may not be agreeable to be Gazd upon."[38]

As the days passed, and the family gathered at his house, Stephen's worries would only deepen. His familiar prayers "yt the Lord be pleasd to direct me" changed to something sharper, more urgent:

> I beg of God to Direct me what to do for my Sister. Be pleasd to incline & dispose her & her Husband to come into, or comply with, Such measures as may . . . promote her Spirituall and Eternall Good & that of her family & off Spring. Oh, that ye vails might be removd from her Eyes!

Again he felt the opportunity, the necessity, the burden of lifting *the veils from her eyes.* And again he faced the dreaded possibility (likelihood?) of failure.[39]

On the 7th that possibility was realized:

> This day . . . I had a Sad discourse with my sister [and her] Husband & find they are not at all Disposed to come & Settle in ye Country. I am at a great loss to Know what course to take, what measures to go into.

A *sad discourse* indeed. The visitors were not—in fact, *not at all*—willing to grasp the chance that once again lay open to them. And Stephen was baffled—in fact, *at a great loss*—about what to do next.[40]

Three days later:

> my poor Sister & company left us. I think I have usd ye best arguments I could to Persuade her to tarry & to come & dwell wth us, but at present they have been ineffectuall. I must leave ye matter wth God.

The best arguments were probably, too, the ones tried several times before. They had not succeeded *at present*—he allowed himself a sliver of hope there—so he must step back, settle his feelings, and *leave the matter with God.*[41]

He could at least take some consolation from the manner of their parting.

> When I took my leave of my Sister & Daughter in the parlour they both Shed tears & Seemd affectd. Oh, yt God wd touch yr Hearts & Encline them to turn to yr Friends & to embrace ye religion of Jesus.

Their tears provided him with an opening in which to reassert—if only to himself—the roots of his own position. Who, after all, are *their* friends? Why, we are—we in Longmeadow, we of the family—not the "savages" of Kahnawake; thus she must someday *turn to us*. And where is *the religion of Jesus*? Surely, it is here, in Protestant New England—not there, in Catholic Canada; eventually she would come to *embrace* it.[42]

But first God must *touch their hearts*, and who could say when that might happen? Three days after their departure, with his siblings and children returning home, he wrote plaintively: "Thus we are in a floating, uncertain world." Still, the latter part of the month found him at his desk "writing to Mr. Secretary Oliver about my poor Sister & family in Canada . . . [in order to] find out a way for her & family to return to this Land of light." Mr. Secretary Oliver was Peter Oliver, a topmost official of the Massachusetts Bay Colony. And Stephen was likely proposing new governmental initiatives to bring Eunice back *to this land of light*, now that Canada was in English hands. Possibly, too, he suggested further inducements—a "present," a stipend, an offering of land—for Eunice *and family* themselves.[43]

There was no apparent result from his letter, and Eunice appears in his diary only infrequently during the next few years. In May 1762, his brother-in-law visited Longmeadow, and "Brot me a letter from my Sister . . . at Canada, by which I learn She & her family are well, & yt Mary & her husband tell of comeing hither this summer." (Mary was the other, younger daughter.) Stephen expressed the hope that "our correspondence . . . may prove really beneficiall to them." And there was, indeed, some ongoing *correspondence*. (Eunice's letters must have been put into English, and into writing, by one or another third party.) On a June day in 1764, Stephen noted that "I have been writing a letter to my Sister at Canada"—this because "I have an affection for her & am concerned fer her welfare."[44]

～

THE FOLLOWING YEAR Eunice's life would change at its center. The repercussions we can only imagine, but the fact itself lies starkly in the mission records: "1765, January 22, died—and was buried on the 23rd—François Xavier Arosen, of an advanced age." They had been married for more than half a century, through the entire span of Eunice's adult life. And her connection to Arosen may well have gone even further back, to the first years of her captivity.[45]

The news would not reach Stephen for a long time. But in November we find this in his diary:

> I hear my Sister Eunice's Husband is dead. Ye Lord mercifully regard my Sister in her widowd Estate & . . . have mercy upon her Soul . . . Oh Lord, thou hast the Hearts of all in thine Hand. If it may be for thine Honour & her reall Good, be pleased to Encline her to return to her native Land.

Did he imagine that the odds of a *return to her native land* were now significantly improved? That just as her marriage long before had cemented her ties to Kahnawake, so, too, her newly *widowed estate* would loosen those ties? He doesn't specifically say, but the implication is clear. It seems, however, improbable that she experienced Arosen's passing this way; though widowed, she was hardly alone. Various bits of evidence suggest close relations with her (now grown) children. They had traveled with her, and would continue to do so. And every communication received from or about her linked her fate and theirs. Moreover, the Kahnawake clan system, with its many-sided obligations among kin, would itself have given comfort and protection. Finally, there was the mission-church: the "offices" of the priests, the support of her fellow worshippers. No, Eunice had many reasons to stay—and few, if any, to leave—even in the face of her loss.[46]

By curious coincidence Stephen was about to undergo a similar change. His own wife (Abigail) had been chronically ill for some years, and now her condition was worsening. In August 1766, he noted that she was "very poorly," and prayed "yt ye Great physcian would help her." His children gathered from their various homes, and waited with him "between hope and Death." Then, on the 27th, he wrote: "We are preparing fer ye funerall of my Dear wife (who Dy'd yesterday); are Getting a Grave Dug & a Coffin made & She is put into it. . . . Our House is now an House of Mourning." On the 28th, they had "ye funerall Exercise" and "Carid the Body of my Dear Consort, and laid it in ye Dark, Silent Grave." On the 29th, his children and friends departed, and "a Great Gap is made in the House"; Stephen was left to ponder his having "livd with her more than 48 years, in the marriage State." He described his nights as "restless" and filled with "disquieting dreams, about Indians."[47]

Yet his grief would subside in the succeeding months, and he remarried barely a year later. His new wife was a Longmeadow widow named Sarah Burt. Perhaps these transitions explain another interval of apparently diminished concern for his "poor sister at Canada." In

1767, he did report a visit by one of the Cuylers "from Allbany," who "brings me account yt my Sister Eunice . . . was alive ye beginning of January & [that] She & her two daughters were well." But otherwise he scarcely mentioned her through a good half-dozen years.[48]

In fact, this same period brought a shift in the substance, as well as the frequency, of his comments about Eunice. No longer did he appeal for her "return to her native country"; in fact, his diary made not a single reference to this theme after 1765. Instead, he expressed the wish that "I might be serviceable to her & hers," that "Some Good may be done" by the letters he wrote her, that his prayers "might be of some advantage [to her] Eternall Soul." The prayers themselves ran strictly to spiritual matters: for example, "ye Ld be pleased to reveal himself in his Son . . . and Grant she may be Savd in ye day of Lord." This, of course, had always been among his central concerns—coupled always with prayers for her return. "Redemption" in two senses, in this world and the next. But now in only one.[49]

Had he actually given up the hope of all his earlier years—the hope, too, of his father and his other Williams kin, not to mention their numerous "friends" throughout New England? Perhaps his most recent disappointment, in the aftermath of Arosen's death and the start of her "widowed estate," seemed somehow final. Or perhaps, with his advancing age (also hers), he was drawn more and more to the prospect of otherworldly reunions. Perhaps, too, he was simply "wearied and fatigued" (the words he had used during her 1761 visit). Whatever the mix of reasons, the shift itself seems palpable—and stunning. A dream of sixty years' duration was gone.

But the story of their lives would continue for some while longer. And, in 1771, it produced something that is otherwise unique in the surviving record: a letter from her to him.

> Coughnawago 12th March 1771
>
> My dr Brother
> We have not Recd aney acct from you Since your Letter of the 19th of Sept. 1761 and are much Surprised that you Cannot find some oppertunity of Letting us know from you by Letter or otherwise. We are all in good helth. My two Daughters are married and well. The one of them has one Child, and the other has not had aney nor any apperance of hir Everey having any. We have a great desire of going down to see you, But dos not know when an oppertunity may offer. We are verey desirous of hering from you, and when you write let us know if all our

Friends are yet alive and if they are in helth and how they Live, with theire names that are alive. I am now growing old and can have but little hopes of seeing you in this woreld. But I pray the Lord that he may give us grace so to Live in this as to be prepared for a happey meeting in the woreld to Come. Doubtless you have herd that my husband is ded. He has been ded this Six yeres. I have nothing more to aquent you with, But am desirous to be Remembred to all Friends and Relations, and Remaine your

> Loving Sister until death,
> Eunice Williams

On the back was written the address: "To Mr. Stephen Williams in Longue medow New England."[50]

Apart from the short Mohawk phrase uttered during her fateful interview with the trader Schuyler more than half a century before, these are her only words that survive today. To be sure, they are not fully hers, since she knew no English—and could not write in any language. The role of a translator/scribe is evident in the phrasing itself—"going down" (presumably the French verb *descendre*) to visit New England, for example, and "the one of them . . . and the other" (*l'un et l'autre*)—not to mention the rendering of the place-name "Longue medow." Still, we can get no closer to her thought and feeling than this.

What, then, is the thought and feeling expressed here? Interest. Affection. And, above all, a wish for connection. The reproach with which she begins: her being *much surprised* that he hasn't written in so long. The recounting of her own family news, followed by the request for his—and that of *all our friends*. The *great desire* to revisit New England, but her *little hopes* of actually managing to do so. The prayer for a *happy meeting* in Heaven. The opening salutation to *my dear brother,* and the farewell from your *loving sister until death*. And the way she identifies herself as, simply, *Eunice Williams*. Connection is indeed her theme, from beginning to end.

Stephen noted his receipt of her letter three weeks after its writing (April 2), and responded with a familiar prayer: "Oh, yt God wd bless hr & hr off Spring, and reveall himself in his Son, in a Saveing manner to yr Souls." This was, of course, his own mode of connection. From now on his diary shows only occasional, intermittent concern with Eunice. At one point he described himself "writing letters to my Sister at Canada." At another, he "receivd a letter from N York (from Col:

P. Schuyler) Giveing me an account yt my sister Eunice was alive & well ye middle of Novembr: last." And, at still another, he was "informed . . . yt my sister Eunice's 2nd Son was come to Hatfield wth a young french wife." This last he found "Surprizeing & cant be true as my Sister has no Son." A week later the information was corrected: "the person yt was Soposd to be my Sister Eunice's Son" proved instead to be the son of another woman also "taken Captive at Deerfield when ye Town was taken."[51]

During this same period a group of Protestant ministers began to proselytize the Indian communities of Canada, and their work would open new channels of communication to New England. Most were young men associated with "Moor's Charity School" (later reorganized and renamed Dartmouth College) in New Hampshire. The Reverend Thomas Kendall, for example, spent the summer of 1773 in Kahnawake, and kept a lengthy journal of his experiences there. He lived in the house of an ex-captive named Stacy, attended at least one mass (in which he "saw more Hypocricy than could posably go with a rational mind"), went occasionally into "counsel with the Chiefs," conducted an informal school for "Indian boys," himself learned to "speak Indian prty fast," and promoted the admission of several of his best pupils to the Charity School the following winter. His journal does not mention Eunice, but certainly he knew her. For, in December, Stephen's diary noted receipt of a letter "from Mr. Thos Kendall . . . who has been (last Summer) at Canada." Kendall offered "Some account of my Sister Eunice & family"; moreover, he "thinks they are willing to come (at least some of ym) & See us if they were invited."[52]

In February, he heard from his friend Henry Cuyler that "Eunice's daughter Katherine & her Husband were with him [in Albany] a few days ago," and that Eunice herself had traveled part of the route south (to within "about 3 miles from fort Edwards"). They had hoped, indeed, "to have come hither [to New England], but . . . winter over takeing them preventd their journey." Stephen found "ye afair . . . difficult" to understand, believing that "they might have come thither Easily in a Sleigh." Still, he "wrote to Mr. Cuyler to Supply them with ye value of ten or twelve Dollars if they need it," and left the rest for God to "mercifully over-rule." Two months later, Cuyler wrote again "yt he has not heard from my Sister Eunice & family Since ye beginning of March." He had been unable, therefore, to "advance [them] some mony (as I desird)," but would do so if and when he had the chance. In July came yet another letter from the same source, and "I learn yt tis probable my Sister returnd to Canada upon ye very breaking up of ye Winter." The question of an "advance" remained unresolved, and Stephen worried "lest my Sister & Children will be Suspicious they are neglectd." He comforted himself with the thought that "I did what I could . . . to have them taken care of," and hoped that "Mr. Kendall [and] Mr. Fisher will see her at Canada and Deliver them ye money yt I sent." His sense of financial obligation seems new—and puzzling. But clearly *ye money* was one of his remaining ties to them.[53]

Kendall and Fisher did not, so far as we know, see Eunice that second summer. But another Dartmouth missionary named James Dean met her, and wrote about her in a subsequent letter to Stephen. "Spent the summer past at Gachnawago [Kahnawake]," Dean began, "and was well acquainted with your Sister." She was living "comfortably and well"; her health seemed remarkably good, "considering her advanced age." Her family consisted of "two daughters and One Grandson, which are all the Descendants she has." She kept an "affectionate remembrance of her friends in New England," but did not expect to see them again since "the fatigues of so long a journey would be too much for her to undergo." Dean added, as a kind of postscript, that Stephen would soon receive a letter "from herself, which Mr. Frisbie [another missionary] brought down." And Stephen's diary recorded its arrival soon thereafter.[54]

꒛

AT THIS POINT—the end of the year 1774—Stephen had passed his eightieth birthday, and Eunice was nearly as old. Yet their story continued still. Or, rather, their two stories—for age was gently widening the distance between them. Stephen went on with his duties as pastor—though the town did hire a younger man to assist him. His family, meanwhile, was attaining virtually patriarchal dimensions. Seven grown children: five sons, three of whom had followed him into the ministry, and two daughters, themselves the wives of ministers. Plus at least forty grandchildren (ranging in age from one to twenty-seven years) and three great-grandchildren.[55]

With Eunice, by contrast, were only her middle-aged daughters Catherine and Mary and her grandson Thomas; these, as James Dean noted, were "all the descendants she has." One imagines, given the circumstances, that Thomas became a particular focus of attention, but not much is known of his childhood years. According to a later account, he was among the "Indian boys" marked for education at

Moor's Charity School—but could not actually go because of illness. He served, on the British side, in the American War of Independence (as did many others from Kahnawake). He became a huntsman and fur trader, and frequently traveled to Albany to ply his wares. He was married, in 1779, to Marie Anne Konwatewentaton; she, too, was the grandchild of a captive (in her case, of the man born Silas Rice and rechristened Jacques Tannhahorens after being taken from the Massachusetts town of Westborough). Soon thereafter Thomas and Marie Anne began to have children of their own, a dozen by the time they were done. These would also be Eunice's great-grandchildren—and her sole blood link to the future.[56]

The Revolutionary War interrupted, but did not entirely foreclose, communication between Canada and New England. In April 1776, Stephen received a report that his sister was "alive and in Health," and wrote to her in reply. In June 1778, he heard the same thing from a Deerfield kinswoman. And in July of that year he heard it again on better authority: "Ye account comes from one yt saw her last winter." He professed satisfaction that she was "comfortably provided for (Says my informer)," and prayed for the "saveing" of her soul "notwithstanding the disadvantages she is undr by a Suprstitious Education."[57]

Stephen was still "in health" as he entered his ninetieth year (and his sixty-sixth in the Longmeadow pastorate). But in the spring of 1782, he began at last to weaken. Sensing that his end was near, he undertook a round of pastoral and personal farewells. His "sons in the ministry . . . [came] in a body" to see him, as did a great many of his local parishioners. And, as a eulogist would later remark, "none who visited him . . . returned without his most affectionate blessing." He "read over ye memorandum I made of my captivity . . . when I returnd to New England," and reflected how "God has done Great & marvellous things for me." His enormous diary ended, literally in mid-sentence, with the entry for June 3: "About one this morning . . ." His last spoken words were a moving spiritual testament to his family, remembered and treasured long thereafter. Death took him on June 10.[58]

A little before, Stephen had noted this:

> I heard of ye death of Lt. Hall of Deerfield who was taken captive when I was & (unless Capt. Carter of Norwalk is liveing) I am ye last Pson yt Survives of those captivatd at yt time.[59]

Captain Carter was, in fact, gone by then. Yet Stephen's claim to be *the last person that survives* from the original *captivated* cohort was wrong; his *sister at Canada* would outlive him by another three years. That he could simply have forgotten her seems unlikely—no, impossible—given all that had gone before. But perhaps he overlooked her for a different reason. Perhaps he had changed his long-standing view—and saw her, in the end, as captive no more.

ENDINGS

ᘰ

HOW DOES THE story end?

> Le vingt six novembre, mil sept cens quatre vingt cinq, j'ai in-
> humé Marguerite, belle-mère d'Annasetegen. Elle était agée de
> quatre vingt quinze ans. . . . L. Ducharme, miss[ionaire].

Translation:

> On the twenty-sixth of November, seventeen hundred and eighty-
> five, I buried Marguerite, the mother-in-law of Annasetegen. She
> was ninety-five years old. . . . L. Ducharme, miss[ionary].[1]

Two very simple, very spare sentences from the mission records.
Marguerite: the name she took in her Catholic re-baptism long ago.
(And the one with which she had been introduced to John Schuyler
soon thereafter.) *Mother-in-law of Annasetegen*: she is identified by
reference to her daughter Catherine's husband, who was himself a
figure of note—a "grand chief." *Ninety-five years old*: an estimate no
doubt; indeed, an overestimate. Actually she was eighty-nine.

And yet, for none of them was this truly an end at all. Not for her;
not for the priest who buried her; not for the mourners who gathered,
that early winter's day, by her grave.

No, in their minds, it would have seemed more nearly a beginning.
From the illusions and vanities of "this world" (as she had put it in
her letter to Stephen some years before) she was going now to the
blessed truths of "the next." Her earthly death was like a barrier falling
to permit her eternal release. Her mortal remains would lie inert and
inhumé in the mission cemetery—though destined, in some remote
future time, for their own "resurrection." Her immortal soul would
fly toward a previously unseen but long-prepared rendezvous.[2]

Indeed, in the deepest sense, they saw her death—like all death—

as neither end nor beginning, but rather a "passing." Continuity, not change, was its central theme. The shape and substance of an entire life would find appropriate afterlife confirmation: sin would be punished, and virtue rewarded, each in its own due measure. The "deathbed" scene should itself be peaceful and dignified. The gathering of family and friends, the arrival of the priest, the administering of last rites ("extreme unction"): these were but encouragements to her soul about to depart. The outcome was already clear and could not now be changed.

And yet her passing would not, they believed, be completed in a single stage. From "this world" she would travel to an intermediate stop known as "Purgatory." There she would linger for a time, poised between the "celestial vault" of Heaven and the "fiery abyss" of Hell. Purgatory had its own fire, but of another sort: its point was exactly the purging, the final preparation, needed for entry into Paradise. Her stay there would depend on the moral record of all her preceding years—and on the "intercessory" efforts of earthbound "friends." Those she had left behind could indeed intercede, with masses and prayers for the "repose" of her soul. She would welcome periods of repose, since Purgatory was—at the very least—an agitated, uncomfortable place. Her views of the inferno below were indescribably horrifying. But, fortunately, she could also look up toward the open gates of Heaven. There she could see the Virgin and Christ child splendidly enthroned. And the various saints beckoning to her. And groups of angels, sprinkling fresh water (to symbolize consolation) on those, like herself, whose time of deliverance was not yet come.

Eventually, they told themselves, her time *would* come. And she would make her final "ascent," accompanied by cherubs, serenaded by celestial choirs, and welcomed by the Savior Himself. Safe at last in paradise, she would enjoy the unspeakable bliss of the holy. And would enjoy, too, a longed-for reunion with other souls important to her: most especially, her Kahnawake parents; her husband Arosen; her daughter Mary; and, yes, her fondly remembered "English" brother Stephen.

⁙

THE EVIDENCE does not show us how, but we may assume that news of her death would in time have reached New England: reached Deerfield first, perhaps, from there to follow the lines of Williams family connection to Longmeadow, to Mansfield and Coventry in

Connecticut, and eventually to Waltham, Roxbury, and Boston. The "unredeemed captive," they might have said, has found at last her resting place.

But their view of this place, and of the resting it allowed, would have differed from the ones that prevailed (concurrently) in Kahnawake. To be sure, Heaven and Hell were also their end points; the difference was in the process, the "passage" thereto. A key element, for example, was "predestination." Though softened over time around some of its edges, this profoundly "Puritan" belief remained strong at its core in much of eighteenth-century New England. Its central premise was simple and daunting: The salvation of individual souls was decided by God irrespective of—and prior to—specific earthly experiences. Humankind was separated into the "chosen" few (the "elect," the future "saints") and all the rest (the "reprobate" masses).[3]

Each person, then, in approaching death was also approaching a climax of self-discovery: In which group would he (or she) henceforth be found? Each had long sought signs of "assurance" in his (or her) daily life, and some went forward with confidence. Stephen Williams, for one, declared in a "last conversation" that he "had a firm hope of future glory, grounded wholly on the mercy of God and merits of the redeemer."[4]

Still: even "firm hope" was well short of certainty, and many who reached this point remained deeply anxious. Moreover, the experience of dying, the moment itself, would likely be an ordeal of great magnitude—as the Bible said, "the wages of sin." The minister who preached at Stephen's funeral described it thus:

> Death is justly stiled the King of Terrors, the most terrible of all terribles. The pains and agonies of a dying hour are very terrifying, the thought of being disembodied and dissolved very disagreeable, the consequences infinitely great and important. Many a good man (some for one reason, and some for another) have stood shuddering upon the brink, afraid to launch out into the bottomless ocean of eternity.[5]

But Eunice had now launched out. And, presumably, she now knew her "eternal destiny." Her peculiar situation as a Catholic convert would, for her New England relatives, have been an added—and major—complication. The stain of "popery" was in some sense indelible, but was it therefore unforgivable? Stephen had remembered to the end "the disadvantages she is under by a superstitious education." And, many years before, her cousin Solomon Williams acknowledged that "her own misery is unfelt and unseen by her," since she had lived since childhood "in the thickness of popish darkness"—this while preaching about her, as well as to her, in his "Awakening" sermon at Mansfield.[6]

So perhaps she might have been saved, after all; God's ways were that unknowable. If so, she was now "sitting at Christ's right hand," in the company of other elected souls. If not, she must be in Hell, enduring the tyranny of Satan and the torments of the damned. In one or the other setting she would remain for an undetermined period of years—ten, a hundred, a thousand, nobody could say for sure—until the final "Day of Judgement." This would mark the end of time (as we know it) and would bring, too, Christ's "Second Coming." Her soul, like all others, would then be summoned anew and joined to her resurrected body. The judgment process would follow directly—at which point (as a Boston clergyman described it) "the heavens shall roar, and there will be terrible thunderings and lightnings, and the earth shall be in flames of fire." Her "carriages" in life, whether righteous or sinful, would be weighed in their turn—indeed, would be "openly declared before the whole world." The result would confirm, a thousandfold, the previous verdict given at the time of her death: either to be "raised up in glory," or to be cast into "an endless eternity of misery."[7]

჻

T W O   E N D I N G S so far: one from her fellow Catholics in the mission-village, the second from her Puritan blood-kin in New England. But these are not quite all. For, here and there in the byways of Kahna-wake, still another tradition lingered, a legacy of the first migrants from the Iroquoian heartland a century before. This, too, offered its own way to end.

"I am quite sure," wrote Lafitau, "that an Iroquois . . . would be embarrassed to specify the nature of his soul." Nevertheless he would "give it spirituality, as much or more than we do"—and would identify it with both "the operations of the mind" and "those of the heart and will." Moreover: "The soul of the Indians is much more independent of their bodies than ours is"; thus it may take "long journeys" of its own—as during sleep, when it provides the stuff of dreams. These same "soul" qualities were shared, so the Iroquois believed, with non-human forms of life. Animals "possess a great deal of reason and intelligence," and "survive their body," and travel after death "to the country of souls."[8]

It was to this "country of souls" that Eunice herself must now have departed. The route was "very long and painful," with "much to suffer because of the rivers which have to be passed over on bridges so shaky and narrow that only disembodied souls can pass over them." Furthermore, the bridges were guarded by ferocious dogs, which "dispute the passage"; as a result, "many of [the travelers] fall into the waters, whose current rolls them from precipice to precipice."[9]

Still, if she should be "fortunate enough" to get through, a sublime reward was waiting. She would find herself in a "great and beautiful" land, approaching a vast "lodge," one part of which was "inhabited by their God Tharonhiaouagon, and the other by Ataentsic, his grandmother." The lodge, apparently, was a palatial version of an Iroquoian longhouse, and its head "in Indian fashion" was the grandmother. Its apartments were sumptuously decorated "with an infinite number of wampum belts, bracelets, and other furnishings," all of them "gifts made . . . by the dead who are under her rule."[10]

While advancing toward this extraordinary place, she would begin to hear "the drum and the sound of the turtle shell rattle [which] mark the cadence of the dead with a charm suitable to win all hearts." The "ravishing music" would excite in her a "keen pleasure" and cause her to "run ardently" toward its source. Soon she would hear as well the sounds of "continual acclamations" uttered by hosts of joyful "dancing souls." When she was very near, "several souls [would] detach themselves" and come out to meet her. Thus escorted she would arrive at the "lodge" itself and "the assembly where the dancing is taking place." There she would receive greetings and "compliments," and would be "satiated with the most delicious viands." And would "mingle with the others to dance and enjoy alternately all the pleasures." And, best of all, would "no longer [be] subject to anger, restlessness, infirmities, or any of the vicissitudes of mortal life."[11]

꒛

THREE DIFFERENT endings, then, representing the three main strands of her long life story. However, in one respect they do converge. Each denies the finality of death—and continues the story toward an endless "next world" future.

EPILOGUE

ᔐ

IN "THIS WORLD," too, the story continued—even without the living presence of its leading protagonists. Their descendants would remain in touch, and at least occasionally in direct contact, for decades yet to come. And would add new twists to the ties of blood and interest that still connected them.

As Eunice's sole surviving grandchild, Thomas Thorakwaneken Williams was a key link to the next stage. His activities as huntsman and trader—and as sometime military scout, negotiator, and middleman in the world of intercolonial politics—took him repeatedly southward from his Kahnawake home. Occasionally, perhaps quite often, he would visit en route with his New England "friends." In the summer of 1785, for example, one of the Longmeadow Williamses wrote to her aunt in Deerfield that "the last Sabbath A Grandson of your Sister Eunice came here & with him a Cousin of his." This was Thomas and a certain Jean Baptiste Toietakherontie (who may also have had some Williams blood). They "propose tarrying here nine or ten days, & are going from here to Deerfield." They had made other stops already; as a result, they carried "letters of Genll Schuyler of Albany [a Revolutionary War hero] and Mr. West of Stockbridge [the current missionary there] informing who they are & recommending them to the kind treatment of their friends."[1]

This evidently cordial encounter followed a pattern that would long endure. In the winter of 1800, Thomas reappeared with two of his children, apparently at the express invitation of Deacon Nathaniel Ely (husband of a granddaughter of Stephen Williams). Deacon Ely recorded their arrival as follows: "January 23 . . . Mr. Thomas Williams with his two Sons, viz. Lazau [short for Eleazer] Aged 11 and John Sunwattis 7, came to my House at Longmeadow." The boys "were in Indian Dress and Could not Speak a word of English. They were put immediately to School." Ely noted also that "These Lads are Great Grandchildren to Eunice Williams who was Carried into Captivity in the year 1704."

Putting the two boys to school was, in fact, the purpose of their visit; subsequently, Ely would describe what "indefatiguable Pains have been Taken to Learn them to Read & Write and also to Give them some knowledge of Agricolture and the Arts of Civil life." The result—he seemed to imply—might even reverse the "capture" of their notorious forebear; gradually, they would be brought back to "civil life."[2]

Deacon Ely declared that "the Lads are well Inclined and in Particular the Oldest Appears to be a Solem youth." However, a short "remembrance" composed years later by a fellow pupil suggests a more complicated story.[3] There was, first, the matter of their "very grotesque and attractive appearance": the colorful "blankets [they wore] . . . worked into the forms of a loose great coat," the "beaded wampum . . . about the loins," the "scarlet gaiters" buttoned up their legs, the moccasins on their feet, and "the hair of their heads carelessly stuck with feathers." In a "country retreat" like Longmeadow "this exhibition excited a wondrous and wondering attention." In church "the whole congregation, on Sunday, instead of looking at the minister . . . could . . . think of little but the Indians." And, in school, they were equally "as much the objects of curiosity." Their teachers were obliged to "humor . . . the wildness of their nature and habits . . . [and] to endure the disorder which their manners at first created." From time to time they would "jump up and cry 'Umph' or some other characteristic and guttural exclamation, and then perhaps spring across the room." Occasionally, they would "dart out" of the schoolhouse altogether "and take to their heels in such a direction as their whims might incline them."

The boys remained in Longmeadow for about five years—and "gradually dropped their Indian dress and manners and adopted those of their new society." They traveled occasionally to the homes of other Williamses, one of whom noted their visits in her diary. ("In the evening our Indian cousins visited us," or: "Today . . . came here . . . our Canada cousins.") Their father "came down" to check on their progress, and later sent a fulsome letter of thanks to Deacon Ely. ("I do think, Sir, that you are a best friend to me I have in the world.") Eventually, the younger boy was taken back to Kahnawake. But

Eleazer stayed on, having become "a universal favorite" (according to the fellow pupil quoted above) and "cherished by everybody as a most promising youth."4

Thenceforth Eleazer was the exclusive focus of this "civilizing" project. He was "extensively introduced into the best society of New England," and acquired "numerous . . . patrons . . . among the best and most influential men of the country." A crucial element—as Eleazer himself acknowledged—was "my being descended of the famous Rev. John Williams." The latter's "captivity, suffering, and the destruction of his whole parish . . . being so noted in that part of the country . . . excited a curiosity among the Rev. clergy to see & converse with me." For their part, the reverend clergy took great satisfaction from the "rapid developments of his intellect and moral virtues and the improvement of his manners." They felt especially gratified that he managed "as the highest finish of his character . . . to embrace and cherish with great sincerity and earnestness the . . . principles of Christian piety." In sum: "he grew up a gentlemen and a Christian." (Whereas—they might well have reflected—a century before, *she* had grown up a "savage" and a "papist"?) Here was a turnabout indeed. (And also a measure of revenge?)5

But however "promising" he seemed as a youth, Eleazer would subsequently confound these selfsame "patrons." An initial disappointment was his abrupt departure from Moor's Charity School (to which he was sent in 1807); a second was his conversion (in 1811) to Episcopalianism. From then on, his career would carry him far from New England. Together with his father he played an obscure part, on the American side, in the War of 1812. (He later claimed to have helped win the battle of Plattsburg, to have carried out numerous secret missions, and to have served as "Superintendant-General" for Indian affairs on the northern frontier—all this in the rank of a commissioned "colonel." But the supporting evidence is nil.)6

After the war Eleazer accepted a position as "lay teacher"—in effect, missionary—among the Oneida Indians of upstate New York. Once there, he was quickly embroiled in tribal politics, as leader of the "Christian Party." In the early 1820s, he planned, promoted, and participated in the removal of several hundred Oneidas from their traditional homeland to a frontier "reserve" in Wisconsin. For a time he attained considerable prominence as a kind of intercultural broker and representative of Indian interests to various governmental authorities. But in the 1830s, he gradually lost favor, even with his "Party" supporters. The following decade found him frequently on the road, pursuing various schemes of missionary enterprise and personal emolument. His numerous detractors became openly scornful; one rebuked him publicly as "a fat, lazy, good-for-nothing Indian."[7]

But Eleazer was about to make a spectacular, if short-lived, comeback. Sometime in the late 1840s, he conceived the idea that he was not, biographically speaking, the man he seemed to be. Instead, he was the "lost Dauphin": Louis XVII, scion of the Bourbon dynasty and rightful heir to the throne of France. In fact, Eleazer was one of at least forty such "pretenders" (worldwide), but his ingeniously argued claim put him near the front of the pack. There was, for a start, no record of his baptism at Kahnawake (in contrast to most of his siblings). From this it followed that his life had begun elsewhere—and from this an extraordinary tale of royal birth, capture in the first bloody wave of the French Revolution, rescue from a Parisian jail, a secret transatlantic journey arranged by monarchist agents, and eventual placement in a safely inconspicuous Indian village. The details were presented in a series of newspaper articles, both in the United States and in France, beginning about 1850; the most provocative and widely read appeared in *Putnam's Magazine* under the heading "Have We A Bourbon Among Us?" The author of this piece, an Episcopalian clergyman named Hanson, soon elaborated his case in a book entitled *The Lost Prince*—he omitted the question mark this time—which made its subject a national celebrity.[8] The "Dauphin Williams" was sought out by journalists, was much in demand as a lecturer, and was invited to meet with important public figures. He sat for portraits by leading painters and photographers—with results that were eagerly studied for traces of "Bourbon" likeness.[9]

But even at the outset his claims aroused deep skepticism. Moreover, his elderly mother bitterly dismissed them all. She had borne him, she explained, "in the woods" while on a hunting trip with her family near Lake George—hence the absence of a baptismal record.[10] Other parts of the story also collapsed under scrutiny. Eleazer died, discredited and in poverty, in 1858, while visiting the Kahnawake of St. Regis. The "Dauphin" controversy would long outlast him—there were renewed bursts of public interest well into the twentieth century—but mostly he was put down as a charlatan.[11]

That issue aside, one senses here yet another variation on the old theme of unusual origins. And perhaps the virulence of Eleazer's critics reflected their own prior stake in the theme. In their minds, the line of his life was supposed to begin with "savagery"—and then ascend toward the level of "civill [and Christian] gentleman." He had let them down, on the second count, through the course of his adult years, and then sought to challenge the first. No—he seemed to be saying—far from starting "savage," he had been born at the absolute pinnacle. Circumstances had forced him down, not up; and, near the end of his days, he wished only to reassert his claim to the heights. It was, by any standard, a bizarre turn of affairs, and, for many in the world of "civility," an unacceptable one.

✒

A N D N O W a truly concluding scene, based on a slim volume (pamphlet really) published in 1837. Here is the volume's long and very descriptive title: *A Sermon, Preached to the First Congregational Society in Deerfield, Mass., and in the Hearing of Several Indians of Both Sexes, Supposed to be Descendants of Eunice Williams, Daughter of Rev. John Williams, First Minister of Deerfield, August 27, 1837.*[12]
An inside page of "prefatory remarks" puts the background in place.

> On the 22nd of last month our village was visited by two or three families of Indians, amounting in all to twenty-three of various ages, calling themselves by the name of Williams on the ground of being descendants of Eunice.

> During their short stay, a little more than a week, they encamped in the vicinity of the village—employed their time not otherwise occupied in making baskets—visited the graves of their ancestors, the Rev. Mr. Williams and wife—and attended divine service on Sunday in an orderly and reverent manner. They refused to receive company on the Sabbath, and at all times and in all respects seemed disposed to conduct themselves decently and inoffensively. During their sojourn with us . . . their encampment was frequented by great numbers of persons, almost denying them time to take their ordinary meals, but affording them, as if to make amends for such inconvenience and privation, a ready sale for their fabrics.

> On the 1st of September they decamped and commenced their homeward progress towards Canada.[13]

Simple enough, on its face. And pleasant. And popular, in the literal sense. The Indians came, and made a *short stay*, and *visited the graves of their ancestors*, and attended *divine service*, and found a *ready sale for their fabrics*, and then *decamped* to return *toward Canada*.

We know nothing, unfortunately, of their personal experience around these events. Did they feel welcome? Were they at all fearful in coming, or regretful on leaving? How much, and in what ways, were they gratified by their sense of contact with *the Rev. Mr. Williams and wife*? The record before us does not, indeed cannot, say.

About the other side—that of the Deerfield (and adjacent) villagers—we know a good deal more. We can immediately sense the interest aroused, in the *great number of persons* who flocked to visit *their encampment*. We can sense, too, a kind of wonderment—that the visitors should have behaved so *decently and inoffensively* and in such *an orderly and reverent manner*.

Moreover: alongside such outward signs, we have the evidence of the sermon itself—the core of the printed volume. And it is powerful. Listen . . .

> *Acts, XVII, 26*. And [the Lord] hath made of one blood all nations of men for to dwell on the face of the earth; and hath determined the times before appointed, and the bounds of their habitation.[14]

Thus a Biblical text, fitted to the occasion. And the themes to be discussed: *blood, nations, times,* and *bounds*.

> The varieties which human nature presents . . . are such as will not allow us, on first inspection . . . to acquiesce in the belief of a common origin.[15]

Appearances—to repeat—*will not allow us*. However:

> the Scriptures . . . assert a common origin for all the differing tribes and races of men . . . [And] Naturalists and Physiologists, . . . who have gone most deeply into the investigation of this subject . . . have in general . . . arrived at the same conclusion.[16]

So the issue is clearly framed: the old, endlessly debated, always compelling issue of *a common origin*. For them, common origin would inescapably mean common species.

The argument moves, step by careful step, from scripture and scientific opinion to culture and reproductive biology.

> One reason . . . in favor of the supposition of a common origin is the general prevalence of such a sentiment among the mass of mankind, notwithstanding the obvious reasons for adopting a different hypothesis.[17]

A widely prevalent *sentiment*, in the face of *obvious reasons* to the contrary: such a sentiment must have some basis in truth.

Another reason . . . perhaps . . . the most conclusive and incontrovertible, . . . is [the] invariably acknowledged law of nature that none of the distinct species of animals . . . are capable of being mingled, blended, or assimilated in the natural progress of propagation or reproduction.[18]

The point is that the various *tribes of men* can indeed be *mingled, blended or assimilated*. And, should anyone wish to doubt the fact, there was irrefutable evidence close at hand—in the flesh and blood of Eunice Williams's descendants. Eunice's life itself offered a precise demonstration of *the natural progress of propagation or reproduction* across racial lines. Furthermore:

With respect to the varieties, which actually exist in the human race . . . much might be said by way of satisfactory explanation. Climate, together with the changes produced upon the human constitution by diet, air, soil, and habits of life, in regions exceedingly unlike each other, is known to be attended with peculiarities which are very considerable.[19]

In short: there are ways to account for racial *varieties* other than actual species difference. Such as environmental influence, in *regions exceedingly unlike each other*.

This fact becomes manifest in instances of migration, in the case of the same individuals.[20]

Again: was not Eunice herself one of those *individuals*? Her personal *migration*—if the term be allowed—had assuredly produced both *changes* and *peculiarities*.

And there is more. The supposition of *a common origin* appears not only plausible, but morally advantageous as well.

For if men were by nature what they have become by custom and various accidental causes, no remedy could be hoped to arrive for those occasions of disaffection and hostility, by which they are divided from, and animated against, each other—no remedy short of that which should effect the extermination of one or the other.[21]

To say it again:

If communities of men, who are made alien to each other by strong lines and marks of diversity, and who are accustomed to regard each other with the utmost jealousy and aversion, had reason to believe that these marks of distinction and sentiments of enmity were founded in nature—were a part of their original constitution—what hope could they entertain that such a terrible evil, such a wasting scourge, could ever be mitigated or removed?[22]

If . . . if . . . Rather, in that case,

blood and carnage must . . . deform and deface the scenes of earth, to the end of time.[23]

Look past the circumlocutions, and one sees here the germ of an immensely forbidding idea. *Marks of distinction*, among the various racial groups, underlie *sentiments of enmity*, which may, in turn, bring efforts at *extermination*. From difference, to hatred, to killing: an apparently logical sequence. Fortunately, however, the sequence is not inevitable.

From this gloomy, repulsive view of human nature, how refreshing the transition to that account of the matter which is presented in revelation![24]

Revelation, of course, meant Christian faith itself. Which:

gathers all the scattered and various kindreds of the earth into a common family; traces all the countless diversities of human shade and feature to the same primeval origin; finds the same life-blood circulating through the veins of every human creature, whether his skin be blanched like the snows by the chill atmosphere of the north, or darkened to a sable hue by the scorching rays of a torrid clime; purifies and reconciles all the discordant and conflicting customs and religions of Greek and Jew, Barbarian and Scythian; invites them all to one hospitable roof . . . the everlasting habitation of the same Common Parent, as brethren of a single, united, harmonious household.[25]

Does this not (in the Shakespearean phrase) protest too much? Certainly, one feels the pressure, the straining toward another *account of the matter*. Thus: *a common family; the same primeval origin; the same life-blood; one hospitable roof; a single, united, harmonious household*. Here lay an urgently necessary antidote to the *gloomy, repulsive view* presented at length just before.

The necessity was underscored by the situation immediately in front of them.

In the consideration of this subject . . . attention has been impressed and directed by a regard to the unusual visit which during the past week has been made to our village.[26]

Remember, too, that the visitors were actually present with the congregation that day, listening (though perhaps not fully understanding) as the preacher went on.

When we consider this remarkable illustration of the truth declared in our text, by which the blood of two races so distinct and unlike and once so hostile and irreconcilable, has been blended together, . . . this event . . . amply justifies . . . that strong expression of interest, curiosity, and attention which has been so generally manifested.[27]

To summarize: How *remarkable* it is—given such *distinct, unlike, hostile, and irreconcilable* elements—that these two groups should ever have been *blended together.*

What a struggle lies uncovered here, in the overheated words of the sermon. What a tumult of wish and feeling. Fascination. And repulsion. And perplexity. A sense of wonderment that they share with "us" an ancestor, and a single origin. An impulse—though this cannot be directly acknowledged—to destroy them. And a feeling of obligation, rooted in faith, to welcome and embrace them. (Just as she had once embraced them, long years before?)

With all this said, there remained a final concern: why had they come to Deerfield at all?

That this visit should have been undertaken principally from the not illaudable motive of paying respect to the grave of an ancestor . . . seems highly probable. Such a motive is a sacred one; it possesses a measure of dignity, . . . and excludes all suspicion of selfish and mercenary views—of unworthy and mendicant expedients.[28]

Yes, they must be taken at their *highly probable* word. *Suspicion* might suggest that they have come for *mendicant* or *mercenary* reasons—that is, to beg or to stake some claim—but they say otherwise. Indeed:

On their part there has not appeared to be any evidence of unreasonable expectation or extravagant demand.[29]

These terms hint at a further question. Why, after all, might the people of Deerfield even imagine their forming an *unreasonable expectation* or making an *extravagant demand*?

The answer lay with history. It came now in the voice of the preacher—and was directed toward the visitors—but it carried the full weight of the past. Deerfield's past, Kahnawake's past, Eunice's past.

> I would say, as ye have buried the hatchet, whose traces still remain visible on the ancient portal to remind us of bygone days of blood and violence, of suffering and captivity, so sleep the sword by which those wrongs—if wrongs they were—have been fully avenged.[30]

He was referring, of course, to the "massacre" of 133 years before. The door (or *portal*) of the old Sheldon house—where Deerfield's finest had made a particularly stout defense—did indeed retain *traces* of the Indian *hatchet*. And the sorrow of it rose yet again.

> We look at the mouldering, moss-covered house of strength . . . and as we behold the deep, indented marks of savage and mortal weapons, the record of "dreadful summoners," at dead of night, storming the bolted doors of maternal tenderness and sleeping infancy, we shudder at the thought of those barbarous cruelties, which were preparing for the defenceless and unsuspecting inmates.[31]

Barbarous cruelties they were. Impossible to forget. And very difficult to forgive.

But wait; this is not quite all. For:

> we are aware that it will be said, on the other side, "Judge not, lest ye be judged."[32]

The other side? In fact, there was more to remember from Deerfield's history. Especially from its beginning.

> The messengers from Dedham, first employed to seek out this location, in their report speak as follows: "Providence led us to that place. It is indeed far away from our plantations, and the Canaanites and Amelekites dwell in that valley, and . . . must delight to live there. But this land must be ours. . . . Let us go and possess the land."[33]

To paraphrase: the *messengers from Dedham*—who became the founders of Deerfield—had simply dispossessed the Indians (*Canaanites and Amelekites*) already living there. Was this not, perhaps, a

prior *cruelty . . . on the other side?* The preacher put the question very
delicately, in his own way.

> Whether the spirit of enterprise that expresses itself in these terms
> is in accordance with that commandment which forbids us "to
> covet anything which is our neighbor's" . . . is a fit subject for
> our serious reflection.[34]

At last the whole sequence lay bare, *a fit subject for our serious reflection.* The coercive, covetous settlement of Deerfield. The massacre,
and its attendant *suffering* and *captivity.* The ensuing campaigns of
vengeance. The eventual, uneasy peace (with *hatched buried* and
sword asleep). And, finally, the arrival, one August morning in 1837,
of the unlooked-for visitors. No, they had not come to reclaim the
land (though indeed they might have). Yes, they did seek (as they
said) simply to venerate *an ancestor, long since departed, and that
ancestor our own no less than theirs.*

What all this led to was a sense of completion—and even of acceptance.

> I would recognize with pious humility . . . the workings of that
> mysterious providence, which has mingled your blood with ours,
> and which . . . admonishes us that God . . . hath made of one
> blood all nations of men, and hath determined the times, the
> places, and circumstances in which they should live, in order
> to accomplish his designs of impartial benevolence and general
> good. . . .[35]

Your blood with ours. Was there not a kind of "redemption" here as
well?

NOTES

꒭

ABBREVIATIONS

AC   Archives des Colonies, Correspondance Générale, microfilm copy at the Public Archives of Canada (Ottawa).

CAI   Joseph François Lafitau, *Customs of the American Indians Compared with the Customs of Primitive Times*, William N. Fenton and Elizabeth L. Moore, eds., 2 vols. (Toronto, 1974).

CM Diary   *Diary of Cotton Mather*, Worthington C. Ford, ed., 2 vols. (Boston, 1908; repr. New York, n.d.).

CSP   *Calendar of State Papers (Great Britain), Colonial Series: America and the West Indies, 1677–1733, Preserved in the Public Record Office*, 30 vols. (1896–1939).

GC   Gratz Collection, The Historical Society of Pennsylvania (Philadelphia).

HD   George Sheldon, *A History of Deerfield, Massachusetts*, 2 vols. (Deerfield, Mass., 1895–96; repr. 1983).

JM   The Judd Manuscripts, Forbes Library (Northampton, Mass.).

JR   *The Jesuit Relations and Allied Documents*, 73 vols., Reuben Gold Thwaites, ed. (Cleveland, Ohio, 1896–1901).

LIR   *The Livingston Indian Records, 1666–1723*, Lawrence Leder, ed. (Gettysburg, Pa., 1956).

LMAD   *Collection de Manuscrits, Contenant Lettres, Mémoires, et Autres Documents Historiques Relatifs à la Nouvelle France*, 2 vols. (Quebec, 1884).

MA	Massachusetts Archives (Boston, Mass.).
NYCD	*Documents Relative to the Colonial History of New York*, 15 vols., E. B. O'Callaghan and Berthold Fernow, eds. (Albany, N.Y., 1856–87).
PIW	Samuel Penhallow, *Penhallow's Indian Wars* (Boston, 1726; repr. with Notes, Index, and Introduction by Edward Wheelock, Freeport, N.Y., n.d.).
PIW Mss	Samuel Penhallow, Penhallow's Indian Wars, ms. version, Library of Congress (Washington, D.C.).
PVMA Mss	Pocumtuck Valley Memorial Association, Manuscript Collection, Historic Deerfield Library (Deerfield, Mass.).
PVMA Procs	*Proceedings and Collections of the Pocumtuck Valley Memorial Association.*
RC	John Williams, *The Redeemed Captive Returning to Zion* (Boston, 1707; repr. and ed. by Edward W. Clark, Amherst, Mass., 1976).
SP	Samuel Partridge, "An account of ye destruction at Derefd, febr 29, 1703/4," in *Proceedings of the Massachusetts Historical Society*, IX, 478–81.
SS Diary	*The Diary of Samuel Sewall, 1674–1729*, M. Halsey Thomas, ed., 2 vols. (New York, 1973).
SS LB	Letterbook of Samuel Sewall, in *Collections of the Massachusetts Historical Society*, sixth series, I–II (1886–88).
SW	Stephen Williams, "What befel Stephen Williams in His Captivity," in Stephen W. Williams, *A Biographical Memoir of the Rev. John Williams* (Greenfield, Mass., 1837), Appendix.
SW Diary	Diary of Stephen Williams, typescript copy, 10 vols., Richard R. Storrs Memorial Library (Longmeadow, Mass.).
SW Mss	Stephen Williams, "An account of what befell Stephen Williams in his captivity," in manuscript collection, Missouri Historical Society (Columbia, Mo.); copy at the Historic Deerfield Library (Deerfield, Mass.). This is a slightly different version of the published Stephen Williams captivity narrative. (See SW, above.)
WP	The Winthrop Papers, in *Collections of the Massachusetts Society*, sixth series, III–V (1889–91).

WP Mss   The Winthrop Papers, manuscript collection at the Massachusetts Historical Society (Boston).

BEGINNINGS

1. For a concise account of the planning of the Massachusetts Bay Colony, see Edmund S. Morgan, *The Puritan Dilemma: The Story of John Winthrop* (Boston, 1958), Ch. 1.

2. The original of this seal is in the Archives of the Commonwealth of Massachusetts (Boston).

3. On the attitudes of the settlers toward Indians, see Neal Salisbury, *Manitou and Providence: Indians, Europeans, and the Making of New England, 1500–1643* (New York, 1982). On the transformation of the early New England environment, see William Cronon, *Changes in the Land: Indians, Colonists, and the Ecology of New England* (New York, 1983).

4. The best accounts of the Massachusetts "praying towns" are Neal Salisbury, "Red Puritans: The 'Praying Indians' of Massachusetts Bay and John Eliot," in *William and Mary Quarterly*, 3d ser., XXXIII (1974), 31–60, and James Axtell, *The Invasion Within: The Contest of Cultures in Colonial North America* (New York, 1985), Ch. 9. See also William Kellaway, *The New England Company, 1649–1776: Missionary Society to the American Indians* (London, 1961) and Henry Warner Bowden, *American Indians and Christian Missions* (Chicago, 1981), Ch. 4.

5. An early, but still useful, study of this theme is Roy Harvey Pearce, *The Savages of America: A Study of the Indian and the Idea of Civilization* (Baltimore, 1953). See also Richard Slotkin, *Regeneration Through Violence: The Mythology of the American Frontier, 1600–1860* (Middletown, Conn., 1973).

6. For an overview of the captivity experience in early New England, see Alden Vaughan and Daniel K. Richter, "Crossing the Cultural Divide: Indians and New Englanders, 1605–1763," in *American Antiquarian Society Proceedings*, XC (1980), 23–99. This work is based, in turn, on the much earlier (and remarkably exhaustive) research of Emma Lewis Coleman; see her *New England Captives Carried to Canada, Between 1677 and 1760*, 2 vols. (Portland, Maine, 1925). For other useful references, see Ch. 3, fn. 56, below.

7. See Axtell, *The Invasion Within*, Ch. 13.

8. A brief account of these events can be found in W. J. Eccles,

The Canadian Frontier, 1534–1760 (Albuquerque, N. Mex., 1969), 62–66. See also George T. Hunt, *The Wars of the Iroquois* (Madison, Wis., 1940); Allen W. Trelease, *Indian Affairs in Colonial New York: The Seventeenth Century* (Ithaca, N.Y., 1960); and Daniel K. Richter, "War and Culture: The Iroquois Experience," in *William and Mary Quarterly*, 3d ser., XL (1983), 528–559.

9. On the extent, and effects, of epidemic disease among the native peoples of northeastern North America, see Bruce G. Trigger, *Natives and Newcomers: Canada's "Heroic Age" Reconsidered* (Montreal, 1985), Ch. 5. On the cultural repercussions of widespread "adoptions," see Denys DeLâge, *Le Pays Renversé: Amerindians et européens en Amérique du nord-est, 1600–1664* (Montreal, 1985), 230ff.

10. See Daniel K. Richter, "Iroquois versus Iroquois: Jesuit Missions and Christianity in Village Politics," in *Ethnohistory*, XXXII (1985), 1–16. Richter's new book *The Ordeal of the Longhouse: The Peoples of the Iroquois League in the Era of European Colonization* (Chapel Hill, N.C., 1992) promises the fullest, most authoritative account of Iroquois history yet available. Unfortunately, it was published too late for use in the present study.

11. On Iroquois participation in the fur trade, see Trelease, *Indian Affairs* and, especially, Thomas Elliot Norton, *The Fur Trade in Colonial New York* (Madison, Wis., 1974). On the broader question of cultural disruption among Iroquoian peoples, see DeLâge, *Le Pays Renversé*.

12. The definitive history of early Deerfield is Richard I. Melvoin, *New England Outpost: War and Society in Colonial Deerfield* (New York, 1989); on the meeting (at Dedham) of 22 May 1670, see ibid., 62. All students of Deerfield's past are indebted to George Sheldon's classic nineteenth-century work, *A History of Deerfield, Massachusetts*, 2 vols. (Deerfield, Mass., 1895–96; repr. 1983).

13. See Melvoin, *New England Outpost*, Ch. 3.

14. On King Philip's War, see Douglas E. Leach, *Flintlock and Tomahawk: New England in King Philip's War* (New York, 1958), and Russell Bourne, *The Red King's Rebellion: Racial Politics in New England, 1675–1678* (New York, 1990). On Deerfield's experience of this war, see Melvoin, *New England Outpost*, Ch. 4.

15. Melvoin, *New England Outpost*, Chs. 5–7.

16. See Ola Winslow, *John Eliot: Apostle to the Indians* (Boston, 1968).

17. Most of these genealogical particulars can be found in Stephen West Williams, *The Genealogy and History of the Family of Williams* (Greenfield, Mass., 1847).

18. For a short account of the War of the Spanish Succession from the standpoint of its English participants, see Maurice Ashley, *England in the Seventeenth Century*, rev. ed. (London, 1960), Ch. 14.

ONE

1. On these preparations to defend Deerfield, see HD, I: 283–84.

2. From an "account" by Stephen Williams, quoted in ibid., I: 287.

3. John Williams to Joseph Dudley, 21 October 1703, in ibid., I: 288–90.

4. Solomon Stoddard to Joseph Dudley, 22 October 1703, in ibid., I: 290–91.

5. See ibid., I: 292, 287.

6. In late January the governor of Connecticut, writing to his counterpart in Massachusetts, spoke of "the terrible season," and described "the snow being neere knee deepe a little way up in the Country"; see John Winthrop to Joseph Dudley, 25 January 1703/4, WP Mss, microfilm reel 16. See also the references to winter weather in the diary of Daniel Fairfield (Braintree, Mass.), in JM, III: 268–73, 365–80.

7. Samuel Partridge to John Winthrop, 21 February 1703/4, WP Mss., microfilm reel 16.

8. PIW, 12, and "Notes," 5. See also PIW Mss., 14. For another account, see Thomas Hutchinson, *The History of the Colony and Province of Massachusetts Bay*, 2 vols. (London, 1765–68), II, 137. The following summer, Lord Cornbury, governor of New York, claimed to have "sent them [the people of Deerfield] notice . . . that the enemy was preparing to attack them . . . [which] was brought to my knowledge by some spys which I have kept in the Indian country"; see Cornbury to the Earl of Nottingham, 22 June 1704, in NYCD, IV: 1099–1100.

9. Partridge to Winthrop, 21 February 1703/4, WP Mss., microfilm reel 16; PIW, 12; Isaac Addington to Fitz-John Winthrop, 6 March 1703/4, in WP, V: 180.

10. RC, 43.

11. On the theme of religious "declension"—and its related sermon-type, the "jeremiad"—the seminal work is still Perry Miller, *The New England Mind: The Seventeenth Century* (New York, 1939) and *The New England Mind: From Colony to Province* (New York, 1953).

12. PIW, 12; PIW Mss., 14.

13. Pierre de Rigaud, Marquis de Vaudreuil, to Jérome de Pontchartrain, 15 November 1703, in AC, file C-11-A, XXI: 13.

14. For a brief historical overview of these communities, see George F. G. Stanley, "The First Indian 'Reserves' in Canada," in *Revue d'Historique de l'Amérique Française*, IV (1950), 178–210; see also W. J. Eccles, *The Canadian Frontier* (Albuquerque, N. Mex., 1969), 88.

15. Vaudreuil to Pontchartrain, 3 April 1704 and 17 November 1704, in AC, file C-11-A, XXII: 45–48, 3–38.

16. The numbers of Frenchmen and Indians in the Canadian attack-force were variously reported by different parties. But the most plausible totals are those given by Claude de Ramezay, governor of the city of Montreal; he, after all, was probably present when the force set out. See Ramezay to Pontchartrain, 14 November 1704, AC, file C-11-A, XXII: 125. On the leadership of Hertel de Rouville, see Vaudreuil to Jacques François de Brouillan, 15 March 1704, translated in WP Mss., microfilm reel 16.

17. On French policy toward New England, see Francis H. Hammang, *The Marquis de Vaudreuil: New France at the Beginning of the Eighteenth Century* (Louvain, 1938), 118–24, and Emma L. Coleman, "Canadian Missions and Deerfield Captives," PVMA Procs, V: 317–36.

18. The probability that John Williams was targeted for capture in advance, is carefully examined in George Sheldon, "New Tracks on an Old Trail," PVMA Procs, IV: 11–28. On the career of Baptiste, see C. Alice Baker, "The Adventures of Baptiste," PVMA Procs, IV: 342–60, 450–77.

19. Some of these details are suggested in the "captivity narratives" by John Williams and his son Stephen. See, for example, RC, 51, and SW, 103. See also the account given in HD, I: 295.

20. PIW, 12.

21. On the moment of entry into the village, and the element of surprise, see the following contemporaneous sources: Joseph Dudley to the Council of Trade and Plantations, 20 April 1704, in CSP (1704–05), 100; Addington to Winthrop, 6 March 1703/4, WP, V:

180; William Whiting to Fitz-John Winthrop, 4 March 1703/4, WP, III: 176; SP, 478; PIW, 12; Hutchinson, *History of . . . Massachusetts Bay*, II: 138; RC, 44. A long-standing local tradition describes the negligence of the watchman as follows: "while on his beat, towards morning . . . [he] heard from one of the houses the soft voice of a woman singing a lullaby to a sick child . . . [whereupon] he stopped, and leaning against the window where the child lay, listened to the soothing tones of the singer until he fell asleep." (See HD, I: 307.)

22. These details were remembered, and carefully described, years later by John Williams. See John Williams to Stephen Williams, 11 March 1728/9, PVMA Mss., Williams Papers, box 1, folder 9. See also HD, I: 605, 609.

23. RC, 44–46.

24. SP, 478–80.

25. RC, 46.

26. SP, 479; RC, 45.

27. Jonathan Wells et al., petition to the Massachusetts General Court, 17 May 1736, in HD, I: 301; Jonathan Wells and Ebenezer Wright to the Massachusetts General Court, in HD, I: 297–98. On this phase of the battle, see also Dudley to the Council of Trade and Plantations, in CSP (1704–05), 100; SP, 479–80; Addington to Winthrop, 6 March 1703/4, WP, V: 180; Whiting to Winthrop, 4 March 1703/4, WP, III: 176; SS LB, I: 299; PIW, 13.

28. Wells et al., petition, in HD, I: 301; SP, 479–80.

29. The most careful, and detailed, of these lists (from the time of the massacre itself) is included in SP, 481–82. The reference to the Nims children is in Stephen Williams, "Names of Those Who Were Slain at the Taking of the Town," in Stephen W. Williams, *A Biographical Memoir of the Rev. John Williams* (Greenfield, Mass., 1837), 101–2. The "stifled" description is in PIW Mss., 15. See also Daniel White, "An Account of the Desolation of Deerfield," manuscript collection, Historical Society of Pennsylvania.

30. Some of these injuries were described in subsequent claims for compensation submitted to the General Court; see HD, I: 306–7, 312.

31. See ibid., I: 605, 609, 315, and *passim*; see also SP, 479. The story of Mary Catlin's "deliverance" was included in a letter from Lucy D. Shearer to George Sheldon, 1 November 1875; see HD, I: 310.

32. These details are included in SP, 480. For other contemporaneous accounts, see the references in note 21 (above).

33. SP. The original of this document is in the manuscript collection of the Massachusetts Historical Society. It is unsigned, but comparison of the handwriting with other (signed) materials establishes that Samuel Partridge was its author.

34. These conclusions, together with the ones in the preceding paragraph, are based on SP, 481–82. The actual percentages are as follows. *Captured*: men, 44 percent; women, 68 percent. *Escaped*: men, 36 percent; women, 10 percent. *Killed*: men, 20 percent; women, 22 percent. *Killed* (by age): infants (under age 3), 63 percent; children (ages 3–12), 33 percent; teenagers (ages 13–19), 3 percent.

35. SP, 481–82.

36. Ibid., 482.

37. Vaudreuil to Pontchartrain, 17 November 1704, AC, file C-11-A, XXII: 33; Ramezay to Pontchartrain, AC, file C-11-A, XXII, 125; SP, 480; RC, 47.

38. Aspects of this "borderland" geography are discussed in Samuel Carter, "The Route of the French and Indian Army That Sacked Deerfield, Feb. 29th, 1703/4 (O.S.), on Their Return March to Canada with the Captives," PVMA Procs, II: 126–51.

39. RC, 46.

40. Ibid., 46; see also SW, 103.

41. RC, 47; SW Mss., 4.

42. This reconstruction of their experience, though conjectural, is based on the author's personal knowledge of wintertime travel in the New England woodlands.

43. RC, 47–48; SW Mss., 6.

44. RC, 50.

45. RC, 46–47.

46. RC, 48–49. See also SW Mss., 6–7.

47. RC, 50. The grave of Eunice Williams (senior) remains, alongside that of her husband, in the cemetery at Deerfield to the present day. A plaque at the side of the Green River a few miles north of Deerfield marks the site of her death.

48. RC, 50. The "tradition" mentioned here is noted in Carter, "The Route of the French and Indian Army That Sacked Deerfield," 151 (note).

49. SW, 103; RC, 47; SW, 103.

50. RC, 50.

51. Ibid., 50; SW, 103.

52. RC, 50.

53. This story is presented in a letter by Louis Davaugour, S. J., to the Superior General, Society of Jesus, 7 October 1710, in JR, LXVII: 168–71.
54. SW Mss., 8–9; RC, 51.
55. RC, 51; SW Mss., 9–13.
56. RC, 51; SW Mss., 10–11.
57. SW Mss., 13–15; RC, 52–53.
58. RC, 53–54.
59. RC, 53–57.
60. RC, 56–57.
61. RC, 57–63.
62. RC, 63–64.
63. RC, 54, 65.
64. SW, 105–110. See also SW Mss., 15–25 (some differences in detail).
65. SW Mss., 40; SW, 109–10. See also RC, 65.
66. RC, 54, 65.
67. RC, 66.
68. RC, 69, 77, 82, 85, 69, 52.
69. These computations are based on an exhaustive review of all sources bearing on the "march." A good starting point is the list (especially the column headed "captivities") included in SP, 481–82. This can be compared with other, more or less contemporaneous lists, such as the one compiled by Stephen Williams, in Stephen W. Williams, *A Biographical Memoir of the Rev. John Williams*, 100–1, and White, "An Account of the Desolation of Deerfield." Much useful information can also be found in HD, *passim*.

Two

1. Jonathan Wells et al., petition to the Massachusetts General Court, 17 May 1736, in HD, I: 301.
2. SP, 480; William Whiting to Fitz-John Winthrop, 4 March 1703/4, in WP, III: 176–77; Wait Winthrop to Fitz-John Winthrop, 4 March 1703/4, in WP, V: 124–25; Isaac Addington to Fitz-John Winthrop, 6 March 1703/4, in WP, V: 180; SS Diary, I: 498; *The Holy Bible*, authorized King James version (Oxford, England, n.d.), 275. Of course, news of the massacre traveled in other directions as well. Sometime in March, for example, the authorities in New York

provided compensation to "3 Messengers from New Ingland that brought the News of the Misfourtun of Dier field kot [i.e., cut] off by the french"; see New York Colonial Manuscripts (New York State Archives, Albany, N.Y.), IL: 34. And, in April, John Schuyler of Albany was writing to Massachusetts governor Joseph Dudley on the same subject; see his letter of 28 April 1704, in WP Mss., microfilm reel 16.

3. *The Holy Bible*, King James version, 275.

4. Rev. Timothy Edwards (Windsor, Conn.), in "The Black Book" (Miscellaneous Documents), PVMA Mss.; MA, CXXII: 200; Wait Winthrop to John Winthrop, 15 March 1704, in WP Mss., microfilm reel 16.

5. Diary of Daniel Fairfield (Braintree, Mass.) in JM, III: 268–73, 365–80; SS LB, I: 299; Benjamin Church, 20 June 1704, quoted in C. Alice Baker, "The Adventures of Baptiste," in PVMA Procs, IV: 459.

6. See Baker, "The Adventures of Baptiste," PVMA Procs, IV: 457–59, and Richard I. Melvoin, *New England Outpost: War and Society in Colonial Deerfield* (New York, 1989), 228–29.

7. Joseph Dudley to Fitz-John Winthrop, 30 March 1704, in WP, V: 188; Lord Cornbury to the Earl of Nottingham, 22 June 1704, in NYCD, IV: 1099; Col. Quary to the Council of Trade and Plantations, 30 May 1704, in CSP (1704–05), 139.

8. Dudley to the Council of Trade and Plantations, 20 April 1704, in CSP (1704–05), 100; Vaudreuil to Pontchartrain, 3 April 1704 and 16 November 1704, in AC, file C-11-A, XXII: 45–48, 3–38.

9. These letters are discussed and quoted in C. Alice Baker, *True Stories of New England Captives* (Cambridge, Mass., 1897), 171–72. The originals, supposed to be in the Massachusetts Archives, could not be located in July 1989. French translations, evidently made by and for the authorities in Canada, can be found in LMAD, II: 410–11, 425–26.

10. John Williams's letter of May 1704 does not survive. But it is specifically noted in Laurence Claese to (unidentified) "Gentn," 20 May 1704, in LIR, 194. The report of Schuyler's meeting with French Indians was included in a letter from William Whiting to Fitz-John Winthrop, 21 August 1704; see WP, III: 260.

11. The quoted passages are from the records of the Council of Massachusetts Bay, as cited in Baker, *True Stories*, 172–73.

12. Dudley to Vaudreuil, 20 December 1704, in Baker, *True Stories*,

174. (A French translation, made for the authorities in Canada, is in LMAD, II: 426–27.)

13. Unidentified writer to John Sheldon, n.d., in PVMA Mss., Sheldon Papers, folder 4; John Sheldon to Hannah Sheldon, 1 April 1705, PVMA Mss., Sheldon Papers, folder 5. See also Baker, *True Stories*, 78–79.

14. Baker, *True Stories*, 179–80; Vaudreuil to Dudley, 26 March 1705, in LMAD, II: 428–29.

15. The ransoming of Stephen is described in SW, 110.

16. John Williams to Mrs. John Livingston, 21 April 1705, in WP, V: 296; Richard Lord to Mrs. John Livingston, 31 May 1705, in WP, V: 296.

17. The details of this sequence are effectively presented in Baker, *True Stories*, 180–92.

18. PIW, 29.

19. The original is in the Massachusetts Archives; see MA, LXXI: 240.

20. PVMA Mss., Williams Papers, box 1, folder 4. The "colledge" to which Mather refers was Harvard—from which Eleazer Williams would graduate in 1706.

21. Samuel Sewall to John Williams, 18 January 1705/6 and 22 August 1706, in SS LB, I: 323–24, 328–30.

22. SS Diary, I: 510–11; CM Diary, I: 555.

23. SS Diary, I: 549; John Williams, petition to the Massachusetts General Court, 10 October 1705, in MA, XI: 198, 198b, and the Court's order of 22 November 1705, MA, XI: 198b; Sewall to John Williams, 22 August 1706, in SS LB, I: 329.

24. CM Diary, I: 567–68; Cotton Mather, *Good Fetch'd Out of Evil*: *A Collection of Memorables Relating to Our Captives* (Boston, 1706).

25. The arrival of this group was widely noted both in newspapers and in private communications. See, for example, *Boston News-letter*, no. 136 (November 18–25, 1706), and diary of Daniel Fairfield (entry for 21 November 1706), JM, III: 269.

26. SS LB, II: 340; RC, 114; CM Diary, I: 575; Thomas Prince, "Historical Observations," in Stephen W. Williams, *A Biographical Memoir of the Rev. John Williams* (Greenfield, Mass., 1837), 211; HD, I: 337–38; SS Diary, I: 555.

27. SS Diary, I: 557; HD, I: 359; HD, I: 360. On the likelihood that John Williams received "invitations" apart from Deerfield, note the comment, in the sermon given at his funeral by the Rev. Isaac

Chauncy of Hatfield, that "when he return'd from Captivity he was importunely invited to settle where his worldly Interests might be more promoted, than if he return'd to Dearfield," quoted in HD, I: 462.

28. *Boston News-letter*, no. 144 (January 13–20, 1706/7).

29. Sewall's comment is in SS Diary, I: 563–64. On the publishing history of Williams's book, see RC, "Textual Introduction," 27–31.

30. The sermon was published by the "printer" B. Green (Boston, 1707). Sewall's comment is in SS LB, I: 351.

31. SS Diary, I: 563.

32. John Williams to Stephen Williams, 21 June 1707, in GC, American Colonial Clergy, case 8, box 25; John Williams to Stephen Williams, 18 August 1707, in PVMA Mss., Williams Papers, box 1, folder 9; John Williams to Stephen Williams, 21 June 1707 (see citation above); John Williams to Stephen Williams, 18 August 1707 (see citation above); Esther Williams to Stephen Williams, 11 September 1707, in PVMA Mss., Williams Papers, box 1, folder 9; Samuel Williams to Stephen Williams, 6 November 1707, in GC, American Miscellany, case 8, box 20.

33. Peter Schuyler to Joseph Dudley, 28 May 1707, in LIR, 200; Peter Schuyler to Samuel Partridge, 11 August 1707, in MA, II: 445, 445a; John Williams to Stephen Williams, 21 June 1707, in PVMA Mss., Williams Papers, box 1, folder 9.

34. Samuel Sewall to John Williams, 18 August 1707, in SS LB, I: 351–53; Samuel Sewall, "Extract of Mr. Williams's Answer to Mine," 29 August 1707, in SS LB, I: 354; Esther Williams to Samuel Williams, 11 September 1707, in PVMA Mss., Williams Papers, box 1, folder 9.

THREE

1. John Williams to "the Honord Generall Court of the province of the Massachusetts Bay in New England," 10 October 1705. This petition was "Read in the House of Representatives" on November 22, and the House promptly resolved that its "prayer . . . be Granted." Williams also sent a covering letter, supplying additional details, to Governor Dudley. See MA, XI: 198, 198b.

2. On this sequence of hope and disappointment, see RC, 78, 80, 108.

3. Ibid., 82–107, 112–13.

4. Ibid., 108–9.

5. Ibid., 112.
6. Ibid., 111–12.
7. Ibid., 111; Cotton Mather, *Good Fetch'd Out of Evil: A Collection of Memorables Relating to Our Captives* (Boston, 1706), 6.
8. See ibid. Williams's "pastoral letter" is one of "three short essays" included there. Cotton Mather's account of preparing the volume can be found in CM Diary, I: 567–68.
9. Cotton Mather, *Good Fetch'd Out of Evil*, 6–7.
10. Ibid., 8–12, 15.
11. Ibid., 18, 15.
12. Ibid., 16–17.
13. See pp. 49–50.
14. See CM Diary, I: 575. See also SS Diary, I: 555.
15. (Boston, 1707); repr. in John Williams, *The Redeemed Captive Returning to Zion*, 6th ed. (Boston, 1795; repr. Springfield, Mass., 1908), 145–69. References to the sermon made here and in the succeeding paragraphs are based on this version.
16. Ibid., 146–47, 151–52.
17. Ibid., 146.
18. Ibid., 146–47.
19. Ibid., 149–50.
20. Ibid., 151–59.
21. Ibid., 159.
22. Ibid., 160–65.
23. Ibid., 167–68.
24. Ibid., 150, 160, 164.
25. "Petition of the Militia of the Town of Dearefeild," to Gov. Joseph Dudley, 6 September 1705, quoted in HD, I: 323; Samuel Partridge to Gov. Dudley and the General Court, 28 May 1707, quoted in ibid., I: 361; Jonathan Wells and John Sheldon "in behalf of ye whole town of Deerfield," to the General Court, 25 October 1707, quoted in ibid., I: 362. On the general condition of Deerfield at this time, see also HD, I: 358–60, and Richard Melvoin, *New England Outpost: War and Society in Colonial Deerfield* (New York, 1989), 246–48.
26. One of the first and most famous of these narratives (preceding Williams's *Redeemed Captive* by some twenty-five years) was Mary Rowlandson, *The Sovereignty and Goodness of God Together with the Faithfulness of His Promises Displayed; Being a Narrative of the Captivity of Mrs. Mary Rowlandson* (Boston, 1682).
27. In the pages that follow, all references are to the most recent

edition of this book (RC). On the book's publishing history, see
ibid., 27–31.

28. Ibid., 39–41.
29. Ibid., 55.
30. Ibid., 74.
31. Ibid., 46.
32. Ibid., 115.
33. Ibid., 52.
34. Ibid., 79.
35. Ibid., 43.
36. Ibid., 49.
37. Ibid., 91.
38. Ibid., 54–55, 58, 64, 83, 85, 108, 80, 62, 58–59, 67.
39. Ibid., 56, 63, 71.
40. Ibid., 73–74, 82–84, 86–106.
41. Ibid., 74, 75–76.
42. The sermon was subsequently published; the full citation is John
    Williams, *God in the Camp; or, The Only Way for a People to Engage
    the Presence of God with Their Armies* (Boston, 1707).
43. Ibid., 1–2.
44. Ibid., 3, 4–5, 7.
45. Ibid., 9–12.
46. Ibid., 14–15.
47. Ibid., 17–18.
48. Ibid., 18–19.
49. Ibid., 19.
50. Ibid., 20.
51. Ibid.
52. Ibid., 21.
53. Ibid., 22.
54. The scholarly literature on "declension" in colonial New England
    is voluminous; much of it is introduced, summarized, and evaluated
    in Robert G. Pope, "New England versus the New England Mind:
    The Myth of Declension," in *Journal of Social History*, III
    (1969–70), 95–108. The originator of this scholarship was Perry
    Miller; see especially his *The New England Mind, From Colony to
    Province* (Cambridge, Mass., 1953), 3–118. The phrase "rhetoric
    of failure" is taken from Harry S. Stout, *The New England Soul:
    Preaching and Religious Culture in Colonial New England* (New
    York, 1986), 77, 85, and *passim*.

55. Thomas Foxcroft, *Eli, the Priest Dying Suddenly* (Boston, 1729), 38.

56. The literature of, and about, captivities is huge—and still growing. For a brief survey, see Alden T. Vaughan and Edward W. Clark, eds., *Puritans Among the Indians: Accounts of Captivity and Redemption, 1676–1724* (Cambridge, Mass., 1981), 1–28. See also Richard VanDerBeets, *The Indian Captivity Narrative: An American Genre* (Lanham, Md., 1984); Richard Slotkin, *Regeneration Through Violence: The Mythology of the American Frontier, 1600–1860* (Middletown, Conn., 1973), esp. 94–145; James Axtell, "The White Indians of Colonial America," in *William and Mary Quarterly*, 3d ser., XXXII (1975), 55–88; and Roy Harvey Pearce, "The Significances of the Captivity Narrative," in *American Literature*, XIX (1947), 1–20. The most recent of these studies, and one of the finest, is June Namias, *White Captives: Gender and Ethnicity on the American Frontier* (Chapel Hill, N.C., 1993).

FOUR

1. C. Alice Baker, *True Stories of New England Captives* (Cambridge, Mass., 1897), 189. See also the account in HD, I: 338–40.

2. "An accompt of the Sums or Disbursements of John Shelden," in MA, LXXI: 438; Vaudreuil to Dudley, 16 August 1707, in AC, file C-11-A, XXVIII: 159–65.

3. The fate of many captives "in French hands" can be learned from Emma Lewis Coleman, *New England Captives Carried to Canada*, 2 vols. (Portland, Maine, 1925), *passim*.

4. Quoted in Coleman, *New England Captives*, II: 99. Kellogg's journey to the Mississippi River was subsequently described in a remarkable document prepared for the Royal Society of London and found today in its "register book" (folios 132–36). A printed version is included in Timothy Hopkins, *The Kelloggs in the Old World and the New*, 2 vols. (San Francisco, Calif., 1903), I: 60–62.

5. Baptismal record of Elisabeth Price, published in Coleman, *New England Captives*, II: 114.

6. Lettres de Naturalité, Louis (King of France), May 1710; published in Coleman, *New England Captives*, I: 125–28.

7. Marriage record of Freedom (Marie Françoise) French; published in Coleman, *New England Captives*, II: 82.

8. Vaudreuil to Pontchartrain, 17 November 1704, in AC, file C-11-A, XXIV, 13.

9. Dudley to Vaudreuil, 10 April 1704; see Baker, *True Stories*, 171–72. (For additional reference information, see Ch. 2, note 9, above.)

10. Baker, *True Stories*, 171; Vaudreuil to Dudley, 28 March 1705, in LMAD, II: 428–29; Dudley to Vaudreuil, 4 July 1705 (French translation), in LMAD, II: 435; Vaudreuil to Dudley, 2 June 1706, in LMAD, II: 454; draft treaty, 6 October 1705 (Quebec), in LMAD, II: 446.

11. In the summer of 1709 one William Moody of Exeter, New Hampshire, was captured, escaped, and then was recaptured by French Indians; the second time "after they had got him over, they Burnt him on the Spot." (This was reported by a party of "scouts" sent out from Deerfield; see HD, I: 371.) The same source also reported "yt wn the Indians got to Canada they Burnt one more of these Captives, Andrew Gilman by name." (HD, I: 371.) Samuel Penhallow expanded this report to include cannibalizing; Moody, he writes, was "most inhumanly tortured,. . . by fastning him unto a Stake and roasting him alive; whose flesh they afterwards devoured." (See PIW, 49.) An account of these two deaths subsequently reached England and was included in the "state papers" there; see CSP (1710–June 1711), 75. On the proposed execution of John Williams, see pp. 30–32.

12. In 1696, for example, a number of Deerfield residents were captured and taken to Kahnawake; when they "came to the fort,. . . the males were obliged to run the gauntlet. Mr. [Daniel] Belding, being a very nimble and light-footed man, received but few blows, save at first setting out, but the other two men were much abused by clubs, firebrands, etc." (See "Extract from Stephen Williams' Journal," in Stephen W. Williams, *A Biographical Memoir of the Rev. John Williams* [Greenfield, Mass., 1837], 115.) In 1709 two more Deerfield men, John Arms and Joseph Clesson, were similarly "abused" at Kahnawake; Arms, indeed, was beaten "so pitifully that . . . [he] could neither stand nor goe . . . [nor] speake." (See Major T. Lloyd, "Names and conditions of all English prisoners taken this year," 3 October 1709, in CSP [1710–June 1711], 76.) The more general description, quoted in the text, of the "practise" of running the gauntlet is also taken from Lloyd, "Names and conditions . . . ," CSP (1710–June 1711), 76.

13. Baptism of Catherine Aouenrat, "register" of the Mission de St.

François Xavier du Sault St. Louis (Kahnawake, Canada), I, leaf 6; burial of Elizabeth Sahiaks [born Abigail Nims, of Deerfield], "register" of the Mission du Lac des Deux Montagnes (Montreal, Canada), I, n.p.; James Smith, *An Account of the Remarkable Occurrences in the Life and Travels of Col. James Smith*, in Archibald Loudon, ed., *Outrages Committed by the Indians* (London, 1808; repr. New York, 1971), 130; Zadock Steele, *The Indian Captive, or a Narrative of the Captivity and Sufferings of Zadock Steele* (Montpelier, Vermont, 1786), 70.

14. One ex-captive described adoption and its *sequelae* as "an awfull School for Children, When We See how Quick they will Fall in with the Indians ways . . . Nothing seems to be more takeing; in Six months time they Forsake Father and mother, forgit thir own Land, Refuess to Speak there own toungue & Seemingly be Holley Swollowed up with the Indians." See Titus King, *Narrative of Titus King of Northampton, Mass.* (Hartford, Conn., 1938), 17. For thoughtful, comprehensive discussion of this and related issues, see James Axtell, *The Invasion Within: The Contest of Cultures in Colonial North America* (New York, 1985), Chs. 12–13.

15. Petition of Benjamin Nason to the Council of Massachusetts Bay, 21 September 1700, quoted in Coleman, *New England Captives*, I: 382; petition of Richard Dollar to the Assembly of New Hampshire, 26 April 1715, quoted in ibid., I: 373.

16. Mary M. B. French, *A New England Pioneer: The Captivity of Mrs. Johnson* (Woodstock, Vt., n.d.), 16; *God's Mercy Surmounting Man's Cruelty, Exemplified in the Captivity . . . of Elizabeth Hanson*, in Samuel G. Drake, *Tragedies of the Wilderness* (Boston, 1846), 124–25; dispatch to *Boston News-letter*, 25 August 1725, repr. in Coleman, *New England Captives*, II: 164.

17. See Coleman, *New England Captives*, II: 263. References to the French "buying back" English captives from the Indians are scattered through the records. For example: "I bought back nine Englishmen from the hands of the savages"; Vaudreuil to Pontchartrain, 13 October 1705, in AC, file no. C-11-A, XXII: 348.

18. Coleman, *New England Captives*, II: 266.

19. John Gyles, *Memoirs of Odd Adventures . . . in the Captivity of John Gyles*, in Drake, *Tragedies of the Wilderness*, 81: King, *Narrative of Titus King*, 20. A visitor to Canada in the mid-eighteenth century discussed this matter in more general terms: "The prisoners they take are either adopted, or made into slaves among them, or even condemned to death. Their slavery consists of doing

the lowest forms of work. . . . Adoption is done by a family which has lost a man to warfare and which wishes to replace him with a captive. . . ." (Trans. from T. C. B., *Voyage au canada, dans le nord de l'Amérique Septentrionale fait depuis 1751 à 1761* [Quebec, 1887], 264.)

20. For example, Sarah Hanson, originally of Dover, New Hampshire, given to an "old squaw . . . [with] a son whom she intended my daughter should in time be prevailed with to marry." See Hanson, *God's Mercy*, 125.

21. This was Nathan Blake, originally of Keene, New Hampshire, captured by French Indians in 1746; see Coleman, *New England Captives*, II: 190–91.

22. Amos Eastman, originally of Rumney, New Hampshire, captured by Abenakis from Canada in 1752; see Coleman, *New England Captives*, II: 293.

23. Silas Rice, originally of Marlborough, Mass., and John Tarbell, originally of Groton, Mass. See Ebenezer Parkman, *The Story of the Rice Boys* (repr. Westboro, Mass., 1906), 4; and Coleman, *New England Captives*, I: 296.

24. This story was widely recounted—and celebrated—at the time (by Cotton Mather, among others). For a short version, see Coleman, *New England Captives*, I: 342–43.

25. See Joseph Petty to Stephen Williams, n.d., printed in HD, I: 353–54. The original is in Memorial Hall, Deerfield, Mass.

26. Joseph Petty's account of his escape, noted in the preceding entry, is one sign of Stephen's role as a collector of such lore. And there are others; see, for example, a letter sent by his father, John Williams, to Stephen, 11 March 1728/9, in PVMA Mss., Williams Papers, box 1, folder 9.

27. On Stephen, see SW, 104–10; on Samuel, see RC, 86ff.; on Esther and Warham, see ibid., 65.

28. RC, 66.

29. RC, 66–67. See also the discussion of John Williams's encounters with Eunice, in Ch. 2 (above).

30. Peter Schuyler to Samuel Partridge, 18 February 1706/7, in MA, II: 443.

31. Samuel Partridge to Peter Schuyler, 2 April 1707, in LIR, 198–99.

32. See LIR, 201. The "sachem" mentioned here was, very probably, not simply "of Canada," but of Kahnawake itself. A French communiqué of a few years later refers to "Onnongaresson, an Indian of

Sault St. Louis [the French name for Kahnawake]"; the spelling seems sufficiently close to mean the same man. See Vaudreuil to Pontchartrain, 31 October 1710, translated in NYCD, IX: 849.

33. LIR, 201; MA, LXXI: 438.

34. Elisha Williams to Stephen Williams, 4 August 1707, in PVMA Mss., Williams Papers, box 1, folder 9.

35. Vaudreuil to Pontchartrain, 28 April 1706, in AC, file C-11-A, XXIV: 5; Dudley to the Council of Trade and Plantations, 8 April 1712, in CSP (July 1711–June 1712), 257–58; Dudley to the Queen, 14 June 1712, in ibid., 299–300.

36. Stephen Williams himself composed a set of "notes" on these events, which were later published under the heading "An account of Some Ancient things" in Stephen W. Williams, *A Biographical Memoir*, 116–21. Another useful, and almost contemporaneous, account is found in PIW, *passim*. See also Melvoin, *New England Outpost*, 247–48, and (for the French side) Francis H. Hammang, *The Marquis de Vaudreuil* (Louvain, 1938), Chs. 5–6.

37. John Williams to Stephen Williams, 8 August 1710, in GC, American Miscellany, case 8, box 20; and John Williams to Stephen Williams, 17 August 1710, in ibid., American Colonial Clergy, case 8, box 25.

38. Hinsdale's family history is described in HD, II: 201–7.

39. This account is by Stephen Williams; see HD, I: 367–68.

40. On the Nicholson expedition, see Bruce T. McCully, "Catastrophe in the Wilderness: New Light on the Canada Expedition of 1709," in *William and Mary Quarterly*, 3rd ser., XI (1954), 441–56. British plans for this campaign are presented in a dispatch from Major T. Lloyd to Solomon Merit, 13 November 1709, in CSP (1710–June 1711), 300–02.

41. Account by Stephen Williams; see HD, I: 368.

42. Lloyd, "Names and conditions," in CSP (1710–June 1711), 75.

43. Vaudreuil to Pontchartrain, 14 November 1709, translated and published in NYCD, IX: 883–84.

44. Account by Stephen Williams; see HD, I: 368.

45. HD, I: 368.

46. Official papers, bearing on the case of John Arms, are conveniently reprinted in Baker, *True Stories*, "Appendix," 360–64.

47. Esther Williams to Stephen Williams, 28 February 1710, in GC, Rev. John Williams and Family, case 8, box 28.

48. Quoted in HD, I: 375; see also Coleman, *New England Captives*, I: 436. (The original of this letter is in MA, LI: 187.)

49. Council of War to Vaudreuil, 11 October 1710, in CSP (1710–June 1711), 230–31.
50. "A Journall of ye Travails of Major John Livingstone . . ." in CSP (July 1712–July 1714), 371–86.
51. Vaudreuil to Nicholson, 14 January 1711, in AC, file C-11-A, XXXI: 100–9; Vaudreuil to Dudley, 14 January 1711, ibid., file C-11-A, XXXI: 110–16.
52. Records of the Council of Massachusetts Bay, 2 April 1711 and 15 November 1711, in MA, V: 365–66, 470.
53. Henri-Antoine de Meriel to Johnson Harmon, 26 June 1711, in MA, LI: 212–13 (published in Baker, *True Stories*, "Appendix," 366–67); Records of the Council of Massachusetts Bay, 15 November 1711, in MA, V: 470.
54. CM Diary, II: 92–93, 104. See also SS Diary, I: 666.
55. John Williams's "service as Chaplain in the late Expedition to Canada" was subsequently acknowledged—and compensated with a grant of £25 for his "Wages & subsistence"—by the Massachusetts authorities. See Records of the Council of Massachusetts Bay, in MA, V: 466. On the disastrous result of this expedition, see "Continuation of Col. King's Journal," 15 August 1711, in CSP (July 1711–June 1712), 92–93.
56. John Williams to Stephen Williams, 3 December 1711, in PVMA Mss., Williams Papers, box 1, folder 9.
57. The experiences of this "scout" were subsequently described by one of its members, Ebenezer Grant; see HD, I: 380–81.
58. Plans for the journey were discussed in a letter from Partridge to Dudley, 1 July 1712; see HD, I: 381–82. Details of the messengers' experience en route are contained in a manuscript journal kept by Samuel Williams; see GC, Rev. John Williams and Family, case 8, box 28. Upon his return, Samuel "communicated . . . [a] letter from Mr. Vaudreuil" to Dudley, and also submitted "An Accompt . . . for expenses"; see Records of the Council of Massachusetts Bay, 26 and 29 September 1712, in MA, V: 607–8.
59. On proclaiming the cease-fire in Boston, see the dispatch from Dudley to the Council of Trade and Plantations, 2 December 1712, in CSP (July 1712–July 1714), 102–3. The "memorial" on English prisoners, undated but received in London in July 1712, can be found in ibid., 8.
60. Dudley to Vaudreuil, 12 November 1712, in MA, II: 627–27a.
61. Peter Schuyler to Dudley, 19 December 1712, in MA, II: 466.
62. CM Diary, II: 191.

63. SS Diary, I: 708.
64. Elisha Williams to Stephen Williams, 29 March 1713, in PVMA Mss., Williams Papers, box 1, folder 9.

FIVE

1. RC, 76. On typical age at marriage among the Kahnawake, see p. 155 and Ch. 7, note 55.
2. Dudley to the Council of Trade and Plantations, 2 December 1712, in CSP (July 1712–July 1714), 103.
3. "Propositions Made by Sarachdowne . . . to the Commissioners of Indian Affairs in Albany," 19 May 1712; see New York Colonial Manuscripts (New York State Archives, Albany, N.Y.), LVII: 152. See also Thomas Elliot Norton, *The Fur Trade in Colonial New York, 1686–1776* (Madison, Wis., 1974), 133.
4. John Schuyler to Dudley, 10 June 1713, in MA, II: 468.
5. The original of this extraordinary document is in MA, II: 468. Printed versions can be found in HD, II: 349–50 and C. Alice Baker, *True Stories of New England Captives* (Greenfield, Mass., 1897), 144–46.
6. On the powers and responsibilities of the French governor (*le gouverneur générale*), see Guy Frégault, *La Civilisation de la Nouvelle France, 1713–1744* (Montreal, 1969), and Marcel Trudel, *Introduction to New France* (Toronto, 1968), 149–51.
7. This building, the Château de Ramezay, still stands in the "old city" of Montreal; it is used now as a museum.
8. This description of the mission's appearance in 1713 is based on reports of archaeological excavations carried out in the 1950s. See Wilfred Jury, "Kahnatakwenke, Fourth Site of Caughnawaga," in *Kateri*, VIII, no. 1 (December 1955), 6–10; Jury, "Caughnawaga's Fourth Site," ibid., IX, no. 1 (December 1956), 4–9; and "Excavations at Caughnawaga," ibid., IX, no. 2 (March 1957), 6–9, and IX, no. 3 (June 1957), 6–9. These results are supplemented by information from CAI, *passim*.
9. See, in this connection, the map included in Jury, "Caughnawaga's Fourth Site," 6.
10. On the life of Cholonec, see David M. Hayne et al., eds., *Dictionary of Canadian Biography*, 12 vols. (Toronto, 1966–90), II: 144. On Garnier, see ibid., II: 237.
11. On the clothing, coiffure, and personal adornments of Kahnawake

women, see CAI, II: 28–29, 38, 43–44, and JR, LXII: 179, 185–87.

12. The "discoverer," in the mission records, of François Xavier Arosen (and of Eunice herself) was Fr. Guillaume Forbes, a priest at Kahnawake in the closing decades of the nineteenth century (and subsequently bishop of Quebec). The results of his research, and the reasoning behind them, are presented in a series of letters to C. Alice Baker, currently in PVMA Mss., Baker Papers; on Arosen, see especially Forbes to Baker, 1 March 1900, box 2, folder 9.

13. See above, pp. 88–91.

14. On Iroquois naming practices, see CAI, I: 71–72. On the avoidance of nominal repetition, see register, Mission de Saint François Xavier du Sault St. Louis (Kahnawake, P. Q., Canada), passim. Material from this document has been published in several volumes of the series entitled Répertoire des actes de baptême, mariage, sépultures, et des recensements du Québec ancien, Hubert Charbonneau et Jacques Légaré, directeurs (Montreal, 1985–); see, for example, XXVIII: 481–515.

15. On age at marriage among the Kahnawake, see p. 155 and Ch. 7, note 55.

16. MA, II: 468 (published in HD, I: 348–49); SS Diary, II: 719; ibid., II: 720.

17. Vaudreuil to Dudley, 12 June 1713, translated in MA, II: 631–34.

18. Dudley to Vaudreuil, 27 June 1713, in MA, II: 635.

19. Dudley to the Earl of Dartmouth, 24 August 1713, in CSP (July 1712–July 1714), 228; SS Diary, II: 730; Dudley and Nicholson to Vaudreuil, 3 November 1713, in AC, file no. C-11-A, XXXIV: 336–38.

20. The entire document is published, under the title "Stoddard's Journal," in The New England Historical and Genealogical Register, V (1851): 21–42. The original is in Houghton Library, Harvard University (Cambridge, Mass.).

21. Ibid., 27–28.

22. Ibid., 28.

23. Ibid., 28–29.

24. Ibid., 28–29 and passim.

25. Ibid., passim; Elisha Williams to Stephen Williams, 2 April 1714, in Beinecke Library, Yale University (New Haven, Conn.).

26. "Stoddard's Journal," 32.

27. Ibid., 33.

28. Ibid., 34.

29. John Williams to Samuel Sewall, 1 June 1714, in WP, V: 295.
30. "Stoddard's Journal," 34.
31. Ibid., 34.
32. Ibid., 34–35.
33. Ibid., 35.
34. Ibid., 34, 37, 40–41.
35. Ibid., 39–41.
36. Sarah Williams to Stephen Williams, 9 September 1714, in PVMA Mss., Williams Papers, box 1, folder 9; Elisha Williams to Stephen Williams, 20 October 1714, PVMA Mss., Williams Papers, box 1, folder 9.
37. Rev. Eleazer Williams, "A Discourse Delivered at Deerfield, 1846, On Commemoration of the Death of the Rev. John Williams," in "The Eleazer Williams Scrapbook," Edward A. Ayer Collection, Newberry Library (Chicago, Ill.), ms. 999a. Similar comments can be found in Solomon Williams, *The Power and Efficacy of the Prayers of the People of God . . . A Sermon Preach'd at Mansfield, Aug. 4, 1741* (Boston, 1742), 18, and also in a letter from Jerusha M. Colton (a Williams descendant) to Stephen W. Williams, 26 May 1836, quoted in Stephen W. Williams, *A Biographical Memoir*, 93.

Six

1. "Mr. Colden's Memoir on the Fur Trade," 10 November 1724, in NYCD, V: 728.
2. Claude Chauchetière, *Narrative of the Mission of Sault St. Louis, 1667–1685*, introduction by David Blanchard (Kahnawake, Canada, 1981), 35. Chauchetière was himself a priest at the mission during the early years—and was also its first historian. His "narrative" was published in JR, LXIII; the reference given here is to its most recent reprinting. For a somewhat updated (twentieth-century) version of the "legend"—mixed with much solid historical information—see Edward J. Devine, *Historic Caughnawaga* (Montreal, 1922). Devine, too, was a Jesuit and longtime mission priest.
3. Chauchetière, *Narrative*, 37.
4. Ibid., 37. The best recent study of the beginnings of LaPrairie is Yvon Lacroix, *Les origines de LaPrairie* (Montreal, 1981).
5. Chauchetière, *Narrative*, 37–39.
6. Ibid., 39.
7. Ibid., 47.

8. On the extraordinary piety manifested by early mission converts, see, for example, ibid., 51, 73, 75, 77 and JR, LIX: 257–65; LX: 277–93; LXIII: 127–33.
9. Chauchetière, *Narrative*, 51.
10. Ibid., 53.
11. Ibid., 55, 65.
12. JR, LIX: 269–91; Chauchetière, *Narrative*, 75–77.
13. JR, LXI: 53.
14. See the references given in "Beginnings," note 8, above.
15. See Bruce G. Trigger and James F. Pendergast, "Saint Lawrence Iroquoians," in William C. Sturtevant, ed., *Handbook of the North American Indians*, XV: *Northeast* (Washington, D.C., 1978), Bruce G. Trigger, volume ed., 357–61. See also Thomas Elliot Norton, *The Fur Trade in Colonial New York, 1687–1776* (Madison, Wis., 1974), Ch. 2; Devine, *Historic Caughnawaga*, 11–12; Lacroix, *Les origines de LaPrairie*, 15–17; Chauchetière, *Narrative*, 39.
16. Chauchetière, *Narrative*, 37–39, 53; JR, LV: 35.
17. See Daniel K. Richter, "Iroquois versus Iroquois: Jesuit Missions and Christianity in Village Politics," in *Ethnohistory*, XXXII (1985), 1–16. For individual cases of Kahnawake converts subjected to persecution in their tribal homelands, see P. F. X. Charlevoix, *History and Gener͡ ' Description of New France*, J. G. Shea, trans., 6 vols. (London, 1902), III, Appendix: "Details on the Life and Death of Some Indian Christians," 283–308.
18. Chauchetière, *Narrative*, 61.
19. Ibid., 47, 67. See also JR, LV: 37.
20. Chauchetière, *Narrative*, 61; JR, LIX: 275.
21. Chauchetière, *Narrative*, 61. See also Lacroix, *Les origines de LaPrairie*, 21, 65–67.
22. Chauchetière, *Narrative*, 61, 67, 101, and *passim*; JR, LXIII: 131. See also Lacroix, *Les origines de LaPrairie*, 32–33.
23. Chauchetière, *Narrative*, 77; Lacroix, *Les origines de LaPrairie*, 30–33.
24. JR, LX: 275; Chauchetière, *Narrative*, 81.
25. Devine, *Historic Caughnawaga*, 41.
26. JR, LXII: 253.
27. Chauchetière, *Narrative*, 95, 115–23, 129; JR, LX: 279–83.
28. JR, LXI: 199; LX: 277; LXII: 173; LXIII: 196.
29. See, for example, Nicolas Burtin, *Vie de Catherine Tekakwitha, vierge iroquoise décédée en odeur de saintée à l'ancien village du Sault St. Louis, le 17 avril 1680* (Quebec, 1894); Ellen H. Wal-

worth, *The Life and Times of Kateri Tekakwitha, The Lily of the Mohawks* (Albany, N.Y., 1926); and Henri Béchard, *The Original Caughnawaga Indians* (Montreal, 1976). The literature on Kateri Tekakwitha is enormous—and still growing. A journal entitled *Kateri*, devoted entirely to this subject, has been published on a quarterly basis at Kahnawake for the past fifty years.

30. JR, LXII: 175–83; Chauchetière, *Narrative*, 103–5.

31. Chauchetière, *Narrative*, 103; JR, LXII: 77; LXIII: 249.

32. For a concise account of Kateri's life (including phrases and sentences quoted in this paragraph), see Charlevoix, *History and Description*, III: 283–96. A recent, interpretive discussion can be found in Norman Clermont, "Catherine Tekakwitha, 1656–1680," in *Culture*, VII (1), 47–53. For a fictionalized treatment, in a distinctly "postmodern" vein, see Leonard Cohen, *Beautiful Losers* (Toronto, 1966).

33. On the concept of cultural "revitalization," see Anthony F. C. Wallace, "Revitalization Movements: Some Theoretical Considerations for Their Comparative Study," in *American Anthropologist*, LVIII (1958), 264–81. In this connection, note the following, striking statement by Lafitau: "The Indians have lost . . . [many] of their customs, a fact which they themselves recognize and regret for, in the misfortunes which have come upon them, they say that they ought not to complain and that they are being punished for having abandoned the practices of retreats and fasts." (CAI, I: 219).

34. Charlevoix, *History and Description*, III: 294; CAI, I: 219–20, 231–35; II, 207–13. For a modern account of Iroquois spirituality, see Anthony F. C. Wallace, *The Death and Rebirth of the Seneca* (New York, 1970), Ch. 3–4, 8, 10. Similar, and related, practices among the Hurons—another Iroquoian group—are carefully described in Bruce G. Trigger, *The Children of Aataensic: A History of the Huron People to 1660* (Montreal, 1976), *passim*.

35. Chauchetière, *Narrative*, 51.

36. On divorce in early Kahnawake, see Chauchetière, *Narrative*, 71. (In the mid-eighteenth century, at least 20 percent of Kahnawake marriages ended in failure: this computation is based on material in the "register," Mission de Saint François Xavier du Sault St. Louis, Kahnawake, Canada.) On Kahnawake burial practices, see Chauchetière, *Narrative*, 69–71; JR, LXI: 207–9. On traditional Iroquoian burial customs, see CAI, II: 216–33.

37. On church singing among the Kahnawake, see JR, LX: 145 and

LXVIII: 273–75; on the naming of mission priests, JR, LXVIII: 269 and CAI, II: 240; on the ceremony of *hotounongannandi*, JR, LXIV: 125.

38. Charlevoix, *History and Description*, III: 304; JR, LXIV: 145; LXV: 33–37. These people, and their sufferings, were long remembered. A visitor to Canada in the mid-eighteenth century noted that "in the area around Montreal they celebrate four ceremonies in honor of four Indian martyrs from the village of St. Louis, and several parishes nearby go there in procession once a year to sing a grand mass." ('Trans. from T. C. B., *Voyage au canada, dans le nord le l'Amérique Septentrionale fait depuis 1751 à 1761* [Quebec, 1887], 68.)

39. For a careful, contemporaneous account of ritual torture among the Iroquois, see CAI, II: 151–63. Individual episodes of torture are described at numerous points in the Jesuit Relations. For a recent scholarly treatment of this subject, see Nathaniel Knowles, *The Torture of Captives by the Indians of Eastern North America* (Philadelphia, Pa., 1940).

40. The best single description (and analysis) of the trade is Jean Lunn, "The Illegal Fur Trade Out of New France, 1713–60," in Canadian Historical Association, *Report of the Annual Meeting, 1939*, 61–76. See also Norton, *The Fur Trade*, Ch. 8; Guy Frégault, "La Compagnie de la Colonie," in *Le XVIIIe Siècle Canadien: Etudes* (Montreal, 1968), 242–88; Frégault, *La Civilisation de la Nouvelle France*, 72–76; Allen W. Trelease, *Indian Affairs in Colonial New York: The Seventeenth Century* (Ithaca, N.Y., 1960), 217–19.

41. Frontenac to the King, 2 November 1681, trans. in NYCD, IX: 145. French law bearing on the fur trade is carefully described in Frégault, "La Compagnie," 243–48.

42. Beauharnois to Maurepas, 21 September 1741, trans. in NYCD, IX: 1071. For a description of a trading "convoy," see Governor Clinton to the Lords of Trade and Plantations, 17 June 1751, ibid., IX: 716. On the mechanics of the trade, see Lunn, "The Illegal Fur Trade," 61–63, and Norton, *The Fur Trade*, 124–27.

43. Among the most useful of the surviving account books are those of Robert Sanders and Evert Wendell, Albany merchants heavily involved in the trade. (Both documents are found today in the manuscript collection of the New-York Historical Society, New York, N.Y.) See also, in the same connection, the Cornelius Cuyler Letter Books (American Antiquarian Society, Worcester, Mass.).

The passages quoted in this paragraph of the text are (in order) from: Sanders Letter Book, 26, 27, 62; Evert Wendell Account Book, 90, 94.

44. Lunn, "The Illegal Fur Trade," 62–63.

45. Ibid., 65–68. The various goods received by the traders in exchange for their furs are clearly indicated in the Evert Wendell Account Book, *passim*. On the advantages of trading at Albany, note this comment by one French official to another: "the English have ruined our Indian trade . . . by means of the cheap bargains they can give of goods, at nearly one half the price our Frenchmen can afford [to give]"; see Callières to Seignelay, January 1689, trans. in NYCD, IX: 405. Similar statements appear in both French and English records, through the middle of the eighteenth century.

46. Discussion of the illegal fur trade, and of measures designed to stop it, is found throughout the correspondence of French colonial officials. See, for example, Vaudreuil and Bégon to Pontchartrain, 12 November 1712, in *Rapports de l'archiviste de la province de Québec*, XXVII (1947–48), 183–84; Vaudreuil and Bégon to Pontchartrain, 20 September 1714, ibid., 275–76; and Beauharnois to Maurepas, 21 September 1741, trans. in NYCD, IX: 1069–71. (The quoted sentences in the text are from ibid., 1071.) For a vivid account of a single confrontation involving Kahnawake leaders, mission priests, and the French governor, see *Mémoires sur le Canada, depuis 1749 jusqu'à 1760* (no author given; Quebec, 1873), 20–23.

47. See, for example, "Conference Between Governor Burnet [of New York] and the Indians," 27 August 1722, in NYCD, V: 668–69, and "Mr. Colden's Memoir on the Fur Trade," ibid., V: 726–33.

48. In 1698 New York officials compiled estimates of the "comparative population of . . . the Indians in 1689 and 1698." The overall decline was thought to be roughly 50 percent; for the Mohawks, in particular, it was more than 60 percent (NYCD, IV: 337). On Anglo-Indian discussion of Iroquois migration to Canada, see, for example, "Governor Sloughter's Address to the Five Nations," 1 June 1691, in NYCD, III: 773–74; "Conference of the Earl of Bellomont with the Indians," 26 August 1700, ibid., IV: 728–46; and "Conference of Lord Cornbury with the Indians," 9 July 1702, ibid., IV: 982–87. (The quoted statement is from ibid., IV: 987.) Comments on the same theme are frequently present in correspondence between British colonial officials; see, for example, NYCD, IV: 168–69; IV: 487–88; IV: 747; V: 571.

49. "Report of the Commissioners of Indian Affairs," 12 November

1724, in NYCD, V: 742. English efforts to regulate the trade with Canada are fully described in Norton, *The Fur Trade*, 135–45.

50. Denonville to Seignelay, 27 October 1687, trans. in NYCD, IX: 353–54; "Observations on the State of Affairs in Canada," trans. in ibid., IX: 433; "Summary of Intelligence from Canada," ibid., IX: 435.

51. Denonville to Seignelay, January 1690, trans. in NYCD, IX: 440–42; Charlevoix, *History and Description*, III: 198. See also "Mémoire sur le Canada," in LMAD, I: 564.

52. Devine, *Historic Caughnawaga*, 89–91.

53. On the Schenectady campaign (from the French perspective), see "Notice of the most Remarkable Occurrences in Canada, 1689, 1690," trans. in NYCD, IX: 466–68. This account mentions "80 Indians of the Sault" taking part, and particularly emphasizes the role of "the Great Mohawk, the chief . . . of the Sault." See also Charlevoix, *History and Description*, III: 122–26.

54. See "Memoir on Behalf of the Christian Iroquois in Canada," 11 November 1692, trans. in NYCD, IX: 539–42; "Information furnished by the Rev. Mr. Miller, respecting New York," December 1696, ibid., IV: 183.

55. For examples of Indian disinclination (or refusal) to follow French commanders, see NYCD, IX: 559 (campaign against the Mohawks, 1692) and AC, file no. C-11-A, XXIX: 88–96 (campaign against Haverhill and other Massachusetts towns, 1708). The pattern would grow stronger as time passed; by the 1740s French leaders routinely excluded the Kahnawake from military planning "as 'twas feared . . . that they are treacherous" (trans. in NYCD, X: 102). On the matter of contacts between Kahnawake and the New York Iroquois, see various French communiqués, trans. in NYCD, IX: 499, 557, 578, 580, 598–99; see also JR, LXIV: 59–63, and LIR, 166–67.

56. On the intercolonial diplomacy of this period, see, for example, Norton, *The Fur Trade*, 18–25, and Trudel, *Introduction to New France*, 73–75.

57. See AC, file no. C-11-A, XXIX: 88–96; LIR, 212; NYCD, IX: 811, 813; ibid., VI: 286.

58. On the complexity of relations between the Kahnawake, French Canada, and New England (in the 1740s), see the long manuscript letter from "Joseph Kellogg Interpreter" to "Your Excellency the Governor of Massachusetts Bay," 3 December 1744, in MA, XXXI: 518–20.

59. On racial mixing at Kahnawake, note the following comment by

Bishop Guillaume Forbes (in the year 1900): "All these captives, . . . once adopted, were considered to be truly part of the
tribe . . . [As a result] today there is not a single purely Iroquois
family at Kahnawake . . . [and] only a couple of individuals who
can claim to be Iroquois without any admixture of white blood."
(Trans. from *Bulletin de Récherches Historiques*, VI: 117.) A century earlier, an American visitor to Kahnawake remarked that "a
great mixture of the blood of whites with that of aborigines is observ-
able in the persons of the inhabitants." (See Isaac Weld, *Travels
Through the States of North America and . . . Upper and Lower
Canada, During the Years 1795, 1796, and 1797*, two vols. [Lon-
don, 1807], II: 24.)

60. The evidence of a "warrior tradition" is too copious (and scattered)
for referencing here. But see, for example, the descriptions of Kahnawake war "feasts" in NYCD, IX: 479, and Kellogg to the Governor of Massachusetts Bay, 3 December 1744, in MA, XXXI: 519.
Note, in the same connection, this comment by a French official:
"men are not esteemed great among those people [the French Indi-
ans] except in so far as they are skilled in killing others by surprise,
and successful in hunting." (Aigremont to Pontchartrain, 14 November 1708, trans. in NYCD, IX: 823.) And this, by one of the
mission priests: "The men . . . make it to be understood that they
are properly born only for great things, especially for warfare. This
exercise, which exposes their courage to the rudest tests, furnishes
them frequent occasions to put in its brightest light all the nobility
of their sentiments." (CAI, II: 98.) Another mission priest declared
that "the Iroquois of Sault St. Louis are looked upon as the most
warlike of all the American tribes." (L. F. Nau to J. Bonin, 2
October 1735, in JR, LXVIII: 275.)

61. On Kahnawake demography, see the figures in "Tableau 3," Lacroix, *Les origines de LaPrairie*, 38, and the graph in R. Cole Harris
et al., eds., *Historical Atlas of Canada*, 3 vols. (Toronto, 1987) I,
plate 47. These conclusions are based on scattered estimates (and
other information) from the time. See, for example, NYCD, IV:
747; VI: 276, 582; IX: 1053, and also AC, file no. C-11-A,
XXXVII: 447; XLIII: 106; LVIII: 145; LXXV: 211.

62. Devine, *Historic Caughnawaga*, 128–29. See also the references
given in Ch. 5, note 8, above.

63. The plans are fully described in a document entitled "Proposed
Change of the Iroquois Indians of the Mission of Sault St. Louis"
(translation), in AC, file no. C-11-A, XXXVI: 203–5.

SEVEN

1. Edited and translated by William N. Fenton and Elizabeth L. Moore; published by the Champlain Society, 2 vols. (Toronto, 1974). The initial publication of the *Moeurs des sauvages* was in Paris in 1724. Fenton and Moore offer, in their modern edition, a lengthy Introduction with much useful discussion of Lafitau's life, career, and later reputation. For a short biographical summary, see also the entry in David M. Hayne et al., eds., *Dictionary of Canadian Biography*, 12 vols. (Toronto, 1966–90), III: 334–38 (written by Fenton). Surprisingly, there is at present no full-scale biography of Lafitau.

2. Lafitau's place in the history of anthropology is discussed at length in Fenton and Moore's Introduction to the *Moeurs des sauvages*; see CAI, xxix–cxix. It should be noted that Lafitau's purpose was never a "scientific" one (in the modern sense). He aimed, at bottom, to prove an ancient link between the peoples of the Old World and the New by adducing specific cultural similarities; this, he hoped, would confirm various Scriptural *dicta*, including the idea of a single "creation." But his method was evidently so painstaking, so "empirical" in its procedural details, that his portrayal of the native Americans seems persuasive—and reliable. He was, moreover, generally careful to distinguish between the various Indian cultures— and between his many different sources. The only Indians he observed from close up (and for an extended period of time) were those at the mission he served. Frequently he refers to them in the first person ("our Iroquois," "I have myself seen," etc.).

3. As noted above (Ch. 5, note 12), the discovery of Eunice Williams's Indian names was the work of Guillaume Forbes, a nineteenth-century mission priest (and later bishop). On "A'ongote," see especially Forbes's letter to C. Alice Baker, 10 December 1896, in PVMA Mss., Baker papers, box 2, folder 9.

4. On the mixed tribal backgrounds of the first Kahnawake settlers, see Claude Chauchetière, *Narrative of the Mission of Sault St. Louis, 1667–1685*, introduction by David Blanchard (Kahnawake, Canada, 1981), 55, and JR, LV: 35; on the subsequent prominence of Mohawk migrants, JR, LXI: 241; LXII: 169; LXIII: 179. The strengthening Mohawk identity of Kahnawake was expressed by frequent, informal contacts between mission residents and their

tribal "kindred" in colonial New York. French officials of the time reported visits by Mohawks from New York to "their relatives at the Sault." (One group decided to stay, "having, as they said, no nearer relatives than those residing here.") See the correspondence trans. in NYCD, IX: 499, 601; see also ibid., IX: 596, 687, and *passim*.

5. P. F. X. Charlevoix, *Journal of a Voyage to North America*, trans. by Louise Phelps Kellogg, 2 vols. (Chicago, 1923), I: 52; CAI, I: 71. The idea of "requickening" and replacing the dead was deeply embedded in Iroquoian tradition—and was continued, in specific cases, at Kahnawake. Thus, for example, the New England captive Timothy Rice was given to a Kahnawake chief "who adopted him to be his son, instead of a son which he . . . had lost." (Ebenezer Parkman, *The Story of the Rice Boys* [repr. Westborough, Mass., 1906], 4–5.) And Zadock Steele (of Connecticut) was, after capture by Kahnawakes, "adopted into one of the Indian families to fill the place of one whom they had lost on their expedition to Royalton." (Zadock Steele, *The Indian Captive* [repr. New York, n.d.], 70.) Additional cases of this type are mentioned in NYCD, VI: 795–96 and IX: 518, 629. Whether Eunice Williams was also adopted to replace a deceased person cannot be determined from the limited evidence available; the probability, however, seems strong.

6. CAI, II: 240; JR, LXVIII: 269.

7. These translations are suggested in Forbes to Baker, 10 December 1896, PVMA Mss., Baker papers, box 2, folder 9. Names given to other captives seem also to have referred to personal circumstances. Sarah Hanson's Indian name, for example, translates to "the woman of the burning of the cooking." (See Emma Lewis Coleman, *New England Captives Carried to Canada*, 2 vols. [Portland, Maine, 1925], II: 165.)

8. CAI, II· 171–72; M. Franquet, *Voyages et Mémoires sur le Canada en 1752–53* (Toronto, 1968), 38. For further description of Iroquois practice in adopting captives, see Charlevoix, *Journal*, I: 352–53, and JR, LXIX: 59–65.

9. The other captive children from Deerfield included Mercy Carter (age 10 when taken), Abigail French (6), Mary Harris (9), Joanna Kellogg (11), Mary Field (7), Martha French (8), Rebecca Kellogg (8), Mary Sheldon (16), William Brooks (5), Daniel Crowfoot (3), Waitstill Warner (3), and Joseph Kellogg (12). Of this group the first five definitely remained in Kahnawake for life, and others may have done so.

10. These passing references to Eunice Williams's adoptive parents are noted in Chs. 4–5 above.

11. On early New England family life, see John Demos, *A Little Commonwealth: Family Life in Plymouth Colony* (New York, 1970), Philip J. Greven, Jr., *Four Generations: Population, Land, and Family in Colonial Andover, Massachusetts* (Ithaca, N.Y., 1970), and Edmund S. Morgan, *The Puritan Family: Religion and Domestic Relations in Seventeenth-Century New England*, rev. ed. (New York, 1966).

12. JR, LXII: 173; M. Franquet, "Plan du fort du Sault St. Louis et du Village des Sauvages Iroquois, 1754," ms. map in archival collections of the Newberry Library (Chicago, Ill.).

13. CAI, I: 70; JR, LXI: 55.

14. CAI, I: 338–39.

15. CAI, I: 339; J. C. B., *Voyage au Canada dans le Nord d'Amérique Septentrionale, Fait Depuis L'An 1751 à 1761* (Québec, 1887), 229; Bacqueville de la Potherie, *Histoire de l'Amérique Septentrionale*, 4 vols. (Rouen, 1722), I: 358–59.

16. Charlevoix, *Journal*, II: 29; J. C. B., *Voyage*, 228; CAI, I: 360–61.

17. Franquet, *Voyages et Mémoires*, 38; Joseph Kellogg, ms. document beginning "When I was Carryed to Canada . . . ," in GC, The Rev. John Williams and Family, case 8, box 28. (This very interesting and revealing document is unsigned. However, a note at the bottom in another hand—apparently that of Stephen Williams—states the following: "this I sopose is capt. Kellogue's acct. I found it among my Father's papers." The internal evidence, as well, points to "Capt." Joseph Kellogg.)

18. CAI, II: 19; Franquet, *Voyages et Mémoires*, 38. See also J. C. B., *Voyage*, 229. The drawing of Kahnawake, made in the mid-eighteenth century by person(s) unknown, is today in the Bibliothèque Nationale (Paris). It is reproduced in several recent books—for example, in David Blanchard, *Kahnawake: A Historical Sketch* (Kahnawake, Canada, 1980), frontispiece. On early New England domestic architecture, see Abbott L. Cummings, *The Framed Houses of Massachusetts Bay, 1675–1725* (Cambridge, Mass., 1979), and Demos, *A Little Commonwealth*, Ch. 1. On Iroquoian "longhouses," see Thomas S. Abler, "Longhouse and Palisade: Northeastern Iroquoian Villages of the Seventeenth Century," in *Ontario History*, LXII (1970), 17–40, and Thomas Grassman, *The Mohawk Indians and Their Valley* (Schenectady, N.Y., 1969), Ap-

pendix C: "The Mohawk-Caughnawaga Excavation," 638–46. (This last is a field report of archaeological work at the site of the first Kahnawake, in the Mohawk Valley.) I am grateful to Dean Snow (Anthropology Dept., State University of New York, Albany) for helpful discussion and correspondence on the matter of Kahnawake housing.

19. Franquet, *Voyages et Mémoires*, 38.

20. Ibid., 38; CAI, II; 21–22; JR, LXVIII: 265.

21. In fact, we have no specific record of the Williams family home prior to the time of the massacre (in which it was destroyed). But it must have been comparable to the house built for John Williams (by the town of Deerfield) three years later—and about that we do have information. See especially the various "inventory" documents made following John Williams's death in 1729, found today in the Registry of Probate, Hampshire County, Northampton, Mass.

22. RC, 66. On Puritan child-rearing more generally, see Demos, *A Little Commonwealth*, Ch. 9, and Morgan, *The Puritan Family*, Ch. 3.

23. RC, 66. Thomas Hutchinson, governor and historian of Massachusetts, commented some years after the fact on the "tenderness" and "affection" shown by Indians to their captives. (See his *The History of the Colony and Province of Massachusetts Bay*, 2 vols. [London, 1765–68], II: 138, footnote.) It is also notable that repatriated captives were sometimes visited at their own homes in New England by their former Indian "masters." (Examples are noted in Coleman, *New England Captives, passim*.)

24. Sewall to Williams, 18 January 1706, in SS LB, I:323.

25. Kellogg, ms. document (see note 17 above). The quotation in the related footnote is from SW, 108.

26. CAI, II: 30; JR, LXVIII: 265; CAI, II: 44. Lafitau's interest in the details of Indian dress is especially striking; see his lengthy description in CAI, II: 28–46. There are additional references to Kahnawake clothing and coiffure in JR, LXII: 179, 185; Franquet, *Voyages et Mémoires*, 36–37; J. C. B., *Voyage*, 222; and James Smith, *An Account of the Remarkable Occurrences in the Life and Travels of Col. James Smith*, in Archibald Loudon, ed., *Outrages Committed by the Indians* (London, 1808; repr. New York, 1971), 154, 169, 181, 187, 233–34. (Smith described his captors as being "very tenacious of their old mode of dressing and painting.") There is, in the holdings of the Pocumtuck Valley Memorial Association (Deerfield, Mass.), an interesting assemblage of personal items from

eighteenth-century Kahnawake. Some of these came through the Williams family, and may well have been acquired during one of Eunice Williams's return visits to Massachusetts; indeed, two of them—a stone "gorget" and a deer-hide mocassin—are attributed to "Amrusus [actually, Arosen] husband of Eunice Williams." Other items in the collection include woven belts, a tobacco pouch, and a burden strap. Several of them are described and illustrated in Jonathan Fairbanks et al., eds., *New England Begins: The Seventeenth Century*, 3 vols. (Boston, Mass., 1982), I: 88–90.

27. Titus King, *Narrative of Titus King of Northampton, Mass.* (Hartford, Conn., 1938), 10; Thomas Hutchinson, quoted in Samuel G. Drake, *A Particular History of the Five Years French and Indian War in New England and Parts Adjacent* (repr. Freeport, N.Y., 1970), 177.

28. JR, LXVIII: 263–65; CAI, II: 15.

29. CAI, II: 124, 128; Smith, *Remarkable Occurrences*, 148; CAI, II: 97, 70. On the excavations at Kahnatakwenke, see the references given in Ch. 5, note 8 (above). Information on the material culture of the Kahnawake is too scattered for easy referencing here. But the most useful sources are, undoubtedly, Lafitau, CAI, *passim*, and Smith, *Remarkable Occurrences*.

30. Franquet, *Voyages et Mémoires*, 35–36. For an instance of the ceremonial etiquette surrounding Anglo-Indian diplomacy (in which the Kahnawake were centrally involved), see the record of "A Conference held at Deerfield . . . the Twenty seventh Day of August . . . 1735," published in *New England Historical and Genealogical Register*, LX (1906), 5–20. For additional examples of ceremonialism within Kahnawake itself, see JR, LIX: 269 and LXIV: 57. On this general subject, see also CAI, I: Ch. 5, *passim*.

31. JR, LX: 289; LXIV: 125; LXI: 175; Smith, *Remarkable Occurrences*, 131; CAI, I: 316–19. For an interesting case of a war feast jointly sponsored by the French governor and the "domiciled Indians" of Canada (including the Kahnawake), see NYCD, IX: 479. Joseph Bartlett, a Kahnawake captive originally from Newbury, Mass., described the menu on such occasions: "squatted corn, . . . the inwards of cattle, . . . the flesh of a beaver . . . [and of] a dog"; see his "Narrative" in Joshua Coffin, *A Sketch of the History of Newbury* (Boston, 1845), 333.

32. Charlevoix, *Journal*, II: 80; CAI, I: 350. See also Smith, *Remarkable Occurrences*, 233.

33. CAI, I: 300.

34. JR, LXI: 59; Bacqueville, *Histoire*, I: 361–63; CAI, I: 351; JR, LXII: 179.
35. Chauchetière, *Narrative*, 51; Smith, *Remarkable Occurrences*, 153. Smith was especially emphatic about the ethic of sharing (among the Kahnawake), and provided numerous specific examples of it; ibid., 143, 155, 233, 241. Lafitau admired their "charitable hospitality, which would confound all the nations of Europe"; CAI, I: 90.
36. JR, LXIV: 131.
37. Charlevoix, *Journal*, II: 29–30; Aigremont to Pontchartrain, 14 November 1708, in NYCD, IX: 823. See also CAI, I: 90.
38. Charlevoix, *Journal*, I: 26 (and, for a similar comment, CAI, II: 98–99); Smith, *Remarkable Occurrences*, 153; CAI, II: 102; ibid., II: 160–61; ibid., II: 158.
39. See, in this connection, RC, 55, 57 and SW, 105–6.
40. Since the mission "register" from before 1735 has been lost (or destroyed), there is no record of her rebaptism. The practice, however, is not in doubt—witness a good many other captive children (in other mission sites) for whom baptismal evidence does survive. A presumably representative case was that of Abigail Nims, taken as a child from Deerfield to the Indian mission-village of Sault-au-Récollet. She was baptized in Montreal, as noted in the following: "On June 15, 1704 the rites of baptism have been administered by me, the undersigned priest, to a little English girl named in her country Abigail, and now Marie Elisabeth, born at Dearfield in New England the 11 June 1700 of the marriage of Geoffroi Nimbs Shoemaker . . . and living [now] in the wigwam of a squaw of the Mountain. . . ." (See Coleman, *New England Captives*, II: 103–4.) For additional examples of captive children rebaptized and (sometimes) renamed, see ibid., II: 13–14, 50, 67, 82–84, 97, 104, and *passim*.
41. Kellogg, ms. document (see note 17 above).
42. JR, LXV: 93, 91; RC, 66.
43. The details of this description are taken especially from Franquet, *Voyages et Mémoires, passim*, and also from the map he drew for his military superiors ("Plan du fort du Sault de St. Louis et du village des Sauvages Iroquois," original in the archival collections of the Newberry Library, Chicago). The Desaunier sisters were evidently the only Europeans to reside in Kahnawake on a regular basis, besides the mission priests. Their presence was a continual source of worry and suspicion for French colonial officials, because

they appeared to be centrally involved in the illicit fur trade. For a short account, see E. P. H., "Unrest at Caughnawaga, or The Lady Fur traders of Sault St. Louis," in *The Bulletin of the Fort Ticonderoga Museum*, XI (1963), 155–60. See also P. C. de Rochemonteix, *Les Jésuites de la Nouvelle France* (Paris, 1906), 19–51, 246–58.

44. JR, LXV: 29; LXVIII: 271; see also JR, LXII, 171ff.

45. JR, LXV: 31. One visitor to the mission claimed, with perhaps pardonable exaggeration, that "Frenchmen just arrived" in Canada—and taken to see the Kahnawake—would typically "weep for joy to behold wolves transformed into lambs, and wild beasts into children of God." (P. F. X. Charlevoix, *History and General Description of New France*, J. G. Shea, trans., 6 vols. [London, 1902], IV: 306.) On the "festivals" honoring Kahnawake's "martyrs," see J. C. B., *Voyage*, 51.

46. This topic is explored at some length in Ch. 6 (pp. 129–31) above.

47. CAI, I: 243, 246.

48. Ibid., I: 218–19.

49. Ibid., I: 231.

50. Ibid., I: 134, 149.

51. Ibid., I: 323, 326.

52. Smith, *Remarkable Occurrences*, 160, 175, 197, 237.

53. The name François Xavier Arosen is linked, in the Kahnawake mission register, to Maria Gannenstenhawi (formerly Eunice Williams); the two are identified as *conjugibus* (married). That Eunice's husband had, as well, a second Indian name is shown by several references in New England records. A letter from Stephen Williams to Joseph Kellogg (16 December 1743) refers to the husband as Tairagie. The records of the Massachusetts assembly (8 February 1743/4) identify him as Terragie. A third rendition—presumably of the same name—appears in a later discussion of Eunice's life composed by the Rev. Richard Storrs (28 March 1811); here he is called Turroger. And, in a short biography of Eunice's grandson (written by her great-grandson Eleazer Williams), the name is given a further, distinctively French twist: De Roguers. Spelling differences aside, one can readily make out the shared phonetic *core* here. See: Stephen Williams to Joseph Kellogg, 16 December 1743, in GC, American Colonial Clergy, case 8, box 25; Records of the House of Representatives of Massachusetts Bay, 8 February 1743, MA, XXXI: 466; Richard Storrs to "Rev. Romeyn," 28 March

1811, in *The Christian Magazine* (June 1811), 343; Eleazer Williams, *Life of Te-ho-ra-gwa-ne-gen, alias Thomas Williams* (Albany, N.Y., 1859), 17.

54. Register, Mission de Saint François Xavier du Sault St. Louis (Kahnawake, Canada), III, n. p.

55. The figures for Kahnawake (in the mid-eighteenth century) are compiled from evidence in ibid. James Smith offered this comment, from his own experience among the Kahnawake: "The age of consent [in marriage] is about fourteen for the women and eighteen for the men" (Smith, *Remarkable Occurrences*, 240). On age at marriage in colonial French Canada, see Louise Dechêne, *Habitants et Marchands de Montreal au XVIIe Siècle* (Montreal, 1974), 104–5, and Jacques Henripin, *La population canadienne au début du XVIIIe siècle* (Paris, 1954), 66.

56. CAI, I: 340–41.

57. Ibid., I: 342, 344. On Iroquois marriage-making, see also Charlevoix, *Journal*, I: 48.

58. CAI, I: 348–49. On the obligations of spouses to one another, see also Charlevoix, *Journal*, I: 51, and Bacqueville *Histoire*, I: 358–59. The conclusions presented here about illegitimacy are based on evidence in the register, Mission . . . du Sault.

59. Smith, *Remarkable Occurrences*, 240; CAI, I: 354.

60. See pp. 104–5.

61. Register, Mission . . . du Sault, I, leaves 8, 19.

62. Stephen Williams's diary makes one explicit reference to "my Br in law & his son." (The brother-in-law mentioned here is Arosen.) See SW Diary, III: 384. On Stephen's reference to Kellogg's "bad news," see ibid., I: 364.

63. The conclusions about "birth intervals" (for Kahnawake mothers) are based on evidence in the register, Mission . . . du Sault. Lafitau's comments are in CAI, I: 355–56. See also Charlevoix, *Journal*, I: 51, Bacqueville, *Histoire*, I: 359, and J. C. B., *Voyage*, 228. The relatively low fertility rate at Kahnawake was part of a larger pattern for Iroquoian women generally. On the latter subject, see William Engelbrecht, "Factors Maintaining Low Population Density Among the Prehistoric Iroquois," in *American Antiquity*, LII (1987), 13–27.

64. CAI, I: 355–56. See also Charlevoix, *Journal*, I: 51. Note the following instance of childbearing by a "Canada Mohawk" woman, as reported in a journal from the time: "Soon after we began our

day's work an old squaw, pregnant, that travelled with us, stoped alone & was delivered of a child & by Monday overtook us with a living child upon her back." Quoted in HD, I: 518.

65. CAI, I: 357; Charlevoix, *Journal*, II: 102. See also J. C. B., *Voyage*, 227–28. A fine collection of early Kahnawake cradleboards can be seen today in the museum collection at the Château de Ramezay, Montreal.

66. These conclusions about infant mortality among the Kahnawake are based on information in the register, Mission . . . du Sault.

67. Charlevoix, *Journal*, I: 53. See also J. C. B., *Voyage*, 227, where "the giving of a name" is described as "the event which concludes the first period of childhood."

68. It is as Maria Gannenstenhawi that Eunice appears in records of the birth of her two daughters; see register, Mission . . . du Sault, I, leaves 8, 19. The translation of this name is suggested by Guillaume Forbes, in his correspondence with C. Alice Baker; see Forbes to Baker, 10 December 1896, in PVMA Mss., Baker Papers, box 2, folder 9.

69. Charlevoix, *Journal*, I: 52. Note the following statement by a leading student of Iroquois culture (today): "When a child is born, he or she is given a name 'not in use.' This 'baby name' is usually later changed for an 'adult name' that is not then 'in use,' that is, one belonging to someone now deceased or to someone whose name has been changed. Certain of these names are associated with particular obligations (in effect, roles) in the society." See Elisabeth Tooker, "Women in Iroquois Society," in Michael K. Foster, Jack Campisi, and Marianne Mithun, eds., *Extending the Rafters: Interdisciplinary Approaches to Iroquoian Studies* (Albany, N.Y., 1986), 112.

70. This cycle was carefully described by Lafitau; see CAI, II: 54–55, 60–64, 105 (Plate VII), 288, 290–91, and *passim*.

71. The term "heavy work" appears in CAI, II: 54. For a sampling of opinion (among English and European observers) about the work responsibilities of Indian women, see James Axtell, ed., *The Indian Peoples of Eastern America: A Documentary History of the Sexes* (New York, 1981), part four.

72. See, for example, Gabriel Sagard, *Le Grand Voyage du Pays des Hurons* (Paris, 1632), Ch. 7, and Baron de Lahontan, *New Voyages to North America*, 2 vols. (London, 1703), II: 421.

73. CAI, II: 54–55, 64–68, 70–71, 94, 97; JR, LXVIII: 275. See also Franquet, *Voyages et Mémoires*, 38, and J. C. B., *Voyage*,

221. For a useful discussion of early European views about gender difference in Iroquoian culture, see Norman Clermont, "La Place de la Femme dans les Sociétés Iroquoiennes," in *Recherches Amérindiennes au Québec*, XIII (1983), 286–90.

74. CAI, II: 15–16.

75. JR, LXVIII: 275. On the annual "hunt," see the lengthy, first-hand account in Smith, *Remarkable Occurrences*, 133–48, and some briefer comments, ibid., 173–74, 184–86, 196. See also JR, LXI: 57, 217–19; J. C. B., *Voyage*, 227; NYCD, III: 815.

76. In October 1735, a mission priest wrote that "we have actually forty warriors out on expeditions to strike at other tribes"; moreover, "last year ninety of our young men joined the French expedition against the Renards [the Fox Indians]." See JR, LXVIII, 275–77.

77. The information is drawn from "Census Data for New France," Archives Nationales (Paris), Section Outre-Mer, G¹, article 463. This material appears as a graph in R. Cole Harris et al., eds., *The Historical Atlas of Canada*, 3 vols. (Toronto, 1987), I, plate 47. The graph is actually the third in a demographic time-series, of which the first and second, dated to 1685 and 1695, show a "sex ratio" (adult females per 100 males) of approximately 135, whereas the last, dated 1716, shows a ratio of 265.

78. JR, LXI: 219; Smith, *Remarkable Occurrences*, 155.

79. Ibid., 154. On the depth and pervasiveness of Iroquoian gender distinctions, an eminent anthropologist has written this: "The most basic distinction [in Iroquoian societies] . . . was that made between the sexes . . . Almost every task was considered to be either exclusively men's work or exclusively women's work." See Bruce G. Trigger, *The Children of Aataentsic*, 2 vols. (Montreal, 1976), I: 34.

80. Register, Mission . . . du Sault, I: leaves 6, 10, 26; II: leaf not numbered (baptism dated 13 October 1754).

81. This was the observation of the nineteenth-century mission priest Guillaume Forbes; see his letter to C. Alice Baker, 10 December 1896, in PVMA Mss., Baker Papers, box 2, folder 9.

82. JR, LXVIII: 269–71.

83. Bacqueville, *Histoire*, I: 360–61. On the clan organization of the Kahnawake, Lafitau is especially informative; see CAI, I: 82, 287, 290–93, 300–1.

84. Ibid., I: 364–65; Bacqueville, *Histoire*, I: 360. See also Charlevoix, *Journal*, II: 83.

85. These connections were traced by Guillaume Forbes, and de-

scribed in his letter to C. Alice Baker, 10 December 1896, in PVMA Mss., Baker Papers, box 2, folder 9. See also Forbes, *Dictionnaire Généalogique des Familles de Caughnawaga*, ms. volume at Archives de la Compagnie de Jésus (St. Jérôme, Canada), 51, and Coleman, *New England Captives Carried to Canada*, II: 59–60.

86. CAI, I: 341.

87. John Henry Lydius to Colonel John Stoddard, 24 October 1744, in MA, XXXI: 510–12; CAI, I: 290. An especially detailed and thoughtful description of Iroquoian village governance can be found in ibid., I: 290–308.

88. CAI, I: 293–94; Charlevoix, *Journal*, II: 26–27; CAI, I: 296.

89. Bacqueville, *L'Histoire*, I: 362; CAI, I: 296.

90. CAI, I: 69.

91. See, for example, Lewis H. Morgan, *Ancient Society*, Leslie A. White, ed. (1877; repr. Cambridge, Mass., 1964), 60–80 and *passim*. The connection to Marxism is briefly explored in ibid., Editor's Introduction, xxxviii–xxxix, and in Thomas R. Trautman, *Lewis Henry Morgan and the Invention of Kinship* (Berkeley, Calif., 1987), 251–55. The key Marxist text, in this connection, is Friedrich Engels, *The Origin of the Family, Private Property, and the State, in Light of the Researches of Lewis H. Morgan*, Aleck West, trans. (1884; repr. New York, 1972).

92. The views of Lafitau have their proponents even today. One scholar argues that Iroquois matrons exercised more authority "than women have enjoyed anywhere at any time" (Judith K. Brown, "Economic Organization and the Position of Women Among the Iroquois," in *Ethnohistory*, XVII [1970], 156). Another has claimed that "of all the peoples of the earth, the Iroquois approach most closely to that hypothetical form of society known as the 'matriarchate' " (George Peter Murdock, *Our Primitive Contemporaries* [New York, 1934], 302). For more qualified and cautious views, see D. Jenness, *Indians of Canada*, 2nd ed. (Ottawa, 1934), 134–37, and Harriet M. Converse, "Women's Rights Among the Iroquois," in A. C. Parker, ed., *Myths and Legends of the New York State Iroquois* (Albany, N.Y., 1908), 135–38. See also W. M. Beauchamp, "Iroquois Women," in *Journal of American Folklore*, XII (1900), 81–91, and Nancy Bonvillain, "Iroquoian Women," in Bonvillain, ed., *Studies in Iroquoian Culture: Occasional Publications in Northeastern Anthropology*, No. 6, 47–58. Finally: for an overview of this entire debate, see Tooker, "Women in Iroquois Society," 109–23.

93. This and related questions are discussed in Alden Vaughan and Daniel K. Richter, "Crossing the Cultural Divide: Indians and New Englanders, 1605–1763," in *American Antiquarian Society Proceedings*, XC (1980), 23–99.
94. See below, chapter entitled "Endings."

EIGHT

1. SW Diary, I: 160.
2. Ibid., I: 12; John Williams to Stephen Williams, 14 May 1716, in Edward E. Ayer Collection, Newberry Library (Chicago, Ill.), ms. no. 1004.5; Samuel Sewall to John Williams, 21 January 1716/17, in SS LB, 66; John Williams to Stephen Williams, 8 December 1719, in GC, American Colonial Clergy, case 8, box 25.
3. Dudley to Vaudreuil, 15 April 1717, in MA, II: 668; Records of the Council of Massachusetts Bay, 7 September 1721, MA, VII: 300; Records of the Ministry of the Marine, 13 October 1720, in AC, file C-11-A, XLI: 232–34.
4. John Williams to Stephen Williams, 17 August 1717, in GC, American Colonial Clergy, case 8, box 25; John Williams to Stephen Williams, 27 November 1718, ibid.
5. The experience of the several Kelloggs is described at some length in Emma Lewis Coleman, *New England Captives Carried to Canada*, 2 vols. (Portland, Maine, 1925) II: 97–102; see also Timothy Hopkins, *The Kelloggs in the New World*, 2 vols. (San Francisco, Calif., 1903), I: 36–38, 55–63. Joseph Kellogg's efforts to repatriate his sisters are noticed at various points in the official records of Massachusetts. In 1718, for example, he presented a "memorial" to the Council, "setting forth that he has several near Relations now in the hands of the French & Indians of Canada, who have professed the Roman Catholic Religion, . . . [and proposing] to undertake a Journey thither to persuade them to return to their country." He asked for "something by the Publick to defray his charges." The Councillors authorized "a suitable reward" if (and only if) he "should succeed in his intention of bringing home any of the English Captives." See Records of the Council of Massachusetts Bay, 25 February 1718, in MA, VII: 18.
6. Records of the Council of Massachusetts Bay, 17 March 1721/22, in ibid., VII: 350; see also ibid., VII: 374–75.
7. SW Diary, I: 27; James Davenport to Abigail and Stephen Wil-

liams, 20 August 1722, in Boston Public Library, Boston, Mass., ms. no. Ch.A.5.51; John Williams to Stephen Williams, 16 March 1718/19, in GC, American Colonial Clergy, case 8, box 25.

8. John Williams to Stephen Williams, 24 May 1718, Fisher Howe misc. letters, folder 1, Williams College Archives (Williamstown, Mass.); *New England Courant* (Boston, Mass.), 12 September 1723.

9. Bill of John Saler of Boston "for Entertaining and Providing for twenty two French Mohawks nineteen days," in MA, XXXI: 186.

10. On the details of this war, see Colin G. Calloway, *The Western Abenakis of Vermont, 1600–1800* (Norman, Okla., 1990), Ch. 6, and Francis Parkman, *A Half-Century of Conflict* (Boston, 1897), Chs. 10–11. For a local perspective on the war, see the entries in the diary of Warham Williams (Eunice's younger brother), especially for the summer of 1723; this document is in the American Antiquarian Society (Worcester, Mass.), Williams Family Papers.

11. Samuel Partridge to William Dummer, 11 July 1724 and 1 October 1724, in MA, II: 118, 217.

12. Deerfield's involvement in the war is summarized in Richard I. Melvoin, *New England Outpost: War and Society in Colonial Deerfield* (New York, 1989), 263–66.

13. On the plans for Stephen's ordination, see John Williams to Stephen Williams, 15 September 1716, in GC, American Colonial Clergy, case 8, box 25; see also John Williams to Stephen Williams, 11 October 1716, in PVMA Mss., Williams Papers, box 1, folder 9. On the plans for his wedding, see M. W. Davis to George Sheldon, 11 April 1902, in ibid., Williams Papers, box 16, folder 2. Sewall's gift is noted in his diary entry for 18 September 1718; see SS Diary, II: 903.

14. John Williams to Samuel Sewall, 11 January 1721/2, in ms. collection of the New England Historic Genealogical Society (Boston, Mass.); John Williams to Stephen Williams, 7 January, 1722/3, in PVMA Mss., Williams Papers, box 1, folder 9; Isaac Chauncey, *A Sermon Preach'd at the Funeral of the Reverend Mr. John Williams* (Boston, 1729); SS Diary, II: 855, 917, 950–51, 1014, and *passim*; Commonplace Book of John Williams, in PVMA Mss., Williams Papers, box 4, folder 2.

15. These activities can be traced through scattered (but numerous) references in his surviving correspondence. See PVMA Mss., Williams Papers, and GC, American Colonial Clergy, and The Reverend John Williams and Family, *passim*.

16. SW Diary, IV: 183; IV: 263; II: 393; V: 351; III: 55; III: 59; II: 278.

17. SW Diary, II: 128–29.

18. Ibid., II: 129–30.

19. Chauncey, *A Sermon Preach'd at the Funeral of the Reverend Mr. John Williams, passim.*

20. *The Boston News-letter* (June 19–26, 1729), no. 130; *The New England Weekly Journal* (June 23, 1729); Thomas Foxcroft, *Eli, the Priest Dying Suddenly* (Boston, 1729).

21. (Boston, 1729).

22. John Williams, *A Serious Word to the Posterity of Holy Men*, 1, 6, 4, 38, 4, 7, 37, 5.

23. Ibid., 38, 37, 33, 31, 32, 39.

24. Ibid., 56–60.

25. Various probate materials pertaining to the Williams family, including the lengthy inventory of John's estate, can be found in the Registry of Probate, Hampshire County, Northampton, Mass., box 161, no. 31. See also the related material in the Probate Court Records, V, leaves 1, 44–45, 51–56, 63, 67, 69, and VI, leaf 78.

26. Ibid., box 161, no. 31.

27. The court's order in this matter is dated 10 March 1729/30; see ibid., box 161, no. 30.

28. SW Diary, II: 146.

29. Ebenezer Hinsdale to Stephen Williams, 21 August 1730, in GC, The Reverend John Williams and Family, case 8, box 28. James Corse was the son of Elizabeth Corse, a widow captured in the "massacre" years before. His mother had remarried in Canada; her new husband was a Frenchman, by whom she had several additional children. (See Coleman, *New England Captives*, II, 74–76.) In the summer of 1730, the Massachusetts Council ordered that James Corse be assisted as he traveled to Canada "to recover [his mother] out of Captivity where she has been for a long time." (See MA, XXXVIIIa: 125–29.) While en route, Corse kept a diary which he subsequently "Communicated to the General Court." (The diary is published in HD, I: 518.) Almost certainly, it was during this journey that Corse met, and traveled with, François Xavier Arosen. Stephen must have known of the journey and hoped that Corse would bring direct news of his sister—hence his "request" to his cousin Hinsdale.

30. Hinsdale to Stephen Williams, 21 April 1730, in GC, The Reverend John Williams and Family, case 8, box 28.

31. Ibid.

32. SW Diary, II: 257.

33. Ibid., II: 283, 318; HD, I: 311. The fascinating detail of the silver cup was, according to George Sheldon, contained in a letter sent to him in 1884 by Charles K. Williams of Rutland, Vermont. Unfortunately, the letter cannot be located today.

34. Warham Williams to Stephen Williams, 5 March 1732, in GC, The Reverend John Williams and Family, case 8, box 28.

35. Eleazer Williams to Stephen Williams, 7 February 1733/34, in Edward E. Ayer Collection, Newberry Library (Chicago, Ill.), ms. no. 998a.

36. Ibid.

37. SW Diary, II: 394–95.

38. *Diary of Joshua Hempstead of New London, Connecticut* (New London, Conn., 1901), 278.

39. SW Diary, II: 300, 417, 440; III: 7; John Sergeant to Benjamin Colman, 1 August 1743, in Colman Papers, Massachusetts Historical Society, Boston. For a full account of the Stockbridge project, see James Axtell, *The Invasion Within: The Contest of Cultures in Colonial North America* (New York, 1985), 196–204.

40. SW Diary, III: 226, 286, 309. The reference to his boyhood experience draws on SW Mss., 110.

41. A "diary" of this conference was kept by a member of the Governor's Council who attended (and who cannot be identified today). The diary is published in George Sheldon, *The Conference at Deerfield, Mass., August 27–31, 1735, Between Gov. Belcher and Several Tribes of Western Indians* (Boston, 1906), 8–20.

42. SW Diary, III: 38.

43. Sheldon, *The Conference at Deerfield, Mass.*, 9–10.

44. Ibid., 9–14; SW Diary, III: 38.

45. Sheldon, *The Conference at Deerfield, Mass.*, 19, 8; SW Diary, III: 38.

46. Hocquart to the Ministry of the Marine, 18 October 1731, 24 October 1731, and 10 October 1732, in AC, file C-11-A, LV: 182, 190–91, and LVIII: 144–45.

47. Beauharnais and Hocquart to the Ministry of the Marine, 15 October 1730, in ibid., LII: 20–22.

48. Hocquart to the Ministry of the Marine, 10 October 1732, in ibid., LVIII: 144–45; Beauharnais and Hocquart to the Ministry of the Marine, 18 October 1731, ibid., LIV: 149.

49. Beauharnais and Hocquart to the Ministry of the Marine, 14 October 1738, in ibid., LXIX: 79–80.
50. Beauharnais and Hocquart to the Ministry of the Marine, 14 October 1738, in ibid., LXIX: 74–76.
51. SW Diary, III: 106.
52. The story of the Carter family, during and after the "massacre," can be found in Coleman, *New England Captives*, II: 68–72.
53. Robert and Ahasueras Wendell to Ebenezer Carter, 6 July 1736, in ibid., II: 72; SW Diary, III: 106.
54. Ibid., III: 239.
55. Thomas Hutchinson, *History of the Colony and Province of Massachusetts Bay*, 2 vols. (London, 1765–68), I: 139 (fn.).
56. Coleman, *New England Captives*, I: 295; SW Diary, III: 247.
57. Ibid., III: 321.
58. Ibid.

NINE

1. The description of Albany—its physical appearance and topographical layout—contained in this and succeeding paragraphs is based largely on primary materials reprinted in Joel Munsell, *Annals of Albany*, 10 vols. (Albany, N.Y., 1854–71) and in Cuyler Reynolds, *Albany Chronicles: A History of the City Arranged Chronologically* (Albany, N.Y., 1906). Early maps, for example, can be found in Munsell, *Annals of Albany*, I: 183; III: 120; IV, frontispiece, 189, 328; VIII: frontispiece. See also Reynolds, *Albany Chronicles*, 133, 165. For drawings and photographs of early buildings, see ibid., 51, 68, 70, 76, 183, 186, 188, 195, 220, 248, 374, 380, 396, and Munsell, *Annals of Albany*, II: 48. For census materials, see ibid., I: 263–64; II: 282–83; III: 334. For travelers' accounts, see ibid., I: 208–11 (Isaac Weld, 1796); I: 281–83 (Samuel F. B. Morse, 1789); II: 48–54 ("Mrs. Grant," 1764); X: 219 (Elkanah Watson, 1788). However, the fullest and best such account—and the most timely for the purposes of this study—is found in Peter Kalm, *Travels into North America* (repr. Barre, Mass., 1972), trans. by John R. Forster, 321–37. The city records are published, in somewhat abridged form, in Munsell, *Annals of Albany, passim*.
2. On the populace of Albany in the 1740s, see Kalm, *Travels into*

North America, 332–35. See also the "List of Freeholders in the City of Albany . . . 1742," in Munsell, *Annals of Albany*, II: 282–83.

3. Kalm, *Travels into North America*, 333–34.

4. SW Diary, III: 321.

5. Ibid., III: 321–22.

6. Ibid., III: 322; Kalm, *Travels into North America*, 326. On the look, population, and cultural aspect of Stockbridge in this period, see Sarah Cabot Sedgwick and Christine Sedgwick Marquand, *Stockbridge, 1739–1939: A Chronicle* (Great Barrington, Mass., 1939), 23, 45–46, and Electa F. Jones, *Stockbridge, Past and Present* (Springfield, Mass., 1854), 64–66. On the missionary work of Sergeant and the (sometimes complicating) presence of Ephraim Williams, see James Axtell, *The Invasion Within: The Contest of Cultures in Colonial North America* (New York, 1985), 196–204. For additional material on the Stockbridge Williamses, see Sedgwick and Marquand, *Stockbridge, 1739–1939*, 30–31, 40–43, 49–71. On the road between Stockbridge and Westfield, see ibid., 283–84.

7. SW Diary, III: 322; *The Holy Bible*, authorized King James version (Oxford University Press, New York, n. d.), 302. For another account of these events, see Alexander Medlicott, Jr., "Return to This Land of Light: A Plea to an Unredeemed Captive," *New England Quarterly*, XXXVIII (1965), 202–16.

8. This reconstruction of the appearance of eighteenth-century Longmeadow is based on materials in *Proceedings of the Centennial Celebration of the Incorporation of the Town of Longmeadow, October 17th, 1883, With Numerous Historical Appendices* (Springfield, Mass., 1884).

9. A collection of early maps of the town can be found in the archival holdings of the Longmeadow Historical Society, Longmeadow, Mass.

10. On the career of Joseph Kellogg, see Timothy Hopkins, *The Kelloggs in the Old World and the New*, 2 vols. (San Francisco, Calif., 1903), I: 59–63.

11. The tradition of Eunice's unwillingness to occupy a bed inside Stephen's home has been variously preserved. One early account reads as follows: "She visited her brother in Longmeadow, but could not be induced to sleep in a house and lived in a wigwam in the orchard east of her brother's house until she returned to Canada. She never sat in a chair, or wore the clothing they provided for her, preferring her Indian garb. This grieved Mr. Williams." See Annie E. Emerson, *Longmeadow Historical Society: Memories, Past and*

Present, typescript at Richard S. Storrs Memorial Library, Long-meadow, Mass., n. p. See also Emma Lewis Coleman, *New England Captives Carried to Canada*, 2 vols. (Portland, Maine, 1925), II: 63; William Wight, *Eleazer Williams: His Forerunners, Himself* (Milwaukee, Wis., 1896), 139; and Medlicott, "Return to This Land of Light," 210. As noted in the Emerson memoir (above), local tradition also made much of Eunice's preference for Indian dress. A nineteenth-century Williams descendant wrote on this point as follows: "She attended meeting [church services] . . . while here, and her friends dressed her in English fashion. She indignantly threw off her clothes in the afternoon, and resumed her Indian blanket." See John Williams, *The Redeemed Captive Returning to Zion* (Northampton, Mass., 1853), ed. by Stephen W. Williams, Appendix (by the editor), 175. These elements of intercultural conflict in Eunice's story are thoughtfully discussed in Dawn Lander Gherman, "From Parlor to Teepee: The White Squaw on the American Frontier," Ph.D. diss., University of Massachusetts (Amherst, Mass., 1975), 70–91.

12. Richard Storrs to Rev. [———] Romeyn, 28 March 1811, reprinted in *The Christian Magazine*, June 1811, 344; SW Diary, III: 322.

13. Ibid., III: 322.

14. Ibid., III: 322–23. The description of the interior of the meeting-house is based on records reprinted in *Proceedings at the Centennial Celebration of . . . Longmeadow*, 150–55; see also the diagrams of the "ground floor" and "gallery" of "the old meeting-house," in ibid., 160–61.

15. SW Diary, III: 323.

16. Ibid.

17. Ibid., III: 323–24.

18. Ibid., III: 324–25.

19. Ibid., III: 325–28.

20. Charles B. De Saileville, *A History of the Life and Captivity of Miss Eunice Williams, Alias, Madam De Roguers, Who Was Styled "The Fair Captive,"* ms. in the holdings of the Missouri Historical Society (St. Louis, Mo.), Eleazer Williams Collection, 95–99. This curious document was written in about the year 1842. (See the "Dedicatory Epistle," dated 12 June 1842, also in the Missouri Historical Society, Eleazer Williams Collection.) Its contents appear to mix solidly grounded (and independently verifiable) fact with elements of local folklore and legend—and some that may be out-

right fantasy. It is impossible to say which category applies to the account presented here of the reasons for Eunice's 1740 visit.

21. The conference at Albany, "towards the end of August 1740," is documented in NYCD, IX: 1062–63. The Rice brothers reached Westborough on August 15, as noted in the diary of Ebenezer Parkman, the town's minister; see the printed version in *Proceedings of the American Antiquarian Society*, LXXII: 124, 130–31. From Westborough the Rices went on to Groton and Boston; they returned to Canada in mid-October. See also Coleman, *New England Captives*, I: 324–27.

22. Joseph Sewall to Stephen Williams, 5 January 1740/41, in GC, American Colonial Clergy, Case 8, Box 24; SW Diary, III: 362. The reference to the money sent to Albany is found in an almanac once owned by Stephen Williams; see Nathaniel Ames, *An Astronomical Diary, Or, An Almanac For the Year 1741* (Boston, 1741), copy at the City Library, Springfield, Mass., n. p.

23. SW Diary, III: 327; Joseph Sewall to Stephen Williams, 5 January 1740/41, in GC, American Colonial Clergy, case 8, box 24.

24. SW Diary, III: 374–75.

25. Ibid., III: 375–76.

26. Ibid., III: 376.

27. Ibid., III: 377–78.

28. Ibid., III: 378–80.

29. Ibid., III: 382–84.

30. Ibid., III: 383–84.

31. Ibid., III: 384.

32. Diary of Jacob Eliot, vol. I, entry for 4 August 1741, in Sterling Library, Yale University (New Haven, Conn.), Manuscripts and Archives, Jacob Eliot Family Papers, Group 193, Box 2. Most of what we know about the Mansfield visit is contained in the published version of Solomon Williams's sermon; see Solomon Williams, *A Sermon Preach'd at Mansfield, Aug. 4, 1741* (Boston, 1742).

33. Ibid., title page, 1; De Saileville, *A History of the Life and Captivity of Miss Eunice Williams*, 110.

34. Williams, *A Sermon Preach'd at Mansfield, Aug. 4, 1741*, title page.

35. Ibid., 14–16.

36. Ibid., 17–18.

37. Ibid., 18.

38. Ibid.

39. Ibid., 20.

40. Ibid., 21, 23.
41. Ibid., 25–26.
42. Ibid., 26.
43. Ibid., 27.
44. Ibid., 17.
45. SW Diary, III: 386–87.
46. Ibid., III: 391, 393.
47. See "fragment of a journal (1742–43–44) of Stephen Williams concerning the visit of his sister Eunice, to Longmeadow, Mass." in State Historical Society of Wisconsin, Area Research Center (Green Bay, Wis.), Eleazer Williams Papers, Box 4, Folder 14. As noted in the text, this "fragment" was made by a later copyist, and there is no way now to check the accuracy of its contents. However, another such fragment—in the same hand, but covering a different (earlier) part of Stephen Williams's life—*can* be checked against the surviving diary; apart from modernization of spelling and punctuation, it matches perfectly. Furthermore, the diction in the first (unchecked) fragment seems fully consistent with all parts of the known diary.
48. Ibid., n. p. (entry for 1 November 1742).
49. Ibid., n. p. (entries for 4, 14, 19, 27, 29 September 1743); John Sergeant to Stephen Williams, 24 October 1743, in Edward E. Ayer Collection, Newberry Library (Chicago, Ill.), ms. no. 800; Peter Reynolds to Eleazer Wheelock, 15 September 1743, in GC, American Colonial Clergy, Case 8, Box 24.
50. "Fragment of a journal of Stephen Williams," n.p. (entry for 5 October 1743); De Saileville, *A History of the Life and Captivity of Miss Eunice Williams*, 117–18. Other accounts of the 1743 visit— also dating from the early nineteenth century—can be found in Richard Storrs to Rev. [————] Romeyn, 6 April 1811, reprinted in *The Christian Magazine*, June 1811, 344, and Jerusha M. Colton to [————], 26 May 1836, reprinted in Stephen West Williams, *The Genealogy and History of the Family of Williams* (Greenfield, Mass., 1847), 93–94.
51. MA, XXXI: 466. Several decades later the Rev. Richard Storrs, a collateral descendant of the Williamses, wrote as follows about the same event: "In one instance the Legislature of this Commonwealth made a very handsome grant and proposed to them [Eunice and her husband] an annual stipend, with a permanent settlement, on condition they would take up their abode in New England"; see *The Christian Magazine*, June 1811, 344. Indeed, the idea of a strategic

"offer" by colony authorities has long been part of the lore surrounding Eunice Williams, but it could not be substantiated until "Tairagie" was recognized as one of the names used by her husband.

52. "Fragment of a journal of Stephen Williams," n.p. (entry for 28 October 1743).

53. Ibid., n.p. (entries for 30 November, and 12 and 13 December, 1743).

54. Stephen Williams to Joseph Kellogg, 16 December 1743, in GC, American Colonial Clergy, Case 8, Box 25.

55. "Fragment of a journal of Stephen Williams," n.p. (entry for 19 December 1743).

56. Ibid., n.p. (entry for 20 December 1743); De Saileville, *A History of the Life and Captivity of Miss Eunice Williams*, 120–21.

57. "Fragment of a journal of Stephen Williams," n.p. (entries for 6 February, and 2 and 6 March, 1743).

58. Ibid., n.p. (entries for 20, 21, 22, 23 March 1743).

59. Ibid., n.p. (entry for 24 March 1743).

60. Richard Storrs to Rev. [———] Romeyn, 6 April 1811, reprinted in *The Christian Magazine*, June 1811, 344; Jerusha M. Colton to [———], 26 May 1836, reprinted in Stephen West Williams, *The Family of Williams*, 94; ibid., 93.

TEN

1. For a useful overview of the war in the northeast, including its immediate antecedents, see Colin G. Calloway, *The Western Abenakis of Vermont, 1600–1800* (Norman, Okla., 1990), Ch. 8. On the preparations made at Deerfield, see HD, I: 529–32.

2. "Fragment of a journal (1742–43–44) of Stephen Williams concerning the visit of his sister Eunice to Longmeadow, Mass.," in State Historical Society of Wisconsin, Area Research Center (Green Bay, Wis.), Eleazer Williams Papers, box 4, folder 14, entry for 6 February 1744; Charles B. De Saileville, *A History of the Life and Captivity of Miss Eunice Williams, Alias Madam De Roguers, Who Was Styled "the Fair Captive,"* ms. volume in the Missouri Historical Society (St. Louis, Mo.), Eleazer Williams Collection, 127. Stephen's final comment on the visit is quoted in ibid., 131 (diary entry for 28 March 1744). For discussion of the provenance and internal characteristics of these two documents, see above, Ch. 9, endnotes 20, 47.

3. The visit of the Harris brothers was described in two long letters, which survive today in the files of the Massachusetts Archives: John Henry Lydius to Colonel John Stoddard, 24 October 1744, MA, XXXI: 510–12, and Joseph Kellogg to Gov. Jonathan Belcher, 3 December 1744, MA, XXXI: 518–20. On the career of Mary Harris, Eunice's fellow captive in the massacre, see George F. Smythe, "Mary Harris, The 'White Woman,' " in PVMA Procs., VII: 288–302, and Emma Lewis Coleman, *New England Captives Carried to Canada*, 2 vols. (Portland, Maine, 1925), II: 87–88.

4. Kellogg to Gov. Belcher, 3 December 1744, MA, XXXI: 519; Lydius to Stoddard, 24 October 1744, MA, XXXI: 510–11.

5. A summary of these efforts, from the English perspective, can be found in Calloway, *The Western Abenakis of Vermont, 1600–1800*, 149–50; for a French perspective, see W. J. Eccles, *The Canadian Frontier, 1534–1760* (Albuquerque, N. Mex., 1969), 151–53. On the attack at Saratoga, see Gov. Clinton to the Lords of Trade, 30 November 1745, in NYCD, VI: 288.

6. See Calloway, *The Abenakis of Western Vermont, 1600–1800*, 151–59.

7. Account of Capt. Phineas Stevens, quoted in ibid., 155; ibid., 149; Deacon Noah Wright, quoted in HD, I: 547.

8. "Autograph Journal of the Rev. Stephen Williams, 1745–48," ms. in the holdings of the Massachusetts Historical Society (Boston, Mass.), Parkman Papers, LXX-A, entries for 30 July 1746 and 6 October 1747. (This portion of Stephen's diary was separated long ago from the rest. It is not included in the typescript which otherwise figures prominently in the present study.) At another point Stephen noted that he had "been preaching abt war: ye Lord be pleasd to affect us suitably wth his frown in this awefull judgmt." See ibid., entry for 11 May 1746.

9. On Stephen's experiences at Louisburg, see ibid., entries covering the period from 18 July to 29 November 1745. When evacuated (on the latter date) he was already "so ill . . . yt I can give little or no acct of any thing yt passed on ye whole voyage." When his ship reached Boston, he was "putt into a cradle & cover'd over" while being carried to a friend's house for an extended period of medical care. See ibid., entries for 29 November and 8 December 1745.

10. "Operations of the French in New England and New York, 1745, 1746," translated and printed in NYCD, X: 32. (The original French version of this writing can be checked in *Collection de Manuscrits, Contenant Lettres, Mémoires, et Autres Documents Histo-*

riques Relatifs à la Nouvelle France, 4 vols. [Quebec, Canada, 1884], III, 274–76.)

11. See "Operations of the French," in NYCD, X: 32–35.
12. Beauharnais to the Ministry of the Marine, 26 June 1746, translated and printed in ibid., X: 86.
13. Kellogg to Gov. Belcher, 3 December 1744, MA, XXXI: 520; Beauharnais to the Ministry of the Marine, 29 November 1747, translated and printed in NYCD, X: 102 (for the French original see *Collection de Manuscrits*, IV: 339–40). For a specific instance of treachery attributed to the Kahnawake, see the dispatch dated 3 June 1747, in ibid., 340–41.
14. *A Narrative of the Captivity of Nehemiah How*, as published in Samuel G. Drake, *Tragedies of the Wilderness, or True and Authentic Narratives of Captives* (Boston, 1846), 129.
15. On these men, and their connection to the war, see HD, I: 533, 536, 538, 550, and Stephen West Williams, *The Genealogy and History of the Family of Williams* (Greenfield, Mass., 1847), 191, 234, 258, and *passim*.
16. See, for example, the incident reported in the *Boston Evening Post*, 26 June 1749, and reprinted in NYCD, VI: 519. The comments by Stephen Williams are taken from yet another piece which was separated long ago from the main body of his diary, and which today is found in the Library of Congress. See "Journal of Stephen Williams, July 15, 1749 to July 14, 1750," photostatic copy at the Massachusetts Historical Society (Boston, Mass.), entries for 23 October and 15 December 1749.
17. Ibid., leaf 62.
18. Ibid.
19. Ibid.
20. Ibid., leaf 63.
21. Ibid.
22. Ibid.
23. Ibid., leaf 71.
24. SW Diary, II: 172.
25. Ibid., VIII: 22–23.
26. Stephen Williams, "An account of Some Ancient Things," as printed in Stephen W. Williams, *A Biographical Memoir of the Rev. John Williams* (Greenfield, Mass., 1837), 126–27.
27. See HD, I: 632, 637, 647, and *passim*. The comment by Elijah Williams is quoted in ibid., I: 639.

28. On the attitude of the Kahnawake in the period immediately preceding the outbreak of war, see Calloway, *The Western Abenakis of Vermont, 1600–1800*, 165–67. Kahnawake participation in French-sponsored "war parties" is noted in various documents translated and published in NYCD, X: 153–54 and *passim*. A variety of English prisoners, taken to Kahnawake during the war years, would subsequently petition New England authorities for financial "relief." A representative case was that of Ebenezer Pratt, captured while on a "scout" in 1757 "and carried in six days to an Indian castle called Cahnawaugo . . . and there continued till . . . he was redeemed from the Indians by the Governor of Montreal . . . [during] all which time . . . he suffered greatly, and . . . came Home almost naked, and . . . in a weakly state"; see MA, LXXVIII: 743. (For other, similar examples, see ibid., LXXVIII: 659–61, 716, and LXXIX: 311, 379, 410–12, 569.) On French suspicions of Kahnawake "fidelity," see, for example, Baron de Dieskau to Count d'Argenson, 14 September 1755, translated in NYCD, X: 316, and M. de Montcalm to M. de Massiac (no date), ibid., X: 810. The famous Montcalm was especially doubtful about the Kahnawake; see his exchange of letters with the Marquis de Vaudreuil, 1 August and 6 August 1758, translated in ibid., X: 811. For a more general account of Kahnawake participation in the French and Indian war, see E. J. Devine, *Historic Caughnawaga* (Montreal, Canada, 1922), 257–71. On the founding of St. Regis by "seceding Kahnawakes," see the Marquis de Duquesne to the Ministry of the Marine, 31 October 1754 and 26 March 1755, translated in NYCD, X: 267, 301. See also Abbé G. Forbes, "Saint Regis," *Bullétin des Recherches Historiques*, VIII: 12–13; George F. G. Stanley, "The First Indian Reserves in Canada," *Révue d'Histoire de L'Amérique Française*, IV, 203–5; Franklin B. Hough, *A History of St. Lawrence and Franklin Counties, New York* (Albany, N.Y., 1853), 110–15; and Devine, *Historic Caughnawaga*, 253–56.

29. Stephen's experience as chaplain, on these two occasions, is briefly described in a ms. autobiography, dated 31 January 1769, and found today in the holdings of the Boston (Mass.) Public Library, ms. 1000.

30. Stephen Williams, ms. sermon notes, in the Stephen Williams Papers, Massachusetts Historical Society (Boston, Mass.); see especially the folder marked "Sermon, January 30, 1756." (In fact, material in this folder represents several different sermons, with

dates of 30 January, 5 February, 12 February, and 11 March 1756, which may have been presented as a running series.) Key phrases quoted here appear on pp. 1, 2, 3; the block quote is from p. 10.

31. Stephen Williams, ms. autobiography, Boston Public Library, ms. 1000.

32. Abigail Williams's estate was introduced in probate court on 8 April 1755; final disposition of her properties was effected on 13 January 1756. See the materials pertaining to this case in Registry of Probates, Hampshire County (Northampton, Mass.).

33. SW Diary, IV: 203–4, 351.

34. On these points of family history, see the correspondence between Guillaume Forbes and C. Alice Baker, in PVMA Mss., Baker Papers. See also William Ward Wight, *Eleazer Williams: His Forerunners, Himself* (Milwaukee, Wis., 1896), 139, and Emma Lewis Coleman, *New England Captives Carried to Canada*, II: 59–64. The mention of Arosen is found in HD, I: 635.

35. SW Diary, V: 288, 290–91, 299, 303.

36. Journal of the Rev. John Ballantine (transcribed and annotated by Joseph D. Bartlett, 1886), typescript copy at the American Antiquarian Society (Worcester, Mass.). See entry for 30 June 1761.

37. SW Diary, V: 345–47.

38. Ibid., V: 346–47.

39. Ibid., V: 346.

40. Ibid., V: 347.

41. Ibid., V: 348.

42. Ibid.

43. Ibid., V: 349, 351.

44. Ibid., V: 409; VI: 142–43.

45. Register, Mission de Saint François Xavier du Sault St. Louis (Kahnawake, Canada), IV, n. p.

46. SW Diary, VI: 256.

47. Ibid., VI: 320–23.

48. The several stages of Stephen's decision to remarry are indicated in his diary; see ibid., VI: 389; VII: 8, 12–15. He described his new wife as "the relict [widow] of my Good friend Deacon Nathll Burt." On Cuyler's "account" of his sister, see ibid., VI: 369.

49. Ibid., VI: 369; VII: 86, 338.

50. The original of this letter is in GC; copy read at the Historic Deerfield Library, Deerfield, Mass., PVMA Mss., Williams Papers.

51. SW Diary, VII: 337; VIII: 86, 138, 8–9.

52. Kendall's experiences are described in his "Diary and Account

book, 1772–1774; Mission to the Caughnawaga Indians, 1772–1774," in Dartmouth College Archives (Dartmouth College Library, Hanover, N. H.), Wheelock Papers, W. P. 772900.3 (no pagination). On the receipt of his letter to Stephen Williams, see SW Diary, VIII: 230.

53. Ibid., VIII: 250, 267, 296.

54. James Dean to Stephen Williams, 12 November 1774, in the Newberry Library (Chicago, Ill.), Edward E. Ayer Collection, no. 221. On the receipt of Eunice's letter by Stephen, see SW Diary, VIII: 338.

55. These connections can be explored, for example, in Stephen West Williams, *The Genealogy and History of the Family of Williams, passim*.

56. On Thomas Thorakwaneken Williams (Eunice's grandson), see Eleazer Williams, *The Life of Te-ho-ra-gwa-ne-gen, alias Thomas Williams* (Albany, N.Y., 1859). See also William Ward Wight, *Eleazer Williams: His Forerunners, Himself*, 143–46.

57. SW Diary, IX: 83.

58. Robert Breck, *A Sermon Preached at the Funeral of the Rev. Stephen Williams* (Springfield, Mass., 1782), 12; SW Diary, X: 349–50. Stephen's reputed last words are quoted in Breck, *A Sermon Preached*, 27.

59. SW Diary, X: 46.

ENDINGS

1. Register, Mission de Saint François Xavier du Sault St. Louis (Kahnawake, Canada), III, n. p.

2. The summary of French Catholic views about death, presented in this and succeeding paragraphs, is based principally on material found in JR, *passim*; A. J. B. Johnston, *Religion in Life at Louisburg* (Montreal, Canada, 1984), 138–50; and Philippe Ariès, *The Hour of Our Death*, trans. by Helen Weaver (New York, 1982), 32, 152–57, 162–65, 305–8, 462–66.

3. On the general subject of this and succeeding paragraphs, see David Stannard, *The Puritan Way of Death: A Study of Religion, Culture, and Social Change* (New York, 1977).

4. Robert Breck, *A Sermon Preached at the Funeral of the Rev. Stephen Williams* (Springfield, Mass., 1782), 17.

5. Ibid., 18.

6. See pp. 235, 204.
7. See "Extracts from the Commonplace Book of Joseph Green," in John Demos, *Remarkable Providences*, rev. ed. (Boston, 1991), 417 ff.
8. CAI, I: 230–31.
9. Ibid., I: 253.
10. Ibid.
11. Ibid., I: 258.

EPILOGUE

1. Lucy Williams to Abigail Silliman, 8 June 1785, in PVMA Mss., Williams Papers, box 1, folder 17. See also Eleazer Williams, *Life of Te-ho-ra-gwa-ne-gen, alias Thomas Williams* (Albany, N.Y., 1859).
2. Nathaniel Ely, ms. memorandum dated 23 January 1800, in Longmeadow (Mass.) Historical Society, Ely Genealogy File. In his personal journal Ely noted the same event: "our Cousins from Connawaga Came." (See journal of Nathaniel Ely, p. 2, in Missouri Historical Society [Columbia, Mo.], film copy in PVMA Mss., Williams Papers, box 15, folder 1.)
3. Ely's comment is in his ms. memorandum dated 23 January 1800, in Longmeadow (Mass.) Historical Society, Ely Genealogy File. For the "remembrance" of the fellow pupil, see C. Colton, *Tour of the American Lakes, and Among the Indians*, 2 vols. (1833; reissued, Port Washington, N.Y., 1972), I: 159–63.
4. Ibid., 163–64; diary of Jerusha Mather Williams, entries for 2 March 1802 and 15 February 1803, in Longmeadow (Mass.) Historical Society, Williams Genealogy File; Thomas Williams to Nathaniel Ely, 19 January 1806, in Longmeadow (Mass.) Historical Society, Williams Genealogy File; Colton, *Tour of the American Lakes*, 164. The experience of these Kahnawake Williamses during their boyhood years in New England can be followed through various manuscript documents; see especially the journal of Nathaniel Ely (citation in fn. 2 above). Efforts were made by a local "missionary society" to raise money for the support of the "two Indian lads"; see the printed circular, dated 21 May 1804 and signed by Joseph Lathrop et al., as well as ms. correspondence on the same subject, in Longmeadow (Mass.) Historical Society, Williams Genealogy File. See also a ms. copybook of Eleazer Williams, describing events between April 1804 and April 1806, and his brief autobiographical

memoir (no date) in the Newberry Library (Chicago, Ill.), Edward
E. Ayer Collection, ms. 999a. Eleazer's younger brother John returned to Canada in January 1804 (as Deacon Ely noted), "having
lived with us 4 years"; see Ely's journal, 97. Apparently John had
not adapted successfully to his New England surroundings; later it
was said that "he much preferred his bow and arrow to his book
. . . [and] he was given up as incorrigible." (See M. W. Davis to
George Sheldon, 11 April 1902, in PVMA Mss., Williams Papers,
box 16, folder 2.)

5. Colton, *A Tour of the American Lakes*, 164; Eleazer Williams,
autobiographical memoir (no date), in the Newberry Library (Chicago, Ill.), Edward E. Ayer Collection, ms. 999a.

6. The best short account of Eleazer Williams's life is Geoffrey E.
Buerger, "Parson, Pretender, Pauper: Eleazer Williams Reconsidered," in *The Voyageur*, winter issue 1988–89, 4–18. (On the years
immediately following his departure from New England, see especially 7–8.) For his own account of his exploits in the War of 1812,
see Williams, *Life of Te-ho-ra-gwa-ne-gen*, 60–88. See also William
Ward Wight, *Eleazer Williams: His Forerunners, Himself* (Milwaukee, Wis., 1896), 154–59.

7. Buerger, "Parson, Pretender, Pauper," 8–12; Wight, *Eleazer Williams*, 166–78. The "rebuke" noted in the text was by John Y.
Smith, his fellow resident at Green Bay, Wisconsin; see the quotation in Wight, *Eleazer Williams*, 176.

8. John H. Hanson, "Have We a Bourbon Among Us?," *Putnam's
Magazine*, February 1853, 194–217; Hanson, *The Lost Prince:
Facts Tending to Prove the Identity of Louis the Seventeenth, of
France, and the Rev. Eleazer Williams, Missionary Among the Indi-
ans of North America* (New York, 1854). Claims to this effect began
to appear in local and national newspapers as early as 1849. On the
details of publication about the "Dauphin controversy," see
Buerger, "Parson, Pretender, Pauper," 13–17.

9. Ibid., 14.

10. See Wight, *Eleazer Williams*, 148–49.

11. Among those who sought to discredit Eleazer Williams's claims
was Mark Twain; see his "The Wild Man Interviewed," in the
Buffalo Express, 18 September 1869. For a detailed analysis of these
claims, see Wight, *Eleazer Williams*, 177–95.

12. (Greenfield, Mass., 1837). The author of the pamphlet (and sermon) was John Fessenden.

13. Ibid., 3–4. The visitors apparently camped on a promontory

above the village, known then as Fort Hill. According to subsequent remembrance, "they came into the village asking for people by the name of Williams. There were several families of that name then, but they chose to go to the house of Ephraim Williams because there they could see a little white Williams papoose [also named] Ephraim." New England Williamses have continued to encounter Indian "cousins" in the twentieth century. In 1922, for example, one Elisabeth Sadoques, a Canadian Indian claiming descent from Eunice, visited Deerfield "and read a very charming paper on her tribe and their ways" to the local historical society. On these matters, see Mary Williams Fuller, "The Williams Family in Deerfield," PVMA Procs., VIII: 100–1.

14. Fessenden, *A Sermon Preached*, 5.
15. Ibid.
16. Ibid.
17. Ibid., 6.
18. Ibid., 7.
19. Ibid., 8.
20. Ibid.
21. Ibid., 10.
22. Ibid.
23. Ibid., 12.
24. Ibid., 10.
25. Ibid., 10–11.
26. Ibid., 12.
27. Ibid., 13.
28. Ibid.
29. Ibid.
30. Ibid., 14.
31. Ibid., 15.
32. Ibid.
33. Ibid. The words attributed here to "the messengers from Dedham" are an invention of a nineteenth-century town historian, trying to imagine how the first English settlers might have looked on the Pocumtuck site. See Erastus Worthington, *History of Dedham, 1635–1827* (Boston, 1827), 19.
34. Fessenden, *A Sermon Preached*, 15.
35. Ibid., 14–15.

INDEX